Third Edition

THE BEDFORD HANDBOOK FOR WRITERS

Diana Hacker

BEDFORD BOOKS of ST. MARTIN'S PRESS | BOSTON

For Bedford Books
Publisher: Charles H. Christensen
Associate Publisher: Joan E. Feinberg
Managing Editor: Elizabeth M. Schaaf
Copyeditor: Barbara G. Flanagan
Text design and typography: Claire Seng-Niemoeller
Cover design: Hannus Design Associates

The Bedford Handbook for Writers, Third Edition, was formerly titled
Rules for Writers.

Library of Congress Catalog Card Number: 89–63901

5   4   3   2   1

f   e   d

For information, write: St. Martin's Press, Inc.
175 Fifth Avenue, New York, NY 10010
Editorial Offices: Bedford Books of St. Martin's Press
29 Winchester Street, Boston, MA 02116

ISBN: 0–312–05599–4

ACKNOWLEDGMENTS

Nelson W. Aldrich, Jr., from *Old Money: The Mythology of America's Upper
Class.* Copyright © 1988 by Nelson W. Aldrich, Jr. Reprinted by permission
of Alfred A. Knopf, Inc.
The American Heritage Dictionary of the English Language, from the entry
under "prevent." Copyright © 1981 by Houghton Mifflin Company. Reprinted
by permission from *The American Heritage Dictionary of the English Language.*
Russell Baker, from *Growing Up.* Copyright © 1982 by Russell Baker. Published by Congden & Weed.

*Acknowledgments and copyrights are continued at the back of the book on
pages 688–689, which constitute an extension of the copyright page.*

Preface for Instructors

The Bedford Handbook for Writers, available in paperback or hardcover, is a major revision of *Rules for Writers,* Second Edition. It retains the quick reference features of *Rules for Writers* and includes more rhetorical material to strengthen the book as a classroom text.

When I began writing this book in 1982, I had been teaching long enough to know just what I wanted in a handbook. Like many of my colleagues, I teach five composition classes a semester, each with twenty-five students of varying abilities, so there is all too little time for individualized grammar lessons. I wanted a handbook so clear and accessible that my students could learn from it on their own. I had in mind a book that would give students what they seem to prefer—straightforward, unambiguous rules—but without suggesting that rules are absolutes or that writing well is simply a matter of following the rules.

Further, because my students have such a range of abilities, I hoped for a book that would be useful for all of them, offering a little help or a lot of help depending on their needs. Finally, I envisioned a handbook that would support the philosophy of composition that I work so hard to convey in the classroom. Writing is a process, I tell my students, and revision is central to that process. Revision is not a punishment for failing to get things right the first time. Nor is it a perfunctory clean-up exercise. It occurs right on the pages of a rough draft, often messily, with cross-outs and insertions, and it requires an active mind, a mind willing to look at a draft from the point of view of the reader, to spot problems, and to choose solutions.

With these aims in mind, then, I began writing this book. And it was with them in mind that I rewrote it again and again, with each draft edging closer to my vision. Now, six years after the initial publication of *Rules for Writers* and after much classroom testing, I have revised the book once again, this time under a new title: *The Bedford Handbook for Writers*. Here are its principal features.

Hand-edited sentences.   Most of the examples appear as they would in a rough draft, with handwritten revisions made in color over typeset faulty sentences. Unlike the usual technique of printing separate incorrect and correct versions of a sentence, hand-edited sentences highlight the revision, allowing students to grasp both the error and its correction at a glance. Further, hand-edited sentences mimic the process of revision as it should appear in the students' own drafts.

Award-winning design, now with a third color.   At the 1985 New England Book Show, the judges presented the first edition of this book (then titled *Rules for Writers*) with a Special Merit Award, remarking that it was a pleasure to see a reference book "designed with taste, clarity, and simplicity." Because the design highlights rules and examples, the book is easy to skim; readers who want more help will find it in full explanations following rules and in small-print comments pegged to examples.

For *The Bedford Handbook,* we have added a third color, used in the part openers and in the new full-page charts.

Quick reference charts. New to this edition are more than twenty full-page charts designed for quick reference. Many of these charts take students back to their own writing, helping them review their drafts for common problems such as comma splices and subject-verb agreement. Other charts summarize important material: guidelines for peer reviewers, a checklist for global revision, strategies for avoiding sexist language, and so on.

An organization reflecting the writing process. *The Bedford Handbook for Writers* moves from the whole paper and paragraphs through sentence rhetoric and diction to grammar, punctuation, and mechanics. This organization puts the stages of the writing process in context, thereby showing students when—as well as how—to revise and edit their drafts.

A problem-solving approach to errors. Where relevant, *The Bedford Handbook for Writers* attends to the linguistic and social causes of errors and to the effect of errors on readers. The examples of errors in the text are realistic, most having been drawn from student essays and local newspapers. The text treats these errors as problems to be solved, often in light of rhetorical considerations, not as violations of a moral code. Instead of preaching at students, it shows them why problems occur, how to recognize them, and how to solve them.

A unique section on ESL problems. Part VI now focuses exclusively on common problems facing speakers of English as a second language. Section 29 discusses ESL problems with verbs; section 30 explains when to use the articles *a,* *an,* and *the*; and section 31 alerts ESL students to a variety of other potential trouble spots.

Special attention to dialect differences.   Most of the material on dialect differences (formerly in Part VI) has been moved to section 27, "Choose standard English verb forms." There students will find help with such matters as omitted *-s* and *-ed* endings and omitted verbs.

Straightforward advice on composing and revising.   Instead of philosophizing about the writing process, Part I of *The Bedford Handbook for Writers* shows students, through a multiplicity of examples on a variety of topics, how to find a process that will work for them. The emphasis, throughout, is on flexibility.

The current edition adds five new charts and includes fuller advice on prewriting and global revision as well as a new section on peer review. Part II, Constructing Paragraphs, contains more on developing and arranging paragraphs, on reasons for combining or dividing paragraphs, and on coherence.

Five chapters on the research paper.   Part X has been substantially revised to make the research material more useful both as a reference and as a classroom text. The material is now divided into five chapters, and the MLA documentation models are easier to find because the edges of the pages are highlighted in color. Many new documentation models for both MLA and APA have been added in this edition.

To make the research paper chapters more useful as a classroom text, I have included further advice on matters most troublesome to students: choosing and narrowing a topic, finding sources, integrating quotations, and avoiding plagiarism both at the note-taking and the drafting stages of the writing process. New full-page charts show students how to handle quotations, summaries, and paraphrases without plagiarizing.

A chapter on writing about literature.   New to this edition is a chapter that takes students through the process of writing about literature: from forming an interpretation and planning the essay to drafting and revising it. Two sample essays are included: one on Langston Hughes's "Ballad of the Landlord" (without secondary sources) and one on Eudora Welty's "Why I Live at the P.O." (with secondary sources).

A chapter on writing arguments.   The chapter on argumentative writing, now illustrated with a variety of examples, has been significantly expanded. Using a process approach, the chapter shows students how to construct an argument that will have some hope of persuading readers who do not already agree with their views. The logical fallacies and common mistakes in inductive and deductive reasoning now appear at the end of the chapter.

Extensive exercises, some with answers.   At least one exercise set accompanies nearly every section of the book. Most sets begin with five lettered sentences with answers so that students can test their understanding independently. The sets then continue with ten numbered sentences whose answers appear only in the *Instructor's Annotated Edition*, so that instructors may use the exercises in class or assign them as homework. New to this edition are many exercises in paragraph or essay form.

A wide array of ancillaries.   To make *The Bedford Handbook for Writers* more useful for both students and instructors, the publisher has greatly expanded the package of resources accompanying the handbook. All are free of charge to instructors, and the workbook and a set of supplemental exercises are available for student purchase as well.

CLASSROOM RESOURCES

Instructor's Annotated Edition

Bedford Basics: A Workbook for Writers (with Answer Key)

Supplemental Exercises for The Bedford Handbook for Writers (with Answer Key)

Diagnostic Tests to Accompany The Bedford Handbook for Writers (with ESL versions)

RESOURCES FOR STUDENTS

MLA and APA Documentation Models (Reprinted from *The Bedford Handbook for Writers*)

Answers to Exercises in The Bedford Handbook for Writers

Preparing for the CLAST with The Bedford Handbook for Writers

Preparing for the TASP with The Bedford Handbook for Writers

SOFTWARE

Grammar Hotline for The Bedford Handbook for Writers (IBM and Mac versions)

Exercise Tutor for The Bedford Handbook for Writers (IBM and Mac versions)

PROFESSIONAL RESOURCES FOR INSTRUCTORS

Background Readings for Instructors Using The Bedford Handbook for Writers

The Bedford Bibliography for Teachers of Writing, Third Edition

Acknowledgments

No author can possibly anticipate the many ways in which a variety of students might respond to a text: Where might students be confused? How much explanation is enough? What is too intimidating? Do the examples appeal to a range of students? Are they free of stereotypes? To help me answer such questions, more than one hundred professors from more than seventy colleges and universities contributed useful insights based on their varied experiences in the classroom.

For their many helpful suggestions, I would like to thank an unusually perceptive group of reviewers:

Dolores Burton, Boston University
Marie Ciconte, California State University, Long Beach
Thomas Copeland, Youngstown State University
Ray Duda, University of Michigan
Gerry Eldred, Long Beach City College
Elaine Engelhardt, Utah Valley Community College
Jean English, University of Tennessee at Martin
Jane Vogel Fischman, State University of New York at
    Buffalo
George Gadda, UCLA
Barbara Gaffney, University of New Orleans
Linda Gajdusek, San Francisco State University
Chrysanthy Grieco, Seton Hall University
Dorothy Harris, Okaloosa-Walton Community College
Iris Hart, Santa Fe Community College
Sandra Hastings, Seattle Central Community College
Dona Hickey, University of Richmond
Barbara Hirschfelder, Santa Fe Community College
Franklin Horowitz, Columbia University
Robert Kantor, Ohio State University
Brian Kennedy, Cedarville College
Charles Kovich, Rockhurst College
Barbara Ladd, University of North Carolina at Chapel Hill

Rosalyn Lomax, Wayne County Community College
Janet Marting, University of Akron
Michael Meyer, University of Connecticut
Terry Miller, Indian River Community College
Mary Moya, Rutgers University
Lolly Ockerstrom, Northeastern University
Jed O'Connor, Florida State University
Pat Parnell, White Pines College
John Patton, University of Toledo
Danielle Roemer, Northern Kentucky University
Walter Shear, Pittsburg State University
Barbara Sloan, Santa Fe Community College
Mira Stillman, Rutgers University
Stephen Sutherland, Northeastern University
David W. Taylor, Moravian College
Thomas Whissen, Wright State University
Phyllis Whitesell, Franklin and Marshall College
Kathy Zambias, Rutgers University

For helping me to see the strengths and deficiencies of the second edition, thanks go to the many instructors who took the time to answer a detailed questionnaire.

Gabriel Bannerman-Richter, California State University, Sacramento
Christine Birdwell, Michigan State University
Karen S. Bowen, Pikes Peak Community College
Lurene Brooks, Golden West College
Greg Brown, Pittsburg State University
Judy Burges, College of Charleston
Marie Ciconte, California State University, Long Beach
Michael Cochran, Santa Fe Community College
Derreatha Corcoran, Moorpark College
Don Coslick, Prince George's Community College
V. M. D'Ortona, St. Johns River Community College
Kevin J. Duffy, University of Virginia
Jane Dugan, Cleveland State University

Richard DuRocher, St. Olaf College
K. Eisele, Onondaga Community College
Diane Ewing, Golden West College
Gerald W. Farrar, James Madison University
Jane Vogel Fischman, State University of New York at Buffalo
Margaret W. Franke, Northern New Mexico Community College
Barbara Gaffney, University of New Orleans
Clifford Garner, Rockland Community College
Dennis Goldsberry, College of Charleston
Craig Hancock, State University of New York at Albany
June Harmon, University of Virginia
Dorothy Harris, Okaloosa-Walton Community College
Jeane Harris, Arkansas State University
Iris Hart, Santa Fe Community College
Louis B. Hillman, State University of New York at Brockport
Barbara Hirschfelder, Santa Fe Community College
Allan Hirsh, Central Connecticut State University
Harv Hopkins-Garriss, James Madison University
Helen Isaacson, University of Michigan, Ann Arbor
Anne Mills King, Prince George's Community College
Peggy Kocoras, Clark University
Monica Laws, Arkansas State University
Mark Levensky, Evergreen State College
Mary Ann Linzmayer, Santa Fe Community College
John D. Magee, Ohio Northern University
John William Martin, Moraine Valley Community College
Patricia McKinney, Oregon State University
Ted McNulty, Towson State University
Karen Meyers, University of North Carolina at Greensboro
Frank Miller, Portland State University
Logan D. Moon, Arkansas State University

Lyle W. Morgan II, Pittsburg State University
William Nichols, Denison University
Lynn Parker, Brandeis University
Don K. Pierstorff, Orange Coast College
John B. Pieters, Santa Fe Community College
Leigh Pomeroy, Mankato State University
Gary D. Pratt, Brandeis University
June Randall, State University of New York at Buffalo
Marsha Rutter, San Diego State University
Theresa P. Santangelo, Fullerton College
Leone Scanlon, Clark University
C. Scholey, Southwestern Oregon Community College
Jo C. Searles, Pennsylvania State University
Walter Shear, Pittsburg State University
Nancy Sheley, California State University, Long Beach
Ray Sherer, Harrisburg Area Community College
Martha Simonsen, William Rainey Harper College
Dennis Slattery, Incarnate Word College
Dorothy Stephens, University of California, Berkeley
Thom Tammaro, Moorhead State University
David W. Taylor, Moravian College
Mary Ann Trevathan, California Polytechnic State
   University
Ray Van Dyke, Radford University
Wanda Van Goor, Prince George's Community College
Phyllis Whitesell, Franklin and Marshall College
Carolyn A. Wood, Santa Fe Community College
Laura Wright, Leeward College
Jonathan Yordy, State University of New York at Buffalo
Gay Zieger, Santa Fe Community College

Writing a handbook is truly a collaborative effort. For their assistance with the chapters on research writing, I would like to thank William Peirce, Lloyd Shaw, and Barbara Flanagan. I am also indebted to William Peirce for helping with the argument chapter, to Julia Sullivan for contributing to the chapter on writing about literature, and to Glenn Blalock for drafting the connected discourse exercises new to this edition.

Several talented editors and editorial assistants at Bedford Books have made invaluable contributions. Riikka Melartin responded to the evolving manuscript in detail and orchestrated much of the book's development with great organizational skill. Ellen Darion helped me get started on parts of the book that I found most difficult: the chapters on research, on argument, and on writing about literature. Ellen Kuhl worked with reviewers, and she and Meredith Weenick and Jane Betz edited many of the ancillaries to accompany *The Bedford Handbook for Writers*.

Special thanks are due to five people who have worked hard to make this handbook a success: to Charles Christensen for his creativity and his wise and expert counsel; to Joan Feinberg for setting a standard of excellence and nudging me toward it, always with intelligence, grace, and good humor; to Elizabeth Schaaf for taking an active interest in all aspects of the book—from its design to its readability—while guiding it expertly through production; to Barbara Flanagan for bringing consistency and grace to the final manuscript (no small task in a handbook); and to Claire Seng-Niemoeller for designing clean, uncluttered pages that highlight the book's hand-edited sentences. From the beginning, Chuck, Joan, Elizabeth, Barbara, Claire, and I have worked as a team. This book—originally *Rules for Writers* and now *The Bedford Handbook for Writers*—belongs to all of us.

Finally, a note of thanks goes to my parents, Clair and Georgiana Tarvin, and to Joseph and Marian Hacker, Robert Hacker, Greg Tarvin, Betty Renshaw, Bill Fry, Bill Mullinix, Joyce Magnotto, Christine McMahon, Anne King, Wanda Van Goor, Joyce McDonald, Tom Henderson, and Robbie and Austin Nichols for their support and encouragement; and to the many students over the years who have taught me that errors, a natural by-product of the writing process, are simply problems waiting to be solved.

Diana Hacker

Prince George's Community College

Introduction
for Students

Though it is small enough to hold in your hand, *The Bedford Handbook for Writers* will answer most of the questions you are likely to ask as you plan, draft, and revise a piece of writing: How do I choose and narrow a topic? What can I do if I get stuck? How do I know when to begin a new paragraph? Should I write *none was* or *none were*? When does a comma belong before *and*? What is the difference between *accept* and *except*?

How to find information

When you are revising an essay that has been marked by your instructor, tracking down information is simple. If your instructor marks problems with a number such as *16* or a number and letter such as *12e*, you can turn directly to the appropriate section of the handbook. Just flip through the colored tabs on the upper corners of the pages until you find the number in question. The number *16*, for example, leads you to the rule "Tighten wordy sentences," and *12e* takes you to the subrule "Repair dangling modifiers." If your instructor uses an abbreviation such as *w* or *dm* instead of a number, consult the list of abbreviations and symbols inside the back cover of the book, where you will find the name of the problems *(wordy; dangling modifier)* and the number of the section to consult.

When consulting the handbook on your own, you may find information in several ways. The alphabetical index at the back is perhaps the most reliable way to find what you're looking for. As you become familiar with the overall plan of the book, however, you can also make use of the full table of contents at the beginning of the book or of the brief table of contents inside the front cover. And as you become accustomed to the headings at the tops of the pages next to the colored tabs, you may be able to find information simply by flipping through the pages.

Many sections of the handbook contain cross-references to other sections of the book. Most of these will lead you to specific sections in Part IX, Grammar Basics, where you will find a discussion of grammatical concepts and terminology necessary for understanding many of the rules in the rest of the book. Whenever the book uses a grammatical term that you don't fully understand, you can also track down its meaning by consulting the list of grammatical terms inside the back cover.

On the very last page of the book, following the index, is a directory of useful charts and lists. Many of the charts help you review your own writing for common problems such as sentence fragments and dangling modifiers. Other charts summarize important material: ways to narrow a subject to a topic, major uses of the comma, parts of speech, and so on.

The plan of the book

A glance at the table of contents will show you that *The Bedford Handbook for Writers* is organized to reflect the writing process. Advice about composing and revising comes first

(Parts I and II), followed by strategies for revising sentences for clarity and style (Parts III and IV) and editing them for grammar, punctuation, and mechanics (Parts V–VIII). If you speak English as a second language (ESL), you will find special help in Part VI, Editing for ESL Problems.

The book ends with several special reference sections. Part IX, a review of grammar basics, defines key grammatical terms and concepts such as nouns and pronouns, subjects and verbs, subordinate clauses, and so on. Part X explains the process of writing and documenting a research paper. Part XI includes advice on argumentative writing, writing about literature, and business writing. Following Part XI is a Glossary of Usage, which lists alphabetically many common problems in word choice.

The process of revision

The Bedford Handbook for Writers shows you how to improve sentences the way practicing writers do it—by working directly on a rough draft. Instead of making corrections as you recopy sentences and paragraphs, try marking up your drafts with cross-outs and insertions. This technique gives you better control over your sentences, and it saves you time as well. To see what a marked-up draft looks like, turn to pages 72–73 or flip through the central sections of this book, which are illustrated with sentences that look just like those in a carefully revised draft.

How to use this book for self-study

In a composition class, most of your time should be spent writing. Therefore it is unlikely that you will want to study all of the chapters in this book in detail. Instead you should focus on the problems that tend to crop up in your own writing. Your instructor (or your college's writing center) will be glad to help you design an individualized program of self-study.

The Bedford Handbook for Writers has been designed so that you can learn from it on your own. By providing answers to some exercise sentences, it allows you to test your understanding of the material. Most exercise sets begin with five sentences lettered a–e and conclude with ten sentences numbered 1–10. Answers to the five lettered sentences appear in an appendix at the end of the book.

Diana Hacker

Contents

Part II

Part IV

Part V

Part VI

Part VIII

Part IX

Part X

PART I

Composing and Revising

Since it's not possible to think about everything all at once, most writers work on a piece of writing in stages. They begin by generating ideas and sketching a plan. When they feel ready to attempt an initial draft, they rough it out imperfectly, concentrating more on content than on style, grammar, and mechanics. If possible, they then get away from the draft for a while.

For most writers, revising is seldom a one-step process. The larger elements of writing receive attention first — the focus, organization, paragraphing, content, and overall strategy. Improvements in sentence structure, word choice, grammar, punctuation, and mechanics usually come later.

Of course, the writing process will not always occur for you quite as simply as just described. While drafting, for example, you may discover an interesting new approach to your topic that demands a revised plan. Or while revising you may need to generate more ideas and draft new material. Although you should generally move from planning to drafting to revising, be prepared to circle back to earlier stages whenever the need arises.

1

Generate ideas and sketch a plan.

Before attempting a first draft, spend some time generating ideas. Mull over your subject while listening to music or driving to work, jot down inspirations on scratch paper, and explore your insights with anyone willing to listen. At this stage you should be collecting information and experimenting with ways of focusing and organizing it to best reach your readers.

1a Assess the writing situation.

Begin by taking a look at the writing situation in which you find yourself. The key elements of the writing situation include your subject, the sources of information available to you, your purpose, your audience, and constraints such as length, format, and deadlines.

It is unlikely that you will make final decisions about all of these matters until later in the writing process — after a first draft, for example. Nevertheless, you can save yourself time by thinking about as many of them as possible in advance. For a quick checklist, see pages 14–15.

Subject

Frequently your subject will be given to you. In a psychology class, for example, you might be asked to explain Bruno Bettelheim's Freudian analysis of fairy tales. Or in a course on the history of filmmaking, you might be assigned an essay on the political impact of D. W. Griffith's silent film *The Birth of a Nation*. In the business world, your assignment might be to draft a quarterly sales report or craft a diplomatic letter to a customer who has complained about your firm's computer software.

Sometimes you will be free to choose your own subject. Then you will be wise to select a subject that you already know something about or one that you can reasonably investigate in the time you have. Students in composition classes have written successfully on all of the subjects listed here, most of which were later narrowed into topics suitable for essays of 500–750 words. By browsing through the lists, perhaps you can pick up some ideas of your own.

> *Education:* computers in the classroom, an inspiring teacher, sex education in junior high school, magnet schools, a learning disability such as dyslexia, programmed instruction,

parochial schools, teacher certification, a local program to combat adult illiteracy, creative means of funding a college education

Careers and the workplace: working in an emergency room, the image versus the reality of a job such as lifeguarding, a police officer's workday, advantages of flex-time for workers and employers, company-sponsored day care, mandatory drug testing by employers, sexual or racial discrimination on the job, the psychological effects of unemployment, the rewards of a part-time job such as camp counseling

Families: an experience with adoption, a portrait of a family member who has aged well, the challenges facing single parents, living with an alcoholic, a portrait of an ideal parent, growing up in a large family, the problems of split custody, an experience with child abuse, the depiction of male-female relationships in a popular TV series, expectations versus the reality of marriage, overcoming sibling rivalry, the advantages or disadvantages of being a twin

Health: a vegetarian diet, weight loss through hypnotism, a fitness program for the elderly, reasons not to smoke, the rights of smokers or nonsmokers, overcoming an addiction, lithium as a treatment for depression, the side effects of a particular treatment for cancer, life as a diabetic, the benefits of an aerobic exercise such as swimming, caring for a person with AIDS

Sports and hobbies: an unusual sport such as free-fall parachuting, surviving a wilderness program, bodybuilding, a sport from another culture, the philosophy of karate, the language of sports announcers, pros and cons of banning boxing, coaching a Little League team, cutting the costs of an expensive sport such as skiing, a portrait of a favorite sports figure, sports for the handicapped, the discipline required for a sport such as gymnastics, the rewards of a hobby such as woodworking

The arts: working behind the scenes at a theater, censorship of rock and roll lyrics, photography as an art form, the

Japanese tea ceremony, the influence of African art on Picasso, the appeal of a local art museum, a portrait of a favorite musician or artist, performing as a musician, a high school for the arts, the colorization of black-and-white films, science fiction as a serious form of literature, a humorous description of romance novels or hard-boiled detective thrillers

Social justice: an experience with racism or sexism, affirmative action, reverse discrimination, making public transportation accessible for the physically handicapped, an experience as a juror, a local program to aid the homeless, discrimination against homosexuals, pros and cons of a national drinking age of twenty-one

Death and dying: working on a suicide hotline, the death of a loved one, a brush with death, caring for terminally ill patients, the Buddhist view of death, explaining death to a child, passive euthanasia, death with dignity, an out-of-body experience

Violence and crime: an experience with a gun, a wartime experience, violence on television news programs, visiting a friend in prison, alternative sentencing for first offenders, victims' rights, a successful program to eliminate violence in a public high school, violence between parents and children or between husband and wife

Nature and ecology: safety of nuclear power plants, solar energy, wind energy, air pollution in our national parks, grizzly bears in Yellowstone, communication among dolphins, organic gardening, backpacking in the Rockies, marine ecology, an experimental farming technique, cleaning up Boston Harbor, the preservation of beaches in Delaware

Many of these subjects are too broad. Part of your challenge as a writer will be whittling broad subjects down to manageable topics. If you are limited to a few pages, for example, you could not possibly do justice to a subject as broad as "sports for the handicapped." You would be wise to restrict your paper to a topic more manageable in the space allowed — perhaps a description of the Saturday morning athletic program your college offers for handicapped children. The chart on page 7 suggests specific ways to narrow a subject to a topic.

Sources of information

Where will your facts, details, and examples come from? Can your topic be illustrated by personal experience, or will you need to search out relevant information through direct observation, interviews, questionnaires, or reading?

PERSONAL EXPERIENCE   You can develop many topics wholly through personal experience, depending of course on your own life experiences. The students who wrote about life-guarding, learning disabilities, weight loss through hypnotism, and free-fall parachuting all spoke with the voice of personal experience, as did those who wrote about flex-time, coaching a Little League team, and company-sponsored day care. When narrowing their subjects, those students chose to limit themselves to information they had at hand. For example, instead of writing about company-sponsored day care in general — a subject that would have required a great deal of research — one student limited her discussion to the successful day-care center at the company for which she worked.

DIRECT OBSERVATION   Direct observation is an excellent means of collecting information about a wide range of subjects, such as male-female relationships on the television program *Cheers*, the language of sports announcers, or the appeal of a local art museum. For such subjects, do not rely on your memory alone; your information will be fresher and more detailed if you actively collect it, with a notebook or tape recorder in hand. As writer Stuart Chase advises young journalists assigned to report on their city's water system, "You will write a better article if you heave yourself out of a comfortable chair and go down in tunnel 3 and get soaked."

Ways to narrow a subject to a topic

SUBDIVIDING YOUR SUBJECT

Many subjects can be subdivided. Instead of writing about censorship of popular songs, for example, you might select a subdivision of this general subject: censorship of rap music. Or instead of writing about homelessness in general, you might focus on homeless families in a particular shelter.

RESTRICTING YOUR PURPOSE

Often you can narrow your subject by restricting your purpose. For example, if your subject is drug testing in the workplace, you might at first hope to persuade readers that it should be banned in all situations. Upon further reflection, however, you might realize that this goal is more than you could hope to accomplish, given your word limit. By adopting a more limited purpose — to show that drug testing is unreliable, to argue that its use by private employers should be banned, or to demonstrate that it violates an innocent person's right to privacy — you would have a better chance of success.

RESTRICTING YOUR AUDIENCE

Another way to narrow your subject is to write for a particular audience. For example, instead of writing to a general audience on a subject such as teenage pregnancy, you might address persons with a special interest in the subject: young people, parents, or counselors working for Planned Parenthood.

CONSIDERING THE INFORMATION AVAILABLE TO YOU

One of the most natural ways to narrow a subject is to look at the information you have collected. If you have gathered a great deal of information on one aspect of your subject (for example, discrimination against persons with AIDS) and less information on other aspects (such as the causes of AIDS or promising treatments for AIDS), you may have found your topic.

INTERVIEWS AND QUESTIONNAIRES Interviews and questionnaires can supply you with detailed and interesting information on a variety of subjects. A nursing student interested in the care of terminally ill patients might interview nurses at a hospice; a political science major might speak with a local judge to learn about alternative sentencing for first offenders; a future teacher might conduct a survey on the classroom use of computers in local schools. It is a good idea to tape interviews to preserve any lively quotations that you might want to weave into your essay. (See page 489.) Keep questionnaires simple and specify a deadline to ensure that you get a reasonable number of responses.

READING Reading will be your primary source of information for many college assignments, which will generally be of two kinds: analytical assignments that call for a close reading of one book, essay, or literary work or research assignments that send you to the library to consult a variety of sources on a particular topic. For analytical essays, you can usually assume that your reader is familiar with the work and has a copy of it at hand. You select details from the work not to inform readers but to support an interpretation. When you quote from the work, page references are often sufficient. For research papers, on the other hand, you cannot assume that your reader is familiar with your sources or has them close at hand. This means that you must formally document all quoted and summarized or paraphrased material (see 54). When in doubt about the need for formal documentation, consult your instructor.

Purpose

Your purpose will often be dictated by the specific writing situation that faces you. Perhaps you have been asked to take minutes for a club meeting, to draft a letter requesting payment from a client, or to describe the results of a biology experiment. Even though your overall purpose is fairly obvious in such situations, a close look at that purpose can help you make a variety of necessary decisions. How detailed should the minutes be? Is your purpose to summarize the meeting or to establish a careful record of discussion in case future controversies arise? How firmly should your letter request payment? Do you need the money at all costs, or do you hope to get it without risking loss of the client's business? How technical is the biology report expected to be?

In many writing situations, part of your challenge will be discovering a purpose. Consider, for example, the topic of magnet schools — schools that draw students from different neighborhoods because of features such as advanced science classes or late-afternoon day care. Your purpose could be to inform parents of the options available in your county. Or you might argue that the county's magnet schools are not promoting racial integration as had been planned. Or you might propose that the board of education create a magnet high school for the arts on your college campus.

Although no precise guidelines will lead you to a purpose, you can begin by asking yourself which one or more of the following aims you hope to accomplish.

PURPOSES FOR WRITING

to inform	to evaluate
to persuade	to recommend
to call readers to action	to request
to change attitudes	to propose
to analyze	to provoke thought
to argue	to express feelings
to theorize	to entertain
to summarize	to give aesthetic pleasure

It is surprising how often writers misjudge their own purposes: informing, for example, when they should be recommending; summarizing when they should be analyzing; or expressing feelings about problems instead of proposing solutions. Before beginning any writing task, therefore, pause to ask, "Why am I communicating with my readers?" And this question will lead you to another important question: "Just who are those readers?"

Audience

Audience analysis can often lead you to an effective strategy for reaching your readers. One writer, whose purpose was to persuade teenagers not to smoke, jotted down the following observations about her audience:

> dislike lectures, especially from older people
> have little sense of their own mortality
> are concerned about physical appearance and image
> want to be socially accepted
> have limited budgets

This analysis led the writer to focus more on the social aspects of smoking (she pointed out, for instance, that kissing a smoker is like licking an ashtray) than on the health risks. Her audience analysis also warned her against adopting a preachy tone that her readers might find offensive. Instead of lecturing to her audience, she decided to draw examples from her own experience as a hooked smoker: burning holes in her best sweater, driving in zero-degree weather late at night in search of an open tavern to buy cigarettes, rummaging through ashtrays for stale butts, and so on. The result was an essay that reached its readers instead of alienating them.

The following checklist will help you decide how to approach your audience.

AUDIENCE CHECKLIST

How well informed are your readers about the subject?

What do you want them to learn about the subject?

How interested and attentive are they likely to be?

Will they resist any of your ideas?

What is your relationship to them: Employee to supervisor? Citizen to citizen? Expert to novice? Scholar to scholar?

How much time are they willing to spend reading?

How sophisticated are they as readers? Do they have large vocabularies? Can they follow long and complex sentences?

Of course, in some writing situations the audience will not be neatly defined for you. Nevertheless, many of the choices that you make as you write will tell readers who you think they are (novices or experts, for example), so it is best to be consistent — even if this means creating an audience that is in some sense a fiction.

Writers in the business world often find themselves writing for multiple audiences. A letter to a client, for instance, might be distributed to sales representatives as well. Readers of a report may include persons with and without technical expertise or readers who want details and those who prefer a quick overview. To satisfy the demands of multiple audiences, business writers have developed a variety of strategies: attaching cover letters to more detailed reports, adding boldface headings, placing summaries in the left margin, and so on.

In the academic world, considerations of audience can be more complex than they seem at first. Your professor will read your essay, of course, but most professors play multiple roles while reading. Their first and most obvious roles are as coach and judge; less obvious is their role as an intelligent and objective reader, the kind of person who might reasonably be informed, convinced, entertained, or called to action by what you have to say.

Some professors create writing assignments that specify an audience, such as a hypothetical supervisor, readers of a local newspaper, or fellow academics in a particular field of study. Other professors expect you to invent an audience appropriate to your purpose and your subject. Still others prefer that you write for a general audience of educated readers — nonspecialists who can be expected to read with an intelligent, critical eye. When in doubt about an appropriate audience for a particular assignment, check with your professor.

Length, format, and deadlines

Writers seldom have complete control over length, format, and deadlines. Journalists usually write within strict word limits set by their editors, businesspeople routinely aim for conciseness, and most college assignments specify an approximate length.

Certain formats may also be required by your writing situation. Specific formats are frequently used in the business world for documents such as letters, memos, reports, budget analyses, and personnel records. In the academic world, you may need to learn precise conventions for lab reports, critiques, research papers, and so on. For most undergraduate papers, a standard format is acceptable (see 46). The conventions for research papers are discussed in 54.

A final constraint is the deadline. The deadline tells you what is possible and helps you plan your time. For complex writing projects, such as research papers, you'll need to manage your time quite carefully. By working backward from the deadline, you can create a schedule of target dates for completing various parts of the process. See page 470 for an example.

EXERCISE 1 – 1

Choose one of the subject areas mentioned on pages 3–5 and add at least five subjects to those already on the list. If other members of your class have also done this exercise, pool the results.

EXERCISE 1–2

Narrow five of the following subjects into topics that would be manageable for an essay of two to five pages.

1. Working behind the scenes at a theater
2. A sport from another culture
3. Violence between parents and children
4. The advantages or disadvantages of being a twin
5. An experience with adoption
6. The side effects of a particular treatment for cancer
7. Computers in the classroom
8. Parochial schools
9. Performing as a musician
10. An experience with racism or sexism

EXERCISE 1–3

Which of the following subjects might be illustrated wholly by personal experience? For the others, suggest possible sources of information: direct observation, interviews, questionnaires, or reading.

1. The problems of split custody
2. Working in an emergency room
3. Backpacking in the Rockies
4. The influence of African art on Picasso
5. Violence on television news programs
6. The discipline required for a sport such as gymnastics
7. Photography as an art form
8. Affirmative action
9. A local program to aid the homeless
10. Visiting a friend in prison

EXERCISE 1–4

Suggest a purpose and audience for five of the following subjects.

1. A vegetarian diet
2. Cutting the costs of an expensive sport such as skiing

Checklist for assessing the writing situation

At the beginning of the writing process, you may not be able to answer all of the questions on this checklist. That's fine. Just be prepared to think about them later.

NOTE: It is not necessary to think about the elements of a writing situation in the exact order listed in this chart.

SUBJECT

— Has a subject (or a range of possible subjects) been given to you, or are you free to choose your own?

— Is your subject worth writing about? Can you think of any readers who might be interested in reading about it?

— How broadly can you cover the subject? Do you need to narrow it to a more specific topic (because of length restrictions, for instance)?

— How detailed should your coverage be?

SOURCES OF INFORMATION

— Where will your information come from: Personal experience? Direct observation? Interviews? Questionnaires? Reading?

— If your information comes from reading, what sort of documentation is required?

PURPOSE

— Why are you writing: To inform readers? To persuade them? To entertain them? To call them to action? Some combination of these?

AUDIENCE

— How well informed are your readers about the subject?

— What do you want them to learn about the subject?

— How interested and attentive are they likely to be?

— Will they resist any of your ideas?

— What is your relationship to them: Employee to supervisor? Citizen to citizen? Expert to novice? Scholar to scholar?

— How much time are they willing to spend reading?

— How sophisticated are they as readers? Do they have large vocabularies? Can they follow long and complex sentences?

LENGTH

— Are you working within any length specifications? If not, what length seems appropriate, given your subject, your purpose, and your audience?

FORMAT

— Must you use a particular format? If so, do you have guidelines or examples that you can consult?

DEADLINE

— What is your deadline? How much time will you need to allow for the various stages of writing, including typing and proofreading the final draft?

3. The challenges facing single parents
4. Advantages of flex-time for workers and employers
5. Growing up in a large family
6. Pros and cons of a national drinking age of twenty-one
7. Science fiction as a serious form of literature
8. An unusual sport such as free-fall parachuting
9. A police officer's workday
10. Working on a suicide hotline

EXERCISE 1–5

For each of the following paired items, choose the sentence or passage that is more effective, given the writer's purpose and audience. Be prepared to explain your choices.

1. Here are two notices sent out by dentists to remind patients to call for an appointment. Which notice is more effective?

   a. Things to do today:
      1. Floss.
      2. Call your dentist.
      It's time again for your regular dental checkup, so please call today for an appointment.

   b. It is the custom of this office to notify patients on record for periodical examination of the mouth. This service is rendered to safeguard previous work and to ensure future good health and appearance. May I suggest you call.

2. If you were writing an instruction booklet for machinists at a tractor manufacturer, which version of the following sentence would you choose?

   a. Move the control lever to the reverse position after the machine stops.

   b. After the machine stops, move the control lever to the reverse position.

3. In an essay written for a general audience, which of the following sentences would be more effective?

   a. When I was ten, my parents sent me to summer camp because they thought I needed peer stuff.

b. When I was ten, my parents sent me to summer camp because they thought I needed to interact more with children my own age.

4. In a business letter promoting the writer's company to an audience aware of the company's former problems, which version of the following sentence is more effective?

    a. At this point in time ours is a revitalized and emergent company no longer attached to outmoded marketing concepts, no longer subject to inbred managerial alliances, and never again dependent on reactionary governmental influences.

    b. Our company has emerged, revitalized, from its outdated marketing ideas, its parochial management, and its dependence on government contracts.

5. Which of the following sentences would be more effective in a campus newspaper article criticizing the food in the cafeteria's vending machines?

    a. First and foremost, the hamburgers that are sold in the cafeteria's machines are dry in texture and cold to the taste.

    b. When I turned to the machine, I decided to try a sizzling hamburger, lean and juicy. Instead, out came a small dry patty so cold that the fat was congealed in tiny globs on top of the meat.

1b   Experiment with ways to explore your subject.

Instead of just plunging into a first draft, experiment with one or more techniques for exploring your subject, perhaps one of these:

listing	freewriting
clustering or branching	keeping a journal
asking questions	talking

For writing based on reading, two other techniques will also prove useful: note taking and annotating (see 52c and 57a).

Whatever technique you turn to, the goal is the same: to generate a wealth of ideas. At this early stage of the writing process, you should aim for quantity, not necessarily quality, of ideas. If an idea proves to be off the point, trivial, or too farfetched, you can always throw it out later.

Listing

You might begin by simply listing ideas, putting them down in the order in which they occur to you — a technique sometimes known as "brainstorming." Here, for example, is a list one student writer jotted down:

Lifeguarding — an ideal summer job?

> my love of swimming and lying in the sun
>
> hired by Powdermill Village, an apartment complex
>
> first, though, there was a test
>
> two weeks of training — grueling physical punishment plus book work
>
> I passed. The work was over — or so I thought.
>
> greeted by manager; handed a broom, hose, bottle of disinfectant
>
> scrubbing bathrooms, cleaning the pool, clearing the deck of dirt and leaves
>
> little kids breaking every pool rule in the book — running on deck, hanging on buoyed ropes, trying to drown each other
>
> spent most of my time blowing the whistle
>
> working the evening shift no better — adults smuggling in gin and tonics, sexual advances from married men
>
> by end of day, a headache and broom-handled hands

The ideas appear here in the order in which they first occurred to the writer. Later she felt free to rearrange them, to cluster them under general categories, to delete some, and to add others. In other words, she treated her initial list as a source of ideas and a springboard to new ideas, not as an outline.

Clustering or branching

Unlike listing, the techniques of clustering and branching highlight relationships among ideas. To cluster ideas, write your topic in the center of a sheet of paper, draw a circle around it, and surround that with related ideas connected to it with lines. If some of the satellite ideas lead to more specific clusters, write them down as well. The writer of the following diagram was exploring ideas for an essay on home uses for computers.

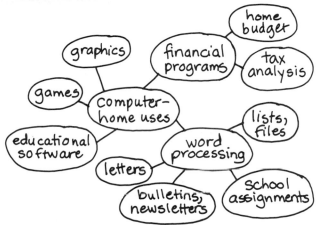

To use the branching technique, put the main idea at the top of a page and then list major supporting ideas beneath it, leaving plenty of space between each one. To the right of each major idea, branch out to minor ideas, drawing lines to indicate the connections. If minor ideas lead to even more specific ideas, continue branching. Here, for example, is a branching diagram for an essay describing an innovative magnet high school called "School without Walls."

School without Walls — an attractive option

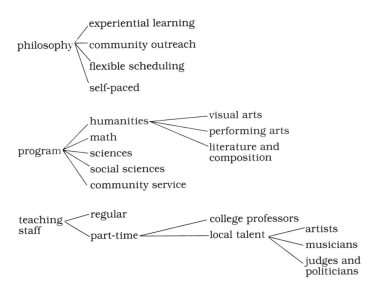

philosophy
- experiential learning
- community outreach
- flexible scheduling
- self-paced

program
- humanities
  - visual arts
  - performing arts
  - literature and composition
- math
- sciences
- social sciences
- community service

teaching staff
- regular
- part-time — local talent
  - college professors
  - artists
  - musicians
  - judges and politicians

Asking questions

By asking relevant questions, you can generate many ideas — and you can make sure that you have adequately surveyed your subject. When gathering material for a story, journalists routinely ask themselves Who? What? When? Where? Why? and How? In addition to helping journalists get started, these questions ensure that they will not overlook an important fact: the date of a prospective summit meeting, for example, or the exact location of a neighborhood burglary.

Whenever you are writing about events, whether current or historical, the journalist's questions are one way to get started. One student, whose subject was the negative reaction in 1915 to D. W. Griffith's silent film *The Birth of a Nation*, began exploring her topic with this set of questions:

Who objected to the film?

What were the objections?

When were protests first voiced?

Where were protests most strongly expressed?

Why did protesters object to the film?

How did protesters make their views known?

In the academic world, scholars often generate ideas with questions related to a specific discipline: one set of questions for analyzing short stories, another for evaluating experiments in social psychology, still another for reporting field experiences in anthropology. If you are writing in a particular discipline, try to discover the questions that scholars typically explore. These are frequently presented in textbooks as checklists. See 57a for an example.

Freewriting

In its purest form, freewriting is simply nonstop writing. You set aside ten minutes or so and write whatever comes to you, without pausing to think about word choice, spelling, or even meaning. If you get stuck, you can write about being stuck, but you should keep your pencil moving. The point is to loosen up, relax, and see what happens. Even if nothing much happens, you have lost only ten minutes. It's more likely, though, that something interesting will emerge on paper — perhaps an eloquent sentence, an honest expression of feeling, or a line of thought worth exploring.

To explore ideas on a particular topic, consider using a technique known as *focused freewriting*. Again, you write quickly and freely — without regard for word choice, spelling, punctuation, or even paragraphing — but this time you focus on a subject and pay some attention to meaning. The following passage was written freely by a student who was recalling childhood visits to his grandparents' farm.

> Memories. Memories of Canton, Mississippi. We called it The Farm, like it was the only farm in the world. There was lots to keep us busy, 90 acres of untamed pastures. One of the first things that comes to mind is playing in the haybarn, climbing through the hay stacked high to the rafters. We would burrough a path between the bails tunnelling our way to the top. This was alot of fun until someone disturbed one of the many wasp nests making everyone scatter. Cruising the pastures, we enjoyed testing sound travel. We would spread out from each other and still talk at a normal tone audibly. I remember once getting over 100 yards away from my brother — although we would have to talk slowly and clearly, we could understand each other. Another game for the pasture was to lie on the ground, be very quiet, slow our breathing, and wait for the buzzards. We could never figure out how they knew we weren't dead.   — David Queen, student

Despite the awkward beginning, the misspellings, and some problems with punctuation, this freewriting has potential. Its writer later polished some of the sentences and included them in an essay.

Keeping a journal

A journal is a collection of personal, exploratory writings. An entry in a journal can be any length — from a single sentence to several pages — and it is likely to be informal and experimental.

In a journal, meant for your eyes only, you can take risks. In one entry, for example, you might do some freewriting or focused freewriting. In another, you might pose a series of interesting questions, whether or not you have the answers. In still another, you might play around with language for the sheer fun of it: writing "purple prose," for instance, or parodying the style of a favorite author or songwriter.

Keeping a journal can be an enriching experience in its own right, since it allows you to explore issues of concern to you without worrying about what someone else thinks. A journal can also serve as a sourcebook of ideas to draw on in future essays; on rare occasions, in fact, a journal entry may emerge as a polished essay of interest to readers other than yourself. Some writers find that they do their best work when writing for themselves, deliberately ignoring the constraints of a formal writing situation.

Should you decide to keep a journal, here are some prompts to help you get started.

SOME IDEAS FOR JOURNAL WRITINGS

— Record some stories from your family's history.

— Describe some of your more interesting dreams.

— Write about a moral dilemma that you (or a friend or relative) once faced or that you now face.

— Describe a turning point in your life.

— Write a history of your involvement with a hobby or an art form; or write about current projects.

— Record your first impressions of a course you are taking this semester.

— Keep a running log of your involvement in a class that features interesting group discussions.

— Write an imaginary dialogue between two major historical figures you have read about, or a scientist and a philosopher, or characters in different novels.

— Comment on an interesting idea encountered in one of your college classes — a historical interpretation, a psychological theory, a new biological breakthrough.

— Parody the style of a favorite author or songwriter. Or mimic the style of a genre with which you are familiar (such as romances, hard-boiled detective novels, or sports writing).

Talking

The early stages of the writing process need not be lonely. Many writers begin a writing project by brainstorming ideas in a group, debating a point with friends, or engaging in conversation with a professor. Others turn to themselves for company — by talking nonstop into a tape recorder.

Talking can be a good way to get to know your audience. If you're planning to write a narrative, for instance, you can test its dramatic effect on a group of friends. Or if you hope to advance a certain argument, you can try it out on listeners who hold a different view.

As you have no doubt discovered, conversation can deepen and refine your ideas before you even begin to set them down on paper. Our first thoughts are not necessarily our wisest thoughts; by talking and listening to others we can all stretch our potential as thinkers and as writers.

EXERCISE 1–6

Generate a list of at least fifteen items for one of the subjects listed on pages 3–5.

EXERCISE 1–7

Using the technique of clustering or branching, explore one of the subjects listed on pages 3–5.

1c Settle on a tentative focus.

As you explore your subject, you will begin to see possible ways to focus your material. At this point, try to settle on a tentative central idea.

For many types of writing, your central idea can be asserted in one sentence, a generalization preparing readers for the supporting details that will follow. Such a sentence, which will ordinarily appear in the opening paragraph of your finished essay, is called a *thesis*. A successful thesis — like the following, all taken from articles in *Smithsonian* — points both the writer and the reader in a definite direction.

> Much maligned and the subject of unwarranted fears, most bats are harmless and highly beneficial.

> Geometric forms known as fractals may have a profound effect on how we view the world, not only in art and film but in many branches of science and technology, from astronomy to economics to predicting the weather.

> Aside from his more famous identities as colonel of the Rough Riders and President of the United States, Theodore Roosevelt was a lifelong professional man of letters.

The thesis sentence usually contains a key word or controlling idea that limits its focus. The preceding sentences, for example, prepare for essays that focus on the *beneficial* aspects of bats, the *effect* of fractals on how we view the world, and Roosevelt's identity as a writer, or *man of letters.*

It's a good idea to formulate a thesis early in the writing process, perhaps by jotting it on scratch paper, by putting it at the head of a rough outline, or by attempting to write an introductory paragraph that includes the thesis. Your tentative thesis will probably be less graceful than the thesis you include in the final version of your essay. Here, for example, is one student's early effort:

> Although they both play percussion instruments, drummers and percussionists are very different.

The thesis that appeared in the final draft of the student's paper was more polished.

> Two types of musicians play percussion instruments — drummers and percussionists — and they are as different as Quiet Riot and the New York Philharmonic.

Don't worry too soon about the exact wording of your thesis, however, because your main point may change as your drafts evolve. (See 2b and 3b.)

For some types of writing, it may be difficult or impossible to express the central idea in a thesis sentence; or it may be unwise or unnecessary to put a thesis sentence in the paper itself. A personal narrative, for example, may have a focus too subtle to be distilled in a single sentence, and such a sentence might ruin the story. Strictly informative writing, like that found in many business memos, may be difficult to summarize in a thesis. In such instances, do not try to force the central idea into a thesis sentence. Instead, think in terms of an overriding purpose, which may or may not be stated directly in the paper itself.

1d   Sketch a tentative plan.

Once you have generated some ideas and formulated a tentative thesis, you may want to sketch an informal outline. Informal outlines can take many forms. Perhaps the most common is simply the thesis followed by a list of major supporting ideas.

Hawaii is losing its cultural identity.

— pure-blooded Hawaiians increasingly rare

— native language diluted

— natives forced off ancestral lands

— little emphasis on native culture in schools

— customs exaggerated and distorted by tourism

Clustering or branching diagrams, often used to generate ideas, can also serve as rough outlines (see pages 19 and 20). And if you began by jotting down a list of ideas (see page 18), you may be able to turn the list into a rough outline by crossing out some ideas, adding others, and numbering the ideas to create a logical order.

Another type of informal outline, the tree diagram, pictures more complex relations among ideas. Here, for example, is a tree diagram on the subject of the disposal of nuclear waste.

When to use a formal outline

Early in the writing process, rough outlines have certain advantages over their more formal counterparts: They can be produced more quickly, they are more obviously tentative, and they can be revised more easily should the need arise. However, a formal outline may be useful later in the writing process, after you have written a rough draft, especially if your subject matter is complex.

The student who sketched the tree diagram about the disposal of nuclear waste later wrote a sentence outline that improved and clarified the structure of his rough draft. Notice that the student's thesis is an important part of the outline. Everything else in the outline supports it, either directly or indirectly.

Thesis: Although various methods for limiting or disposing of nuclear wastes have been proposed, each has serious drawbacks.

I. The process of limiting nuclear waste through partitioning and transmutation has serious drawbacks.
   A. The process is complex and costly.
   B. Nuclear workers' exposure to radiation would increase.

II. Antarctic ice sheet disposal is problematic for scientific and legal reasons.
   A. Our understanding of the behavior of ice sheets is too limited.
   B. An international treaty prohibits disposal in Antarctica.

III. Space disposal is unthinkable.
   A. The risk of an accident and resulting worldwide disaster is great.
   B. The cost is prohibitive.
   C. The method would be unpopular at home and abroad.

IV. Seabed disposal is unwise because we do not know enough about the procedure or its impact.
   A. Scientists have not yet solved technical difficulties.
   B. We do not fully understand the impact of such disposal on the ocean's ecology.

V. Deep underground disposal endangers public safety and creates political problems.
   A. Geologists disagree about the safest disposal sites, and no sites are completely safe.
   B. There is much political pressure against the plan from citizens who do not want their states to become nuclear dumps.

In constructing a formal outline, keep the following guidelines in mind.

1. Put the thesis at the top.
2. Make items at the same level of generality as parallel as possible (see 9).
3. Use sentences unless phrases are clear.
4. Use the conventional system of numbers and letters for the levels of generality.

    I.
      A.
      B.
         1.
         2.
            a.
            b.
               (1)
               (2)
                  (a)
                  (b)
    II.

5. Always use at least two subdivisions for a category, since nothing can be divided into fewer than two parts.
6. Limit the number of major sections in the outline; if the list of roman numerals begins to look like a laundry list, find some way of clustering the items into a few major categories with more subcategories.
7. Be flexible; in other words, be prepared to change your outline as your drafts evolve.

EXERCISE 1-8

Draft a preliminary thesis and rough outline on the subject of the growing influence of computers on our daily lives. The following list is meant to prompt your thoughts. If some items do not support your thesis, eliminate them; if you can think of other items that do, add them.

Topic: The growing influence of computers on our daily lives

Automatic banks
Personal computers installed in every dorm room in colleges
Computers in grade schools
Computer literacy as a job requirement in many fields
Computers in scholarship
Computer games
Isolation of many "hackers"
Mechanization of society
Fear of computers
Robots
Liberal arts education made obsolete by computers
Computer cash registers in stores
Robot actors at EPCOT Center and Disney World
Revenge of computers as the subject for science fiction films
Computer dating
Computers eliminating jobs
Computers eliminating tedious work
Computer art
Computer mail
Lap-top computers

2

Rough out an initial draft.

As long as you treat an initial draft as a rough draft, you can focus your attention on ideas and organization, knowing that problems with sentence structure and word choice can always be dealt with later.

2a Let it be rough and keep it moving.

Before beginning a first draft, gather together your prewriting materials — lists, diagrams, outlines, freewriting, and so on. In addition to helping you get started, such notes and blueprints will encourage you to keep moving. With your earlier thoughts close by, you won't need to pause so frequently, staring at a blank page in search of ideas. Writing tends to flow better when it is drafted relatively quickly, without many stops and starts. The trick, of course, is to relax — to overcome the fear that grips many of us as we face that blank page.

At one time or another, we all experience writer's block. But if writer's block is a chronic problem for you, consider whether you're being too hard on yourself. Do you demand that your sentences all be stylish and perfectly grammatical right from the start? Do you expect your ideas to emerge full-blown, like Athena from the head of Zeus?

Professional writers are not so tough on themselves. Jacques Barzun, for example, lets his rough-draft sentences be "as stupid" as they wish. Joan Didion acknowledges that she discovers ideas *as she writes;* for her, writing is a way of learning, not just a means of revealing already known truths. As Didion puts it, "I write entirely to find out what I'm thinking, what I'm looking at, what I see and what it means."

2b For most types of writing, draft an introduction that includes a thesis.

The introduction announces the main point; the body develops it, usually in several paragraphs; the conclusion drives it home. You can begin drafting, however, at any point. If you find it difficult to introduce a paper that you have not yet written, you can write the body first and save the introduction for later.

For most writing tasks, your introduction will be a paragraph of 50 to 150 words. Perhaps the most common strategy is to open the paragraph with a few sentences that engage the reader and to conclude it with a statement of the essay's main point. The sentence stating the main point is called a *thesis.* (See 1c.) In the following examples, the thesis has been italicized.

> To the Australian aborigines, the Dreamtime was the time of creation. It was then that the creatures of the earth, including man, came into being. There are many legends about that mystical period, but unfortunately, the koala does not fare too well in any of them. *Slow-witted though it is in life, the koala is generally depicted in myth and folklore as a trickster and a thief.*   — Roger Caras, "What's a Koala?"

> When I was sixteen, I married and moved to a small town to live. My new husband nervously showed me the house he had rented. It was after dark when we arrived there, and I remember wondering why he seemed so apprehensive about my reaction to the house. I thought the place seemed shabby but potentially cozy and quite livable inside. The morning sun revealed the reason for his anxiety by exposing the squalor outdoors. Up to that point, my contact with any reality but that of my own middle-class childhood had come from books. *The next four years in a small Iowa town taught me that reading about poverty is a lot different from living with it.*
> — Julie Reardon, student

Ideally, the sentences leading to the thesis should hook the reader, perhaps with one of the following:

a startling statistic or unusual fact

a vivid example

a description

a paradoxical statement

a quotation or bit of dialogue

a question

an analogy

a joke or an anecdote

Such hooks are particularly important when you cannot assume your reader's interest in the subject. Hooks are less necessary in scholarly essays and other writing aimed at readers with a professional interest in the subject.

Although the thesis frequently appears at the end of the introduction, it can just as easily appear at the beginning. Much work-related writing, in which a straightforward approach is most effective, commonly begins with the thesis.

> *Flex-time scheduling, which has proved its effectiveness at the Library of Congress, should be introduced on a trial basis at the main branch of the Montgomery County Public Library.* By offering flexible work hours, the library can boost employee morale, cut down on absenteeism, and expand its hours of operation.   — David Warren, student

In narrative and descriptive writing, it is not always necessary to have an explicitly stated thesis. (See 1c.) However, an introduction without a thesis should clearly suggest the purpose and direction of the essay to follow. For example, even though a thesis has not been directly stated in the following introduction, readers understand that they are about to hear a gripping story about danger at sea.

> At the Coast Guard Training Center in Alameda, California, our instructors stressed that we still had much to learn about the sea's moods and temperaments. Our training, they said, was only inadequate preparation for what could happen to us in open water. "The ocean humbles even the most experienced skipper!" warned one teacher ominously. He often spoke of the *Edmund Fitzgerald*, an ore carrier which had foundered in a winter storm on Lake Superior. Even

though the ship was over seven hundred feet from stem to stern and equipped with the latest technology, she went down in less than a sweep of the radar's antenna. But it made no difference to me. After all, those men on the *Fitzgerald* were only civilians; I was a Coast Guardsman. After fifteen weeks at the Center, after long hours delving into the art of navigation and piloting, I could deal with any emergency. Steering — "wheeling" as we called it — was my forte. Several times, in fact, in less-than-perfect conditions, I had brought ships through narrow entrances in the breakwall. I could handle any ship of any tonnage. There was nothing that I couldn't do.

— Jonathan Schilk, student

Characteristics of an effective thesis

An effective thesis should be a generalization, not a fact; it should be limited, not too broad; and it should be sharply focused, not too vague.

Because a thesis must prepare readers for facts and details, it cannot itself be a fact. It must always be a generalization demanding proof or further development.

TOO FACTUAL   The first polygraph was developed by Dr. John A. Larson in 1921.

REVISED   Because the polygraph has not been proved reliable, even under the most controlled conditions, its use by private employers should be banned.

Although a thesis must be a generalization, it must not be *too* general. You will need to narrow the focus of any thesis that you cannot adequately develop in the space allowed. Unless you were writing a book or a very long research paper, the following thesis would be too broad.

TOO BROAD   Many drugs are now being used successfully to treat mental illnesses.

You would need to restrict the thesis, perhaps like this:

REVISED   Despite its risks and side effects, lithium is an effective treatment for depression.

Finally, a thesis should be sharply focused, not too vague. Beware of any thesis containing a fuzzy, hard-to-define word such as *interesting, good,* or *disgusting.*

TOO VAGUE   Many of the songs played on station WXQP are disgusting.

The word *disgusting* is needlessly vague. To sharpen the focus of this thesis, the writer should be more specific.

REVISED   Of the songs played on station WXQP, all too many depict sex crudely, sanction the beating or rape of women, or foster gang violence.

In the process of making a too-vague thesis more precise, you may find yourself outlining the major sections of your paper, as in the previous example. This technique, known as *blueprinting,* helps readers know exactly what to expect as they read on. It also helps you, the writer, control the shape of your essay. Here is another example of blueprinting, taken from a student essay.

From the moment she can understand her parents' commands through her own marriage and childbearing, a Vietnamese female tries to establish a good name as a diligent daughter, a submissive wife, and an altruistic mother.

2c Fill out the body.

Before drafting the body of an essay, take a careful look at your introduction, focusing especially on your thesis sentence. What does the thesis promise readers? Try to keep this focus in mind.

It's a good idea to have a plan in mind as well. If your thesis sentence outlines a plan (see 2b) or if you have sketched a preliminary outline, try to block out your paragraphs accordingly. If you do not have a plan, you would be wise to pause for a moment and sketch one (see 1d). Of course it is also possible to begin without a plan — assuming you are prepared to treat your first attempt as a "discovery draft" that will almost certainly be tossed (or radically rewritten) once you discover what you really want to say.

2d Attempt a conclusion.

The conclusion should echo the main idea, without dully repeating it. Often the concluding paragraph can be relatively short. By the end of the essay, readers should already understand your main point; your conclusion simply drives it home and perhaps suggests its significance.

In addition to echoing your main idea, a conclusion might summarize the essay's key points, pose a question for future study, offer advice, or propose a course of action. To end an essay detailing the social skills required of a bartender, one writer concludes with some advice:

> If someone were to approach me one day looking for the secret to running a good bar, I suppose I would offer the following advice: Get your customers to pour out their ideas at a greater rate than you pour out the liquor. You will both win in the end. — Kathleen Lewis, student

To make the conclusion memorable, consider including a detail, example, or image from the introduction to bring readers full circle; a quotation or bit of dialogue; an anecdote; or a humorous, witty, or ironic comment. To end a narrative describing a cash register holdup, one student uses an anecdote that includes some dialogue:

> It took me a long time to get over that incident. Countless times I found myself gasping as someone "pointed" a dollar bill at me. On one such occasion, a jovial little man buying a toy gun for his son came up to me and said in a Humphrey Bogart impression, "Give me all your money, Sweetheart." I didn't laugh. Instead, my heart skipped a beat, for I had heard those words before.   — Diana Crawford, student

Whatever concluding strategy you choose, avoid introducing wholly new ideas at the end of an essay. Also avoid apologies and other limp, indeterminate endings. The essay should end crisply, preferably on a positive note.

Do not become discouraged if the perfect conclusion eludes you at the rough-draft stage of the writing process. Because the conclusion is so closely tied to the rest of the essay in both content and tone, you may well decide to rework it (or even replace it) as your drafts evolve.

EXERCISE 2–1

The following are paired introductory paragraphs written by students. One is a rough-draft version, and the other is a revision. Decide which paragraph in each pair is the revision, and be prepared to discuss how it has been improved. Feel free to make further suggestions for improvement.

1a.   Tucked away in the corner of my cellar, dimly illuminated by a naked swaying bulb, sit row upon row of dust-laden mason jars. These once filled but long unused jars are befriended in their dejection by two huge blue enameled kettles and one nearly new gleaming stainless steel pressure canner. These dusty relics are mementos of my gardening years. Seeing them, I am reminded that after hours of planting, nurturing, and harvesting, a gardener's reward is a bountiful array of fresh, succulent produce that for taste and color cannot be equaled by any that is purchased at an uptown supermarket. But while it is true that Home-Grown-Picked-at-the-Peak vegetables are unbeatable, it has been my unfortunate experience to find that an overabundant supply of table-ready vegetables can be frustrating, exhausting, and costly.   — Rita Hollingsworth

b.   After hours of nurturing and harvesting, a gardener's reward is a bountiful array of fresh, succulent produce. For taste and color these "picked-at-the-peak" vegetables cannot be equaled by those purchased at the local Safeway. It has been my unfortunate experience, however, that an overabundant supply of table-ready vegetables can be frustrating, exhausting, and costly.   — Rita Hollingsworth

2a.   Crickets chirped in the grass surrounding the compound as four men, dressed only in white government-issue underwear, made their way through the dark barracks. Airman Goodrich woke as the rough military blanket settled over his head and chest. He tried to move, but the four men held the blanket securely, pinning him to his bunk. His feet kicked as a fifth man rose from his neighboring bunk and began to pummel him to unconsciousness. Goodrich's screams shattered the night, yet no one moved a muscle to help. Though the snoring, which was incessant at night, had stopped abruptly and completely, everyone pretended to sleep. When the screaming and pleading had finally died away, Goodrich was motionless. The moonlight poured through the windows, casting unearthly shadows across his body.

— Terry L. Burns

b.   Screams shattered the sleep of one hundred men in the dark barracks as Airman Goodrich pleaded for help. Everyone knew what was happening. Three men were holding a blanket over Goodrich's upper torso and head as the fourth pummeled him into unconsciousness, yet no one moved a muscle to help. Everyone pretended to be asleep, though the snoring, which was incessant at night, had stopped abruptly and completely. When the screaming finally stopped, the room was deadly silent. The only sounds to be heard were the chirping of the crickets in the grass surrounding the compound and the ominous buzz of the locust in the trees. Goodrich lay still on his bunk, the moonlight pouring through the windows, casting eerie shadows across his body.　　　— Terry L. Burns

3a.　　　I am approached quite often by people who are curious about my handicap. Because the questions are so common, I should carry a tape recorder that will play, "Beep! This is a recording. I had my right leg amputated when I was five due to osteogenic sarcoma." There have been times, however, when the tape recorder would have been of little value since the questions asked were extraordinary.　　　— Annie Glaven

b.　　　I am approached quite often by people who are curious about my handicap. For the most part, because the questions are so common, I feel as if I should carry a tape recorder that I can press start and it will play beep! this is a recording and continue with my monologue. However, there have been times when the tape recorder would have been of little value since the questions were quite out of the ordinary.　　　— Annie Glaven

4a.　　　On June 2, 1972, at 10:57 A.M., the driver of Checker Cab #43 picked up a thirty-four-year-old, neatly dressed, pretty woman from a veterans hospital and dropped her off a short time later in the downtown section of the city. The woman walked to a nearby hotel, checked in, and paid for her room in advance. The woman was my sister, Laura, and the hotel clerk was the last person to see her alive. Sometime between the time she checked into the hotel and 11:57 P.M. the following evening, Laura committed suicide. The profound sorrow I felt after Laura's tragic death has gradually subsided. The indignant anger that consumed me following her death, however, has not. I was not only angry at my own naiveté and the senselessness of her death, but at the uncaring attitude of the people I encountered following the tragedy.　　　— Doris Egnor

b.　　　I was much more naive and trusting ten years ago than I am today. I believed that all policemen were good, all doctors were caring, and all people shared my concern for their fellow man. I realized with anguish the folly of making such generalizations when my sister, Laura, committed suicide. I was not only angered about my own naiveté but also outraged by the uncaring attitude of the people I encountered following the tragedy.　　　— Doris Egnor

3

Make global revisions: Think big.

Revising is not just a matter of moving words around and correcting grammar. It involves much larger changes, global improvements that can be quite dramatic. Whole paragraphs might be dropped, others added. Material once stretched over two or three paragraphs might be condensed into one. Entire sections could be rearranged. Even the content may change dramatically, for the process of writing stimulates thought.

Major revising can be difficult, sometimes even painful. You might discover, for example, that an essay's first three paragraphs are nothing but padding, that its central argument tilts the wrong way, and that you sound like a stuffed shirt throughout. But the sheer fact that you can see such problems in your writing is a sign of hope. Those opening paragraphs can be dropped, the argument's slant realigned, the voice made more human.

3a Get some distance, perhaps with the help of reviewers.

Many of us resist global revisions because we find it difficult to distance ourselves from a draft. We tend to review our work from our own, not from our audience's, perspective.

To distance yourself from a draft, begin by putting it aside for a while, preferably overnight or even longer. When you return to it, try to play the role of your audience as you read. Mark any places where your readers are likely to be confused, misled, or annoyed; look too for sentences and paragraphs that are not likely to persuade.

If at all possible, enlist the help of reviewers — persons

willing to play the role of audience for you. Possible reviewers include peers, such as family members, friends, and other students; and professionals, such as professors, trained writing center tutors, and practicing writers. Ask your reviewers to focus on the larger issues of writing, not on the fine points. If they are at first captivated by fine points such as grammar and spelling — and many peer reviewers often are — remind them that you are not ready to think about such matters. For the moment, you are interested in their response to the essay as a whole.

Many professors set aside class time for peer review sessions in which students respond to each other's drafts in written comments, discussions, or both. For guidelines on being a peer reviewer, see the chart on pages 42–43.

3b Approach global revision in cycles.

The process of global revision can be complex, so it is best to approach it in cycles, with each cycle encompassing a particular purpose for revising. Five common cycles of global revision are discussed in this section:

- Strengthening the content
- Sharpening the focus
- Improving the organization
- Clarifying the point of view
- Refining the tone

You can handle these cycles in nearly any order, and you may be able to combine some of them.

If you have asked someone to review your draft, you have already begun to see which of these cycles most need your attention. And by giving some thought to your overall purpose and audience, you'll discern even more clearly where your essay does — and does not — need major reworking.

Guidelines for peer reviewers

READING THE ESSAY

As you read, you may want to pencil a few marks in the margin: perhaps a check mark (√) for sentences or passages that seem especially effective, a question mark (?) for spots that confused you, a plus mark (+) for places where you'd like to hear more details. Don't get carried away, however. Remember that you are not "grading" a finished essay; you are helping a fellow writer get distance from a rough draft. Above all, do not mark errors in grammar, punctuation, and spelling. The writer can deal with such matters later.

WRITING COMMENTS

Although some professors may ask you to write comments on the draft of an essay, most prefer that you respond on a separate sheet of paper. Here are some ideas for written responses:

1. In a sentence, describe the writer's apparent purpose and audience.
2. In a sentence, explain what the introduction promises readers; in other words, explain what you, as a reader, expect to hear in the rest of the essay.
3. List the two or three passages that best fulfill the promise of the introduction.
4. List a few things that you would like to hear more about.
5. Try to sketch a very simple outline of the draft. (If this is difficult, the writer may need to work on organization.)
6. Write down two or three sentences from the draft that you found particularly interesting or well written.

DISCUSSING YOUR IDEAS WITH THE WRITER

If you have the opportunity to discuss your ideas with the writer, here are some guidelines to keep in mind:

1. Try to open your conversation with descriptive, rather than evaluative, comments. For example, if the writer's subject is physical handicaps, you might begin by saying, "I think your point is that many adults are insensitive and patronizing when they encounter persons with physical handicaps."

2. When you turn to evaluative comments, make the first ones positive. For example, you might mention that you found the writer's second paragraph a powerful example of insensitivity toward handicapped persons.

3. An effective peer review session is a dialogue, not a monologue. Try to get the writer talking by asking questions — about the draft-in-progress and about the subject. As writers talk about their subject with an interested listener, they often recall useful details and vivid examples that might be included in the essay.

4. If you have suggestions for improvement, try to tie them to the writer's goals. For instance, you might advise the writer to put the most dramatic example of insensitivity toward the handicapped last, where it will have maximum impact on readers. Or you might suggest that a descriptive passage would gain power if abstractions were replaced with concrete details.

5. Throughout the review session, look on yourself as a coach, not a judge, as a proposer of possibilities, not a dictator of revisions. It is the writer, after all, who will have to grapple with the task of improving the essay.

6. At the end of the review session, you might want to express interest in reading the writer's next revision or final draft. Such interest — if it is sincere — can be a powerful motivation for a writer.

Strengthening the content

In reviewing the content of a draft, consider whether any text (sentences, paragraphs, or longer passages) should be added or deleted, keeping in mind your readers' needs. Then, if your purpose is to argue a point, consider how persuasively you have proved your point to an intelligent, discerning audience. When necessary, rethink your argument.

ADDING TEXT   If any paragraphs or sections of the essay are developed too skimpily to be clear and convincing (a common flaw in rough drafts), you will need to add specific facts, details, and examples. This necessity will take you back to the beginning of the writing process: listing specifics, perhaps clustering them, and then roughing out new sentences and paragraphs. Many writers deliberately overwrite a first draft, filling it out with more details than they will probably need, to avoid having to produce new material later. The process of cutting and rearranging is almost always easier than beginning again from scratch.

DELETING TEXT   Look for sentences and paragraphs that can be cut without serious loss of meaning. Perhaps you have repeated yourself or strayed from your point. Maybe you have given undue emphasis to minor ideas. Cuts may also be necessitated by word limits, such as those imposed by a college assignment or by the realities of the business world, where readers are often pressed for time.

RETHINKING YOUR ARGUMENT   A first draft presents you with an opportunity for rethinking your argument. You can often deepen your ideas on a subject by asking yourself some hard questions. Is your claim more sweeping than the evidence allows? Have you left out an important step in the argument? Have you dealt with the arguments of the opposition? Is your thinking flawed by logical fallacies? The more challenging your subject, the more likely you will find yourself adjusting your early thoughts. (For more about argumentative writing, see 56.)

Sharpening the focus

A draft is clearly focused when it fixes the reader's attention on one central idea and does not stray from that idea. You can sharpen the focus of a draft by clarifying the introduction (especially the thesis) and by deleting any text that is off the point.

CLARIFYING THE INTRODUCTION First you will want to make sure that your introduction looks and reads like an introduction. Can readers tell where the introduction stops and the body of the essay begins? Have you perhaps included material in the introduction that really belongs in the body of the essay? Is your introduction long-winded?

Next check to see whether the introduction focuses clearly on the main point of the essay. Does it let readers know what to expect as they read on? Does it make the significance of the subject clear so that readers will want to read on?

The most important sentence in the introduction is the thesis. (See 2b.) If your essay lacks a thesis, make sure that you have a good reason for not including one. If your thesis is poorly focused or if it doesn't accurately state the real point of the essay, you'll need to revise it.

DELETING TEXT THAT IS OFF THE POINT Compare the essay's introduction, particularly its thesis statement, with the body of the essay. Does the body of the essay fulfill the promise of the introduction? If not, one or the other must be adjusted. Either rebuild the introduction to fit the body of the paper or keep the introduction and delete any sentences or paragraphs that stray from its point.

Improving the organization

A draft is well organized when its major divisions are logical and easy for readers to follow. To improve the organization of your draft, consider taking one or more of the following actions: adding or sharpening topic sentences, moving blocks of text, reparagraphing, and considering headings.

ADDING OR SHARPENING TOPIC SENTENCES Topic sentences, as you probably know, state the main ideas of the paragraphs in the body of an essay. (See 5a.) Topic sentences act as signposts for readers, announcing ideas to come.

You can review the organization of a draft by reading only the topic sentences. Do they clearly support the essay's main idea? Do they make a reasonable sentence outline of the paper? If your draft lacks topic sentences, make sure you have a good reason for omitting these important signposts. (See 5a.)

MOVING BLOCKS OF TEXT Improving the organization of a draft can be as simple as moving a few sentences from one paragraph to another or switching the order of paragraphs. Often, however, the process is more complex. As you move blocks of text, you may need to supply transitions to make them fit smoothly in their new positions; you may also need to rework topic sentences to make your new organization clear.

Before moving text, consider sketching a revised outline. Divisions in the outline might become topic sentences in the restructured essay. (See 1d.)

REPARAGRAPHING AND CONSIDERING HEADINGS Occasionally you can clarify the organization of a draft simply by combining choppy paragraphs or by dividing those that are too long for easy reading. (See 6d.)

In long documents, such as research papers or business reports, you may be able to clarify your organization by inserting headings above blocks of text. Possible headings include phrases, declarative or imperative sentences, and questions. To draw attention to headings, consider centering them, putting them in boldface, underlining them, using all capital letters, or some combination of these.

Clarifying the point of view

If the point of view of a draft shifts confusingly or if it seems not quite appropriate for your purpose, audience, and subject, consider adjusting it.

There are three basic points of view to choose from: the first person (*I* or *we*), the second person (*you*), and the third person (*he/she/it/one* or *they*). Each point of view is appropriate in at least some contexts, and you may need to experiment before discovering which one best suits your needs.

THE THIRD-PERSON POINT OF VIEW Much academic and professional writing is best presented from the third-person point of view (*he/she/it/one* or *they*), which puts the subject in the foreground. The *I* point of view is usually inappropriate in such contexts because, by focusing attention on the writer, it pushes the subject into the background. Consider, for example, one student's first-draft description of the behavior of a species of frog that he had observed in the field.

> Each frog that *I* was able to locate in trees remained in its given tree during the entirety of *my* observation period. However, *I* noticed that there was considerable movement within the home tree.

Here the *I* point of view is distracting, as the student himself noticed when he began to revise his report. His revision focuses more on the frogs, less on himself.

Each frog located in a tree remained in that tree throughout the observation period. The frogs moved about considerably, however, within their home trees.

Just as the first-person pronoun *I* can draw too much attention to the writer, the second-person pronoun *you* can focus unnecessarily on the reader. One biology manual, for example, in an exercise meant to focus on the skeletal system, shifts the attention instead to the reader:

Give at least two functions of the backbone from *your* reading.

This exercise would be clearer and more direct if presented without the distraction of the *you* point of view.

What are two functions of the backbone?

Although the third-person point of view is often a better choice than the *I* or *you* point of view, it is by no means trouble-free. Writers who choose it can run into problems when they want to use singular pronouns in an indefinite sense. For example, when Miss Piggy says that a reason for jogging is "to improve *one's* emotional health and make *one* feel better about *oneself*," one wishes she wouldn't use quite so many *one*'s, doesn't one? The trouble is that American English, unlike British English, does not allow this pronoun to echo unself-consciously throughout a sentence. The repetitions sound stuffy.

Some years ago Americans would have said "to improve a person's emotional health and to make *him* feel better about *himself*," with the understanding that *him* really meant *him or her*. Today, however, this use of *him* is offensive to many readers and is best avoided. On the other hand, "to make *him or her* feel better about *himself or herself*" is distinctly awkward. So what is poor Miss Piggy to say?

Her only hope, it turns out, is a flexible and inventive mind. She might switch to the plural: *Joggers run to improve their emotional health and to make them feel better about themselves.* Or she could restructure the sentence altogether: *Jogging improves a person's emotional health and self-image.* (See 17f and 22a.)

THE SECOND-PERSON POINT OF VIEW The *you* point of view, which puts the reader in the foreground, is appropriate if the writer is advising readers directly, as in giving tips on raising children or instructions on flower arranging. All imperative sentences, such as the advice for writers in this book, are written from the *you* point of view, although the word itself is frequently omitted and understood. "Sketch a plan" means "*You* should sketch a plan"; everyone knows this, so the *you* is not expressed.

In the course of giving advice or instructions, the actual word *you* may be appropriate and even desired. In advising gardeners about walkways, for example, newspaper columnist Henry Mitchell feels free to use the words *you* and *your* as the need arises:

> If *your* main walk is less than four feet wide, and if it is white concrete, then widen it, no matter what has to be sacrificed . . . and resurface it with brick, stone, or something less glaring and dull. Three flowers against a good-looking pavement will do more for *you* than thirty flowers against white concrete. [Italics added.]

Mitchell might have written this passage from the third-person point of view instead ("If *the gardener's* walk is less than four feet wide . . ."), but the effect would have seemed oddly indirect. Even at the risk of sounding a bit bossy, Mitchell has wisely selected the imperative stance instead.

Notice that Mitchell's *you* means "you, the reader." It does not mean "you, anyone in general." Indefinite uses of *you*, such as the following example, are inappropriate in formal writing (see 23d).

> Young Japanese women wired together electronic products on a piece-rate system: The more *you* wired, the more *you* were paid.

Here the writer should have stayed with the third-person point of view instead.

> The more *they* wired, the more *they* were paid.

THE FIRST-PERSON POINT OF VIEW If much of a writer's material comes from personal experience, the *I* point of view will prove most natural. It is difficult to imagine, for example, how James Thurber could have avoided the word *I* in describing his early university days:

> *I* passed all the other courses that *I* took at my university, but *I* could never pass botany. This was because all botany students had to spend several hours a week in a laboratory looking through a microscope at plant cells, and *I* could never see through a microscope. *I* never once saw a cell through a microscope. This used to enrage my instructor. [Italics added.]
> — "University Days"

Thurber's *I* point of view puts the writer in the foreground, and since the writer is in fact the subject, this makes sense.

Writers who are aware that the first-person point of view is sometimes viewed as inappropriate in academic writing often overgeneralize the rule. Concluding that the word *I* is never appropriate, they go to extreme lengths to avoid it.

> Mama read with such color and detail that *one* could fancy *oneself* as the hero of the story.

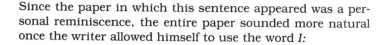
Since the paper in which this sentence appeared was a personal reminiscence, the entire paper sounded more natural once the writer allowed himself to use the word *I:*

> Mama read with such color and detail that *I* could fancy *myself* as the hero of the story.

Refining the tone

The tone of a piece of writing expresses the writer's feelings about the subject and audience, so it is important to get it right. If the tone seems too flippant — or too stuffy, bossy, patronizing, or hostile — obviously it should be modified.

Any piece of writing drafted in anger or frustration will almost certainly need to be toned down. The following rough draft, for example, was written by a secretary in response to criticisms of a newsletter sent out by the organization for which she worked:

> Dear Mr. Martin:
>
> I know our newsletter is crudely laid out, the reason being that I type it from rough drafts under a tight enough deadline that only major errors of judgment get retyped. Perhaps we'd do better if we had a word processor.
>
> I think you were wrong to dismiss the offending story as bragging about *Nuclear War: What's in It for You?* The book was nominated for the prize, a fact worthy of mention despite the fact that it did not win.
>
> In any case, I am glad to hear that you liked the open letter to the president. Would that the *Philadelphia Inquirer* had liked it as well.
>
> Sincerely,
>
> Robbie Nichols

As she reached the last paragraph of the rough draft, the writer saw the need to be more diplomatic. Later, in a calmer mood, she revised the letter like this:

Dear Mr. Martin:

We are glad to hear that you liked Roger Molander's "An Open Letter to the President." Would that the *Philadelphia Inquirer* had liked it as well.

I do think you were wrong to dismiss the sentence about *Nuclear War: What's in It for You?* as "bragging." It is a fairly direct sentence, and there may well be those among the faithful who wouldn't otherwise have known about its nomination for the prize.

Your comments about the physical layout of the story were, in fact, echoed by the staff here. The layout could not be changed, however, because it was typed under a tight deadline that allowed retyping only in cases of major errors of judgment.

Thank you for writing. Even though our newsletter has a limited circulation, we hope that Roger's open letter will elicit serious thought about the president's March 23 address on the Soviet Union and weapons in space.

Sincerely,

Robbie Nichols

EXERCISE 3 – 1

Imagine that Joan Bradley, the writer of the following rough draft, has come to you for advice about global revisions: possible improvements in content, focus, organization, point of view, and tone. (See the chart on page 53.) Try to resist commenting on sentence structure, punctuation, and other sentence-level matters that Bradley can deal with later.

Euthanasia for Animals

Active euthanasia is legal and accepted with animals. It is helping an animal to die by administering certain drugs. It is

Cycles of global revision

STRENGTHENING THE CONTENT

Look for opportunities

- to add specific facts, details, and examples
- to delete repetitious or ineffective text
- to rethink your argument

SHARPENING THE FOCUS

Look for opportunities

- to clarify the introduction (especially the thesis)
- to delete text that is off the point

IMPROVING THE ORGANIZATION

Look for opportunities

- to add or sharpen topic sentences
- to move blocks of text
- to reparagraph and perhaps add headings

CLARIFYING THE POINT OF VIEW

Look for opportunities

- to make the point of view more consistent
- to use a more appropriate point of view
- to avoid the problem of sexist English

REFINING THE TONE

Look for opportunities

- to approach your audience more diplomatically
- to use language more appropriate for your subject and your audience

also the hardest part of my job as a technician in an animal hospital. Sometimes I feel it is justifiable to put an animal to sleep because it is suffering and is being put out of misery, but other times I feel it is a waste of a life of an animal.

An animal brought to the hospital to be put to sleep is called an "E and D" patient. "E and D" means "euthanasia and disposal," meaning we euthanize the animal and then dispose of the body. This is the worst and hardest part of my job.

It is done by injecting the drug T-61 into the animal. It is usually put directly into the vein. I am not a professionally trained technician, but I was taught how to inject drugs into the vein of an animal. It isn't easy, so sometimes I would get out of administering the drug by claiming I couldn't do it. Putting an animal to sleep is a very hard thing for me to do, and it took a long time for me to get used to it.

The process is done by tying the foreleg off above the elbow with a tourniquet. The fur is wetted down with a moist cotton ball and the needle is inserted. The tourniquet is then loosened and the drug is injected. I was surprised to find that animals don't close their eyes and look peacefully asleep when they die. Cats and small dogs have very small veins which are hard to find, so T-61 is injected directly into the chest cavity. This is easier for the technician but harder for the animal because it takes longer for the drug to take effect and to go through the body. I often wonder what the animal feels, and sometimes I have nightmares of a burning sensation going throughout my body, with animals all around me asking, "Why?"

Animals are put to sleep for many different reasons. As I mentioned, some are justifiable, some are not. A good example of just euthanasia is Trixie. She was a thirteen-year-old fox terrier who began to feel her age of ninety-one in dog years. Her owners wanted to do all that was possible to keep her alive but each day she became weaker. Soon she gave up eating and drinking and waited painfully for her time to come. There was nothing anyone could do for Trixie. Veterinarians can cure sickness but cannot restore youth. Instead of watching Trixie suffer, the owner brought her to the hospital for euthanasia.

Another example was the litter of three puppies that some idiot had abandoned in a burlap sack along a roadside. After the sack had been struck by a car, a passerby found the puppies and brought them to the hospital. One puppy was in shock, one had a broken pelvis, the other had serious internal injuries. They were going through much pain and suffering so each puppy was euthanized. I believe these two examples are justifiable because these animals were better off being put to sleep than being allowed to suffer.

Some humans are pig-headed and cruel. Those people who have their pets put to sleep for selfish reasons. Ms. Olsen brought two beautiful cats to the hospital to be euthanized. An adult blue point Siamese that someone had given her and a young healthy black cat. When asked why, she replied, "I've just bought a new beige carpet for my living room and these cats are constantly shedding hair on it that could simply ruin it!" And then there was the woman who wanted her beagle put to sleep because she was moving and couldn't find a suitable home for it. By coincidence a man came in at the same time who just happened to be looking for a beagle. He was looking for one to train into a hunting dog to add to the few he already had. The woman didn't want her to be trained to hunt and proceeded to deprive her dog of a good long, happy life. These examples of euthanasia are the hardest for me to perform because the animal seems to know that it hasn't had a full life and fights the euthanasia.

Whenever I must euthanize an animal, I tell myself that it is part of my job and that I must do it, no matter what the reason. I certainly can't save them all or give them homes. But I can't help wondering who or what can give the right to me do this. I can see where it is needed in some cases, but why not then in people? If euthanasia was allowed with people, perfectly healthy people wouldn't be put to sleep, so why are perfectly healthy animals allowed to be? My point is that euthanasia on animals should have restrictions. I do it as part of my job, then try to forget it, but the look in an animal's unclosed eye and the nightmares will be impossible to forget.

4

Revise and edit sentences; proofread the final draft.

When you revise sentences, you focus on effectiveness; when you edit, you check for correctness. As with global revision, sentence revision may be approached in cycles, with each cycle focusing on a different purpose for making changes. The main purposes for revising sentences — to strengthen, clarify, vary, and refine them — are detailed in the chart on page 58. A checklist on editing for grammar, punctuation, and mechanics appears on page 59.

To save yourself time, you should ordinarily revise and edit sentences right on the pages of an earlier draft, like this:

> Finally ~~we decided~~ *deciding* that perhaps our dream
> needed ~~some~~ prompting, ~~and~~ we visited a fertility
> doctor and began the expensive, time-consuming
> round of procedures that held out ~~the~~ *some* promise of
> ~~fulfilling our dream.~~ *our dream's fulfillment. Our efforts, however, were*
> ~~All this was~~ to no avail/. *As*
> ~~and as~~ we approached the sixth year of our mar-
> riage, we ~~had reached the point where we couldn't~~ *could no longer*
> even discuss our childlessness without becoming
> very depressed. We questioned why this had hap-
> pened to us/. Why had we been singled out for ~~this~~ *such a*
> major disappointment?

The original paragraph was flawed by wordiness and an excessive reliance on structures connected with *and.* Such problems can be addressed through any number of acceptable revisions. The first sentence, for example, could have been changed like this:

> Finally we decided that perhaps our dream
> needed ~~some~~ prompting. ^After visiting^ ~~and we visited~~ a fertility
> ^we^
> doctor, ~~and~~ began the expensive, time-consuming
> round of procedures that ^promised hope^ ~~held out the promise~~ of
> fulfilling our dream.

Though some writers might argue about the effectiveness of these improvements compared with the previous revision, most would agree that both versions are better than the original.

Some of the paragraph's improvements involve less choice and are not so open to debate. The hyphen in *time-consuming* is necessary; a noun must be substituted for the pronoun *this,* which was being used more loosely than grammar allows; and the question mark in the next-to-last sentence must be changed to a period.

Proofreading

After revising and editing, you are ready to prepare the final manuscript. (See 46 for guidelines.) At this point, make sure to allow yourself enough time for proofreading — the final and most important step in manuscript preparation.

Proofreading is a special kind of reading: a slow and methodical search for misspellings, typographical mistakes, and omitted words or word endings. Such errors can be difficult to spot in your own work because you may read what you intended to write, not what is actually on the page. To fight this tendency, try proofreading out loud, articulating each word as it is actually written. You might also try proofreading your essay backward, a strategy that takes your attention

Cycles of sentence-level revision

The numbers in this chart refer to sections in this handbook.

STRENGTHENING SENTENCES

Look for opportunities

- — to use more active verbs (14a)
- — to prune excess words (16)

CLARIFYING SENTENCES

Look for opportunities

- — to balance parallel ideas (9)
- — to supply missing words (10)
- — to untangle mixed constructions (11)
- — to repair misplaced or dangling modifiers (12)
- — to eliminate confusing shifts (13)

INTRODUCING VARIETY

Look for opportunities

- — to combine choppy sentences (8a)
- — to restructure weak compounds (8b)
- — to vary sentence openings (15a)

REFINING THE STYLE

Look for opportunities

- — to choose language more appropriate for the subject and audience (17)
- — to choose more exact words (18)

An editing checklist

At first this checklist may seem overwhelming, but as your instructor responds to your writing and as you become familiar with the rules in this handbook, you'll begin to see which problems, if any, tend to cause you trouble. You can then devise a personal checklist of errors to look for as you edit. (The numbers in the chart refer to sections in this handbook.)

GRAMMAR

Sentence fragments (19)
Comma splices and fused sentences (20)
Subject-verb agreement (21)
Pronoun-antecedent agreement (22)
Pronoun reference (23)
Case of nouns and pronouns (24)
Case of *who* and *whom* (25)
Adjectives and adverbs (26)
Standard English verb forms (27)
Verb tense, mood, and voice (28)
ESL problems (29, 30, 31)

PUNCTUATION

The comma and unnecessary commas (32, 33)
The semicolon (34)
The colon (35)
The apostrophe (36)
Quotation marks (37)
End punctuation (38)
Other punctuation marks (39)

MECHANICS

Abbreviations and numbers (40, 41)
Italics (underlining) (42)
Spelling and the hyphen (43, 44)
Capital letters (45)

away from the meanings you intended and forces you to think about small surface features instead.

Although proofreading may be dull, it is crucial. Errors strewn throughout an essay are distracting and annoying. If the writer doesn't care about this piece of writing, thinks the reader, why should I? A carefully proofread essay, on the other hand, sends a positive message: It shows that you value your writing and respect your readers.

EXERCISE 4 – 1

On a piece of scratch paper, jot down notes describing how you typically approach a writing task. Then, on another sheet of paper, list ways in which you might improve your handling of the writing process. Be prepared to discuss your notes in class. The following questions are meant to prompt your thoughts; don't feel that your notes must address them all.

1. What do you do, if anything, before you begin a first draft? For example, do you jot down notes on scratch paper, talk about your ideas with a friend, or come up with insights late at night and then sleep on them?
2. How do you organize your ideas — in your head or on paper? Do you use outlines or diagrams and, if so, how formal are they?
3. Where and when are you most comfortable writing?
4. Do you type rough drafts, write them in longhand, or use a word processor? Are you addicted to any sort of paper and pen? Do you single-space or double-space a draft? Do you write on both sides of the paper?
5. Do you use a dictionary, a thesaurus, or a reference such as *The Bedford Handbook for Writers*? If so, when do you usually consult these references — while writing the first draft or later?
6. How do you "get distance" from a draft? Do you have someone read what you have written, get advice, and then rewrite? Or do you usually handle revision all on your own? Which of your friends and relatives can be trusted to offer helpful advice? Have you ever asked for feedback from an instructor or a writing center tutor?

7. Do you make major revisions in a rough draft — revisions that go beyond the level of the sentence? For example, do you consider adding, deleting, or moving whole paragraphs? If so, how do you handle such changes — by making them on a word processor, by cutting and taping, by using circles and arrows, or by recopying the whole draft?
8. What sorts of sentence-level revisions do you make?
9. How do you handle proofreading?
10. How much time do you usually spend on a writing assignment? Do you spread your work over several days or wait until the last minute? What proportion of your time is devoted to each stage of the writing process: planning, writing, and revision?

EXERCISE 4–2

This exercise gives you practice finding information in *The Bedford Handbook for Writers*. Each of the following "rules" violates the principle it expresses. Find the handbook section that explains the principle (by using the chart inside the front cover or the index at the back) and then correct the error. Example:

> *its*
> Each pronoun agrees with ~~their~~ antecedent.
> ∧

1. A verb have to agree with its subject.
2. A writer must be careful not to shift your point of view.
3. Don't use no double negatives.
4. When dangling, watch your modifiers.
5. Discriminate careful between adjectives and adverbs.
6. In the writing center, they say that vague pronoun reference is unacceptable.
7. Don't write a comma splice, you must connect the clauses with a comma and a coordinating conjunction or with a semicolon.
8. About sentence fragments. You should avoid them.
9. In most contexts, the passive voice should be avoided.
10. Watch out for *-ed* endings that have been drop.
11. The distinction between *which* and *that* is a matter which some writers take very seriously.
12. In choosing the proper case, follow the example of we teachers, whom are the experts.

13. Its important to use apostrophe's correctly.
14. Watch out for irregular verbs that have came to you in the wrong form.
15. Last but not least, avoid clichés like the plague.

COMPOSING AND REVISING ON A WORD PROCESSOR

A word processor, as you probably know, is a computer equipped with software that allows writers to compose and revise text with ease. Although a word processor cannot think for you, it can be a useful tool at all stages of the writing process: planning, drafting, and revising.

Planning

You can list or "brainstorm" ideas as easily on a word processor as with pencil and paper, especially if you are a fast typist. Later you can delete ideas, add others, and rearrange the order, all with a few keystrokes. And as you begin to perceive relationships among ideas, you may be able to turn your list into an informal outline.

You can create outlines quite easily on a word processor. Some software packages will generate a formal outline structure for you — not the words, of course, but the conventional system of numbers and letters at appropriate indent levels.

If you like to begin a writing task by asking yourself questions, consider keeping sets of questions on file in your computer. A college student, for example, might use one set of questions for writing about literature, another for science reports, another for case studies in sociology or psychology, and so on. In some disciplines, sets of questions have been developed on software by experts in the field. Check with a professor or with your school's writing center to learn about such computer programs.

Software has also been developed to speed the process of academic research. Instead of taking notes on note cards, you can type notes on the computer, code them to reflect the divisions of your outline, and later print the notes in sorted batches. To rearrange the notes, you simply change their codes.

Although the computer can be a useful tool for planning, its advantages over pencil and paper should not be overstated. Not all planning techniques can be done on a word processor (clustering and branching cannot, for example), and a computer will not always be available when an idea strikes. Many writers find that they plan just as easily with pencil and paper; they turn to the computer primarily for drafting and revising.

Drafting

Whether to write a first draft on a word processor is a matter of personal preference. Some writers prefer the sensation of a pencil or pen moving on paper; others like to get their fingers moving on a keyboard.

One advantage of drafting at a keyboard, if you are a good typist, is speed: Your thoughts are not likely to race ahead of your fingers, as they sometimes do when you are drafting by hand. Another advantage is legibility. As you draft, you will find yourself reviewing from time to time what you have already written. Typed copy — whether on a screen or printed out on paper — is more legible than most handwriting.

A third advantage is flexibility. Because changes are so easy to make, a word processor encourages experimentation. If you get stuck while writing the opening paragraph, for example, you can skip ahead, knowing that it will be easy to insert the introduction later. Or you can switch screens and use an empty screen for brainstorming. Or if you have a creative but unusual idea for the introduction, you can try it out, confident that if it doesn't work, you can make it disappear in seconds.

If you decide to type an initial draft on a word processor, it's a good idea to print out hard copy as you go along so that you can easily review what you have written. (Otherwise you will need to scroll from screen to screen.) Be sure to save your draft in the computer's memory periodically as you are working and before turning off the computer.

Revising

The word processor is an excellent tool for revision. As mentioned earlier, revising is nearly always a two-step process. Global revisions, those that affect blocks of text longer than a sentence, generally should be handled first. They include changes in focus, organization, paragraphing, and content. Sentence-level revisions — improvements in sentence structure, word choice, grammar, punctuation, and mechanics — can come later.

GLOBAL REVISIONS Let's assume that you have typed and saved your rough draft on a computer equipped with word processing software. You have printed a copy of the draft, reviewed it for global revisions, and indicated on it where you need to add, delete, and move chunks of text.

Once you have called up the text onto the computer's screen, you move the cursor to the place where you want to add, delete, or move text. Most word processing packages allow you to add text simply by typing it in and to delete text by hitting a delete key. Moving blocks of text is a bit more complicated, usually requiring several keystrokes, but with practice it too is relatively simple.

Because the computer saves time, it encourages you to experiment with global revisions. Should you combine two paragraphs? Would your conclusion make a good introduction? Might several paragraphs be rearranged for greater impact? Will boldface headings improve readability? With little risk, you can explore the possibilities. When a revision misfires, it is easy to restore your original draft.

SENTENCE-LEVEL REVISIONS   Some writers handle sentence-level revisions directly at the computer, but most prefer to print out a hard copy of the draft, mark it up, and then return to the computer. Once you've indicated changes on the hard copy, you can enter them into the computer in a matter of minutes.

Software can provide help with sentence-level revisions. Many word processing programs have spelling checkers that will catch most but not all spelling errors, and some have thesauruses to help with word choice. Other programs, called *text analyzers* or *style checkers,* will flag a variety of possible problems: wordiness, jargon, weak verbs, long sentences, and so on. Be aware, however, that a text analyzer can only point out *possible* problems. It can tell you that a sentence is long, for example, but you must decide whether your long sentence is effective.

To proofread your final text, either read the words on the screen or, if this is too hard on your eyes, print a new copy and proofread the hard copy. Enter any necessary corrections into the computer, print a final copy, and you are done. To preserve the final draft, be sure to save it before you turn off the computer.

SAMPLE STUDENT ESSAY

The essay on pages 67–69 was written by Gary Laporte for an English class assignment. Laporte thought about the assignment for several days, but he was unable to come up with a subject. He was still pondering the question when he watched a basketball playoff game on television. Besides interviewing the stars of each team, the sportscaster spoke with a ten-year-old fan whose ambition was to become a famous athlete. Why famous? thought Laporte. Why not a *good* athlete? Don't people who see games on TV understand that winning depends on good play and teamwork, not on competing with one another for fame and the camera's attention?

Laporte decided that television sports might make a good essay subject since he knew something about it. He jotted down ideas during breaks in the game and came up with the following list:

Cooperation should be focus, not competition

TV creates stars — cameras follow them, commentators interview them

TV doesn't show whole game, only most dramatic shots, slow-motion replays

More people admire sports stars than admire the president of U.S.

Sports stars make more money than president, also do commercials for money

Money becomes purpose of sport

Sports should represent American values — teamwork, shared enthusiasm — easier to see in live games where spectators participate

Cheering, choosing what to watch, buying beer & hot dogs, catching fly balls

Later, Laporte reread his list and concluded that his focus should be the effect of television on both athletes and spectators. With this focus in mind, he formulated a tentative thesis and sketched a rough outline.

Although it is convenient, TV creates a distance between the sport and its fans and between the athletes and the team.

    — television's convenience to fans
        — no need to travel and spend money
        — ability to see more games
    — television's damage to sports
        — creates distance between the sport and fans
        — creates distance between the athletes and the team

Working from his list and outline, Laporte wrote a rough draft. He wrote quickly, focusing more on his ideas than on grammar, punctuation, and spelling. As you read his rough draft, which follows, consider what changes (aside from grammar, punctuation, and spelling) you would recommend.

LAPORTE'S ROUGH DRAFT

Sports on TV--A Win or a Loss?

Team sports are as much a part of Americain
life as Mom and apple pie, and they have a good
tendency to bring people together.   They encourage
team members to cooperate with one another, they
also create shared enthusiasm among fans.   Thanks
to television, this togetherness now seems available to nearly all of us at the flick of a switch.
We do not have to buy tickets, and travel to a
stadium, to see the World Series or the Super
Bowl, these games are on television.   We can enjoy
the game in the comfort of our own living room.
After Thanksgiving or Christmas dinner, the whole
family may gather around the TV set to watch football together.   It would appear that television
has done us a great service.   But is this really
the case?

It is necessary to look at the differences
between live and televised sports.   We can see
more games than if we had to attend each one in
person, and we can follow greater varieties of

sports. On the other hand, television creates a distance between the sport and the fans and between athletes and the teams they play for.

The gap between a game and those who watch it on television has two major aspects. One is that the armchair audience sees only what the camera shows. The advantage of this is that we get a clear look at important plays; also, if we miss a play, we can fall back on the commentator's explanation or the instant replay, which often shows us exactly what happened in slow motion. The disadvantage is that we have no choice about what to watch. If a viewer would rather follow someone in the backfield than the quarterback or would rather look at a batter warming up than a commercial, they are out of luck. The other aspect of observing a game on television is that we miss all the sights, sounds, and smells that link live viewers with the players and one another. When a fly ball comes over the fence, the television audience cannot try to catch it. The roar of cheers after a touchdown is less exciting from the living room sofa than when you are sitting in the bleachers. Someone watching a televised game may feel silly cheering at all, since there is no chance those tiny figures on the screen will hear it.

TV creates a gap between athletes and their teams, in addition. Traditionally, sports have been viewed as arenas where teamwork is essential, and the goals of the group overshadow personal ambition. TV cameras, however, find it more dramatic and more convenient to focus on individual achievements than something as intangible as teamwork. Interviews with sports stars are often part of a televised game. Athletes make more money than the president of the United States, and they appear in the media more often, and they are universally admired. In addition, sports stars have the extra added benefit of endorsing products on TV commercials for large bonus payments.

Team sports are a major part of American life. All the more so since television has brought them into most of our homes. The challenge for sports fans is to support their favorite teams in ways to encourage the best values represented by sports. One way is to continue to attend live games rather than watch games on television.

Before beginning to revise this draft, Laporte brought it to class for a peer review session. Three of Laporte's classmates read the draft and responded to it, using the chart on pages 42–43 as a guideline for their discussion. Here are some of their comments and suggestions:

> I like your details describing the distance between the spectator and the sport (in the third paragraph). You make me experience what you mean.

> Why did you put your thesis at the end of the second paragraph? Wouldn't it be more effective in the introduction?

> You talk about advantages to televised sports in the first and second paragraphs. Maybe this should all be in one place.

> You do a good job of acknowledging that TV does have its advantages.

> Your language seems too stiff in places. Does your audience really require such a formal approach?

> Two of your paragraphs are pretty long. Maybe you could tighten up the third paragraph, which seems wordy. The fourth paragraph probably needs to be divided.

> You haven't convinced me that television separates the players from their team. An example or two would help.

> You're tending to shift from the *we* point of view to the *they* point of view and back again. I'd use the *we* point of view because it is more personal. And after all, most of us are fans.

> You seem to have two introductory paragraphs. Shouldn't you get to the point faster?

> I like the way you pull the essay together in the concluding paragraph.

Notice that Laporte and his classmates were focusing on global matters, not on sentence-level revisions. Because the draft needed a fair amount of work, it made little sense to tinker with its sentences, some of which would be thrown out anyway. For an example of Laporte's global revisions, see page 72.

Once Laporte had written the second draft, he felt ready to devote his full attention to matters of style and correctness. He tightened wordy sentences, combined sentences for better flow, chose his words more carefully, and brought consistency to his style. Finally, with his handbook and dictionary close by, he corrected errors in grammar, punctuation, and spelling. For an example of Laporte's sentence-level revisions, see page 73.

Laporte's final draft appears on pages 74–76.

EXAMPLE OF GLOBAL REVISIONS

Sports on TV--A Win or a Loss?

Team sports are as much a part of Americain
life as Mom and apple pie, and they have a good
tendency to bring people together.   They encourage
team members to cooperate with one another, they
also create shared enthusiasm among fans.   Thanks
to television, this togetherness now seems available to nearly all of us at the flick of a switch.
We do not have to buy tickets, and travel to a
stadium, to see the World Series or the Super
Bowl, these games are on television.   We can enjoy
the game in the comfort of our own living room.
~~After Thanksgiving or Christmas dinner, the whole~~
~~family may gather around the TV set to watch foot-~~
~~ball together.~~   It would appear that television
has done us a great service.   But is this really
the case? *Although television does make sports
more accessible, it also creates a distance between
the sport and the fans and between athletes and
the teams they play for.*
   *The advantage of television is that it provides
sports fans with greater convenience.*
                    [insert] ←
*We can see more games than if we had to attend
each one in person, and we can follow a greater
variety of sports.*

EXAMPLE OF SENTENCE-LEVEL REVISIONS

Televised
∧Sports ~~on TV~~ --A Win or a Loss?

Team sports, ~~are~~ as much a part of American
tend
life as Mom and apple pie, ~~and they have a good~~
us
~~tendency~~ to bring ~~people~~ together. They encourage
and
team members to cooperate with one another, they
Because of
~~also~~ create shared enthusiasm among fans. ∧~~Thanks~~
~~to~~ television, this togetherness now seems avail-
twist of a dial.
able ~~to nearly all of us~~ at the ~~flick of a switch.~~
∧
~~It would appear that television has done us a~~
~~great service.~~ But is this really the case? Al-
makes
though television ~~does make~~ sports more accessible, it also creates a distance between the sport
their
and the fans and between athletes and ~~the~~ teams.
∧   ∧
~~they play for.~~

The advantage of television is that it provides sports fans with greater convenience. We do
not have to buy tickets/ and travel to a stadium/
but
to see the World Series or the Super Bowl/ ~~these~~
any'∧
~~games are on television.~~ ~~We~~ can enjoy ∧~~the~~ game in
rooms. ∧
the comfort of our own living ~~room.~~ We can see
more games than if we had to attend each one in
a   *variety*
person, and we can follow greater ~~varieties~~ of
∧   ∧
sports.

LAPORTE'S FINAL DRAFT

Televised Sports--A Win or a Loss?

Team sports, as much a part of American life as Mom and apple pie, tend to bring us together. They encourage team members to cooperate with one another, and they create shared enthusiasm among fans. Because of television, this togetherness now seems available at the twist of a dial. But is this really the case? Although television makes sports more accessible, it also creates a distance between the sport and the spectator and between athletes and their teams.

The advantage of television is that it provides sports fans with greater convenience. We do not have to buy tickets and travel to a stadium to see the World Series or the Super Bowl but can enjoy any game in the comfort of our own living rooms. We can see more games than if we had to attend each one in person, and we can follow a greater variety of sports.

The price paid for this convenience, however, is high. Television changes the role of the fans who watch the game, making their participation more passive and distant. As television spectators, we see only what the camera shows. Yes, we do get a clearer look at important plays, and if we miss a detail, the commentator's explanation or the instant replay will fill us in. But we have no choice about what to watch. We cannot decide to follow the wide receiver rather than the quarterback or to watch a batter warming up rather than a commercial. Moreover, we miss all the sights, sounds, and smells that link live viewers with the players and with one another. When a fly ball comes over the fence, we cannot try to catch it. The roar of cheers after a touchdown is less exciting from the living room sofa than from the bleachers. We may feel silly cheering at all, since there is no chance those tiny figures on the screen will hear us.

The distance television has created between viewers and players does little more than reduce excitement and perhaps cheapen the experience of watching a game, but the unwholesome gap television creates between athletes and their teams threatens the foundation of team sports. Teamwork has always been paramount in team sports; the goals of the group have always overshadowed personal ambition. Television cameras, however, find it more dramatic to focus on individuals rather than on something as intangible as teamwork. In addition, the economics of television advertising and of team sports as big business create a situation in which players compete with one another for astronomical salaries and the chance to endorse products on television commercials.

Not surprisingly, the competition fostered by television causes players to try to make themselves look good, sometimes at the expense of the team. For example, a basketball player might take --and miss--a difficult shot instead of passing the ball to a teammate left unguarded closer to the basket. Or a star hockey player might work behind the scenes to keep a promising rookie from replacing him.

Team sports are a major part of American life, all the more so since television has brought them into our homes. The challenge for sports fans is to support their favorite teams in ways that encourage the best values represented by sports. One way to do this is to attend more live games rather than watch games on television. Attendance at live games may give the teams, the players, and the television networks the message that teamwork, not individual achievement and financial success, is what matters most about sports.

PART II

Constructing Paragraphs

¶

Except for special-purpose paragraphs, such as introductions and conclusions (see 2b and 2d), paragraphs are clusters of information supporting an essay's main point (or advancing a story's action). Aim for paragraphs that are clearly focused, well developed, organized, coherent, and neither too long nor too short for easy reading.

5

Focus on a main point.

A paragraph should be unified around a main point. The point should be clear to readers, and all sentences in the paragraph must relate to it.

5a   State the main point in a topic sentence.

As readers move into a paragraph, they need to know where they are — in relation to the whole essay — and what to expect in the sentences to come. A good topic sentence, a one-sentence summary of the paragraph's main point, acts as a signpost pointing in two directions: backward toward the thesis of the essay and forward toward the body of the paragraph.

Like a thesis statement (see 1c), a topic sentence is more general than the material supporting it. Often the topic sentence comes first:

> *Nearly all living creatures manage some form of communication.* The dance patterns of bees in their hive help to point the way to distant flower fields or announce successful foraging. Male stickleback fish regularly swim upside-down to indicate outrage in a courtship contest. Male deer and lemurs

mark territorial ownership by rubbing their own body secretions on boundary stones or trees. Everyone has seen a frightened dog put his tail between his legs and run in panic. We, too, use gestures, expressions, postures, and movement to give our words point. [Italics added.]

— Olivia Vlahos, *Human Beginnings*

Frequently the topic sentence is introduced by a transitional sentence linking it to earlier material. In the following paragraph, the topic sentence (italicized) has been delayed to allow for a transition.

But flowers are not the only source of spectacle in the wilderness. *An opportunity for late color is provided by the berries of wildflowers, shrubs, and trees.* Baneberry presents its tiny white flowers in spring but in late summer bursts forth with clusters of red berries. Bunchberry, a ground-cover plant, puts out red berries in the fall, and the red berries of wintergreen last from autumn well into winter. In California, the bright red, fist-sized clusters of Christmas berries can be seen growing beside highways for up to six months of the year. [Italics added.]

— James Crockett et al., *Wildflower Gardening*

Occasionally the topic sentence may be withheld until the end of the paragraph — but only if the earlier sentences hang together so well that the reader perceives their direction, if not their exact point. The opening sentences of the following paragraph state facts, making them supporting material rather than topic sentences, but they strongly suggest a central idea. The topic sentence at the end is hardly a surprise.

Tobacco chewing starts as soon as people begin stirring. Those who have fresh supplies soak the new leaves in water and add ashes from the hearth to the wad. Men, women, and children chew tobacco and all are addicted to it. Once there was a shortage of tobacco in Kaobawa's village and I was plagued for a week by early morning visitors who requested permission to collect my cigarette butts in order to make a wad of chewing tobacco. Normally, if anyone is short of tobacco, he can request a share of someone else's already chewed wad, or simply borrow the entire wad when its owner puts it down somewhere. *Tobacco is so important to them that their word for "poverty" translates as "being without tobacco."* [Italics added.]

      — Napoleon A. Chagnon, *Yanomamo: The Fierce People*

Although it is generally wise to use topic sentences, at times they are unnecessary. A topic sentence may not be needed if a paragraph continues developing an idea clearly introduced in a previous paragraph, if the details of the paragraph unmistakably suggest its main point, or if the paragraph appears in a narrative of events where generalizations might interrupt the flow of the story.

5b Do not stray from the point.

Sentences that do not support the topic sentence destroy the unity of a paragraph. If the paragraph is otherwise well focused, such offending sentences can simply be deleted or perhaps moved elsewhere. In the following paragraph describing the inadequate facilities in a high school, the information about the typing instructor (in italics) is clearly off the point.

As the result of tax cuts, the educational facilities of Lincoln High School have reached an all-time low. Some of the books date back to 1970 and have long since shed their covers. The lack of lab equipment makes it necessary for four to five students to work at one table, with most watching rather than performing experiments. The few typewriters in working order have not been cleaned in so long that most letters come out blotchy and hard to read. There is only one self-correcting typewriter and no prospect of the school's ordering a word processor or computer anytime soon. *Also, the typing instructor left to have a baby at the beginning of the*

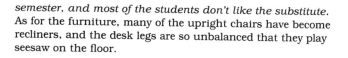
semester, and most of the students don't like the substitute. As for the furniture, many of the upright chairs have become recliners, and the desk legs are so unbalanced that they play seesaw on the floor.

Sometimes the cure for a disunified paragraph is not as simple as deleting or moving material. Writers often wander into uncharted territory because they cannot think of enough evidence to support a topic sentence. Feeling that it is too soon to break into a new paragraph, they move on to new ideas for which they have not prepared the reader. When this happens, the writer is faced with a choice: Either find more evidence to support the topic sentence or adjust the topic sentence to mesh with the evidence that is available.

EXERCISE 5 – 1

Underline the topic sentence in the following paragraph and eliminate any material that does not clarify or develop the central idea.

A recent plan of the mayor's threatens to destroy one of the oldest and most successfully integrated neighborhoods in our city, replacing it with luxury condominiums and a shopping mall. This neighborhood, Thompson's Fields, was settled by a mixture of immigrants from Ireland, Italy, Poland, and Austria in the early part of the twentieth century. Over the years black and Hispanic families have also moved in and have become part of the community. When the mayor designated a five-block area along the neighborhood's main street as the location for a redevelopment program, the community decided to take the mayor to court. The mayor has hired the best urban planners and architects in the country to design and build three large skyscrapers along with parking facilities for the area. One woman has even moved to the city from California to work on the project. If the court accepts the case, the lawyer for the residents will be Ann Tyson, who grew up in Thompson's Fields. The residents have seen a great deal of change over the years, but they refuse to stand by while their homes are razed for some gentrification project that they will never enjoy.

6

Develop the main point.

Topic sentences are generalizations in need of support, so once you have written a topic sentence, ask yourself, "How do I know that this is true?" Your answer will suggest how to develop the paragraph.

6a Flesh out skimpy paragraphs.

Though an occasional short paragraph is fine, particularly if it functions as a transition or emphasizes a point, a series of brief paragraphs suggests inadequate development. How much development is enough? That varies, depending on the writer's purpose and audience.

For example, when she wrote a paragraph attempting to convince readers that it is impossible to lose fat quickly, health columnist Jane Brody knew that she would have to present a great deal of evidence because many dieters want to believe the opposite. She did *not* write:

> When you think about it, it's impossible to lose — as many diets suggest — 10 pounds of *fat* in ten days, even on a total fast. Even a moderately active person cannot lose so much weight so fast. A less active person hasn't a prayer.

This three-sentence paragraph is too skimpy to be convincing. But the paragraph that Brody wrote contains enough evidence to convince even skeptical readers:

> When you think about it, it's impossible to lose — as many diets suggest — 10 pounds of *fat* in ten days, even on a total fast. A pound of body fat represents 3,500 calories. To lose 1

¶

pound of fat, you must expend 3,500 more calories than you consume. Let's say you weigh 170 pounds and, as a moderately active person, you burn 2,500 calories a day. If your diet contains only 1,500 calories, you'd have an energy deficit of 1,000 calories a day. In a week's time that would add up to a 7,000-calorie deficit, or 2 pounds of real fat. In ten days, the accumulated deficit would represent nearly 3 pounds of lost body fat. Even if you ate nothing at all for ten days and maintained your usual level of activity, your caloric deficit would add up to 25,000 calories. . . . At 3,500 calories per pound of fat, that's still only 7 pounds of lost fat.

— Jane Brody, *Jane Brody's Nutrition Book*

6b Choose a suitable pattern of development.

Although paragraphs may be patterned in an almost infinite number of ways, certain patterns of development occur frequently, either alone or in combination: examples and illustrations, narration, description, process, comparison and contrast, analogy, cause and effect, classification or division, and definition. There is nothing magical about these methods of development. They simply reflect some of the ways in which we think.

Examples and illustrations

Examples, perhaps the most common pattern of development, are appropriate whenever the reader might be tempted to ask, "For example?" Though examples are just selected instances, not a complete catalog, they are enough to suggest the truth of many topic sentences, as in the following paragraph.

Normally my parents abided scrupulously by "The Budget," but several times a year Dad would dip into his battered, black strongbox and splurge on some irrational, totally satisfying luxury. Once he bought over a hundred comic books at a flea market, doled out to us thereafter at the tantalizing rate of two a week. He always got a whole flat of pansies, Mom's favorite flower, for us to give her on Mother's Day. One day a boy stopped at our house selling fifty-cent raffle tickets on a sailboat and Dad bought every ticket the boy had left — three books' worth.   — Connie Hailey, student

Illustrations are extended examples, frequently presented in story form. Because they require several sentences apiece, they are used more sparingly than examples. When well selected, however, they can be a vivid and effective means of developing a point. The writer of the following paragraph uses illustrations to demonstrate that Harriet Tubman, famous conductor on the underground railway for escaping slaves, was a genius at knowing how and when to retreat.

Part of Harriet Tubman's strategy of conducting was, as in all battle-field operations, the knowledge of how and when to retreat. Numerous allusions have been made to her moves when she suspected that she was in danger. When she feared the party was closely pursued, she would take it for a time on a train southward bound. No one seeing Negroes going in this direction would for an instant suppose them to be fugitives. Once on her return she was at a railway station. She saw some men reading a poster and she heard one of them reading it aloud. It was a description of her, offering a reward for her capture. She took a southbound train to avert suspicion. At another time when Harriet heard men talking about her, she pretended to read a book which she carried. One man remarked, "This cannot be the woman. The one we want can't read or write." Harriet devoutly hoped the book was right side up.   — Earl Conrad, *Harriet Tubman*

Narration

A paragraph of narration tells a story or part of a story. Narrative paragraphs are usually arranged in chronological order, but they may also contain flashbacks, interruptions that take the story back to an earlier time. The following paragraph, from Jane Goodall's *In the Shadow of Man,* recounts one of the author's experiences in the African wild.

> One evening when I was wading in the shallows of the lake to pass a rocky outcrop, I suddenly stopped dead as I saw the sinuous black body of a snake in the water. It was all of six feet long, and from the slight hood and the dark stripes at the back of the neck I knew it to be a Storm's water cobra — a deadly reptile for the bite of which there was, at that time, no serum. As I stared at it an incoming wave gently deposited part of its body on one of my feet. I remained motionless, not even breathing, until the wave rolled back into the lake, drawing the snake with it. Then I leaped out of the water as fast as I could, my heart hammering.
>
> — Jane Goodall, *In the Shadow of Man*

Description

A descriptive paragraph sketches a portrait of a person, place, or thing by using concrete and specific details that appeal to one or more of our senses — sight, sound, smell, taste, and touch. Consider, for example, the following description of a sea lion.

> To our right, a sea lion slipped from the ocean. It was a young bull; in another few years he would be dangerous, bellowing at intruders and biting off great dirty chunks of the ones he caught. Now this young bull, which weighed maybe 120 pounds, sprawled silhouetted in the late light, slick as a drop of quicksilver, his glistening whiskers radii of gold like any crown. He hauled his packed bulk toward us up the long beach; he flung himself with an enormous surge of fur-clad muscle onto the boulder where I sat. "Soames," I said — very quietly, "he's here because *we're* here, isn't he?" The naturalist nodded. I felt water drip on my elbow behind me, then the fragile scrape of whiskers, and finally the wet warmth and weight of a muzzle, as the creature settled to sleep on my arm. I was catching on to sea lions.
>
> — Annie Dillard, *Teaching a Stone to Talk*

Process

A process paragraph is patterned in time order, usually chronologically. A writer may choose this pattern either to describe a process or to show readers how to perform a process. The following paragraph, taken from a biography of Thomas Jefferson, describes the process of electing a president during the early years of the United States.

> A presidential election in those days was neither simple nor direct. In each State the Electoral College voted for both offices, without designating which of the candidates was to get first place (the Presidency) and which second (the Vice-Presidency). The votes were then sent to the national capital to be counted. The candidate who had the highest number of votes was declared President and the next highest, Vice-President. If the two leading candidates had an equal number of votes, the election was to be decided in the House of Representatives, wherein each State cast one vote. Communication being slow and uncertain, it took several weeks for all the votes to come in from States so far apart as Georgia and Massachusetts.   — Saul K. Padover, *Jefferson*

Here is a paragraph that shows readers how to perform a process — that of opening an oyster.

> An oyster has an irregular shape. The valves are rough and their lips hard to find. Crooked and wrinkled, the hairline crack between the valves can't be widened with the blade of a knife; the point must enter first. Furthermore, a big Chincoteague doesn't fit the left hand. One must hold the animal slanting against the edge of the kitchen sink and poke around, seeking the slot by touch as much as by sight. It takes painful practice. When the knifepoint finds a purchase, push carefully and quickly before the oyster realizes what's afoot and gets a firmer grip on itself. Push in the wrong place — it's easy to mistake a growth line for the groove — and the knife takes on a life of its own. It can skid and open up your hand. This delicate work requires patient agility to find the groove, push

the knife in, then slit the muscle and open the critter without losing too much juice. (Restaurants serve oysters on their flat shell. It's better to throw that one away and lay the delicacies on a bed of crushed ice in the roundest half-shell which holds its delicious liquor. Sprinkle each one with lemon juice — a healthy oyster will wriggle the slightest bit at this to prove it's alive — lift the dishlike shell to the lips, and drink the oyster down. It's a delicious, addicting experience.)

— Philip Kopper, "How to Open an Oyster"

Comparison and contrast

To compare two subjects is to draw attention to their similarities, although the word *compare* also has a broader meaning that includes a consideration of differences. To contrast is to focus only on differences.

Whether a comparison-and-contrast paragraph stresses similarities or differences, it may be patterned in one of two ways. The two subjects may be presented one at a time, block style, as in the following paragraph of contrast.

So Grant and Lee were in complete contrast, representing two diametrically opposed elements in American life. Grant was the modern man emerging; beyond him, ready to come on the stage, was the great age of steel and machinery, of crowded cities and a restless burgeoning vitality. Lee might have ridden down from the old age of chivalry, lance in hand, silken banner fluttering over his head. Each man was the perfect champion of his cause, drawing both his strengths and weaknesses from the people he led.

— Bruce Catton, "Grant and Lee: A Study in Contrasts"

Or a paragraph may proceed point by point, treating two subjects together, one aspect at a time. The following paragraph uses the point-by-point method to both compare and contrast.

Wilson brought qualities as unusual as those of Theodore Roosevelt to American politics. The two men had much in common: cultivation, knowledge, literary skill, personal magnetism, relentless drive. But, where Roosevelt was unbuttoned and expansive, Wilson was reserved and cool; no one known to history ever called him "Woody" or "W.W." Both were lay preachers, but where Roosevelt was a revivalist, bullying his listeners to hit the sawdust trail, Wilson had the severe eloquence of a Calvinist divine. Roosevelt's egotism overflowed his personality; Wilson's was a hard concentrate within. Roosevelt's power lay in what he did, Wilson's in what he held in reserve.

— Arthur M. Schlesinger, Jr., *The Age of Roosevelt:*
The Crisis of the Old Order

Analogy

Analogies draw comparisons between items that appear to have little in common. Writers turn to analogies for a variety of reasons: to make the unfamiliar seem familiar, to provide a concrete understanding of an abstract topic, or to provoke fresh thoughts or changed feelings about a subject. In the following paragraph, physician Lewis Thomas draws an analogy between the behavior of ants and that of humans. Thomas's analogy helps us to understand the social behavior of ants and forces us to question the superiority of our own human societies.

Ants are so much like human beings as to be an embarrassment. They farm fungi, raise aphids as livestock, launch armies into wars, use chemical sprays to alarm and confuse enemies, capture slaves. The families of weaver ants engage in child labor, holding their larvae like shuttles to spin out the thread that sews the leaves together for their fungus gardens. They exchange information ceaselessly. They do everything but watch television.

— Lewis Thomas, "On Societies as Organisms"

Although analogies can be a powerful tool for illuminating a subject, they should be used with caution in arguments. Just because two things may be alike in one respect, we cannot conclude that they are alike in all respects. (See *false analogy,* page 616.)

Cause and effect

When causes and effects are a matter of argument, they are too complex to be reduced to a simple pattern (see page 617). However, if a writer wishes merely to describe a cause-and-effect relationship that is generally accepted, then the effect may be stated in the topic sentence, with the causes listed in the body of the paragraph.

> The fantastic water clarity of the Mount Gambier sinkholes results from several factors. The holes are fed from aquifers holding rainwater that fell decades — even centuries — ago, and that has been filtered through miles of limestone. The high level of calcium that limestone adds causes the silty detritus from dead plants and animals to cling together and settle quickly to the bottom. Abundant bottom vegetation in the shallow sinkholes also helps bind the silt. And the rapid turnover of water prohibits stagnation.
> — Hillary Hauser, "Exploring a Sunken Realm in Australia"

Or the paragraph may move from cause to effects, as in this paragraph from a student's essay on the effects of her family's formal manners on her friends.

> My family's formality often made visitors uncomfortable. Before coming to my house for dinner, my friends used to beg me to teach them to say grace the way we did, because they worried about not fitting in. During the meal they would watch anxiously to see which fork I used, and sometimes they could only stammer when my father asked them questions about world events. It wasn't long before I came to wonder if the purpose of good table manners was really to give guests indigestion. Friends who came to my house for dinner often didn't come again; more often, I went to their houses.
> — Jane Betz, student

Classification and division

Classification is the grouping of items into categories according to some consistent principle. Philosopher Francis Bacon was using classification when he wrote that "some books are to be tasted, others to be swallowed, and some few to be chewed and digested." Bacon's principle for classifying books is the degree to which they are worthy of our attention, but books of course can be classified according to other principles. For example, an elementary school teacher might classify children's books according to the level of difficulty, or a librarian might group them by subject matter. The principle of classification that a writer chooses ultimately depends on the purpose of the classification.

In the following paragraph, essayist E. B. White groups the people of New York City into three categories, according to their reasons for being there.

> There are roughly three New Yorks. There is, first, the New York of the man or woman who was born here, who takes the city for granted and accepts its size and its turbulence as natural and inevitable. Second, there is the New York of the commuter — the city that is devoured by locusts each day and spat out each night. Third, there is the New York of the person who was born somewhere else and came to New York in quest of something. Of these three trembling cities the greatest is the last — the city of final destination, the city that is a goal. It is this third city that accounts for New York's high-strung disposition, its poetical deportment, its dedication to the arts, and its incomparable achievements. Commuters give the city its tidal restlessness, natives give it solidity and continuity, but the settlers give it passion. And whether it is a farmer arriving from Italy to set up a small grocery store in a slum, or a young girl arriving from a small town in Mississippi to escape the indignity of being observed by her neighbors, or a boy arriving from the Corn Belt with a manuscript in his suitcase and a pain in his heart, it makes no difference: each

embraces New York with the intense excitement of first love,
each absorbs New York with the fresh eyes of an adventurer,
each generates heat and light to dwarf the Consolidated
Edison Company.   — E. B. White, "Here Is New York"

Division takes one item and divides it into parts. As with
classification, division should be made according to some
consistent principle. To divide a tree into roots, trunk,
branches, and leaves makes sense; to list its components as
branches, wood, water, and sap does not, for the categories
overlap.

The following paragraph describes the parts of a lemon
and their uses.

> Absolutely every part of a lemon is useful in some way,
> from its seeds to its outermost peel. Lemon-pip oil,
> unsaturated and aromatic, is important in the soap industry
> and in special diets. The pulp left over from squeezed lemons
> is evaporated and concentrated into "citrus molasses" which is
> sold as a base for making vinegar and as an ingredient in
> bland syrups and alcohol. The remains of the "rag" or pulp is
> also sold as cattle feed. Most of the pectin used to thicken and
> solidify jams, jellies, and marmalades comes from the white
> pith of citrus fruits. Among these, lemon and lime pectin has
> the highest "jelly grade" or capacity to thicken liquids. It is
> widely used in medicines taken to combat diarrhea. The
> flavedo, or outer yellow layer of lemon peel, is invaluable for its
> intense taste and scent. (The word *zest,* which originally
> meant "skin or peel," then specifically "citrus peel," is now in
> common use as signifying "lively enjoyment.")
>   — Margaret Visser, *Much Depends on Dinner*

Definition

A definition puts a word or concept into a general class and
then provides enough details to distinguish it from others in
the same class. For example, in one of its senses the term *grit*
names the class of things that birds eat, but it is restricted

to those items — such as small pebbles, eggshell, and ashes — that help the bird grind food.

Many definitions may be presented in a sentence or two, but abstract or difficult concepts may require a paragraph or even a full essay of definition. In the following paragraph, the writer defines envy as a special kind of desire.

> Envy is so integral and so painful a part of what animates human behavior in market societies that many people have forgotten the full meaning of the word, simplifying it into one of the synonyms of desire. It is that, which may be why it flourishes in market societies: democracies of desire, they might be called, with money for ballots, stuffing permitted. But envy is more or less than desire. It begins with the almost frantic sense of emptiness inside oneself, as if the pump of one's heart were sucking on air. One has to be blind to perceive the emptiness, of course, but that's just what envy is, a selective blindness. *Invidia,* Latin for envy, translates as "nonsight," and Dante had the envious plodding along under cloaks of lead, their eyes sewn shut with leaden wire. What they are blind to is what they have, God-given and humanly nurtured, in themselves.
>
> — Nelson W. Aldrich, Jr., *Old Money*

Extended definitions frequently make use of other patterns of development, such as examples, illustrations, or comparison and contrast. Here, for example, is a paragraph that uses a number of illustrations to define the typical teenage victim in a "slasher" film.

> Since teenagers are the target audience for slasher films, the victims in the films are almost always independent, fun-loving, just-out-of-high school partygoers. The girls all love to take late-night strolls alone through the woods or to skinny-dip at midnight in a murky lake. The boys, eager to impress the girls, prove their manhood by descending alone into musty cellars to restart broken generators or by chasing psychotic

killers into haylofts and attics. Entering dark and gloomy houses, young men and women alike decide suddenly that now's a good time to save a few bucks on the family's electric bill — so they leave the lights off. After hearing a noise within the house, they always foolishly decide to investigate, thinking it's one of their many missing friends or pets. Disregarding the "safety in numbers" theory, they branch off in separate directions, never to see each other again. Or the teenagers fall into the common slasher-movie habit of walking backward, which naturally leads them right into you-know-who. Confronted by the ax-wielding maniac, the senseless youths lose their will to survive, close their eyes, and scream.

— Matthew J. Holicek, student

EXERCISE 6 – 1

Write a paragraph modeled on one of the patterns discussed in this section. Some possible topics — most of which you'll need to restrict — are listed here.

Examples or illustrations: sexism in a comic strip, ways to include protein in a vegetarian diet, the benefits of a particular summer job, community services provided by your college, violence on the six o'clock news, educational software for children

Narration: the active lifestyle of a grandparent, life with an alcoholic, working in an emergency room, the benefits (or problems) of intercultural dating, growing up in a large family, the rewards of working in a nursing home, an experience that taught you a lesson, a turning point in your life

Description: your childhood home, an ethnic neighborhood, a rock concert, a favorite painting in an art gallery, a garden, a classic car, a hideous building or monument, a style of dress, a family heirloom (such as a crazy quilt or a collection of Christmas tree ornaments), a favorite park or retreat

Process: how to repair something, how to develop a successful job interview style, how to meet someone of the opposite sex, how to practice safe scuba diving, how to build a set for a play, how to survive in the wilderness, how to train a dog, how to quit smoking, how to make bread

Comparison and contrast: two neighborhoods, teachers, political candidates, colleges, products; country living versus city living; the stereotype of a job versus the reality; a change in attitude toward your family's religion or ethnic background

Analogy: between a family reunion and a circus, between training for a rigorous sport and boot camp, between settling an argument and being a courtroom judge, between a dogfight and a boxing match, between raising a child and tending a garden

Cause and effect: the effects of water pollution on a particular area, the effects of divorce on a child, the effects of an illegal drug, why a particular film or television show is popular, why an area of the country has high unemployment, why early training is essential for success as a ballet dancer, violinist, or athlete

Classification: types of clothing worn on your college campus, types of people who go to college mixers, types of dieters, types of television weather reports, types of rock bands, types of teachers

Definition: a computer addict, an ideal parent or teacher, an authoritarian personality, an intellectual, a sexist, anorexia nervosa, a typical heroine in a Harlequin romance, a typical blind date

6c Consider possible ways of arranging information.

In addition to choosing a pattern of development (or a combination of patterns), you may need to make decisions about arrangement. If you are developing a paragraph with examples, for instance, you'll need to decide how to order the examples. Or if you are contrasting two items point by point, you'll need to decide which points to discuss first, second, and so on. Often considerations of purpose and audience will help you make these choices.

Three of the most common ways of arranging information are treated in this section: time order, spatial order, and order of climax. Other possible arrangements include order of complexity (from simple to complex), order of familiarity (from most familiar to least familiar), and order of audience appeal (from "safe" ideas to those that may challenge the audience's views).

Order of time

Time order, usually chronological, is appropriate for a variety of purposes such as narrating a personal experience, telling an anecdote, describing an experiment, or explaining a process. The following paragraph, arranged in chronological order, appears in *Blue Highways,* an account of the author's travels on the back roads of America.

> Onion Saddle Road, after I was committed to it, narrowed to a single rutted lane affording no place to turn around; if I met somebody, one of us would have to back down. The higher I went, the more that idea unnerved me — the road was bad enough driving forward. The compass swung from point to point, and within five minutes it had touched each of the three hundred sixty degrees. The clutch started pushing back, and ruts and craters and rocks threw the steering wheel into nasty jerks that wrenched to the spine. I understood why, the day before, I'd thought there could be no road over the Chiricahuas: there wasn't. No wonder desperadoes hid in this inaccessibility.   — William Least Heat Moon

Time order need not be chronological. For example, you might decide to arrange events in the order in which they were revealed to you, not in the order in which they happened. Or you might choose to begin with a dramatic moment and then flash back to the events that led up to it.

Order of space

For descriptions of a location or a scene, a spatial arrangement will seem natural. Imagine yourself holding a video camera and you'll begin to see the possibilities. Might you pan the scene from afar and then zoom to a close-up? Would you rather sweep the camera from side to side — or from top to bottom? Or should you try for a more impressionistic effect, focusing the camera on first one and then another significant feature of the scene?

The writer of the following paragraph describes the contents of a long, narrow pool hall by taking us from the front to the back.

> The pool tables were in a line side by side from the front to the back of the long, narrow building. The first one was the biggest, and the best snooker players used it. Beyond it were the other tables used by lesser players, except for the last one. This was the bank's pool table, used only by the best players in the county.   — William G. Hill, student

Order of climax

When ideas are presented in the order of climax, they build toward a conclusion. Consider the following paragraph describing the effects on workers of long-term blue-collar employment. All of the examples have an emotional impact, but the final one — even though it might at first seem trivial — is the most powerful. It shows us just how degrading blue-collar work can become.

> I met people who taught me about human behavior. I saw people take amphetamines to keep up with ever-rising production rates. I saw good friends, and even relatives, physically attack each other over job assignments that would mean a few cents' difference. I observed women cheating on their husbands and men cheating on their wives. I watched

women hand over their entire paycheck to a bookie. I saw
pregnant women, their feet too swollen for shoes, come to
work in slippers. I saw women with colds stuff pieces of tissue
up their nostrils so they wouldn't have to keep stopping to
blow their nose.   — Linda Lavelle, student

Because the order of climax saves the most dramatic examples for the end, it is appropriate only when readers are
likely to persist until the end. In much business writing, for
example, you cannot assume that readers will read more than
the first couple of sentences of a paragraph. In such cases,
you will be wise to open with your most powerful examples,
even at the risk of allowing the paragraph to fizzle at the end.

6d If necessary, adjust paragraph length.

Most readers feel comfortable reading paragraphs that range
between 100 and 200 words. Shorter paragraphs force too
much starting and stopping, and longer ones strain the reader's attention span. There are exceptions to this guideline,
however. Paragraphs longer than 200 words frequently appear in scholarly writing, where they suggest seriousness and
depth. Paragraphs shorter than 100 words occur in newspapers because of narrow columns; in informal essays to
quicken the pace; and in business letters, where readers routinely skim for main ideas.

In an essay, the first and last paragraphs will ordinarily
be the introduction and conclusion. These special-purpose
paragraphs are likely to be shorter than the paragraphs in
the body of the essay. Typically, the body paragraphs will
mimic the essay's organization: one paragraph per point in
short essays, a group of paragraphs per point in longer ones.
Some ideas require more development than others, however,
so it is best to be flexible. If an idea stretches to a length
unreasonable for a paragraph, you should divide it, even if

you have presented comparable points in the essay in single paragraphs.

Paragraph breaks are not always made for strictly logical reasons. Writers use them as well to create emphasis, to mark a shift in time or place, to indicate a contrast, to signal a change in speakers (in dialogue), to provide readers a needed pause, or simply to improve the look of a page. Here is a summary of reasons for beginning a new paragraph.

REASONS FOR BEGINNING A NEW PARAGRAPH

— to mark off the introduction and the conclusion

— to signal a shift to a new idea

— to indicate an important shift in time or place

— to emphasize a point (by placing it at the beginning or the end, not in the middle, of a paragraph)

— to highlight a contrast

— to signal a change of speakers (in dialogue)

— to provide readers a needed pause

— to break up text that looks too dense

Beware of using too many short, choppy paragraphs, however. Readers want to see how your ideas connect, and they become irritated when you break their momentum by forcing them to pause every few sentences. Here are some reasons you might have for combining some of the paragraphs in a rough draft.

REASONS FOR COMBINING PARAGRAPHS

— to clarify the essay's organization

— to connect closely related ideas

— to maintain momentum

— to bind together text that looks too choppy

7

Link sentences to sentences, paragraphs to paragraphs.

When sentences and paragraphs flow from one to another without discernible bumps, gaps, or shifts, they are said to be coherent. Coherence can be improved by strengthening the various ties between old information and new: in other words, between sentences that have been read and those that are about to be read. A number of techniques for strengthening those ties are detailed in this section.

7a Link ideas clearly.

In the first draft of a paragraph or essay, writers do not always link their ideas as clearly as possible. To check a draft for clear connections among ideas, try to look at it from the point of view of a reader.

Think in terms of the reader's expectations. As you know, readers usually expect to learn a paragraph's main point in a topic sentence early in the paragraph. Then, as they move into the body of the paragraph, they expect to encounter specific details, facts, or examples that support the topic sentence — either directly or indirectly. Consider the following example, in which all of the sentences following the topic sentence directly support it.

> A passenger list of the early years of the Orient Express would read like a *Who's Who of the World,* from art to politics. Sarah Bernhardt and her Italian counterpart Eleonora Duse used the train to thrill the stages of Europe. For musicians

there were Toscanini and Mahler. Dancers Nijinsky and
Pavlova were there, while lesser performers like Harry Houdini
and the girls of the Ziegfeld Follies also rode the rails.
Violinists were allowed to practice on the train, and
occasionally one might see trapeze artists hanging like bats
from the baggage racks.

— Barnaby Conrad III, "Train of Kings"

If a sentence does not directly support the topic sentence,
readers expect it to support another sentence in the paragraph and therefore to support the topic sentence indirectly.
Composition scholar Francis Christensen has invented a useful system for numbering the sentences in a paragraph to
depict the hierarchic connections among sentences that readers look for. The topic sentence, being most general, receives
the number 1, and any sentences that directly support it receive the number 2. Sentences that support level 2 sentences
receive the number 3, and so on. Here, for example, is Christensen's numbering system as applied to a paragraph by columnist Ellen Goodman.

1. In the years since Kitty Genovese's murder, social scientists
   have learned a great deal about bystander behavior.
   2. They've learned that the willingness to intervene
      depends on a number of subtle factors beyond fear.
      3. It turns out that people are less likely to help if they
         are in a crowd of bystanders than if they are the only
         one.
         4. Their sense of responsibility is diffused.
         4. If the others aren't helping, they begin to
            reinterpret what they are seeing.
      3. People are also more passive in urban neighborhoods
         or crowded city spots where they suffer from
         "excessive overload" or simply turn off.
      3. They rarely get involved if they believe that the victim
         knows the assailant.
         4. This is especially true if the crime being
            witnessed is . . . a rape or attempted rape.

Because the sentences in this paragraph are arranged in a clear hierarchy, readers can easily follow the writer's train of thought.

To check one of your own paragraphs for clear connections among ideas, look to see if the hierarchic chain has been broken at any point. The topic sentence should announce the main idea, and the rest of the sentences should support it either directly or indirectly. When a sentence supports the topic sentence indirectly, it must support an earlier sentence that is clearly linked (directly or indirectly) to the topic sentence. If you can't find such a sentence, you'll need to add one or rethink the entire chain of ideas.

Like the sentences within paragraphs, the paragraphs within an essay should be arranged in a clear hierarchy. Readers expect to learn the essay's main point in the first paragraph, often in a thesis statement (see 1c). And by scanning the topic sentence of each paragraph in the body of the essay, readers hope to understand how each paragraph connects with what has come before. As a rule, a topic sentence should tell readers whether the information they are about to read supports the thesis statement directly or supports a key idea in the essay, which in turn supports the thesis.

7b Repeat key words.

Repetition of key words is an important technique for gaining coherence, because if too much information seems new, a paragraph will be hard to read. To prevent repetitions from becoming dull, you can use variations of a key word (*hike, hiker, hiking*), pronouns referring to the word (*hikers . . . they*), or synonyms (*walk, trek, wander, tramp, climb*).

In the following paragraph describing plots among indentured servants in seventeenth-century America, historian Richard Hofstadter binds sentences together by repeating the key word *plots* and echoing it with variations (all in italics).

Plots hatched by several servants to run away together occurred mostly in the plantation colonies, and the few recorded servant *uprisings* were entirely limited to those colonies. Virginia had been forced from its very earliest years to take stringent steps against *mutinous plots,* and severe punishments for *such behavior* were recorded. Most servant *plots* occurred in the seventeenth century: a contemplated *uprising* was nipped in the bud in York County in 1661; apparently led by some left-wing offshoots of the *Great Rebellion,* servants *plotted* an *insurrection* in Gloucester County in 1663, and four leaders were condemned and executed; some discontented servants apparently joined *Bacon's Rebellion* in the 1670's. In the 1680's the planters became newly apprehensive of discontent among the servants "owing to their great necessities and want of clothes," and it was feared that they would *rise up* and *plunder* the storehouses and ships; in 1682 there were plant-cutting *riots* in which servants and laborers, as well as some planters, took part. [Italics added.]   — Richard Hofstadter, *America at 1750*

7c   Use parallel structures for parallel ideas.

Parallel grammatical structures are frequently used within sentences to underscore the similarity of ideas (see 9). They may also be used to bind together a series of sentences expressing similar information. In the following passage describing folk beliefs, anthropologist Margaret Mead presents similar information in parallel grammatical form.

Actually, almost every day, even in the most sophisticated home, something is likely to happen that evokes the memory of some old folk belief. The salt spills. A knife falls to the floor. Your nose tickles. Then perhaps, with a slightly embarrassed smile, the person who spilled the salt tosses a pinch over his left shoulder. Or someone recites the old rhyme, "Knife falls, gentleman calls." Or as you rub your nose you think, That means a letter. I wonder who's writing?

— Margaret Mead, "New Superstitions for Old"

A less skilled writer might have varied the structure, perhaps like this: *The salt gets spilled. Mother drops a knife on the floor. Your nose begins to tickle.* But these sentences are less effective; Mead's parallel structures help tie the paragraph together.

7d Maintain consistency.

Coherence suffers whenever a draft shifts confusingly from one point of view to another or from one verb tense to another. (See 13.) In addition, coherence suffers when the subjects of sentences keep introducing new information. As a rule, a sentence's subject should echo a subject or object in the previous sentence.

The following rough-draft paragraph is needlessly hard to read because so few of the sentences' subjects are tied to earlier subjects or objects. The subjects appear in italics.

> *One* goes about trapping in this manner. At the very outset *one* acquires a "trapping" state of mind. A *library* of books must be read, and preferably *someone* with experience should educate the novice. *Preparing* for the first expedition takes several steps. The *purchase* of traps is first. A *pair* of rubber gloves, waterproof *boots*, and the grubbiest *clothes* capable of withstanding human use come next to outfit the trapper for his adventure. The *decision* has to be made on just what kind of animals to seek, what sort of bait to use, and where to place the traps. Finally, the *trapper* needs a heavy stick, in case it is necessary to club the animal and drown him.

Although the writer repeats a number of key words, such as *trapping,* the paragraph seems disconnected because new information keeps appearing as subjects.

To improve the paragraph, the writer used the first-person pronoun as the subject of every sentence. The revision is much easier to read.

> *I* went about trapping in this manner. To acquire a
> "trapping" state of mind, *I* read a library of books and talked
> at length with an experienced trapper, my father. Then *I*
> purchased the traps and outfitted myself by collecting a pair of
> rubber gloves, waterproof boots, and the grubbiest clothes
> capable of withstanding human use. Next *I* decided just what
> kinds of animals to seek, what sort of bait to use, and where
> to place my traps. Finally, *I* found a heavy stick, in case it
> would be necessary to club the animal and drown it.
>
> — John Clyde Thatcher, student

Notice that Thatcher combined some of his original sentences. By doing so, he was able to avoid excessive repetitions
of the pronoun *I*. Notice, too, that he varied his sentence
openings (most sentences do not begin with *I*) so that readers
are not likely to find the repetitions tiresome.

7e Provide transitions.

Certain words and phrases signal connections between ideas,
connections that might otherwise be missed. Included in the
following list are coordinating conjunctions, such as *and,
but,* and *or;* subordinating conjunctions, such as *although*
and *if;* conjunctive adverbs, such as *however* and *therefore;*
and transitional phrases, such as *in addition* and *for example.*

TO SHOW ADDITION
and, also, besides, further, furthermore, in addition,
moreover, next, too, first, second

TO GIVE EXAMPLES
for example, for instance, to illustrate, in fact, specifically

TO COMPARE
also, in the same manner, similarly, likewise

TO CONTRAST
but, however, on the other hand, in contrast, nevertheless, still, even though, on the contrary, yet, although

TO SUMMARIZE OR CONCLUDE
in other words, in short, in summary, in conclusion, to sum up, that is, therefore

TO SHOW TIME
after, as, before, next, during, later, finally, meanwhile, then, when, while, immediately

TO SHOW PLACE OR DIRECTION
above, below, beyond, farther on, nearby, opposite, close, to the left

TO INDICATE LOGICAL RELATIONSHIP
if, so, therefore, consequently, thus, as a result, for this reason, since

Skilled writers use transitional expressions with care, making sure, for example, not to use *consequently* when *also* would be more precise. They are also careful to select transitions with an appropriate tone, perhaps preferring *so* to *thus* in an informal piece, *in summary* to *in short* for a scholarly essay.

In the following paragraph, taken from an argument that dinosaurs had the " 'right-sized' brains for reptiles of their body size," biologist Stephen Jay Gould uses transitions (italicized) with skill:

> I don't wish to deny that the flattened, minuscule head of the large bodied "Stegosaurus" houses little brain from our subjective, top-heavy perspective, *but* I do wish to assert that we should not expect more of the beast. *First of all,* large animals have relatively smaller brains than related, small animals. The correlation of brain size with body size among kindred animals (all reptiles, all mammals, *for example*) is remarkably regular. *As* we move from small to large animals, from mice to elephants *or* small lizards to Komodo dragons,

brain size increases, *but* not so fast as body size. *In other words,* bodies grow faster than brains, *and* large animals have low ratios of brain weight to body weight. *In fact,* brains grow only about two-thirds as fast as bodies. *Since* we have no reason to believe that large animals are consistently stupider than their smaller relatives, we must conclude that large animals require relatively less brain to do as well as smaller animals. *If* we do not recognize this relationship, we are likely to underestimate the mental power of very large animals, dinosaurs in particular. [Italics added.]

        — Stephen Jay Gould, "Were Dinosaurs Dumb?"

EXERCISE 7 – 1

Use Francis Christensen's numerical system (see 7a) to indicate the coordinate and subordinate relations among sentences in the following paragraph.

Once children have learned to read, they go beyond their textbooks and explore the popular books written just for them. In order to see how these books portray men and women, I decided to visit the St. Peter Public Library. One book I found, *The Very Worst Thing,* tells of the adventures of a little boy on his first day in a new school. He arrives at school wearing the new sweater his mother has knit for him and is greeted by his teacher, Miss Pruce, and his male principal. At recess, the girls jump rope and toss a ball back and forth while the boys choose football teams and establish a tree house club. For show-and-tell that day, Henry, his new friend, brings a snake and some mice; Alice shows her foreign dolls, and Elizabeth demonstrates how to make fudge with Rice Krispies. In another book, *Come Back, Amelia Bedelia,* Amelia is fired from her job of baking for Mrs. Rogers, so she tries to find work as a beautician, a seamstress, a file clerk, and an office girl for a doctor. After trying all of these jobs unsuccessfully, she goes back to Mrs. Rogers and gets back her old job by making cream puffs. The rest of the books I looked at contained similar sex-role stereotypes — boys wear jeans and

T-shirts, set up lemonade stands, and play broomball, while girls wear dresses, play dress-up, and jump rope. Men are businessmen, soldiers, veterinarians, and truck drivers. Women are housewives, teachers, and witches who make love potions for girls wanting husbands.

— Patricia Klein, student

EXERCISE 7–2

If you were to divide the paragraph in Exercise 7–1 into two paragraphs, at what point would you make the break? Why?

EXERCISE 7–3

Looking again at the paragraph in Exercise 7–1, find examples of the following techniques for gaining coherence: repetition of key words, parallel structures, and transitions.

PART III

Crafting Sentences

8

Coordinate equal ideas; subordinate minor ideas.

When combining two or more ideas in one sentence, you have two choices: coordination or subordination. Choose coordination to indicate that the ideas are equal or nearly equal in importance. Choose subordination to indicate that one idea is less important than another.

Coordination

Coordination draws attention equally to two or more ideas. To coordinate single words or phrases, join them with a coordinating conjunction or with a pair of correlative conjunctions (see 47g). To coordinate independent clauses, join them with a comma and a coordinating conjunction or with a semicolon:

, and   , but   , or   , nor
, for   , so   , yet   ;

The semicolon is often accompanied by a conjunctive adverb such as *moreover, furthermore, therefore,* or *however* or by a transitional phrase such as *for example, in other words,* or *as a matter of fact.* (See the chart on page 112 for a more complete list.)

Assume, for example, that your intention is to draw equal attention to the following two ideas.

Grandmother lost her sight. Her hearing sharpened.

To coordinate these ideas, you can join them with a comma and the coordinating conjunction *but* or with a semicolon and the conjunctive adverb *however.*

Grandmother lost her sight, but her hearing sharpened.

Grandmother lost her sight; however, her hearing sharpened.

It is important to choose a coordinating conjunction or conjunctive adverb appropriate to your meaning. In the preceding example, the two ideas contrast with one another, calling for *but* or *however.*

Subordination

To give unequal emphasis to two or more ideas, express the major idea in an independent clause and place any minor ideas in subordinate clauses or phrases. (For specific subordination strategies, see the chart on page 113.)

Deciding which idea to emphasize is not a matter of right and wrong but is determined by the meaning you intend. Consider the two ideas mentioned earlier.

Grandmother lost her sight. Her hearing sharpened.

If your purpose were to stress your grandmother's acute hearing rather than her blindness, you would subordinate the idea concerning her blindness.

As she lost her sight, Grandmother's hearing sharpened.

The less important idea appears in an adverb clause modifying the verb *sharpened.*

To focus on your grandmother's growing blindness, you would subordinate the idea concerning her hearing.

Though her hearing sharpened, Grandmother gradually lost her sight.

Here the less important idea appears in an adverb clause modifying the verb *lost.*

Using coordination to combine sentences of equal importance

1. Consider using a comma and a coordinating conjunction. (See 32a.)

   | , and | , but | , or | , nor |
   | , for | , so | , yet | |

   ▶ In Orthodox Jewish funeral ceremonies, the shroud is a simple linen vestment, ~~The~~ *and the* coffin is plain wood with no adornment.

2. Consider using a semicolon and a conjunctive adverb or transitional phrase. (See 34b.)

also	in addition	now
as a result	in fact	of course
besides	in other words	on the other hand
consequently	in the first place	otherwise
finally	meanwhile	still
for example	moreover	then
for instance	nevertheless	therefore
furthermore	next	thus
however		

   ▶ Tom Baxter has been irritating me lately, *therefore,* I avoid him whenever possible.

   ▶ Tom Baxter has been irritating me lately, I avoid him, *therefore,* whenever possible.

3. Consider using a semicolon alone. (See 34a.)

   ▶ Nicklaus is like fine wine, ~~He~~ *he* gets better with time.

Using subordination to combine sentences of unequal importance

1. Consider putting the less important idea in a subordinate clause beginning with one of the following words. (See 49b.)

after	before	that	which
although	even though	unless	while
as	if	until	who
as if	since	when	whom
because	so that	where	whose

▶ ~~My~~ *When my* son asked his great-grandmother if she had been a slave*,* *she* ~~She~~ became very angry.

▶ My sister owes much of her recovery to a bodybuilding program*.* *that she* ~~She~~ began ~~the program~~ three years ago.

2. Consider putting the less important idea in a phrase. (See 49a, 49c, 49d, and 49e.)

▶ Karate*,* ~~is~~ a discipline based on the philosophy of nonviolence*,* ~~It~~ teaches the art of self-defense.

▶ ~~Alvin was~~ *E* encouraged by his professor to apply for the job*,* *Alvin* ~~He~~ filed an application on Monday morning.

▶ I reached for the knife out of habit*,* *my eyes scanning* ~~My eyes scanned~~ the long shiny blade for a price sticker. In a low, steady voice, my customer said, "This is a holdup."

p. 457

8a Combine choppy sentences.

Short sentences demand attention, so you should use them primarily for emphasis. Too many short sentences, one after the other, make for a choppy style.

If an idea is not important enough to deserve its own sentence, try combining it with a sentence close by. Put any minor ideas in subordinate structures such as phrases or subordinate clauses.

> **CHOPPY**   The huts vary in height. They measure from ten to fifteen feet in diameter. They contain no modern conveniences.
>
> **IMPROVED**   The huts, which vary in height and measure from ten to fifteen feet in diameter, contain no modern conveniences.

Three sentences have become one, with minor ideas expressed in an adjective clause beginning with *which*.

▶ Agnes ，was another student I worked with／，She was a hyperactive child.

The revision emphasizes that Agnes was a hyperactive child and de-emphasizes the rest of the information, which appears in an appositive phrase.

Although the
▶ The Market Inn ，is located at 2nd and E Streets／，It doesn't look very impressive from the outside／，The food，however， is

excellent.

Three sentences have become one, with minor ideas expressed in a subordinate clause (*Although . . . outside*), which in turn contains a participial phrase (*located . . . Streets*) modifying *Market Inn*.

Although subordination is ordinarily the most effective technique for combining short, choppy sentences, coordination is appropriate when the ideas are equal in importance.

▶ The hospital decides when patients will sleep and wake/. It
                            and
  dictates what and when they will eat/, It tells them when

  they may be with family and friends.

Three sentences have become one, with equivalent ideas expressed in a coordinate series.

ESL NOTE: When you combine sentences, be careful not to repeat subject or object pronouns in subordinate constructions. See 31b.

EXERCISE 8 – 1

In the following paragraphs, combine choppy sentences by subordinating minor ideas or by coordinating ideas of equal importance. More than one effective revision is possible.

    Some scientists favor continued research to advance the technology of genetic engineering. They argue that they are only refining the process of selective breeding that has benefited society for many years. For centuries, they claim, scientists have recognized variations in plant and animal species from generation to generation. In the early nineteenth century, scientists explained those variations as part of an evolutionary process. They called this process natural selection. Later scientists found ways to duplicate this process of natural selection. They did not want to leave the process to chance. They developed the technique of selective breeding.

    Dairy farmers use selective breeding. They do it to increase production from their herds. They choose the best milk-producing cows for breeding. These cows have certain genetic traits. These traits make them top producers. Breeding them selectively increases the chance that the offspring will inherit those same genetic traits. Then they will be top producers too. For the same reasons, farmers identify the cows that are low producers. They choose not to use them for breeding.

Scientists argue that genetic engineering is not much different from selective breeding. They claim that it can produce similar positive results. Society, they say, should support their research. Society can only benefit, as it has in the past.

8b Avoid ineffective coordination.

Coordinate structures are appropriate only when you intend to draw the reader's attention equally to two or more ideas: *Schwegler praises loudly, and he criticizes softly.* If one idea is more important than another — or if a coordinating conjunction does not clearly signal the relation between the ideas — you should subordinate the lesser idea.

INEFFECTIVE   Closets were taxed as rooms, and most colonists stored their clothes in chests or clothes presses.

IMPROVED   Because closets were taxed as rooms, most colonists stored their clothes in chests or clothes presses.

The revision subordinates the less important idea by putting it in a subordinate clause. Notice that the subordinating conjunction *Because* signals the relation between the ideas more clearly than the coordinating conjunction *and.*

▶ *On Death and Dying,* ~~was written~~ by Dr. Elisabeth Kübler-
Ross, ~~and it~~ describes the experiences of terminally ill
patients.

The minor idea has become a prepositional phrase.

noticing
▶ My uncle ˏ ~~noticed~~ my frightened look ˏ~~and~~ told me

that Grandma had to feel my face because she was

blind.

The less important idea has become a participial phrase modifying the noun *uncle*.

After four hours,
▶ ~~Four hours went by, and~~ a rescue truck finally arrived, but

by that time we had been evacuated in a helicopter.

Three independent clauses were excessive. The least important idea has become a prepositional phrase.

EXERCISE 8 – 2

Combine or restructure the following sentences by subordinating minor ideas or by coordinating ideas of equal importance. You must decide which ideas are minor because the sentences are given out of context. Revisions of lettered sentences appear in the back of the book. Example:

The team rowed until their strength nearly gave out and
where they   *to*
finally returned to shore ˏ ~~and~~ had a party on the beach ~~and~~
celebrate
~~celebrated~~ the start of the season.

a. A couple of minutes went by, and the teacher walked in smiling.
b. The losing team was made up of superstars. These superstars acted as isolated individuals on the court.
c. We keep our use of insecticides, herbicides, and fungicides to a minimum. We are concerned about the environment.
d. The aides help the younger children with reading and math. These are the children's weakest subjects.
e. My first sky dive was from an altitude of 12,500 feet, and it was the most frightening experience of my life.

1. The American crocodile could once be found in abundance in southern Florida. It is now being threatened with extinction.
2. I noticed that the sky was glowing orange and red. I bent down to crawl into the bunker.
3. Sister Consilio was enveloped in a black robe with only her face and hands visible. She was an imposing figure.
4. Cocaine is an addictive drug and it can seriously harm you both physically and mentally, if death doesn't get you first.
5. We met every Monday morning in the home of one of the members. These meetings would last about three hours.
6. Marta was her father's favorite. She felt free to do whatever she wanted.
7. He walked up to the pitcher's mound. He dug his toe into the ground. He swung his arm around backward and forward. Then he threw the ball and struck the batter out.
8. Alan walked over to his car, and he noticed a few unusual dark spots on the hood.
9. The lift chairs were going around very fast. They were bumping the skiers into their seats.
10. The first football card set was released by the Goudey Gum Company in 1933. The set featured only three football players. They were Red Grange, Bronko Nagurski, and Knute Rockne.

8c Do not subordinate major ideas.

If a sentence buries its major idea in a subordinate construction, readers may not give it enough attention. Express the major idea in an independent clause and subordinate any minor ideas.

▶ Lanie, who *had polio as a child,* now walks with the help of braces. ~~had polio as a child.~~

The writer wanted to focus on Lanie's ability to walk, but the original sentence buried this information in an adjective clause.

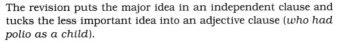

The revision puts the major idea in an independent clause and tucks the less important idea into an adjective clause (*who had polio as a child*).

As
▶ I was driving home from my new job, heading down New
  ∧

York Avenue, ~~when~~ my car suddenly overheated.

The writer wanted to emphasize that the car was overheating, not the fact of driving home. The revision expresses the major idea in an independent clause, the less important idea in an adverb clause (*As I was driving home from my new job*).

8d Do not subordinate excessively.

In attempting to avoid short, choppy sentences, writers sometimes move to the opposite extreme, putting more subordinate ideas into a sentence than its structure can bear. If a sentence collapses of its own weight, occasionally it can be restructured. More often, however, such sentences must be divided.

▶ Our job is to stay between the stacker and the tie machine
                                        If they do,
  watching to see if the newspapers jam/. ~~in which case~~ we
                                      ∧

  pull the bundles off and stack them on a skid, because

  otherwise they would back up in the stacker.

EXERCISE 8 – 3

In each of the following sentences, the idea that the writer wished to emphasize is buried in a subordinate construction. Restructure each sentence so that the independent clause expresses the major idea and lesser ideas are subordinated. Revisions of lettered sentences appear in the back of the book. Example:

Though

Catherine has weathered many hardships, ~~though~~ she has

rarely become discouraged. [*Emphasize that Catherine has*

rarely become discouraged.]

a. Our team finally acquired an expert backstroker, who enabled us to win every relay for the rest of the season. [*Emphasize the wins, not acquiring the backstroker.*]

b. The senator was planning a trip to Spain and Portugal when the travel agent canceled the trip because of terrorist activities. [*Emphasize the cancellation.*]

c. I presented the idea of job sharing to my supervisors, who to my surprise were delighted with the idea. [*Emphasize the supervisors' response to the idea.*]

d. Although native Hawaiians try to preserve their ancestors' sacred customs, outsiders have forced changes on them. [*Emphasize the Hawaiians' attempt to preserve their customs.*]

e. Sharon's country kitchen, which overlooks a field where horses and cattle graze among old tombstones, was formerly a lean-to porch. [*Emphasize that the kitchen overlooks the field.*]

1. My grandfath   ho raised his daughters the old-fashioned way, was bo   ty-six years ago in Puerto Rico. [*Emphasize how the grandj   er raised his daughters.*]

2. The building hou d a school, a grocery store, an auto repair shop, and two families when it burned to the ground last week. [*Emphasize that the building burned down.*]

3. Louis's team worked with the foreign mission by building new churches and restoring those damaged by hurricanes. [*Emphasize the building and restoring.*]

4. We were traveling down I-94 when we were hit in the rear by a speeding Oldsmobile. [*Emphasize the accident.*]

5. Although Sarah felt that we lacked decent transportation, our family owned a Jeep, a pickup truck, and a sports car. [*Emphasize Sarah's feeling that the family lacked decent transportation.*]

9

Balance parallel ideas.

If two or more ideas are parallel, they are more readable when expressed in parallel grammatical form. Single words should be balanced with single words, phrases with phrases, clauses with clauses.

A kiss can be a comma, a question mark, or an exclamation point.   — Mistinguett

This novel is not to be tossed lightly aside, but to be hurled with great force.   — Dorothy Parker

In matters of principle, stand like a rock; in matters of taste, swim with the current.   — Thomas Jefferson

I don't want to achieve immortality through my work. I want to achieve it through not dying.   — Woody Allen

Writers often use parallelism to create emphasis. (See 14c.)

9a Balance parallel ideas linked with coordinating conjunctions.

Coordinating conjunctions (and, but, or, nor, for, so, yet) are used to connect a pair or a series of items. When those items are closely parallel in content, they should be expressed in parallel grammatical form.

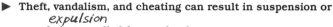

▶ Theft, vandalism, and cheating can result in suspension or
    expulsion
  even ~~being expelled~~ from school.
     ∧

The revision balances the noun *expulsion* with the noun *suspension*.

▶ Mary told the judge that she had been pulled out of a line of
            that she had a
  fast-moving traffic and ~~of her~~ perfect driving record.
          ∧

A *that* clause is now paired with a *that* clause, not with an *of* phrase.

                            repairing
▶ David is responsible for stocking merchandise, ~~all in-store~~
  items in the store,   *selling* ∧
  ~~repairs,~~ writing orders for delivery, and ~~sales of~~ computers.
                                  ∧

The revision uses *-ing* forms for all items in the series.

▶ After assuring us that he was sober, Sam drove down the
                        went through
  middle of the road, ran one red light, and two stop signs
                            ∧

before we persuaded him to pull over.

The revision adds a verb to make the three items parallel: *drove . . . , ran . . . , went through. . . .*

NOTE: Clauses beginning with *and who* or *and which* should be balanced with an earlier *who* or *which,* or the conjunction *and* should be dropped.

▶ Austin is a young man of many talents ~~and~~ who promises to

be a successful artist.

Deleting *and* is the best way to revise this sentence, because repeating *who* leads to unnecessary words: *Austin is a young man who has many talents and who promises to be a successful artist.*

9b   Balance parallel ideas linked with correlative conjunctions.

Correlative conjunctions come in pairs: *either . . . or, neither . . . nor, not only . . . but also, both . . . and, whether . . . or.* Make sure that the grammatical structure following the second half of the pair is the same as that following the first half.

▶ The shutters were not only too long but also ~~were~~ too

wide.

The words *too long* follow *not only,* so *too wide* should follow *but also.* Repeating *were* creates an unbalanced effect.

▶ I was advised either to change my flight or ∧^(*to*) take the train.

To change my flight, which follows *either,* should be balanced with *to take the train,* which follows *or.*

9c   Balance comparisons linked with *than* or *as.*

In comparisons linked with *than* or *as,* the elements being compared should appear in parallel grammatical structure.

▶ It is easier to speak in abstractions than ~~grounding~~ ∧^(*to ground*) one's

thoughts in reality.

▶ Mother could not persuade me that giving is as much a joy
as ~~to receive.~~ ∧^(*receiving.*)

NOTE: Comparisons should also be logical and complete. See 10c.

9d   Repeat function words to clarify parallels.

Function words such as prepositions (*by, to*) and subordinating conjunctions (*that, because*) signal the grammatical
nature of the word groups to follow. Although they can sometimes be omitted, include them whenever they signal parallel
structures that might otherwise be missed by readers.

▶ Many smokers try switching to a brand they find distasteful
                                          to
or a low tar and nicotine cigarette.
   ∧

In the original sentence the prepositional phrase was too complex for easy reading. The repetition of the preposition *to* prevents readers from losing their way.

▶ The ophthalmologist told me that Julie was extremely
                              that
farsighted but corrective lenses would help considerably.
          ∧

A second subordinating conjunction helps readers sort out the
two parallel ideas: *that* Julie was extremely farsighted and *that*
corrective lenses would help.

NOTE: If it is possible to streamline the sentence, repetition
of the function word may not be necessary.

▶ The board reported that its investments had done well in the

first quarter but ~~that they~~ had since dropped in value.

Instead of linking two subordinate clauses beginning with *that*,
the revision balances the two parts of a compound predicate —
had done well in the first quarter and *had since dropped in
value.*

EXERCISE 9-1

Edit the following sentences to correct faulty parallelism. Revisions of lettered sentences appear in the back of the book. Example:

> We began the search by calling the Department of Social
> Services and ~~requested~~ *requesting* a list of licensed day-care centers in
> our area. ∧

a. The system has capabilities such as communicating with other computers, processing records, and mathematical functions.

b. The personnel officer told me that I would answer the phone, welcome visitors, distribute mail, and some typing.

c. This summer I want a job more than to go to Disney World.

d. How ideal it seems to raise a family here in Luray instead of the air-polluted suburbs.

e. Nancy not only called the post office but she checked with the neighbors to see if the package had come.

1. Many states are reducing property taxes for homeowners as well as extend financial aid in the form of tax credits to renters.

2. Arch-ups are done on the floor face down, with arms extended over the head, toes pointed, and knees stay straight.

3. The boys decided that either Carla had hidden the money or had never had it in the first place.

4. During basic training, I was not only told what to do but also what to think.

5. The Food and Drug Administration has admitted that sodium nitrite can deform the fetuses of pregnant women and it can cause serious harm to anemic persons.

6. Bill finds it harder to be fair to himself than being fair to others.

7. More plants fail from improper watering than any other cause.

8. Your adviser familiarizes you with the school and how to select classes appropriate for your curriculum.

9. To administer the poison, the tribe's sorcerers put it in their victims' food, throw it into their huts, or it can be dropped into their mouths or nostrils while they sleep.

10. The babysitter was expected to feed two children, entertain them, take phone messages, and some cleaning in the kitchen.

EXERCISE 9–2

Describe the parallel structure in the following passages and discuss how the use of parallelism contributes to the effectiveness of each. (Also see 14c, which discusses parallel structure.)

1. All respect we may have had for politicians, preachers, lawyers, governors, Presidents, senators, congressmen was utterly destroyed as we watched them temporizing and compromising over right and wrong, over legality and illegality, over constitutionality and unconstitutionality.   — Eldridge Cleaver

2. One of the devastating weaknesses of university learning, of the store of knowledge and opinion that has been handed down through academic training, has been its almost total erasure of women's experience and thought from the curriculum, and its exclusion of women as members of the academic community.

    — Adrienne Rich

3. Knowing others is wisdom; knowing the self is enlightenment. Mastering others requires force; mastering the self needs strength.   — Lao Tsu

4. How can I love the man who raped my mother, killed my father, enslaved my ancestors, dropped atomic bombs on Japan, killed off the Indians and keeps me cooped up in the slums?

    — Malcolm X

5. That modern science, like all things, contains its own share of corruption, that men of science only too often fail to live up to its standards, that science can be used for violent and criminal ends, that man will steal, plunder, abuse, and kill to gain knowledge — all this is no argument against science.

    — Karl Jaspers

10

Add needed words.

Do not omit words necessary for grammatical or logical completeness. Readers need to see at a glance how the parts of a sentence are connected.

10a Add words needed to complete compound structures.

In compound structures, words are often omitted for econ- omy: *The first half of our life is ruined by our parents, [and] the second half [is ruined] by our children.* Such omissions are perfectly acceptable as long as the omitted words are com- mon to both parts of the compound structure.

If the shorter version defies grammar or idiom because an omitted word is not common to both parts of the com- pound structure, the word must be put back in.

▶ Some of the regulars are acquaintances whom we see at
who
work or live in our community.
∧

The word *who* must be included because *whom live in our com- munity* is not grammatically correct.

accepted
▶ I never have and never will accept a bribe.
∧

Have . . . accept is not grammatically correct.

in
▶ Many of these tribes still believe and live by ancient laws.
∧

Believe . . . by is not idiomatic in English.

NOTE: Even when the omitted word is common to both parts of the compound structure, occasionally it must be inserted to avoid ambiguity. The sentence *My favorite English profes- sor and mentor influenced my choice of a career* suggests that the professor and mentor are the same person. If they are not, *my* must be repeated: *My favorite English professor and my mentor influenced my choice of a career.*

10b Add the word *that* if there is any danger of misreading without it.

If there is no danger of misreading, the word *that* may be omitted when it introduces a subordinate clause. *The value of a principle is the number of things* [that] *it will explain.* Occasionally, however, a sentence might be misread without *that.*

▶ As Joe began to prepare dinner, he discovered the oven ^*that*^

wasn't working properly.

Joe didn't discover the oven; he discovered that the oven wasn't working properly.

▶ Many civilians believe the air force has a vigorous exercise ^*that*^

program.

The subordinating conjunction tells readers to expect a clause, not just *the air force*, as the direct object of *believe*.

10c Add words needed to make comparisons logical and complete.

Comparisons should be made between items that are alike. To compare unlike items is illogical and distracting.

▶ Christopher had an attention span longer than the other ^*that of*^

children.

It is illogical to compare an attention span and children. Since repeating the words *attention span* would be awkward, inserting *that of* corrects the problem.

► Henry preferred the hotels in Pittsburgh to ^*those in* Philadelphia.

Hotels must be compared with hotels.

Sometimes the word *other* must be inserted to make a comparison logical.

► Chicago is larger than any ^*other* city in Illinois.

Since Chicago is not larger than itself, the original comparison was not logical.

Sometimes the word *as* must be inserted to make a comparison grammatically complete.

► Ben is as talented, ^*as* if not more talented than, the other actors.

The construction *as talented . . . than* is not grammatical. Adding *as* corrects the problem: *as talented as . . . the other actors.*

Finally, comparisons should be complete enough to ensure clarity. The reader should understand what is being compared.

> **INCOMPLETE**   Brand X is a lighter beer.
>
> **COMPLETE**   Brand X is a lighter beer than Brand Y.

Also, there should be no ambiguity. In the following sentence, two interpretations are possible.

> **AMBIGUOUS**   Kelly helped me more than my roommate.
>
> **CLEAR**   Kelly helped me more than *he helped* my roommate.
>
> **CLEAR**   Kelly helped me more than my roommate *did.*

10d Add the articles *a, an,* and *the* where necessary
for grammatical completeness.

Articles are sometimes omitted in recipes and other instructions that are meant to be followed while they are being read.
Such omissions are inappropriate, however, in nearly all
other forms of writing, whether formal or informal.

> Blood can be drawn from ^*a* patient's femoral bone only by ^*a*
> doctor or by ^*an* ^ authorized person who has been trained in ^*the*
>
> procedure.

ESL NOTE: Articles can cause problems for speakers of English
as a second language. See 30.

EXERCISE 10–1

Add any words needed for grammatical or logical completeness in the
following sentences. Revisions of lettered sentences appear in the
back of the book. Example:

The officer at the desk feared *that* ^ the prisoner in the

interrogation room would escape.

a. Dip paintbrush into paint remover and spread thick coat on
   small section of door.
b. Some say that Ella Fitzgerald's renditions of Cole Porter's songs
   are better than any singer.
c. SETI (the Search for Extraterrestrial Intelligence) has and will
   continue to excite interest among space buffs.
d. Samantha got along better with the chimpanzees than Albert.
e. Gunther Gebel-Williams, whom we watched today and is a star
   of the Ringling Brothers and Barnum & Bailey Circus, is well
   known for his training of circus animals.

1. Their starting salaries are higher than other professionals with more seniority.
2. For many years Americans had trust and affection for Walter Cronkite.
3. We invited all the neighbors whom we knew and enjoyed football as much as we did.
4. Our nursing graduates are as skilled, if not more skilled than, those of any other state college.
5. Jupiter is larger than any planet in our solar system.
6. State officials were more concerned with the damage than what caused it.
7. Great-uncle John's car resembled other bootleggers: it had a smoke screen device useful in case of pursuit by the sheriff.
8. Thomas decided to join the army after his freshman year and been in it ever since.
9. Many citizens do not believe the leaders of this administration are serious about reducing the deficit.
10. It was obvious that the students liked the new teacher more than the principal.

11

Untangle mixed constructions.

A mixed construction contains parts that do not sensibly fit together. The mismatch may be a matter of grammar or of logic.

11a Untangle the grammatical structure.

Once you head into a sentence, your choices are limited by the range of grammatical patterns in English. (See 48 and 49.) You cannot begin with one grammatical plan and switch without warning to another.

> **MIXED** For most drivers who have a blood alcohol content of .05 percent double their risk of causing an accident.

> **REVISED** For most drivers who have a blood alcohol content of .05 percent, the risk of causing an accident is doubled.

> **REVISED** Most drivers who have a blood alcohol content of .05 percent double their risk of causing an accident.

The writer began with a long prepositional phrase that was destined to be a modifier but then tried to press it into service as the subject of the sentence. This cannot be done. If the sentence is to begin with the prepositional phrase, the writer must finish the sentence with a subject and verb (*risk . . . is doubled*). The writer who wishes to stay with the original verb (*double*) must head into the sentence another way: *Most drivers. . . .*

> *Being*
> ~~When an employee is~~ promoted without warning can be
>   ʌ
> alarming.

The adverb clause *When an employee is promoted without warning* cannot serve as the subject of the sentence. The revision replaces the adverb clause with a gerund phrase, a word group that can function as the subject. (See 49b and 49c.)

> Although I feel that Mr. Dawe is an excellent calculus
>
> instructor~~, but~~ a few minor changes in his method would
>
> benefit both him and the class.

The *although* clause is subordinate, so it cannot be linked to an independent clause with the coordinating conjunction *but.*

Occasionally a mixed construction is so tangled that it defies grammatical analysis. When this happens, back away from the sentence, rethink what you want to say, and then say it again as clearly as you can.

> **MIXED** In the whole-word method children learn to recognize entire words rather than by the phonics method in which they learn to sound out letters and groups of letters.

> **REVISED** The whole-word method teaches children to recognize entire words; the phonics method teaches them to sound out letters and groups of letters.

11b Straighten out the logical connections.

The subject and the predicate should make sense together; when they don't, the error is known as *faulty predication.*

▶ The ~~growth in the~~ number of applications is increasing

rapidly.

It is not the growth that is increasing but the number of applications.

▶ Under the revised plan, the elderly, /~~who now receive a~~

∧ *double personal exemption for the*

~~double personal exemption,~~ will be abolished.

The exemption, not the elderly, will be abolished.

An appositive and the noun to which it refers should be logically equivalent. When they are not, the error is known as *faulty apposition.*

▶ *Tax accounting,*

~~The tax accountant,~~ a very lucrative field, requires

∧

intelligence, patience, and attention to detail.

The tax accountant is a person, not a field.

11c Avoid *is when, is where,* and *reason . . . is because* constructions.

In formal English many readers object to *is when, is where,* and *reason . . . is because* constructions on either grammatical or logical grounds. Grammatically, the verb *is* (as well as *are, was,* and *were*) should be followed by a noun that renames the subject or by an adjective that describes it, not by an adverb clause beginning with *when, where,* or *because.* (See 48b and 49b.) Logically, the words *when, where,* and *because* suggest relations of time, place, and cause — relations that do not always make sense with *is, was,* or *were.*

▶ Anorexia nervosa is ~~where people~~ believing they are too fat,

  a disorder suffered by people who,

  diet to the point of starvation.

  Anorexia nervosa is a disorder, not a place.

▶ ~~The reason~~ I missed the exam ~~is~~ because my motorcycle

  broke down.

  The writer might have changed *because* to *that* (*The reason I missed the exam is that my motorcycle broke down*), but the revision above is more concise.

EXERCISE 11–1

Edit the following sentences to untangle mixed constructions. Revisions of lettered sentences appear in the back of the book. Example:

  ~~By~~ loosening the soil around your jade plant will help the air

  and nutrients penetrate to the roots.

a. My instant reaction was filled with anger and disappointment.

b. I brought a problem into the house that my mother wasn't sure how to handle it.

c. It is through the misery of others that has made old Harvey rich.

d. A cloverleaf is when traffic on limited-access freeways can change direction.

e. Bowman established the format in which future football card companies would emulate for years to come.

1. The more experienced pilots in the system Zeke assigned two aircraft to them.

2. Depending on the number and strength of drinks, the amount of time that has passed since the last drink, and one's body weight determines the concentration of alcohol in the blood.

3. The decline in the rate of live births in the country was decreasing.

4. By pushing the button for the insert mode opens the computer's memory.

5. The reason the Eskimos were forced to eat their dogs was because the caribou, on which they depended for food, migrated out of reach.

6. To look at rolling hills of virgin snow or snow-capped evergreens is far more beautiful than the brown slush on city streets.

7. Pat had to train herself on a mainframe computer that was designed for data entry but it was not intended for word processing.

8. One service available to military personnel living on base, the Special Services Building, provides half-price tickets to local movie theaters.

9. In the section of the perimeter for which my unit was responsible came under fire.

10. The little time we have together we try to use it wisely.

12

Repair misplaced and dangling modifiers.

Modifiers, whether they are single words, phrases, or clauses, should point clearly to the words they modify. As a rule, related words should be kept together.

12a   Put limiting modifiers in front of the words they modify.

Limiting modifiers such as *only, even, almost, nearly,* and *just* should appear in front of a verb only if they modify the verb: *At first, I couldn't even touch my toes, much less grasp them.* If they limit the meaning of some other word in the sentence, they should be placed in front of that word.

▶ You will ~~only~~ need to plant ⟨*only*⟩ one package of seeds.

▶ Our team didn't ~~even~~ score ⟨*even*⟩ once.

▶ Bob ~~almost~~ ate ⟨*almost*⟩ the whole chicken.

> *Only* limits the meaning of *one,* not *need. Even* modifies *once,* not *score; almost* modifies *the whole chicken,* not *ate.*

12b   Place phrases and clauses so that readers can see at a glance what they modify.

Although phrases and clauses can appear at some distance from the words they modify, make sure your meaning is clear. When phrases or clauses are oddly placed, absurd misreadings can result.

MISPLACED	The king returned to the clinic where he had undergone heart surgery in 1986 in a limousine sent by the White House.
REVISED	Traveling in a limousine sent by the White House, the king returned to the clinic where he had undergone heart surgery in 1986.

The revision corrects the false impression that the king underwent heart surgery in a limousine.

On the walls

▶ ~~There~~ are many pictures of comedians ~~on the walls~~ who have

performed at Gavin's.

The walls didn't perform at Gavin's; the comedians did. The writer at first revised the sentence like this: *There are many pictures of comedians who have performed at Gavin's on the walls.* But this creates another absurd effect. The comedians weren't performing on the walls.

150-pound,

▶ The robber was described as a six-foot-tall man with a heavy

mustache ~~weighing 150 pounds.~~

The robber, not the mustache, weighed 150 pounds. The revision makes this clear.

Occasionally the placement of a modifier leads to an ambiguity, in which case two revisions will be possible, depending on the writer's intended meaning.

AMBIGUOUS	We promised when the play was over that we would take Charles to an ice cream parlor.
CLEAR	When the play was over, we promised Charles that we would take him to an ice cream parlor.
CLEAR	We promised Charles that we would take him to an ice cream parlor when the play was over.

The first revision suggests that the promising occurred when the play was over, the second that the taking would occur when the play was over.

12c Move awkwardly placed modifiers.

As a rule, a sentence should flow from subject to verb to object, without lengthy detours along the way. When a long adverbial element separates a subject from its verb, a verb from its object, or a helping verb from its main verb, the result is usually awkward.

▶ ~~Kilmer,~~ ^A^ ^after^ doctors told him that he would never walk again, ^Kilmer^ initiated on his own an intensive program of rehabilitation.

There is no reason to separate the subject *Kilmer* from the verb *initiated* with a long adverb clause.

▶ ~~Oscar Lewis spent,~~ ^I^ ^in^ researching *The Children of Sanchez*, ^Oscar Lewis spent^ hundreds of hours living with the Sanchez family in a slum of Mexico City.

The *in* phrase needlessly separates the verb *spent* from its object, *hundreds of hours*.

▶ ~~Many students have,~~ ^B^ ^by^ the time they reach their senior year, ^many students have^ completed all the requirements for their major.

The helping verb *have* should be closer to its main verb *completed*.

EXCEPTION: Occasionally a writer may choose to delay a verb or an object to create suspense. In the following passage, for example, Robert Mueller inserts the *after* phrase between the subject *women* and the verb *walk* to heighten the dramatic effect.

> I asked a Burmese why women, after centuries of following their men, now walk ahead. He said there were many unexploded land mines since the war.   — Robert Mueller

12d Do not split infinitives needlessly.

An infinitive consists of *to* plus a verb: *to think, to breathe, to dance.* When words appear between its two parts, an infinitive is said to be "split": *to carefully balance.* If a split infinitive is obviously awkward, it should be revised.

▶ ~~The~~ patient should try to ~~if possible~~ avoid going up and   *If possible, the*

down stairs.

Usage varies when a split infinitive is less awkward than the preceding one. To be on the safe side, however, you should not split such infinitives, especially in formal writing.

▶ The candidate decided to ~~formally~~ launch her campaign.   *formally*

When a split infinitive is more natural and less awkward than alternative phrasing, most readers find it acceptable: *We decided to actually enforce the law* is a perfectly natural construction in English. *We decided actually to enforce the law* is not.

EXERCISE 12–1

Edit the following sentences to correct misplaced or awkwardly placed modifiers. Revisions of lettered sentences appear in the back of the book. Example:

Answering questions *in a telephone survey* can be annoying. ~~in a telephone survey.~~

a. He only wanted to buy three roses, not a dozen.
b. Within the next few years, orthodontists will be using the technique Kurtz developed as standard practice.

c. Celia received a flier about a workshop on making a kimono from a Japanese nun.
d. Jurors are encouraged to carefully and thoroughly sift through the evidence.
e. Each state would set a program into motion of recycling all reusable products.

1. We hope Monica will realize that providing only for her children's material needs is harmful before it is too late.
2. The orderly confessed that he had given a lethal injection to the patient after ten hours of grilling by the police.
3. Eric took a course at the university that represents a new low in education.
4. Mike, as the next wave rolled in, dropped in easily and made a smooth turn, but the wave closed out.
5. He promised never to remarry at her deathbed.
6. The purpose of EST is to resolve local crises without loss of life in a tactical manner.
7. Though he is seventy-three, my uncle can lift a load of bricks without a thought that would have most twenty-five-year-olds straining.
8. It just took experience with two clients to convince my mother to avoid interior design.
9. The Secret Service was falsely accused of mishandling the attempted assassination by the media.
10. The adoption agency informed us that we would be able to at long last get a child.

12e   Repair dangling modifiers.

A dangling modifier fails to refer logically to any word in the sentence. Dangling modifiers are usually introductory word groups (such as verbal phrases) that suggest but do not name an actor. When a sentence opens with such a modifier, readers expect the subject of the following clause to name the actor. If it doesn't, the modifier dangles.

DANGLING   Deciding to join the navy, the recruiter enthusiastically pumped Joe's hand. [*Participial phrase*]

DANGLING   Upon seeing the barricade, our car screeched to a halt. [*Preposition followed by a gerund phrase*]

DANGLING   To please the children, some fireworks were set off a day early. [*Infinitive phrase*]

DANGLING   Though only sixteen, UCLA accepted Martha's application. [*Elliptical clause with an understood subject and verb*]

These dangling modifiers falsely suggest that the recruiter decided to join the navy, that the car saw the barricade, that the fireworks intended to please the children, and that UCLA is only sixteen years old.

To repair a dangling modifier, you must restructure the sentence in one of two ways: (1) change the subject of the sentence so that it names the actor implied by the introductory modifier or (2) turn the modifier into a word group that includes the actor.

DANGLING   When watching a classic film such as *Gone With the Wind*, commercials are especially irritating.

REPAIRED   When watching a classic film such as *Gone With the Wind*, I find commercials especially irritating.

REPAIRED   When I am watching a classic film such as *Gone With the Wind*, commercials are especially irritating.

A dangling modifier cannot be repaired simply by moving it: *Commercials are especially irritating when watching. . . .* Readers still don't know who is doing the watching.

Reviewing your writing for dangling modifiers

First look for the most common trouble spots:

SENTENCES OPENING WITH A VERBAL

There are three kinds of verbals (see also 49c):

> *-ing* verb forms such as *walking* (present participles)
>
> *-ed, -d, -en, -n,* or *-t* verb forms such as *planted, eaten, taught* (past participles)
>
> *to* verb forms such as *to become* (infinitives)

▶ Excited about winning the championship, ~~a~~ *we held* raucous

celebration ~~was held~~ in the locker room.

SENTENCES OPENING WITH A WORD GROUP CONTAINING A VERBAL

▶ After ~~swimming~~ *I swam* across the lake, the lifeguard scolded

me for risking my life.

SENTENCES OPENING WITH AN ELLIPTICAL CLAUSE (A CLAUSE WITH OMITTED WORDS)

▶ Although *I was* only four years old, my father insisted that I

learn to read.

Dangling modifiers (continued)

Next test your sentences for dangling modifiers:

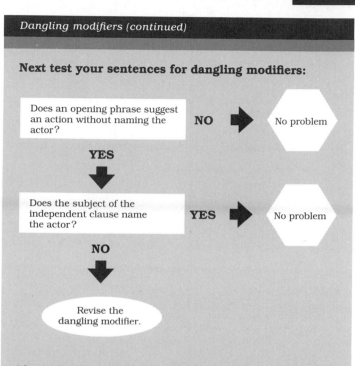

Does an opening phrase suggest an action without naming the actor?

NO → No problem

YES ↓

Does the subject of the independent clause name the actor?

YES → No problem

NO ↓

Revise the dangling modifier.

If you find a dangling modifier, revise the sentence in one of two ways:

1. Change the subject of the independent clause so that it names the actor implied by the modifier.
2. Turn the modifier into a word group that includes the actor.

When the driver opened
▶ ~~Opening~~ the window to let out a huge bumblebee, the car
  ∧

accidentally swerved into the lane of oncoming cars.

The car didn't open the window; the driver did. The writer corrected the problem by turning the opening participial phrase
into an adverb clause, a word group naming the actor.

women have often been denied
▶ After completing seminary training, ~~women's~~ access to the
  ∧

pulpit ~~has often been denied.~~
       ∧

The modifier dangled because the subject of the sentence, *access*, did not name those who had completed seminary training.
(The word *women's* simply modifies *access*.) The writer corrected the problem by making *women* the subject of the sentence.

EXERCISE 12–2

Edit the following sentences to correct dangling modifiers. Most sentences can be revised in more than one way. Revisions of lettered
sentences appear in the back of the book. Example:

a student must complete
To acquire a degree in almost any field, ~~two~~ science courses ,
                                          ∧   ∧

~~must be completed.~~

a. Reaching the heart, a bypass was performed on the severely
   blocked arteries.
b. Nestled in the cockpit, the pounding of the engine was muffled
   only slightly by my helmet.
c. Feeling unprepared for the exam, the questions were as hard as
   June's instructor had suggested they would be.
d. While still a beginner at tennis, the coaches recruited my sister
   to train for the Olympics.
e. To protest the arms buildup, bonfires were set throughout the
   park.

1. When flashing, do not speed through a yellow light.
2. Exhausted from battling the tide and the undertow, a welcome respite appeared in the swimmer's view — the beach!
3. When pouring a carbonated liquid from a can to an ice-filled glass, the glass should be tilted so that the liquid hits the side of the glass, not the ice.
4. As president of the missionary circle, one of Grandmother's duties is to raise money for the church.
5. Shortly after being seated, a waiter approached our table with a smile.
6. Spending four hours on the operating table, a tumor as large as a golf ball was removed from the patient's stomach.
7. To become an attorney, two degrees must be earned and a bar examination must be passed.
8. At the age of twelve, my mother entered me in a public speaking contest.
9. Although too expensive for her budget, Joan bought the lavender skirt.
10. While looking at the map, a police officer approached and asked if she could help.

13

Eliminate distracting shifts.

13a Make the point of view consistent in person and number.

The point of view of an essay is the perspective from which it is written: first-person singular (*I*), first-person plural (*we*), second-person singular or plural (*you*), third-person singular (*he, she, it, one*), or third-person plural (*they*). Writers who are having difficulty settling on an appropriate point of view sometimes shift confusingly from one to another. The solution is to choose a suitable perspective and then stay with it. (See page 47.)

▶ One week our class met in a junkyard to practice rescuing a

victim trapped in a wrecked car. We learned to dismantle the

car with the essential tools. ~~You~~ *We* were graded on ~~your~~ *our* speed

and ~~your~~ *our* skill in extricating the victim.

The writer should have stayed with the *we* point of view. *You* is inappropriate because the writer is not addressing the reader directly. *You* should not be used in a vague sense meaning *anyone*. (See 23d.)

▶ ~~Everyone~~ *You* should purchase a lift ticket unless you plan

to spend most of your time walking or crawling up a steep

hill.

Here *you* is an appropriate choice because the writer is giving advice directly to readers.

▶ ~~A police officer is~~ *Police officers are* often criticized for always being there

when they aren't needed and never being there when they

are.

The writer shifted from the third-person singular (*police officer*) to the third-person plural (*they*), probably in an effort to avoid the wordy *he or she* construction: *A police officer is often criticized for always being there when he or she is not needed and never being there when he or she is.* The most effective revision, this writer decided, was to draft the sentence in the plural. (See 22a and 17f.)

13b Maintain consistent verb tenses.

Consistent verb tenses clearly establish the time of the actions being described. When a passage begins in one tense and then shifts without warning and for no reason to another, readers are distracted and confused.

▶ My hopes ~~rise~~ *rose* and ~~fall~~ *fell* as Joseph's heart started and
stopped. The doctors ~~insert~~ *inserted* a large tube into his chest,
and blood ~~flows~~ *flowed* from the incision onto the floor. The tube
drained some blood from his lung, but it was all in vain.

At 8:35 P.M. Joseph was declared dead.

The writer had tried to make his narrative vivid by casting it in the present tense, but he found this choice too difficult to sustain. A better approach, he decided, was to draft the whole narrative in the past tense.

Writers often encounter difficulty with verb tenses when writing about literature. Because fictional events occur outside the time frames of real life, the past and the present tenses may seem equally appropriate. The literary convention, however, is to describe fictional events consistently in the present tense.

▶ The scarlet letter is a punishment sternly placed upon
Hester's breast by the community, and yet it ~~was~~ *is* an
extremely fanciful and imaginative product of Hester's
own needlework.

13c Make verbs consistent in mood and voice.

Unnecessary shifts in the mood of a verb can be as distracting as needless shifts in tense. There are three moods in English: the *indicative,* used for facts, opinions, and questions; the *imperative,* used for orders or advice; and the *subjunctive,* used in certain contexts to express wishes or conditions contrary to fact (see 28b).

The following passage shifts confusingly from the indicative to the imperative mood.

▶The officers advised us against allowing anyone into our
They also suggested that we
homes without proper identification. ~~Also,~~ alert neighbors to
∧
vacation schedules.

Since the writer's purpose was to report the officers' advice, the revision puts both sentences in the indicative.

A verb may be in either the active voice (with the subject doing the action) or the passive voice (with the subject receiving the action). (See 28c.) If a writer shifts without warning from one to the other, readers may be left wondering why.

▶When the tickets are ready, the travel agent notifies the
lists each ticket
client./~~Each ticket is then listed~~ on a daily register form ∧,
files ∧
and a copy of the itinerary ~~is filed.~~
∧   ∧

The passage began in the active voice (*agent notifies*) and then switched to the passive (*ticket is listed, copy is filed*). Because the active voice is clearer and more direct, the writer put all the verbs in the active voice.

13d Avoid sudden shifts from indirect to direct questions or quotations.

An indirect question reports a question without asking it: *We asked whether we could take a swim.* A direct question asks directly: *Can we take a swim?* Sudden shifts from indirect to direct questions are awkward. In addition, sentences containing such shifts are impossible to punctuate because indirect questions must end with a period and direct questions must end with a question mark. (See 38b.)

▶ I wonder whether the sister knew of the murder and, if so, *whether she reported* ~~did she report~~ it to the police.

> The revision poses both questions indirectly. The writer could also ask both questions directly: *Did the sister know of the murder and, if so, did she report it to the police?*

An indirect quotation reports someone's words without quoting word for word: *Annabelle said that she is a Virgo.* A direct quotation presents the exact words of a speaker or writer, set off with quotation marks: *Annabelle said, "I am a Virgo."* Unannounced shifts from indirect to direct quotations are distracting and confusing, especially when the writer fails to insert the necessary quotation marks, as in the following example.

▶ Mother said that she would be late for dinner and *asked me not to* ~~please do~~ ~~not~~ leave for choir practice until Dad *came* ~~comes~~ home.

> The revision reports all of the mother's words. The writer could also quote directly: *Mother said, "I will be late for dinner. Please do not leave for choir practice until Dad comes home."*

EXERCISE 13-1

Edit the following sentences to eliminate distracting shifts. Revisions of lettered sentences appear in the back of the book. Example:

> For most people it is not easy to quit smoking once ~~you~~ are
>   they
>   ^
>
> hooked.

a. We waited in the emergency room for about an hour. Finally, the nurse comes in and tells us that we are in the wrong place.
b. Newspapers put the lurid details of an armed robbery on page 1, and the warm, human interest stories are relegated to page G-10.
c. A minister often has a hard time because they have to please so many different people.
d. We drove for eight hours until we reached the South Dakota Badlands. You could hardly believe the eeriness of the landscape at dusk.
e. The question is whether ferrets bred in captivity have the instinct to prey on prairie dogs or is this a learned skill.

1. Police officers always follow strict codes of safety. For example, always point the barrel of the gun upward when the gun is not in use.
2. For a minimal fee one may join the class. Once you arrive for class, a medical form is filled out by each person and submitted to the instructor.
3. According to Dr. Winfield, a person who wants to become a doctor must first earn a B.S. degree. After this they must take a medical aptitude test called the MCAT.
4. The principal asked whether I had seen the fight and, if so, why didn't you report it.
5. A single parent often has only their ingenuity to rely on.
6. When the director travels, you will make the hotel and airline reservations and you will arrange for a rental car. A detailed itinerary must also be prepared.
7. As I was pulling in the decoys, you could see and hear the geese heading back to the bay.

8. Rescue workers put water on her face and lifted her head gently onto a pillow. Finally, she opens her eyes.

9. With a little self-discipline and a desire to improve oneself, you too can enjoy the benefits of running.

10. We always follow a strict routine at the campground. First we erected the tent, rolled out the sleeping bags, and set up the kitchen; then we all head for the swimming pool.

14

Emphasize your point.

Within each sentence, emphasize your point by expressing it in the subject and verb, the words that receive the most attention from readers. As a rule, choose an active verb and pair it with a subject that names the person or thing doing the action.

Within longer stretches of discourse, you can draw attention to ideas deserving special emphasis by using a variety of techniques, usually involving some element of surprise.

14a Prefer active verbs.

Active verbs express meaning more emphatically and vigorously than their weaker counterparts — forms of the verb *be* or verbs in the passive voice. Forms of the verb *be (be, am, is, are, was, were, being, been)* lack vigor because they convey no action. Verbs in the passive voice lack strength because their subjects receive the action instead of doing it (see 28c and 48c). The forms of *be* and passive verbs have legitimate uses, but if an active verb can carry your meaning, use it.

BE VERB   A surge of power *was* responsible for the destruction of the coolant pumps.

PASSIVE   The coolant pumps *were destroyed* by a surge of power.

ACTIVE   A surge of power *destroyed* the coolant pumps.

▶ The moods of a manic-depressive ~~are unpredictable~~. *fluctuate without warning.*

Although the original version (with the linking verb *are*) is correct, the active verb *fluctuate* makes the point more powerfully.

▶ ~~The transformer was struck by a bolt of lightning,~~ *A bolt of lightening struck the transformer,* plunging us into darkness.

The active voice (*struck*) makes the point more forcefully than the passive (*was struck*). See 28c.

Even among active verbs, some are more active — and therefore more vigorous and colorful — than others. Carefully selected verbs can energize a piece of writing.

▶ The goalie crouched low, ~~reached~~ *swept* out his stick, and ~~sent~~ *hooked* the rebound away from the mouth of the net.

14b As a rule, choose a subject that names the person or thing doing the action.

In weak, unemphatic prose, both the actor and the action may be buried in sentence elements other than the subject and the verb. In the following sentence, for example, the actor and the action both appear in prepositional phrases, word groups that do not receive much attention from readers.

WEAK   Exposure to Dr. Patterson's excellent teaching had the effect of inspiring me to major in education.

EMPHATIC   Dr. Patterson's excellent teaching inspired me to major in education.

Consider the subjects and verbs of the two versions — *exposure had* versus *teaching inspired.* Clearly the latter expresses the writer's point more emphatically.

> ~~The use of cocaine~~ by pregnant women can ~~be a major~~ ~~contributor to~~ severe brain damage in infants.

Cocaine used ... *cause*

In the original version, the subject and verb — *use can be* — express the point blandly. The revision, with *cocaine can cause* as the subject and verb, alerts us to the dangers of cocaine more emphatically.

EXERCISE 14–1

Revise any weak, unemphatic sentences by replacing *be* verbs or passive verbs with active alternatives and, if necessary, by naming in the subject the person or thing doing the action. Some sentences are emphatic; do not change them. Revisions of lettered sentences appear in the back of the book. Example:

The ranger doused the campfire before giving us
~~The campfire was doused by the ranger before we were given~~
a ticket for unauthorized use of a campsite.

a. The practice of disposing of nuclear waste in Antarctica would be in violation of an international treaty.
b. The entire operation is managed by the producer.
c. Finally the chute caught air and popped open with a jolt at about 2,000 feet.

d. Escaping into the world of drugs, I was rebellious about anything and everything laid down by the establishment.

e. At the crack of rocket and mortar blasts, I jumped from the top bunk and landed on my buddy below, who was crawling on the floor looking for his boots.

1. The maintaining of an accurate and orderly log by the radiologist is required according to hospital protocol.
2. Sam was unsuccessful in his attempt to pass the first performance test.
3. The bomb bay doors rumbled open and freezing air whipped through the plane.
4. C.B.'s are used to find parts, equipment, food, lodging, and anything else that is needed by a trucker.
5. There were exploding firecrackers all around us.

14c Experiment with techniques for gaining special emphasis.

By experimenting with certain techniques, usually involving some element of surprise, you can draw attention to ideas that deserve special emphasis. Use such techniques sparingly, however, or they will lose their punch. The writer who tries to emphasize everything ends up emphasizing nothing.

Using sentence endings for emphasis

You can highlight an idea simply by withholding it until the end of a sentence. The technique works something like a punch line. In the following example, written by the English novelist Aldous Huxley, the sentence's meaning is not revealed until its very last word.

> The only completely consistent people are dead.
>
> — Aldous Huxley

Two types of sentence that withhold information until the end deserve special mention: the inversion and the periodic sentence. The *inversion* reverses the normal subject-verb order, placing the subject at the end, where it receives unusual emphasis. (Also see 15c.)

> In golden pots are hidden the most deadly poisons.
> — Thomas Draxe

The *periodic* sentence opens with a pile-up of modifiers and withholds the subject and verb until the end. It draws attention to itself because it contrasts with the cumulative sentence, which is used more frequently. A *cumulative* sentence begins with the subject and verb and adds modifying elements at the end.

PERIODIC
Twenty-five years ago, at the age of thirteen, while hiking in the mountains near my hometown of Vancouver, Washington, I came face to face with the legendary Goat Woman of Livingston Mountain. — Tom Weitzel, student

CUMULATIVE
A metaphysician is one who goes into a dark cellar at midnight without a light, looking for a black cat that is not there. — Baron Bowan of Colwood

Using parallel structure for emphasis

Parallel grammatical structure draws special attention to paired ideas or to items in a series. (See 9.) When parallel ideas are paired, the emphasis falls on words that underscore comparisons or contrasts, especially when they occur at the end of a phrase or clause.

> We must *stop talking* about the *American dream* and *start listening* to the *dreams of Americans.* — Reubin Askew

In a parallel series, the emphasis falls at the end, so it is generally best to end with the most dramatic or climactic item in the series.

> Sister Charity enjoyed passing out writing punishments: translate the Ten Commandments into Latin, type a thousand-word essay on good manners, copy the New Testament with a quill pen. — Marie Visosky, student

Using punctuation for emphasis

Obviously the exclamation point can add emphasis, but you should not overuse it. As a rule, the exclamation point is more appropriate in dialogue than in ordinary prose.

> I oozed a glob of white paint onto my palette, whipped some medium into it, loaded my brush, and announced to the class, "Move over, Michelangelo. Here I come!"
> — Carolyn Goff, student

A dash or a colon may be used to draw attention to word groups worthy of special attention. (See 35a, 35b, and 39a.)

> The middle of the road is where the white line is — and that's the worst place to drive. — Robert Frost

> I turned to see what the anemometer read: The needle had pegged out at 106 knots. — Jonathan Shilk, student

Occasionally, a pair of dashes may be used to highlight a word or an idea.

> [My friend] was a gay and impudent and satirical and delightful young black man — a slave — who daily preached sermons from the top of his master's woodpile, with me for sole audience. — Mark Twain

Using an occasional short sentence for emphasis

Too many short sentences in a row will fast become monotonous (see 8a), but an occasional short sentence, when played off against longer sentences in the same passage, will draw attention to an idea.

> The great secret, known to internists and learned early in marriage by internists' wives [or husbands], but still hidden from the general public, is that most things get better by themselves. Most things, in fact, are better by morning.
>
> — Lewis Thomas

EXERCISE 14–2

Discuss the methods used to achieve emphasis in the following paragraphs.

> Unseen in the jungle, but present, are tapirs, jaguars, many species of snake and lizard, ocelots, armadillos, marmosets, howler monkeys, toucans and macaws and a hundred other birds, deer, bats, peccaries, capybaras, agoutis, and sloths. Also present in this jungle, but variously distant, are Texaco derricks and pipelines, and some of the wildest Indians in the world, blowgun-using Indians, who killed missionaries in 1956 and ate them.   — Annie Dillard

> My Uncle Tom worked as a blacksmith in the B & O yards near Harpers Ferry. That was a good job too. Though he walked the four-mile round trip to and from the shop daily in sooty railroader's clothes, Uncle Tom was well off. His house contained a marvel I had never seen before: an indoor bathroom. This was enough to mark Uncle Tom a rich man, but in addition he had a car. And such a car. It was an Essex, with windows that rolled up and down with interior hand cranks, not like my father's Model T with the isinglass windows in side curtains that had to be buttoned onto the frame in bad weather. Uncle Tom's Essex even had cut-glass

flower vases in sconces in the backseat. He was a man of substance. When he rolled up in his Essex for Ida Rebecca's command appearances on Sunday afternoons in Morrisonville, wearing a white shirt and black suit, smoking his pipe, his pretty red-haired wife Goldie on the seat beside him, I felt pride in kinship to so much grandeur.   — Russell Baker

15

Provide some variety.

When a rough draft is filled with too many same-sounding sentences, try injecting some variety — as long as you can do so without sacrificing clarity or ease of reading.

15a Vary your sentence openings.

Most sentences in English begin with the subject, move to the verb, and continue along to the object, with modifiers tucked in along the way or put at the end. For the most part, such sentences are fine. Put too many of them in a row, however, and they become monotonous.

Adverbial modifiers, being easily movable, can often be inserted ahead of the subject. Such modifiers might be single words, phrases, or clauses.

▶ A̶ few drops of sap e̶v̶e̶n̶t̶u̶a̶l̶l̶y̶ began to trickle into the pail.
Eventually a

Like most adverbs, *eventually* does not need to appear close to the verb it modifies (*began*).

Just as the sun was coming up, a
▶ ~~A~~ pair of black ducks flew over the blind. ~~just as the sun was coming up.~~

The adverb clause, which modifies the verb *flew*, is as clear at the beginning of the sentence as it is at the end.

Adjectives and participial phrases can frequently be moved to the beginning of a sentence, as long as the subject of the sentence names the person or thing being described in the introductory phrase.

Dejected and withdrawn,
▶ Edward, ~~dejected and withdrawn,~~ nearly gave up his search for a job.

The single-word adjectives *dejected* and *withdrawn* can be moved ahead of the subject, *Edward*, which they modify.

A *John and I*
▶ ~~John and I,~~ Anticipating a peaceful evening, sat down at the campfire to brew a cup of coffee.

Many participial phrases can be moved without mishap. *Anticipating a peaceful evening* can open the sentence as long as the subject of the sentence names the persons doing the anticipating. If the words *John and I* were not the subject of the sentence, the modifier would dangle. (See 12e.)

15b Use a variety of sentence structures.

A writer should not rely too heavily on simple sentences and compound sentences, for the effect tends to be both monotonous and choppy. (See 8a and 8b.) Too many complex or compound-complex sentences, however, can be equally monotonous. If your style tends to one or the other extreme, try to achieve a better mix of sentence types.

The major sentence types are illustrated in the following sentences, all taken from Flannery O'Connor's "The King of the Birds," an essay describing the author's pet peafowl.

SIMPLE   Frequently the cock combines the lifting of his tail with the raising of his voice.

COMPOUND   Any chicken's dusting hole is out of place in a flower bed, but the peafowl's hole, being the size of a small crater, is more so.

COMPLEX   The peacock does most of his serious strutting in the spring and summer when he has a full tail to do it with.

COMPOUND- **COMPLEX**   The cock's plumage requires two years to attain its pattern, and for the rest of his life, this chicken will act as though he designed it himself.

For a fuller discussion of sentence types, see 50a.

15c Try inverting sentences occasionally.

A sentence is inverted if it does not follow the normal subject-verb-object pattern. Many inversions sound artificial and should be avoided except in the most formal contexts. But if an inversion sounds natural, it can provide a welcome touch of variety.

▶ *Opposite the produce section is a* ~~A~~ refrigerated case of mouth-watering cheeses; ~~is opposite the produce section;~~ a friendly attendant will cut off just the amount you want.

The revision inverts the normal subject-verb order by moving the verb, *is*, ahead of its subject, *case*.

> *Set at the top two corners of the stage were huge*
> ~~Huge~~ lavender hearts outlined in bright white lights. ~~were~~
> Λ .   Λ
> ~~set at the top two corners of the stage.~~

In the revision the subject, *hearts,* appears after the verb, *were set.* Notice that the two parts of the verb are also inverted — and separated from one another — without any awkwardness or loss of meaning.

Inverted sentences are used for emphasis as well as for variety. See 14c.

15d Consider adding an occasional question or quotation.

An occasional question can provide a welcome change of pace, especially at the beginning of a paragraph, where it engages the reader's interest.

> Virginia Woolf, in her book *A Room of One's Own,* wrote that in order for a woman to write fiction she must have two things, certainly: a room of her own (with key and lock) and enough money to support herself.
> *What then are we to make of Phillis Wheatley, a slave, who owned not even herself?* This sickly, frail black girl who required a servant of her own at times — her health was so precarious — and who, had she been white, would have been easily considered the intellectual superior of all the women and most of the men in the society of her day. [Italics added.]
> — Alice Walker

Quotations can also provide variety, for they add other people's voices to your own. These other voices might be bits of dialogue:

> When we got back upstairs, Dr. Haney and Captain Shiller, the head nurse, were waiting for us by the elevator. As

the nurse hurried off, pushing Todd, the doctor explained to us what would happen next.

"Mrs. Barrus," he began, "this last test is one we do only when absolutely necessary. It is very painful and hard on the patient but we have no other choice." Apologetically, he went on. "I cannot give him an anesthetic." He waited for the statement to sink in.   — Celeste L. Barrus, student

Or they might be quotations from written sources:

> Even when she enters the hospital on the brink of death, the anorexic will refuse help from anyone and will continue to deny needing help, especially from a doctor. At this point, reports Dr. Steven Levenkron, the anorexic is most likely "a frightened, cold, lonely, starved, and physically tortured, exhausted person — not unlike an actual concentration camp inmate" (29). In this condition she is ultimately force-fed through a tube inserted in the chest.   — Jim Drew, student

Notice that the quotation from a written source is documented with a citation in parentheses. See 54.

EXERCISE 15–1

Edit the following paragraph to increase variety in sentence structure.

> I have spent thirty years of my life on a tobacco farm, and I cannot understand why people smoke. The whole process of raising tobacco involves deadly chemicals. The ground is treated for mold and chemically fertilized before the tobacco seed is ever planted. The seed is planted and begins to grow, and then the bed is treated with weed killer. The plant is then transferred to the field. It is sprayed with poison to kill worms about two months later. Then the time for harvest approaches, and the plant is sprayed once more with a chemical to retard the growth of suckers. The tobacco is harvested and hung in a barn to dry. These barns are havens for birds. The birds

defecate all over the leaves. After drying, these leaves are divided by color, and no feces are removed. They are then sold to the tobacco companies. I do not know what the tobacco companies do after they receive the tobacco. I do not need to know. They cannot remove what I know is in the leaf and on the leaf. I don't want any of it to pass through my mouth.

EXERCISE 15–2

Discuss how the writers of the following paragraphs provide variety.

I was then a listening child, careful to hear the very different sounds of Spanish and English. Wide-eyed with hearing, I'd listen to sounds more than to words. First, there were English (*gringo*) sounds. So many words were still unknown to me that when the butcher or the lady at the drugstore said something, exotic polysyllabic sounds would bloom in the midst of their sentences. Often the speech of people in public seemed to me very loud, booming with confidence. The man behind the counter would literally ask, "What can I do for you?" But by being so firm and clear, the sound of his voice said that he was a *gringo*; he belonged in public society.

— Richard Rodriguez

Our own house was an appalling sight from the outside. The siding, originally white, sprouted leprous gray patches where the paint was peeling away. Bark hung down from the huge dead elm in the front yard like long, limp scabs. The tree and a doorless garage leaned ominously toward our house. To the north, weeds grew up around a lonely, abandoned shack. To the south, a run-down house covered with rotting, gray asbestos shingles crouched, a weathered outhouse several steps from the back door. Farther south along the frozen, muddy road huddled a tiny one-room dwelling isolated in a swampy hollow. Barely glimpsed through a sea of stiffly dried weeds, the roofs of two ramshackle chicken coops rounded out the view from our yard. Our forgotten lane lacked street lamps and house numbers and was denied even the dignity of a street sign at the corner.   — Julie Reardon, student

PART IV

Choosing Words

16

Tighten wordy sentences.

In a rough draft we are rarely economical: We repeat ourselves, we belabor the obvious, we cushion our thoughts in verbiage. As a general rule, advises writer Sidney Smith, "run a pen through every other word you have written; you have no idea what vigor it will give your style."

Long sentences are not necessarily wordy, nor are short sentences always concise. A sentence is wordy if it can be tightened without loss of meaning.

16a Eliminate redundancies.

Writers often repeat themselves unnecessarily. Afraid, perhaps, that they won't be heard the first time, they insist that a teacup is small *in size* or yellow *in color,* that married people should cooperate *together,* that a fact is not just a fact but a *true* fact. Such redundancies may seem at first to add emphasis. In reality they do just the opposite, for they divide the reader's attention.

▶ Mr. Barker still hasn't paid last month's rent. ~~yet.~~
                                                      ∧

▶ Black slaves were ~~called or~~ stereotyped as lazy even though

  they were the main labor force of the South.

Though modifiers ordinarily add meaning to the words they modify, occasionally they are redundant.

W

▶ Sylvia ~~very hurriedly~~ scribbled her name, address, and phone number on the back of a greasy napkin.

▶ Joel was determined ~~in his mind~~ to lose weight.

The words *scribbled* and *determined* already contain the notions suggested by the modifiers *very hurriedly* and *in his mind.*

16b Avoid unnecessary repetition of words.

Though words may be repeated deliberately, for effect, repetitions will seem awkward if they are clearly unnecessary. When a more concise version is possible, choose it.

▶ Our fifth patient, in room six, is ~~a~~ mentally ill. ~~patient.~~

▶ The best teachers help each student to ~~become a better~~ *grow* ~~student~~ both academically and emotionally.

16c Cut empty or inflated phrases.

An empty phrase can be cut with little or no loss of meaning. Common examples are introductory word groups that apologize or hedge: *in my opinion, I think that, it seems that, one must admit that,* and so on.

▶ ~~In my opinion, our~~ *Our* current policy in Central America is misguided on several counts.

▶ ~~It seems that~~ *Lonesome Dove* is one of Larry McMurtry's

most ambitious novels.

Readers understand without being told that they are hearing the writer's opinion or educated guess.

Inflated phrases can be reduced to a word or two without loss of meaning.

INFLATED	CONCISE
along the lines of	like
as a matter of fact	in fact
at all times	always
at the present time	now, currently
at this point in time	now, currently
because of the fact that	because
by means of	by
by virtue of the fact that	because
due to the fact that	because
for the purpose of	for
for the reason that	because
have the ability to	be able to
in light of the fact that	because
in the nature of	like
in order to	to
in spite of the fact that	although, though
in the event that	if
in the final analysis	finally
in the neighborhood of	about
until such time as	until

▶ We will file the appropriate papers ~~in the event that~~ *if* we are

unable to meet the deadline.

▶ *Because* ~~Due to the fact that~~ the guest of honor is ill, the party is

being postponed until next Saturday.

16d Simplify the structure.

If the structure of a sentence is needlessly indirect, try simplifying it. Look for opportunities to strengthen the verb.

▶ The financial analyst claimed that because of volatile market

conditions she could not ~~make an~~ estimate ~~of~~ the company's

future profits.

The verb *estimate* is more vigorous and more concise than *make an estimate of*.

The colorless verbs *is*, *are*, *was*, and *were* frequently generate excess words.

monitors and balances
▶ The secretary ~~is responsible for monitoring and balancing~~
⌃
the budgets for travel, contract services, and personnel.

The revision is more direct and concise. Actions originally appearing in subordinate structures have become verbs replacing *is*.

The expletive constructions *there is* and *there are* (or *there was* and *there were*) can also generate excess words. The same is true of expletive constructions beginning with *it*. (See 48c.)

A
▶ ~~There is~~ another module ~~that~~ tells the story of Charles

Darwin and introduces the theory of evolution.

H   *must*
▶ ~~It is important that~~ hikers remain inside the park
⌃
boundaries.

Reviewing your writing for wordy sentences

Look especially for these common trouble spots:

REDUNDANCIES (16a)

▶ Passive euthanasia is the ~~act or~~ practice of allowing

terminally ill patients to die.

▶ The colors of the reproductions were ~~precisely~~ exact.

UNNECESSARY REPETITION OF WORDS (16b)

▶ ~~The quilt that was~~ *T*he highlight of grandmother's

collection was a crazy quilt dating from 1889.

EMPTY OR INFLATED PHRASES (16c)

▶ Although ~~it seemed that~~ it was unlikely that the call

was for me, I was so excited that I ran to the phone.

▶ The ring costs ~~in the neighborhood of~~ *about* sixty dollars.

NEEDLESSLY INDIRECT STRUCTURES (16d)

▶ The institute was established to ~~develop and provide~~ *train*

~~training for~~ highway agency employees.

Wordy sentences (continued)

▶ ~~There was a~~ $\overset{A}{}$ deranged vagrant $\overset{was}{}$ pestering the persons in line, spouting biblical quotations one minute and shouting obscenities the next.

▶ ~~It is imperative that~~ $\overset{A}{}$ll police officers $\overset{must}{}$ follow strict procedures when apprehending a suspect.

▶ Last summer, a horse, $\overset{my\ parents\ gave\ me}{}$ ~~was given to me by my parents.~~

NEEDLESSLY COMPLEX STRUCTURES (16e)

▶ We took a side trip to Monticello, ~~which was~~ the home of Thomas Jefferson.

▶ Our landlord was an elderly bachelor/ $\overset{who\ taught\ us}{}$ ~~and it was through his guidance that we were able~~ to appreciate country life.

▶ When I approached the window, the guard took the form/ ~~He~~ asked me a few questions, and then ~~he~~ told me to see another guard, who would do a physical search.

Expletive constructions do have legitimate uses, however. For example, they are appropriate when a writer has a good reason for delaying the subject. (See 48c.)

Finally, verbs in the passive voice may be needlessly indirect. When the active voice expresses your meaning as well, prefer it. (See 14a and 28c.)

▶ All too often, athletes with marginal academic skills . ~~have been recruited by our coaches.~~

our coaches have recruited (inserted after "All too often,")

16e Reduce clauses to phrases, phrases to single words.

Word groups functioning as modifiers can often be made more compact. Look for any opportunities to reduce clauses to phrases or phrases to single words.

▶ Thermography, ~~which is~~ a method of detecting breast cancer, records heat patterns on black-and-white or color-coded film.

A subordinate clause has been reduced to an appositive phrase.

▶ For her birthday we gave Jessica a stylish vest ~~made of leather.~~

leather

A verbal phrase has become a single word.

▶ The Lanier ~~was~~ one of the first word processors on the market. ~~/ It~~ was much more limited than those available now.

Part of an independent clause has become an appositive phrase. (See also 8a.)

EXERCISE 16 – 1

Edit the following sentences for wordiness. Revisions of lettered sentences appear in the back of the book. Example:

> The Wilsons moved into the house ~~in spite of the fact that~~ *even though* the back door was only ten yards from the train tracks.

a. When visitors come to visit her, Grandmother just stares at the wall.

b. Dr. Sandford has seen problems like yours countless numbers of times.

c. In my opinion, Bloom's race for the governorship is a futile exercise.

d. If there are any new fares, then they must be reported by message to all of our transportation offices.

e. In Biology 10A you will be assigned a faculty tutor who will be available to assign you eight taped modules and help you clarify any information on the tapes.

1. Seeing the barrels, the driver immediately slammed on his brakes.

2. The thing data sets are used for is communicating with other computers.

3. The town of New Harmony, located in Indiana, was founded as a utopian community.

4. In the early eighties, some analysts viewed Soviet expansion as an effort to achieve nothing less than world dominance, if not outright control of the world.

5. You will be the contact person for arranging interviews between the institute and the office of personnel.

6. Martin Luther King, Jr., was a man who set a high standard for future leaders to meet.

7. Your job will be the transportation of luggage from the carts to the conveyor belts.

8. A typical autocross course consists of at least two straightaways, and the rest of the course is made up of numerous slaloms and several sharp turns.

9. The program is called the Weight Control Program, and it has been remarkably successful in helping airmen and airwomen lose weight.
10. The price of driving while drunk or while intoxicated can be extremely high.

EXERCISE 16–2

Edit the following paragraph for wordiness.

We examined the old house from top to bottom. In fact, we started in the attic, which was hot and dusty, and made our way down two flights of stairs, and down one more descent, which was a spiral staircase, into the basement. On our way back up, we thought we heard the eerie noise, the one that had startled us from our sound sleep in the first place. This time the noise was at the top of the staircase that led to the second-floor hallway. We froze and stood quietly at exactly the same moment, listening very intently. Finally, after a few moments, someone said, "Why don't we all go in together and see what it is?" Cautiously, with great care, we stepped over the threshold into the dark hallway, which disappeared into darkness in front of us. There was an unearthly emanating light shining from underneath the door that led into the kitchen. All at once we jumped when we heard a loud crashing sound from behind that door. Before we could rush into the kitchen at high speed, the light went out suddenly, and instantly we were in total pitch black darkness. I thought I heard someone's teeth chattering; then I realized with a shock that it was my own teeth I heard chattering. Without saying a word, we backed silently away from the kitchen door — no one wanted to go in now. Then it was as if someone had shot off a gun, because before we realized what we were doing, we tore up the stairs as fast as we could, and we dove into our beds and pulled the covers up and over us to shut out any more frightening sounds and thoughts.

17

Choose appropriate language.

Language is appropriate when it suits your subject, conforms to the needs of your audience, and blends naturally with your own voice.

17a Stay away from jargon.

Jargon is specialized language used among members of a trade, profession, or group. Use jargon only when readers will be familiar with it; even then, use it only when plain English will not do as well.

Sentences filled with jargon are likely to be long and lumpy. To revise such sentences, you must rewrite them, usually in fewer words.

> **JARGON** For years the indigenous body politic of South Africa attempted to negotiate legal enfranchisement without result.

> **REVISED** For years the native population of South Africa negotiated in vain for the right to vote.

Though a political scientist might feel comfortable with the original version, jargon such as *indigenous body politic* and *legal enfranchisement* is needlessly complicated for ordinary readers.

Broadly defined, jargon includes puffed-up language designed more to impress readers than to inform them. The following are common examples from business, government, higher education, and the military, with plain English translations in parentheses.

ameliorate (improve)	indicator (sign)
commence (begin)	optimal (best, most favorable)
components (parts)	parameters (boundaries, limits)
endeavor (try)	peruse (read, look over)
exit (leave)	prior to (before)
facilitate (help)	utilize (use)
factor (consideration, cause)	viable (workable)
impact on (affect)	

▶ ~~In order that I may increase my expertise in the area of~~

~~delivery of services to clients, I feel that participation in this~~
This   *train me to serve clients better.*
~~conference will~~ ~~be beneficial.~~
  ∧   ∧

At first the writer tinkered with this sentence — changing *in order that I may* to *to, the area of delivery of* to *delivering,* and so on. The sentence was improved, but it still sounded unnatural. A better solution, this writer discovered, was to rethink what he wanted to say and then rewrite the sentence. Notice that only three words of the original have been preserved.

17b   Avoid pretentious language, most euphemisms, and "doublespeak."

Hoping to sound profound or poetic, some writers embroider their thoughts with large words and flowery phrases, language that in fact sounds pretentious. Pretentious language is so ornate and often so wordy that it obscures the thought that lies beneath.

                parents become old,
▶ When our ~~progenitors reach their silver-haired and~~
        ∧   *entomb*
~~golden years,~~ we frequently ~~ensepulcher~~ them in ~~homes~~
                            ∧

old-age homes
~~for senescent beings~~ as if they were already among the
^ dead.
~~deceased.~~
^

The writer of the original sentence had turned to a thesaurus (a dictionary of synonyms and antonyms) in an attempt to sound educated. When such a writer gains enough confidence to speak in his or her own voice, pretentious language disappears.

Related to pretentious language are euphemisms, nice-sounding words or phrases substituted for words thought to sound harsh or ugly. Like pretentious language, euphemisms are wordy and indirect. Unlike pretentious language, they are sometimes appropriate. It is our social custom, for example, to use euphemisms when speaking or writing about death (*Her sister passed on*), excretion (*I have to go to the bathroom*), sexual intercourse (*They did not sleep together until they were married*), and the like. We may also use euphemisms out of concern for someone's feelings. Telling parents, for example, that their daughter is "unmotivated" is more sensitive than saying she's lazy. Tact or politeness, then, can justify an occasional euphemism.

Most euphemisms, however, are needlessly evasive or even deceitful. Like pretentious language, they obscure the intended meaning.

EUPHEMISM	PLAIN ENGLISH
adult entertainment	pornography
preowned automobile	used car
economically deprived	poor
selected out	fired
negative savings	debts
strategic withdrawal	retreat or defeat
revenue enhancers	taxes
chemical dependency	drug addiction
nuclear engagement	nuclear war
correctional facility	prison

The term *doublespeak,* coined by George Orwell in his novel *1984,* applies to any deliberately evasive or deceptive language, including euphemisms. Doublespeak is especially common in politics, where missiles are named "Peace-keepers," airplane crashes are termed "uncontrolled contact with the ground," and a military retreat is described as "tactical redeployment." Business also gives us its share of doublespeak. When the manufacturer of a pacemaker writes that its product "may result in adverse health consequences in pacemaker-dependent patients as a result of sudden 'no output' failure," it takes an alert reader to grasp the message: The pacemakers might suddenly stop functioning and cause a heart attack or even death.

EXERCISE 17–1

Edit the following sentences to eliminate jargon, pretentious or flowery language, euphemisms, and doublespeak. You may need to make substantial changes in some sentences. Revisions of lettered sentences appear in the back of the book. Example:

> After two weeks in the legal department, Sue has ~~worked~~ *mastered*
> ~~into~~ the routine, ~~of the office,~~ *office* and her ~~functional and self-~~ *performance has*
> ~~management skills have~~ exceeded all expectations.

a. It is a widespread but unproven hypothesis that the parameters of significant personal change for persons in midlife are extremely narrow.

b. All employees functioning in the capacity of work-study students will be required to give evidence of current enrollment.

c. Utilizing my elbows, I was able to crawl about ten yards to the trench.

d. When our father was selected out from his high-paying factory job, we learned what it was like to be economically depressed.

e. In the event that the recipient of the computer is unable to complete the installation, guidance may be obtained by getting in touch with the firm's main office by using its 800 telephone number.

1. Sam's arguments failed to impact positively on his parents or his male siblings.
2. As I approached the edifice of confinement where my brother was incarcerated, several inmates loudly vocalized a number of lewd remarks.
3. The nurse announced that there had been a negative patient-care outcome due to a therapeutic misadventure on the part of the surgeon.
4. When we returned from our evening perambulation, we shrank back in horror as we surmised that our domestic dwelling was being swallowed up in hellish flames.
5. The bottom line is that the company is experiencing a negative cash flow.

17c Avoid obsolete, archaic, or invented words.

Obsolete words are words found in the writing of the past that have dropped out of use entirely. Archaic words are old words that are still used, but only in special contexts such as literature or advertising. Although dictionaries list obsolete words such as *recomfort* and *reechy* and archaic words such as *anon* and *betwixt*, these words are not appropriate for current use.

Invented words (also called *neologisms*) are words too recently created to be part of standard English. Many invented words fade out of use without becoming standard. *Build-down*, *throughput*, and *palimony* are neologisms that may not last. *Scuba*, *disco*, *sexist*, *software*, and *spinoff* are no longer neologisms; they have become standard English. Avoid using invented words in your writing unless they are given in the dictionary as standard or unless there is no other word to express your meaning.

17d In most contexts, avoid slang, regional expressions, and nonstandard English.

Slang is an informal and sometimes private vocabulary that expresses the solidarity of a group such as teenagers, rock musicians, or football fans; it is subject to more rapid change than standard English. For example, the slang teenagers use to express approval changes every few years; *cool, groovy, neat, wicked,* and *awesome* have replaced one another within the last three decades. Sometimes slang becomes so widespread that it is accepted as standard vocabulary. *Jazz,* for example, started out as slang but is now generally accepted to describe a style of music.

Although slang has a certain vitality, it is a code that not everyone understands, and it is very informal. Therefore, it is inappropriate in most written work.

▶ If we don't begin studying for the final, a whole semester's
        will be wasted.
    work ~~is going down the tubes.~~
        ∧

                                                    disgust you.
▶ The government's "filth" guidelines for food will ~~gross you~~
                                                    ∧
    ~~out.~~

Regional expressions are common to a group in a geographical area. *Let's talk with the bark off* (for *Let's speak frankly*) is an expression in the southern United States, for example. Regional expressions have the same limitations as slang and are therefore inappropriate in most writing.

▶ John was four blocks from the house before he remembered
        turn on
    to ~~cut~~ the headlights ~~.on.~~
        ∧   ∧

▶ I'm not ~~for~~ sure, but I think the dance has been postponed.

As you probably know, many people speak two varieties of English — standard English, used in academic and business situations, and a nonstandard dialect, spoken with close acquaintances who share a regional or social heritage. In written English, a dialect may be used in dialogue, to reflect actual speech, but in most other contexts it is out of place. Like slang and regionalisms, nonstandard English is a language shared by only a few. Standard English, by contrast, is accessible to all.

If you speak a nonstandard dialect, try to identify the ways in which your dialect differs from standard English. Look especially for the following features of nonstandard English, which commonly cause problems in writing.

Misuse of verb forms such as *began* and *begun* (See 27a.)

Omission of -*s* endings on verbs (See 27c.)

Omission of -*ed* endings on verbs (See 27d.)

Omission of necessary verbs (See 27e.)

Double negatives (See 26d.)

17e Choose an appropriate level of formality.

In deciding on a level of formality, consider both your subject and your audience. Does the subject demand a dignified treatment, or is a relaxed tone more suitable? Will the audience be put off if you assume too close a relationship with them, or might you alienate them by seeming too distant?

Formal writing emphasizes the importance of its subject and the exactness of its information. Its tone is dignified, and it maintains a certain distance between writer and audience.

A sophisticated vocabulary and complex sentence structures are compatible with a formal writing style, although simple words and short sentences do not necessarily destroy it. Contractions (*don't, he'll*) and colloquial words (*kids, buddy*) tend to be out of place.

For most college and professional writing, some degree of formality is appropriate. In a letter applying for a job, for example, it is a mistake to sound too breezy and informal.

> **TOO INFORMAL**   I'd like to get that receptionist's job you've got in the paper.
>
> **MORE FORMAL**   I would like to apply for the receptionist's position listed in the *Peoria Journal Star.*

Informal writing is appropriate for private letters, articles in popular magazines, and business correspondence between close associates. Like spoken conversation, it allows contractions and colloquial words. Vocabulary and sentence structure are rarely complex.

In choosing a level of formality, above all be consistent. When a writer's voice shifts from one level of formality to another, readers receive mixed messages.

▶ Once a pitcher for the Cincinnati Reds, Bob shared with me
  began
  the secrets of his trade. His lesson ~~commenced~~ with his
  thrown   ∧
  famous curveball, ~~implemented~~ by tucking the little finger
  ∧
  behind the ball instead of holding it straight out. Next he
  revealed
  ~~elucidated~~ the mysteries of the sucker pitch, a slow ball
  ∧
  coming behind a fast windup.

Words such as *commenced* and *elucidated* are inappropriate for the subject matter, and they clash with informal terms such as *sucker pitch* and *fast windup.*

EXERCISE 17-2

Edit the following paragraph to eliminate slang and maintain a consistent level of formality.

>   The graduation speaker really blew it. He should have discussed the options and challenges facing the graduating class. Instead, he shot his mouth off at us and trashed us for being lazy and pampered. He did make some good points, however. Our profs have certainly babied us by not holding fast to deadlines, by dismissing assignments that the class ragged them about, by ignoring our tardiness, and by handing out easy C's like hotcakes. Still, we resented this speech as the final word from the college establishment. It should have been the orientation speech when we entered as freshmen.

17f Avoid sexist language.

Sexist language is language that stereotypes or demeans men or women, usually women. Some sexist language reflects genuine contempt for women: referring to a woman as a "broad," for example, or calling a lawyer a "lady lawyer," or saying in an advertisement, "If our new sports car were a lady, it would get its bottom pinched."

Other forms of sexist language, while they may not suggest conscious sexism, reflect stereotypical thinking: referring to nurses as women and doctors as men, using different conventions when naming or identifying women and men, or assuming that all of one's readers are men. (See the chart on page 185.)

Still other forms of sexist language result from outmoded traditions. The pronouns *he, him,* and *his,* for instance, were traditionally used to refer indefinitely to persons of either sex.

TRADITIONAL   A journalist is stimulated by *his* deadline.

Today, however, such usage is widely viewed as sexist because it excludes women and encourages sex-role stereotyping — the view that men are somehow more suited than women to be journalists, doctors, and so on.

One option, of course, is to substitute *his or her* for *his: A journalist is stimulated by his or her deadline.* This strategy is fine in small doses, but it generates needless words that become awkward when repeated throughout an essay. A better strategy, many writers have discovered, is simply to write in the plural.

> **REVISED** *Journalists* are stimulated by *their* deadlines.

Yet another strategy is to recast the sentence so that the problem does not arise:

> **REVISED** A journalist is stimulated by *a* deadline.

When sexist language occurs throughout an essay, it is sometimes possible to adjust the essay's point of view. If the essay might be appropriately rewritten from the *I,* the *we,* or the *you* point of view, the problem of sexist English will not arise. (See pages 47–51.)

Like the pronouns *he, him,* and *his,* the nouns *man* and *men* were once used indefinitely to refer to persons of either sex. Current usage demands gender-neutral terms instead.

INAPPROPRIATE	APPROPRIATE
chairman	chairperson, moderator, chair, head
clergyman	member of the clergy, minister, pastor
congressman	member of Congress, representative, legislator
fireman	firefighter
foreman	supervisor
mailman	mail carrier, postal worker, letter carrier
mankind	people, humans
manpower	personnel
policeman	police officer
salesman	salesperson, sales associate, salesclerk
to man	to operate, to staff
weatherman	weather forecaster, meteorologist
workman	worker, laborer

Avoiding sexist language

1. Avoid occupational stereotypes.

▶ After the nursing student graduates, ~~she~~ *he or she* must face a

difficult state board examination.

2. When naming and identifying men and women, be consistent.

▶ Running for city council are Jake Stein, an attorney,

and ~~Mrs.~~ Cynthia Jones, a professor of English~~, and~~

~~mother of three.~~

3. Do not write to an audience of men alone.

▶ If you are a senior government official, your ~~wife~~ *spouse* is

required to report any gifts ~~she~~ *he or she* receives that are

valued at more than $100.

4. Avoid using *he* to mean *he or she* or *him* to mean *him or her.* (For a variety of revision strategies, see the chart on page 241.)

▶ ~~Every applicant wants~~ *All applicants want* to know how much ~~he~~ *they* will

make.

5. Avoid using *-man* words to refer to persons of either sex.

▶ A ~~fireman~~ *firefighter* must always be on call, even when ~~he is~~ off

duty.

EXERCISE 17−3

Edit the following sentences to eliminate sexist language or sexist assumptions. Revisions of lettered sentences appear in the back of the book. Example:

Scholarship athletes   *their*
~~A scholarship athlete~~ must be as concerned about ~~his~~
   ∧   *they are*   *their*   ∧
academic performance as ~~he is~~ about ~~his~~ athletic
                          ∧   ∧

performance.

a. Mrs. Harriet Glover, who is a doctor's wife, is the defense attorney appointed by the court. Al Jones has been assigned to work with her on the case.

b. If a young graduate is careful about investments, he can accumulate a significant sum in a relatively short period.

c. An elementary school teacher should understand the concept of nurturing if she intends to be a success.

d. Because Dr. Brown and Dr. Dorothy Coombs were the senior professors in the department, they served as co-chairmen of the promotion committee.

e. If man does not stop polluting his environment, mankind will perish.

1. I have been trained to doubt an automobile mechanic, even if he has an excellent reputation.

2. When a professor enters the lecture hall, he expects the students to be ready for class to begin.

3. Elizabeth Moore, a mother of three and a judge's wife, will be the next dean of the medical school.

4. In my hometown, the lady mayor has led the fight for a fair share of federal funds for new schools.

5. As partners in a successful real estate firm, John Crockett and Sarah Cooke have been an effective sales team; he is particularly skillful at arranging attractive mortgage packages; she is a vivacious blonde who stays fit by doing aerobics daily.

18

Find the exact words.

Whatever you want to say, claimed French writer Gustave Flaubert, "there is but one word to express it, one verb to give it movement, one adjective to qualify it; you must seek until you find this noun, this verb, this adjective." Even if you are not reaching for such perfection in your writing, you will sometimes find yourself wishing for better words. The dictionary is the obvious first place to turn, a thesaurus the second.

A good desk dictionary — such as *The American Heritage Dictionary, The Random House College Dictionary,* or *Webster's New Collegiate* or *New World Dictionary of the American Language* — lists synonyms and antonyms for many words, with helpful comments on shades of meaning. Under *fertile,* for example, *Webster's New World Dictionary* carefully distinguishes the meanings of *fertile, fecund, fruitful,* and *prolific:*

> SYN. —*fertile* implies a producing, or power of producing, fruit or offspring, and may be used figuratively of the mind; *fecund* implies the abundant production of offspring or fruit, or, figuratively, of creations of the mind; *fruitful* specifically suggests the bearing of much fruit, but it is also used to imply fertility (of soil), favorable results, profitableness, etc.; *prolific,* a close synonym for *fecund,* more often carries derogatory connotations of overly rapid production or reproduction — ANT. *sterile, barren*

If the dictionary doesn't yield the word you need, try a book of synonyms and antonyms such as *Roget's International Thesaurus.* In the back of *Roget's* is an index to the groups of synonyms that make up the bulk of the book. Look up the adjective *still*, for example, and you will find references to lists containing the words *dead, motionless, silent,* and *tranquil.* If *tranquil* is close to the word you have in mind, turn to its section in the front of the book. There you will find a long list of synonyms, including such words as *quiet, quiescent, reposeful, calm, pacific, halcyon, placid,* and *unruffled.* Unless your vocabulary is better than average, the list will contain words you've never heard or with which you are only vaguely familiar. Whenever you are tempted to use one of these words, look it up in the dictionary first to avoid misusing it.

On discovering the thesaurus, many writers use it for the wrong reasons, so a word of caution is in order. Do not turn to a thesaurus in search of exotic, fancy words — such as *halcyon* — with which to embellish your essays. Look instead for words that exactly express your meaning. Most of the time these words will be familiar to both you and your readers. *Tranquil* was probably the word you were looking for all along.

18a Select words with appropriate connotations.

In addition to their strict dictionary meanings (or *denotations*), words have *connotations,* emotional colorings that affect how readers respond to them. The word *steel* denotes "made of or resembling commercial iron that contains carbon," but it also calls up a cluster of images associated with steel, such as the sensation of touching it. These associations give the word its connotations — cold, smooth, unbending.

If the connotation of a word does not seem appropriate for your purpose, your audience, or your subject matter, you should change the word. When a more appropriate synonym does not come quickly to mind, consult a dictionary or a thesaurus.

slender
▶ The model was ~~skinny~~ and fashionable.
          ʌ

The connotation of the word *skinny* is too negative.

sweat
▶ As I covered the boats with marsh grass, the ~~perspiration~~ I
                                                  ʌ
had worked up evaporated in the wind, making the cold

morning air seem even colder.

The term *perspiration* was too dainty for the context, which suggests vigorous exercise.

EXERCISE 18-1

Use a dictionary or thesaurus to find at least four synonyms for each of the following words. Be prepared to explain any slight differences in meaning.

1. decay (verb)
2. difficult (adjective)
3. hurry (verb)
4. pleasure (noun)
5. secret (adjective)
6. talent (noun)

EXERCISE 18-2

For each of the words italicized in the following passages, consider alternatives that the writer might have chosen instead. (A dictionary and a thesaurus will lead you to other possibilities.) Then discuss why the author probably selected the word he or she did.

1. The forest, *choked* by growth and *shadow*, was like a jungle; the air hung thick with heat, *muting* the sound of their progress.

Breathing in a *pungent steam* of sweet grasses and tangy needles, rotting wood and sunbaked fungi, she followed as best she could, *plunging* through the thicket to keep up with the young man ahead.   — Diana West

2. A change of just a few degrees in atmospheric temperature over the next century would be *catastrophic*. A *parade* of scientists appearing before a senate committee in June *painted* a *graphic* picture of what that could mean: melting icecaps and rising sea levels that would *inundate* seaboard cities and drown thousands in *fierce* storms; rainfall shifts that would make the deserts *bloom* and turn *breadbaskets* into *dustbowls*; and, of course, heat everywhere.   — Matthew L. Wald

18b Prefer specific, concrete nouns.

Unlike general nouns, which refer to broad classes of things, specific nouns point to definite and particular items. *Film*, for example, names a general class, *horror film* names a narrower class, and *Carrie* is more specific still. Other examples: *team, football team, New York Jets; music, symphony, Beethoven's Ninth; work, carpentry, cabinetmaking.*

Unlike abstract nouns, which refer to qualities and ideas (*justice, beauty, realism, dignity*), concrete nouns point to immediate, often sensory experience and to physical objects (*steeple, asphalt, lilac, stone, garlic*).

Specific, concrete nouns express meaning more vividly than general or abstract ones. Although general and abstract language is sometimes necessary to convey your meaning, ordinarily prefer specific, concrete alternatives.

▶ The senator spoke about the challenges of the future: *of famine, pollution, dwindling resources, and arms control.*
problems ~~concerning the environment and world peace.~~
            ∧

Nouns such as *thing, area, aspect, factor,* and *individual* are especially dull and imprecise.

rewards.
▶ A career in transportation management offers many ~~things.~~
                                                    ∧

experienced technician.
▶ Try pairing a trainee with an ~~individual with technical~~
                                                      ∧
~~experience.~~

18c Do not misuse words.

If a word is not in your active vocabulary, you may find yourself misusing it, sometimes with embarrassing consequences. Imagine the chagrin of the young woman who wrote
that the "aroma of pumpkin pie and sage stuffing acted as an
aphrodisiac" when she learned that aphrodisiacs are drugs
or foods stimulating sexual desire. Such blunders are easily
prevented: When in doubt, check the dictionary.

climbing
▶ The fans were ~~migrating~~ up the bleachers in search of good
                  ∧
seats.

avail.
▶ Mrs. Johnson tried to fight but to no ~~prevail.~~
                                          ∧
permeated
▶ Drugs have so ~~diffused~~ our culture that they touch all
                  ∧
segments of society.

EXERCISE 18–3

Edit the following sentences to correct misused words. Revisions of
lettered sentences appear in the back of the book. Example:

all-absorbing.
The training required for a ballet dancer is ~~all-absorbent.~~
                                              ∧

a. Many of us are not persistence enough to make a change for the better.
b. Mrs. Altman's comments were meant to invoke a response from the class.
c. Sam Brown began his career as a lawyer, but now he is a real estate mongrel.
d. When Robert Frost died at age eighty-eight, he left a legacy of poems that will make him immortal for years to come.
e. This patient is kept in isolation to prevent her from obtaining our germs.

1. In 1776, the United States acclaimed its independence from England.
2. Trifle, a popular English dessert, contains a ménage of ingredients that do not always appeal to American tastes.
3. Washington's National Airport is surrounded on three sides by water.
4. Frequently I cannot do my work because the music blaring from my son's room detracts me.
5. Tom Jones is an illegal child who grows up under the care of Squire Western.

18d Use standard idioms.

Idioms are speech forms that follow no easily specified rules. The English say "Maria went *to hospital,*" an idiom strange to American ears, which are accustomed to hearing *the* in front of *hospital.* Native speakers of a language seldom have problems with idioms, but prepositions sometimes cause trouble, especially when they follow certain verbs and adjectives. When in doubt, consult a good desk dictionary.

UNIDIOMATIC	IDIOMATIC
according with	according to
abide with (a decision)	abide by (a decision)
agree to (an idea)	agree with (an idea)
angry at (a person)	angry with (a person)
capable to	capable of
comply to	comply with

UNIDIOMATIC	IDIOMATIC
desirous to	desirous of
different than	different from
intend on doing	intend to do
off of	off
plan on doing	plan to do
preferable than	preferable to
prior than	prior to
superior than	superior to
sure and	sure to
try and	try to
type of a	type of

EXERCISE 18–4

Edit the following sentences to eliminate errors in the use of idiomatic expressions. If a sentence is correct, write "correct" after it. Answers to lettered sentences appear in the back of the book. Example:

We agreed to abide ~~with~~ *by* the decision of the judge.

a. I was so angry at the salesperson that I took her bag of samples and emptied it on the floor in front of her.
b. Prior to the Russians' launching of *Sputnik*, *nik* was not an English suffix.
c. Try and come up with the rough outline, and we will find someone who can fill in the details.
d. "Your prejudice is no different than mine," she shouted.
e. The parade moved off of the street and onto the beach.

1. Be sure and report on the danger of releasing genetically engineered bacteria into the atmosphere.
2. Why do you assume that embezzling bank assets is so different than robbing the bank?
3. Most of the class agreed to Sylvia's view that nuclear proliferation is potentially a very dangerous problem.
4. What type of a wedding are you planning?
5. I intend on writing letters to my representatives in Congress demanding that they do something about homelessness in this state.

18e Avoid worn-out expressions.

The frontiersman who first announced that he had "slept like a log" no doubt amused his companions with a fresh and unlikely comparison. Today, however, that comparison is a cliché, a saying that has lost its dazzle from overuse. No longer can it surprise.

To see just how dully predictable clichés are, put your hand over the right-hand column below and then finish the phrases on the left.

cool as a	cucumber
beat around	the bush
blind as a	bat
busy as a	bee, beaver
crystal	clear
dead as a	doornail
from the frying pan	into the fire
light as a	feather
like a bull	in a china shop
playing with	fire
nutty as a	fruitcake
selling like	hotcakes
starting out at the bottom	of the ladder
water over the	dam
white as a	sheet, ghost
avoid clichés like the	plague

The cure for clichés is frequently simple: Just delete them. When this won't work, try adding some element of surprise. One student, for example, who had written that she had butterflies in her stomach, revised her cliché like this:

> If all of the action in my stomach is caused by butterflies, there must be a horde of them, with horseshoes on.

The image of butterflies wearing horseshoes is fresh and unlikely, not dully predictable like the original cliché.

18f Use figures of speech with care.

A figure of speech is an expression that uses words imaginatively (rather than literally) to invigorate an idea or make abstract ideas concrete. Most often, figures of speech compare two seemingly unlike things to reveal surprising similarities. For example, Richard Selzer compares an aging surgeon who has lost his touch to an old lion whose claws have become blunted. Readers enjoy such fresh comparisons, and you will find that creating them is one of the greatest pleasures in writing.

In a *simile,* the writer makes a comparison explicitly, usually by introducing it with *like* or *as.* One student, for instance, writes of his grandfather, "By the time cotton had to be picked, his neck was as red as the clay he plowed." In one of his short stories, William Faulkner describes the eyes of a plump old woman who had locked herself in her house for years as "like two small pieces of coal pressed into a lump of dough." J. D. Salinger's troubled adolescent Holden Caulfield in *The Catcher in the Rye* finds one of his fellow students "as sensitive as a goddam toilet seat," and actress Mae West tells us that men are "like streetcars. There's always another one around the corner."

In a *metaphor,* the *like* or *as* is omitted, and the comparison is implied. For example, Mark Twain's Huck Finn describes his drunken father's face as "fish-belly white." In the Old Testament's Song of Solomon, a young woman compares the man she loves to a fruit tree: "With great delight I sat in his shadow, and his fruit was sweet to my taste." And a student poet describes a fierce summer storm like this: "It growls and barks at me, / jumping at its leash, / as if it guards the gates of heaven."

Although figures of speech are useful devices, writers sometimes use them without thinking through the images they evoke. This can result in a *mixed metaphor,* the combination of two or more images that don't make sense together.

▶ Crossing Utah's salt flats in his new Corvette, my father flew
  at jet speed.
  ~~under a full head of steam.~~
  ∧

Flew suggests an airplane, while *under a full head of steam*
suggests a steamboat or a train. To clarify the image, the writer
should stick with one comparison or the other.

▶ Our office had decided to put all controversial issues on a

back burner **.** ~~in a holding pattern.~~
            ∧

Here the writer is mixing stoves and airplanes. Simply deleting
one of the images corrects the problem.

EXERCISE 18–5

Edit the following sentences to replace worn-out expressions and
clarify mixed figures of speech. Revisions of lettered sentences appear
in the back of the book. Example:

the color drained from his face.
When he heard about the accident, ~~he turned white as a~~
                                  ∧

~~sheet.~~

a. His fellow club members deliberated very briefly; all agreed that
   his behavior was unacceptable beyond the shadow of a doubt.
b. The president thought that the scientists were using science as
   a sledgehammer to grind their political axes.
c. Architect I. M. Pei gave our city a cultural shot in the arm that
   rubbed off in other areas.
d. We ironed out the sticky spots in our relationship.
e. Mel told us that he wasn't willing to put his neck out on a limb.

1. I could read him like a book; he had egg all over his face.
2. Tears were strolling down the child's face.
3. High school is a seething caldron of raw human emotion.
4. There are too many cooks in the broth here at corporate head-
   quarters.

5. Once she had sunk her teeth into it, Helen burned through the assignment.

EXERCISE 18—6

Identify the figurative language in the following sentences. Be prepared to discuss why you think these passages are effective.

1. The kitchen was a great machine that set our lives running; it whirred down a little only on Saturdays and holy days.
— Alfred Kazin

2. If growing up is painful for the Southern Black girl, being aware of her displacement is the rust on the razor that threatens the throat.
— Maya Angelou

3. She sat looking about her with eyes as impersonal, almost as stony, as those with which the granite Rameses in a museum watches the froth and fret that ebbs and flows about his pedestal.
— Willa Cather

4. As the sweeping scythe of plague turned bustling towns into sepulchers and emptied the countryside, it reshaped European history.
— Nicole Duplaix

5. In a word, we [Afro-Americans] are bringing down the curtain on this role you have cast us in and we will no longer be a party to our own degradation.
— John Oliver Killens

PART V

Editing for Grammar

19

Repair sentence fragments.

A sentence fragment is a word group that pretends to be a sentence. Some fragments are clauses that contain a subject and a verb but begin with a subordinating word. Others are phrases that lack a subject, a verb, or both.

To be a sentence, a word group must consist of at least one full independent clause. An independent clause has a subject and a verb, and it either stands alone or could stand alone. To test a word group for sentence completeness, use the flow chart on page 207.

You can repair most fragments in one of two ways: Either pull the fragment into a nearby sentence, making sure to punctuate the new sentence correctly, or turn the fragment into a sentence.

ESL NOTE: Unlike some languages, English does not allow omission of subjects (except in imperative sentences); nor does it allow omission of verbs. See 31a.

19a Attach fragmented subordinate clauses or turn them into sentences.

A subordinate clause is patterned like a sentence, with both a subject and a verb, but it begins with a word that marks it as subordinate. The following words commonly introduce subordinate clauses:

after	even though	so that	when	whom
although	how	than	where	whose
as	if	that	whether	why
as if	in order that	though	which	
because	rather than	unless	while	
before	since	until	who	

Subordinate clauses function within sentences as adjectives, as adverbs, or as nouns. They cannot stand alone. (See 49b.)

Most fragmented clauses beg to be pulled into a sentence nearby.

▶ Jane will address the problem of limited on-campus

parking. *if* ~~If~~ she is elected special student adviser.

If introduces a subordinate clause that modifies the verb *will address.* For punctuation of subordinate clauses appearing at the end of a sentence, see 33f.

▶ Although we seldom get to see wildlife in the city. *at* ~~At~~ the

zoo we can still find some of our favorites.

Although introduces a subordinate clause that modifies the verb *can find.* For punctuation of subordinate clauses appearing at the beginning of a sentence, see 32b.

If a fragmented clause cannot be attached to a nearby sentence or if you feel that attaching it would be awkward, try rewriting it. The simplest way to turn a subordinate clause into a sentence is to delete the opening word or words that mark it as subordinate.

▶ Violence has produced a great deal of apprehension among

teachers at Dean Junior High. ~~So that~~ *S*elf-preservation, in

fact, has become their primary aim.

19b Attach fragmented phrases or turn them into sentences.

Like subordinate clauses, phrases function within sentences as adjectives, as adverbs, or as nouns. They cannot stand alone. Fragmented phrases are often prepositional or verbal phrases; sometimes they are appositives, words or word groups that rename nouns or pronouns. (See 49a, 49c, and 49d.)

Many fragmented phrases may simply be pulled into nearby sentences.

▶ On Sundays James read the newspaper's employment

listings scrupulously/, ~~Scrutinizing~~ *scrutinizing* every position that held

even the remotest possibility.

Scrutinizing every position that held even the remotest possibility is a verbal phrase modifying *James*. For punctuation of verbal phrases, see 32e.

▶ Wednesday morning Phil allowed himself half a grapefruit/,

~~T~~*t*he only food he had eaten in two days.

The only food he had eaten in two days is an appositive renaming the noun *grapefruit*. For punctuation of appositives, see 32e.

If a fragmented phrase cannot be pulled into a nearby sentence effectively, turn the phrase into a sentence. You may need to add a subject, a verb, or both.

▶ In the study skills workshop, we learned the value of

discipline and hard work. ~~Also~~ *We also learned how* to organize our time, take

meaningful notes, interpret assignments, pinpoint trouble

spots, and seek help.

The word group beginning *Also to organize* is a fragmented verbal phrase. The revision turns the fragment into a sentence by adding a subject and a verb.

19c Attach other fragmented word groups or turn them into sentences.

Other word groups that are commonly fragmented include parts of compound predicates, lists, and examples introduced by *such as, for example,* or similar expressions.

Parts of compound predicates

A predicate consists of a verb and its objects, complements, and modifiers (see 48b). A compound predicate includes two or more predicates joined by a coordinating conjunction such as *and, but,* or *or.* Because the parts of a compound predicate share the same subject, they should appear in the same sentence.

▶ Aspiring bodybuilders must first ascertain their strengths and weaknesses/ ~~A~~nd then decide what they want to achieve.

Notice that no comma appears between the parts of a compound predicate. (See 33a.)

Lists

When a list is mistakenly fragmented, it can often be attached to a nearby sentence with a colon or a dash. (See 35a and 39a.)

▶ The side effects of lithium are many/: ~~N~~ausea, stomach cramps, thirst, muscle weakness, vomiting, diarrhea, confusion, and tremors.

Examples introduced by such as, for example,
or similar expressions

Transitional expressions that introduce examples (or explanations) can lead to unintentional fragments. Although you
may begin a sentence with some of the following transitions,
just make sure that what you have written is a sentence, not
a fragment.

also	for instance	or
and	in addition	such as
but	like	that is
especially	mainly	
for example	namely	

Sometimes fragmented examples can be attached to the
preceding sentence.

▶ The South has produced some of our greatest twentieth-
century writers,/₂ ~~Such~~ *such* as Flannery O'Connor, William

Faulkner, Alice Walker, Tennessee Williams, and Thomas

Wolfe.

At times, however, it may be necessary to turn the fragment into a sentence.

▶ If Eric doesn't get his way, he goes into a fit of rage. For
example, ~~lying~~ *he lies* on the floor screaming or ~~opening~~ *opens* the cabinet
doors and then ~~slamming~~ *slams* them shut.

The writer corrected this fragment by adding a subject—*he*—
and substituting verbs for the verbals *lying, opening,* and
slamming.

19d Exception: Occasionally a fragment may be used deliberately, for effect.

Skilled writers occasionally use sentence fragments for emphasis. In the following passage, Richard Rodriguez uses a fragment (italicized) to draw attention to his mother.

> Following the dramatic Americanization of their children, even my parents grew more publicly confident. *Especially my mother.* She learned the names of all the people on our block.
> —*Hunger of Memory*

Fragments are occasionally used to save words. For example, a fragment may be a concise way to mark a transition (*And now the opposing arguments*) or to answer a question (*Are these new drug tests 100% reliable? Not in the opinion of most experts*).

When deciding whether to risk using a fragment, consider your writing situation. Are readers likely to object to fragments, even when used deliberately? Does your subject demand a formal approach? If the answer to either of these questions is yes, you will find it safer to write in complete sentences.

EXERCISE 19 – 1

Repair any fragment by attaching it to a nearby sentence or by rewriting it as a complete sentence. If a word group is correct, write "correct" after it. Revisions of lettered sentences appear in the back of the book. Example:

One Greek island that should not be missed is Mykonos, ̶a̶ vacation spot for Europeans and a playpen for the rich.

a. As I stood in front of the microwave, I recalled my grandmother bending over her old black stove. And remembered what she

Reviewing your writing for sentence fragments

First look for the most common trouble spots:

WORDS INTRODUCING SUBORDINATE CLAUSES (19a)

although	even though	that	where	who
as if	if	though	whether	whom
before	how	unless	which	whose
because	so that	when	while	why

▶ Pat could not come skiing with us/ ~~B~~ᵇecause she had

broken her leg.

PHRASES (19b)

▶ I was exhausted/, ~~H~~ʰaving studied for twelve hours
∧
straight.

▶ Mary is suffering from agoraphobia/, ~~A~~ᵃ fear of the
∧
outside world.

PARTS OF COMPOUND PREDICATES (19c)

▶ Pressing the gun to my shoulder, I laid my cheek to

the stock/ ~~A~~ᵃnd sighted the target.

WORDS INTRODUCING LISTS OR EXAMPLES (19c)

also	especially	in addition	namely	such as
and	for example	like	or	that is
but	for instance	mainly		

Sentence fragments (continued)

Next test possible fragments for sentence completeness:

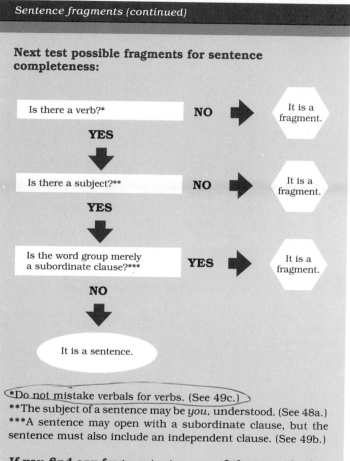

Is there a verb?* → **NO** → It is a fragment.

YES

Is there a subject?** → **NO** → It is a fragment.

YES

Is the word group merely a subordinate clause?*** → **YES** → It is a fragment.

NO

It is a sentence.

*Do not mistake verbals for verbs. (See 49c.)
**The subject of a sentence may be *you*, understood. (See 48a.)
***A sentence may open with a subordinate clause, but the sentence must also include an independent clause. (See 49b.)

If you find any fragments, try one of these methods of revision:

1. Attach the fragment to a nearby sentence.
2. Turn the fragment into a sentence.

taught me: that any food can have soul if you love the people you are cooking for.

b. It has been said that there are only three indigenous American art forms. Jazz, musical comedy, and soap opera.

c. I stepped on some frozen moss and started sliding down the face of a flat rock toward the falls. Suddenly I landed on another rock.

d. Myra did not tell us about her new job for six weeks. Although she saw one or the other of us every day.

e. While on a tour of Italy, Maria and Kathleen sneaked away from their group to spend some quiet minutes with Leonardo da Vinci's *Last Supper*. A stunning fresco painted in the fifteenth century in a Milan monastery.

1. Recently I visited a friend who was confined in Occoquan II. A correctional facility located in Lorton, Virginia.

2. Mother loved to play all our favorite games. Canasta, Monopoly, hide-and-seek, and even kick the can.

3. Underneath all his brashness, Henry is really a thoughtful person. Few of his colleagues realize how sensitive he is.

4. I had pushed these fears into one of those quiet places in my mind. Hoping they would stay there asleep.

5. To give my family a comfortable, secure home life. That is my most important goal.

6. If a woman from the desert tribe showed anger toward her husband, she was whipped in front of the whole village. And shunned by the rest of the women.

7. A tornado is a violent whirling wind. One that produces a funnel-shaped cloud and moves over land in a narrow path of destruction.

8. With machetes, the explorers cut their way through the tall grasses to the edge of the canyon. Where they began to lay out their tapes for the survey.

9. Bill is a disciplined yet adventurous player. Unlike his brother Ken.

10. Theodosia had hated her name for as long as she could remember. Because it sounded so old-fashioned.

EXERCISE 19–2

Repair each fragment in the following paragraphs by attaching it to a sentence nearby or by rewriting it as a complete sentence.

Until recently, Maria thought that studying a foreign language would not be very useful. Because she was going to be a business major, training for management. Even if she worked for a company with an office overseas, she was sure that international clients would communicate in English. The accepted language of the world marketplace. But Maria's adviser, Professor Will, told her that many U.S. firms are owned by foreign corporations. Or rely on the sales of subsidiaries in foreign markets. English is therefore not always the language of preference.

Professor Will advised Maria to learn a foreign language. Such as French, German, or Japanese. These are the most useful languages, he told her. In addition to preparing her to use the language, the classes would expose her to the history, culture, and politics of another country. Factors that often affect business decisions. After talking with Professor Will, Maria was convinced. To begin immediately to prepare for her business career by studying a foreign language.

EXERCISE 19–3

Look through a draft-in-progress for inappropriate fragments, using the chart on pages 206–207. Revise each fragment by attaching it to a nearby sentence or by turning it into a sentence.

EXERCISE 19–4

If fragments are a recurring problem for you, look through your past writings for your own common trouble spots. Begin by compiling a list of fragments and your revisions. Then study the list to learn when you are most tempted to write a fragment. Make a note of these trouble spots and be especially alert to them in future writing.

20

Revise comma splices and fused sentences.

Comma splices and fused sentences occur when independent clauses have been too weakly separated. An independent clause is a word group that can stand alone as a sentence. (See 50a.)

When a writer puts no mark of punctuation between independent clauses, the result is a fused sentence (also called a *run-on sentence*).

> ┌─INDEPENDENT CLAUSE─┐ ┌─INDEPENDENT CLAUSE─┐
> **FUSED**   Power tends to corrupt absolute power corrupts
> ────────────
> absolutely.

A far more common error is the comma splice—independent clauses separated by only a comma or by a comma and a conjunctive adverb or transitional phrase. Conjunctive adverbs include words like *however, therefore,* and *moreover;* transitional phrases are expressions such as *in fact* and *for example.* (See the chart on page 214 for a more complete list.)

> **COMMA**   Power tends to corrupt, absolute power corrupts
> **SPLICE**   absolutely.

> **COMMA**   Power tends to corrupt, moreover, absolute power
> **SPLICE**   corrupts absolutely.

If two independent clauses are to appear in one sentence, they must be firmly separated in one of three ways: (1) by a comma and a coordinating conjunction (*and, but, or, nor, for, so, yet*); (2) by a semicolon (or occasionally a colon) alone; or (3) by a semicolon and a conjunctive adverb or transitional phrase. (See 8, especially the chart on page 112.)

REVISED Power tends to corrupt, and absolute power corrupts absolutely.

REVISED Power tends to corrupt; absolute power corrupts absolutely.

REVISED Power tends to corrupt; moreover, absolute power corrupts absolutely.

Unlike coordinating conjunctions, conjunctive adverbs and transitional phrases are frequently movable: *Power tends to corrupt; absolute power, moreover, corrupts absolutely.* Notice that the semicolon still goes between the clauses. (See 34b.)

To correct a comma splice or a fused sentence, you have four choices:

1. Use a comma and a coordinating conjunction.
2. Use a semicolon (or, if appropriate, a colon).
3. Make the clauses into separate sentences.
4. Restructure the sentence, perhaps by subordinating one of the clauses.

One of these revision techniques will usually work better than the others for a particular sentence. The fourth technique, the one requiring the most extensive revision, is frequently the most effective.

20a Consider separating the clauses with a comma and a coordinating conjunction.

There are seven coordinating conjunctions in English: *and, but, or, nor, for, so,* and *yet.* When a coordinating conjunction joins independent clauses, it must be preceded by a comma. (See 32a.)

▶ Minh did not understand our language, *and* he was unfamiliar with our customs.

▶ Many government officials privately admit that the polygraph

      yet

is unreliable, ~~however~~ they continue to use it as a security

     ∧

measure.

However is a conjunctive adverb, not a coordinating conjunction, so it cannot be used with only a comma to join independent clauses. (See 20b.)

20b Consider separating the clauses with a semicolon (or, if appropriate, with a colon).

When the independent clauses are closely related and their relation is clear without a coordinating conjunction, a semicolon is an acceptable method of revision. (See 34a.)

▶ Tragedy depicts the individual confronted with the fact of

death/; comedy depicts the adaptability and ongoing survival

   ∧

of human society.

A semicolon is required between independent clauses that have been linked with a conjunctive adverb (such as *however, therefore,* or *moreover*) or with a transitional phrase (such as *in fact,* or *for example*). For a longer list, see the chart on page 216. (See also 34b.)

▶ The timber wolf looks much like a large German shepherd/;

                         ∧

however, the wolf has longer legs, larger feet, a wider head,

and a long, bushy tail.

▶ Everyone in my outfit had a specific job/; as a matter of fact,

                    ∧

most of the officers had three or four duties.

If the first independent clause introduces the second or if the second clause summarizes or explains the first, a colon may be an appropriate method of revision. (See 35b.)

▶ The experience taught Juanita a lesson/: ~~she~~ *She* could not

always rely on her parents to bail her out of trouble.

20c Consider making the clauses into separate sentences.

▶ Why shouldn't divorced wives receive half of their husbands'

pensions and other retirement benefits|? ~~they~~ *They* were partners

for many years.

Since one independent clause is a question and the other is a statement, they should be separate sentences.

▶ I gave the necessary papers to the police officer. ~~then~~ *Then* he

said I would have to accompany him to the police station,

where a counselor would talk with me and call my parents.

Because the second independent clause is quite long, a sensible revision is to use separate sentences.

20d Consider restructuring the sentence, perhaps by subordinating one of the clauses.

If one of the independent clauses is less important than the other, turn it into a subordinate clause or phrase. (For more about subordination, see 8, especially the chart on page 113.)

who
▶ Lindsey is a top competitor ~~she~~ has been riding since the
∧
age of seven.

When the
▶ ~~The~~ new health plan was explained to the employees in my
∧
division, everyone agreed to give it a try.

▶ Saturday afternoon Julie came running into the house/~~she~~

~~wanted~~ to get permission to go to the park.

Minor ideas in these sentences are now expressed in subordinate
clauses or phrases.

EXERCISE 20–1

Revise any comma splices or fused sentences using the method of
revision suggested in brackets. Revisions of lettered sentences appear
in the back of the book. Example:

Because
∧Orville was obsessed with his weight, he rarely ate anything

sweet and delicious. [*Restructure the sentence.*]

a. The city had one public swimming pool, it stayed packed with
   children all summer long. [*Restructure the sentence.*]
b. Theo and Fanny had hoped to spend their final days in the old
   homestead, they had to change their plans and move together
   to a retirement home. [*Use a comma and a coordinating
   conjunction.*]
c. Why should we pay taxes to support public transportation, we
   prefer to save energy dollars by carpooling. [*Make two sentences.*]
d. Suddenly there was a loud silence, the shelling had stopped. [*Use
   a semicolon.*]
e. As I walked into the living room, a special report flashed onto
   the TV screen, the space shuttle had exploded. [*Use a colon.*]

1. For the first time in her adult life, Lisa had time to waste, she could spend a whole day curled up with a good book. [*Use a semicolon.*]

2. It is impossible for parents to monitor all the television their children see, therefore, many parents just give up and offer no supervision at all. [*Restructure the sentence.*]

3. The next time an event is canceled because of bad weather, don't blame the meteorologist, blame nature. [*Make two sentences.*]

4. While we were walking down Grover Avenue, Gary told us about his Aunt Elsinia, she was an extraordinary woman. [*Restructure the sentence.*]

5. The president of Algeria was standing next to the podium he was waiting to be introduced. [*Restructure the sentence.*]

6. On most days I had only enough money for bus fare, lunch was a luxury I could not afford. [*Use a semicolon.*]

7. There was one major reason for John's wealth, his grandfather had been a multimillionaire. [*Use a colon.*]

8. In one episode viewers saw two people smashed by a boat, one person choked, and another shot to death, what purpose does this violence serve? [*Make two sentences.*]

9. It was too late to catch a bus after the party, therefore, four of us pooled our money and called a cab. [*Use a comma and a coordinating conjunction.*]

10. Wind power for the home is a supplementary source of energy, it can be combined with electricity, gas, or solar energy. [*Restructure the sentence.*]

EXERCISE 20 – 2

Revise any comma splices or fused sentences using a technique that you find effective. If a sentence is correct, write "correct" after it. Revisions of lettered sentences appear in the back of the book. Example:

but

I ran the three blocks as fast as I could, ~~however~~ I still
                                          ∧

missed the bus.

a. The trail up Mount Finegold was declared impassable, therefore, we decided to return to our hotel a day early.

Reviewing your writing for comma splices and fused sentences

First look for the most common trouble spots:

CONJUNCTIVE ADVERB OR TRANSITIONAL PHRASE

also	in addition	now
as a result	in fact	of course
besides	in other words	on the other hand
consequently	in the first place	otherwise
finally	meanwhile	still
for example	moreover	then
for instance	nevertheless	therefore
furthermore	next	thus
however		

▶ We usually think of children as innocent and

guileless/; however, they are often cruel and unjust.
  ^

EXAMPLE OR EXPLANATION IN SECOND CLAUSE

▶ Martin looked out the window in astonishment: *H*e had
  ^

never seen snow before.

CLAUSES EXPRESSING CONTRAST

▶ Most of his contemporaries had made plans for their
  but
retirement, Tom had not.
  ^

PRONOUN AS SUBJECT OF SECOND CLAUSE
  who
▶ Claudia, was full of energy and enthusiasm, ~~she~~
  ^

tackled the job at once.

Comma splices and fused sentences (continued)

Next test your sentences for correctness:

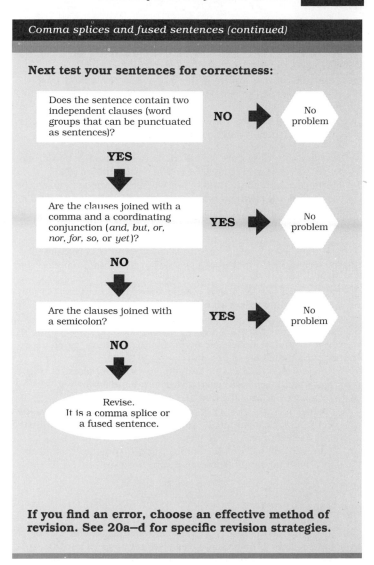

Does the sentence contain two independent clauses (word groups that can be punctuated as sentences)?

NO ➡ No problem

YES ⬇

Are the clauses joined with a comma and a coordinating conjunction (*and, but, or, nor, for, so,* or *yet*)?

YES ➡ No problem

NO ⬇

Are the clauses joined with a semicolon?

YES ➡ No problem

NO ⬇

Revise.
It is a comma splice or a fused sentence.

If you find an error, choose an effective method of revision. See 20a–d for specific revision strategies.

b. The duck hunter set out his decoys in the shallow bay and then settled in to wait for the first real bird to alight.

c. The officer must enforce the laws, this is true even when the laws seem unfair.

d. Researchers were studying the fertility of Texas land tortoises they X-rayed all the female tortoises to see how many eggs they had.

e. The suburbs seemed cold, they lacked the warmth and excitement of our Italian neighborhood.

1. Are you able to endure boredom, isolation, and potential violence, then the army may well be the adventure for you.

2. Maria gave her mother half of her weekly pay then she used the rest as a down payment on a stereo system at Brown's Sounds.

3. If one of the dogs should happen to fall through the ice, it would be cut loose from the team and left to its fate, the sled drivers could not endanger the rest of the team for just one dog.

4. The volunteers worked hard to clean up and restore calm after the tornado, as a matter of fact, many of them did not sleep for the first three days of the emergency.

5. Taking drugs to keep alert on the job or in school can actually cause a decline in work performance, and it can lead to severe depression as well.

6. Pablo had not prepared well for his first overseas assignment, but luck was with him, he performed better than the more experienced members of his unit.

7. It was obvious that Susan had already been out walking in the woods, her boots were covered with mud and leaves.

8. We didn't trust her, she had lied before.

9. I pushed open the first door with my back, turning to open the second door, I encountered a young woman in a wheelchair holding it open for me.

10. If you want to lose weight and keep it off, consider this advice, don't try to take it off faster than you put it on.

EXERCISE 20–3

In the following rough draft, repair any sentence fragments and revise any comma splices or fused sentences. (See sections 19 and 20, especially the charts on pages 206 and 216.)

Teri, Karen, and I took introductory foreign language courses last year. Each of us was interested in learning a different language, however, we were all trying to accomplish the same goal. To begin mastering a new language. When we compared our classes and the results, we found that each course used a quite different approach to language learning.

In my Spanish course, Professor Cruz introduced lists of new vocabulary words every week, she devoted half of each class to grammar rules. I spent most of my time memorizing lists and rules. In addition to vocabulary and grammar study, I read passages of Spanish literature. Translating them into English. And wrote responses to the reading in Spanish. The only time I spoke Spanish, however, was when I translated a passage or answered questions in class. Although Professor Cruz spoke Spanish for the entire class period.

Instead of memorizing vocabulary lists and grammar rules and translating reading selections, Teri's Portuguese class rehearsed simple dialogues useful for tourists. Conducting every class in Portuguese, Teri's professor asked students to recite the dialogues, she corrected the students' pronunciation and grammar as they spoke. Teri's homework was to go to the language lab, she listened to various dialogues and practiced ordering meals, asking for directions to a train station, and so on. Teri learned to pronounce the language well, she mastered the simple dialogues. But she did not get much practice in reading.

Karen took a course in Russian, her experience was different from Teri's and from mine. Her professor asked the students to read articles from the Soviet press. And to listen to recent news programs from the Soviet Union. In class, students discussed the articles and programs. Teri's professor encouraged the students to use Russian as much as possible in their discussions, she also allowed them to use English. Other class activities included writing letters in response to articles in Soviet publications and role playing to duplicate real-life situations. Such as a discussion with a neighbor about the lack of meat in the shops. Karen learned to understand spoken Russian and to speak the language, in addition, she regularly practiced reading and writing. Although her Russian course was difficult, Karen thinks it will help her when she visits the Soviet Union this summer.

Of the three of us, Karen is the most positive about her course. She is certain that she will further develop her language skills when visiting the Soviet Union, moreover, she is confident that she can communicate without struggling too much with a dictionary. Teri and I feel less positive about our courses. Because we both have forgotten the vocabulary and grammar rules. If I were asked to read a passage in Spanish now, I couldn't, Teri says she would not understand Portuguese or be able to respond to a single dialogue if she had to.

EXERCISE 20−4

Look through a draft-in-progress for comma splices and fused sentences, using the chart on pages 216 − 217 as a guide. Choose an effective method of revision for any problem sentences that you find.

EXERCISE 20−5

If comma splices and fused sentences are a recurring problem for you, look through your past writings for your own common trouble spots. Begin by compiling a list of your errors and appropriate revisions. Then study the list to learn when you are most tempted to join independent clauses incorrectly. Make a note of these trouble spots and be especially alert to them in future writing.

21

Make subjects and verbs agree.

In the present tense, verbs agree with their subjects in number (singular or plural) and in person (first, second, or third). The present-tense ending -s is used on a verb if its subject is third-person singular; otherwise the verb takes no ending.

Consider, for example, the present-tense forms of the verb *give:*

	SINGULAR	**PLURAL**
FIRST PERSON	I give	we give
SECOND PERSON	you give	you give
THIRD PERSON	he/she/it gives	they give
	Alison gives	parents give

The verb *be* varies from this pattern; unlike any other verb, it has special forms in *both* the present and the past tense.

PRESENT-TENSE FORMS OF *BE*		**PAST-TENSE FORMS OF *BE***	
I am	we are	I was	we were
you are	you are	you were	you were
he/she/it is	they are	he/she/it was	they were

Speakers of standard English know by ear that *he talks, she has,* and *it doesn't* (not *he talk, she have,* and *it don't*) are the standard forms. For such speakers, problems with subject-verb agreement arise only in certain tricky situations, which are detailed in this section.

If you don't trust your ear, consult 27c, which contrasts the present-tense verb systems of standard and nonstandard English. Also see 48a and 48b on subjects and verbs.

21a Make the verb agree with its subject, not with a word that comes between.

Word groups often come between the subject and the verb. Such word groups, usually modifying the subject, may contain a noun that at first appears to be the subject. By mentally stripping away such modifiers, you can isolate the noun that is in fact the subject.

The *tulips* in the pot on the balcony *need* watering.

▶ High levels of air pollution causes damage to the respiratory

tract.

The subject is *levels*, not *pollution*. Strip away the phrase *of air pollution* to hear the correct verb: *levels cause*.

Costs
▶ A good set of golf clubs ~~cost~~ about three hundred dollars.
⌃

The subject is *set*, not *clubs*. Strip away the phrase *of golf clubs* to hear the correct verb: *set costs*.

NOTE: Phrases beginning with the prepositions *as well as, in addition to, accompanied by, together with,* and *along with* do not make a singular subject plural.

was
▶ The governor, as well as his press secretary, ~~were~~ shot.
⌃

To emphasize that two people were shot, the writer could use *and* instead: *The governor and his press secretary were shot.*

21b Treat most compound subjects connected by *and* as plural.

A subject with two or more parts is said to be compound. If the parts are connected by *and*, the subject is nearly always plural.

Leon and *Jan* often *jog* together.

are
▶ Remember that your safety and welfare ~~is~~ in your own
⌃

hands.

The compound subject *safety and welfare* is plural, requiring the verb *are*.

▶ Jill's natural ability and her desire to help others ~~has~~ *have* led to

a career in the ministry.

Ability and desire is a plural subject, so its verb should be *have*.

EXCEPTIONS: When the parts of the subject form a single unit or when they refer to the same person or thing, treat the subject as singular.

Strawberries and cream was a last-minute addition to the menu.

Sue's friend and adviser was surprised by her decision.

When a compound subject is preceded by *each* or *every*, treat it as singular.

Each tree, shrub, and vine needs to be sprayed.

Every car, truck, and van is required to pass inspection.

This exception does not apply when a compound subject is followed by *each: Alan and Marcia each have different ideas.*

21c With compound subjects connected by *or* or *nor* (or by *either . . . or* or *neither . . . nor*), make the verb agree with the part of the subject nearer to the verb.

A driver's *license* or credit *card is* required.

A driver's *license* or two credit *cards are* required.

▶ If a relative or neighbor ~~are~~ *is* abusing a child, notify the police

immediately.

▶ Neither the instructor nor her students ~~was~~ *were* able to find the classroom.

▶ Neither the students nor the instructor ~~were~~ *was* able to find the classroom.

The verb must be matched with the part of the subject closer to it: *neighbor is* in the first sentence, *students were* in the second, *instructor was* in the third.

21d Treat most indefinite pronouns as singular.

Indefinite pronouns are pronouns that do not refer to specific persons or things. The following commonly used indefinite pronouns are singular:

any	each	everybody	none	someone
anyone	either	everything	no one	something
anybody	everyone	neither		

Many of these words appear to have plural meanings, and they are often treated as such in casual speech. In formal written English, however, they are nearly always treated as singular.

Everyone on the team *supports* the coach.

▶ Each of the furrows ~~have~~ *has* been seeded.

▶ Everybody who signed up for the ski trip ~~were~~ *was* taking lessons.

The subjects of these sentences are *each* and *everybody*. These indefinite pronouns are third-person singular, so the verbs must be *has* and *was*.

The indefinite pronouns *none* and *neither* are considered singular when used alone.

None is immune from this disease.

Neither is able to attend.

When these pronouns are followed by prepositional phrases with a plural meaning, however, usage varies. Some experts insist on treating the pronouns as singular, but many writers disagree. It is safer to treat them as singular.

None of these trades *requires* a college education.

Neither of those pejoratives *fits* Professor Brady.

A few indefinite pronouns (*all, any, some*) are singular or plural depending on the noun or pronoun they refer to.

Some of the *lemonade has* disappeared.

Some of the *rocks were* slippery.

21e Treat collective nouns as singular unless the meaning is clearly plural.

Collective nouns such as *jury, committee, audience, crowd, class, troop, family,* and *couple* name a class or a group. In American English, collective nouns are nearly always treated as singular: They emphasize the group as a unit. Occasionally, when there is some reason to draw attention to the individual members of the group, a collective noun may be treated as plural. (Also see 22b.)

SINGULAR The *class respects* the teacher.

PLURAL The *class are* debating among themselves.

To underscore the notion of individuality in the second sentence, many writers would add a clearly plural noun such as *members:*

PLURAL   The class *members are* debating among themselves.

▶ The scout troop ~~meet~~ in our basement on Tuesdays.
    meets

The troop as a whole meets in the basement; there is no reason to draw attention to its individual members.

▶ A young couple ~~was~~ arguing about politics while holding hands.
    were

The meaning is clearly plural. Only individuals can argue and hold hands.

NOTE: The phrase *the number* is treated as singular, *a number* as plural.

SINGULAR   *The number* of school-age children *is* declining.

PLURAL   *A number* of children *are* attending the wedding.

NOTE: When units of measurement are used collectively, treat them as singular; when they refer to individual persons or things, treat them as plural.

SINGULAR   *Three-fourths* of the pie *has* been eaten.

PLURAL   *One-fourth* of the drivers *were* drunk.

21f   Make the verb agree with its subject even when the subject follows the verb.

Verbs ordinarily follow subjects. When this normal order is reversed, it is easy to become confused. Sentences beginning with *there is* or *there are* (or *there was* or *there were*) are inverted; the subject follows the verb.

There *are* surprisingly few *children* in our neighborhood.

▶ There ~~was~~ *were* a social worker and a crew of twenty volunteers at the scene of the accident.

> The subject *worker and crew* is plural, so the verb must be *were.*

Occasionally you may decide to invert a sentence for variety or effect. When you do so, check to make sure that your subject and verb agree. (See 15c.)

▶ At the back of the room ~~is~~ *are* a small aquarium and an enormous terrarium.

> The subject *aquarium and terrarium* is plural, so the verb must be *are.*

21g Make the verb agree with its subject, not with a subject complement.

One basic sentence pattern in English consists of a subject, a linking verb, and a subject complement: *Jack is a securities lawyer.* Because the subject complement names or describes the subject (*Jack*), it is sometimes mistaken for the subject. (See 48b on subject complements.)

These *problems are* a way to test your skill.

▶ A tent and a sleeping bag ~~is~~ *are* the required equipment.

> *Tent and bag* is the subject, not *equipment.*

▶ A major force in today's economy $\overset{is}{\cancel{are}}$ women — as earners,

consumers, and investors.

Force is the subject, not *women*. If the corrected version seems awkward, make *women* the subject: *Women are a major force in today's economy — as earners, consumers, and investors.*

21h *Who, which,* and *that* take verbs that agree with their antecedents.

Like most pronouns, the relative pronouns *who, which,* and *that* have antecedents, nouns or pronouns to which they refer. Relative pronouns used as subjects of subordinate clauses take verbs that agree with their antecedents.

Take a *suit that travels* well.

Problems can arise with the constructions *one of the* and *only one of the.* As a rule, treat *one of the* constructions as plural, *only one of the* constructions as singular.

▶ Our ability to use language is one of the things that sets us

apart from animals.

The antecedent of *that* is *things*, not *one*. Several things set us apart from animals.

▶ Dr. Barker knew that Frank was the only one of his sons

who $\overset{was}{\cancel{were}}$ responsible enough to handle the estate.

The antecedent of *who* is *one*, not *sons*. Only one son was responsible enough.

21i Words such as *athletics, economics, mathematics, physics, statistics, measles, mumps,* and *news* are usually singular, despite their plural form.

▶ Statistics ~~are~~ *is* among the most difficult courses in our program.

EXCEPTION: When they describe separate items rather than a collective body of knowledge, words such as *athletics, mathematics, physics,* and *statistics* are plural: *The statistics on school retention rates are impressive.*

21j Titles of works and words mentioned as words are singular.

▶ *Lost Cities* ~~describe~~ *describes* the discoveries of many ancient civilizations.

▶ *Controlled substances* ~~are~~ *is* a euphemism for illegal drugs.

EXERCISE 21–1

Underline the subject (or compound subject) and then select the verb that agrees with it. (If you have difficulty identifying the subject, consult 48a.) Answers to lettered sentences appear in the back of the book. Example:

Someone in the audience (has/have) volunteered to

participate in the experiment.

a. Your friendship over the years and your support on a wide variety of national issues (has/have) meant a great deal to us.

Reviewing your writing for problems with subject-verb agreement

First look for the most common trouble spots:

WORDS BETWEEN THE SUBJECT AND VERB (21a)

A *line* of cars behind the snowplows *stretches* over a mile.

COMPOUND SUBJECTS WITH *and*—USUALLY PLURAL (21b)

Naomi's *skills and experience* certainly *qualify* her for the job.

COMPOUND SUBJECTS WITH *or* OR *nor* (21c)

Dr. Brown or *Dr. Mullings* usually *works* the late shift.

Neither Ms. Cox nor her *students want* to support the principal.

SINGULAR INDEFINITE PRONOUNS (21d)

any	each	everybody	none	someone
anyone	either	everything	no one	something
anybody	everyone	neither		

None of the suspects *has* confessed.

COLLECTIVE NOUNS—USUALLY SINGULAR (21e)

audience	club	couple	family	troop
class	committee	crowd	jury	

The philosophy *club* usually *meets* in the seminar room.

SUBJECT AFTER THE VERB (21f)

There *are* several street *people* living under Key Bridge.

Then test for the correct verb form.

Once you have found the subject and decided whether it is singular or plural, your ear will probably tell you which form of the verb to choose. If you don't trust your ear, consult the models here. (See also 27c.)

PRESENT-TENSE FORMS OF *LOVE* (A TYPICAL VERB)

	SINGULAR		**PLURAL**	
FIRST PERSON	I	love	we	love
SECOND PERSON	you	love	you	love
THIRD PERSON	he/she/it	loves	they	love

PRESENT-TENSE FORMS OF *HAVE*

	SINGULAR		**PLURAL**	
FIRST PERSON	I	have	we	have
SECOND PERSON	you	have	you	have
THIRD PERSON	he/she/it	has	they	have

PRESENT-TENSE FORMS OF *DO*

	SINGULAR		**PLURAL**	
FIRST PERSON	I	do/don't	we	do/don't
SECOND PERSON	you	do/don't	you	do/don't
THIRD PERSON	he/she/it	does/doesn't	they	do/don't

PRESENT- AND PAST-TENSE FORMS OF *BE*

	SINGULAR		**PLURAL**	
FIRST PERSON	I	am/was	we	are/were
SECOND PERSON	you	are/were	you	are/were
THIRD PERSON	he/she/it	is/was	they	are/were

b. Two-week-old onion rings in the ashtray (is/are) not a pretty sight.

c. Each of these court documents (has/have) been carefully proof-read by two readers.

d. The main source of income for Trinidad (is/are) oil and pitch.

e. We felt especially confined because there (was/were) no windows in the classroom.

1. Neither my cousin nor his rowdy friends (was/were) accused of the prank.

2. Quilts made by the Amish (commands/command) high prices.

3. Sitting in the back seat of the car parked in the driveway (was/were) John and the class clown, Philip.

4. The most significant lifesaving device in automobiles (is/are) seatbelts.

5. The old iron gate and the brick wall (makes/make) our court-house appear older than its fifty years.

6. The dangers of smoking (is/are) well documented.

7. There (was/were) a Peanuts cartoon and a few Mother Goose rhymes pinned to the bulletin board.

8. When food supplies (was/were) scarce, the slaves had to make do with the less desirable parts of the animals.

9. The slaughter of pandas for their much-sought-after pelts (has/have) caused the panda population to decline dramatically.

10. Zena's family (realizes/realize) that repaying these debts will be difficult.

EXERCISE 21-2

Edit the following sentences for problems with subject-verb agreement. If a sentence is correct, write "correct" after it. Answers to lettered sentences appear in the back of the book. Example:

Jack's first days in the infantry ~~was~~ *were* grueling.

a. High concentrations of carbon monoxide results in headaches, dizziness, unconsciousness, and even death.

b. Not until my interview with Dr. Harvey were other possibilities opened to me.

c. After hearing the evidence and the closing arguments, the jury was sequestered.

d. Crystal chandeliers, polished floors, and a new oil painting has transformed Sandra's apartment.

e. Either Alice or Jan usually work the midnight shift.

1. The board of directors, most of whose members were appointed by the mayor, have just released a report on affirmative action.

2. Of particular concern are penicillin and tetracycline, antibiotics used to make animals more resistant to disease.

3. The presence of certain bacteria in our bodies is one of the factors that determine our overall health.

4. Nearly everyone on the panel favor the arms control agreement.

5. Every year a number of kokanee salmon, not native to the region, is introduced into Flathead Lake.

6. Until recently, economics was not considered a major academic field.

7. All of the witnesses claimed that neither Tom nor his partner was at the scene of the crime.

8. Steve Winwood, as well as Paul Simon, were attending the Grammy Award ceremony.

9. SEACON is the only one of our war games that emphasize scientific and technical issues.

10. The key program of Alcoholics Anonymous are the twelve steps to recovery.

EXERCISE 21 – 3

In the following paragraphs, circle the verb in parentheses that agrees with its subject.

Natalie, together with many other students in her educational philosophy class, (supports/support) a program to standardize cultural literacy in the high school curriculum. Natalie and those who agree with her (argues/argue) that students should have a broad background of shared knowledge. This shared knowledge (helps/help) bind a culture together and (encourages/encourage) pride in our country's heritage. In deciding which knowledge to include in a standardized curriculum, advocates of cultural literacy (looks/look) primarily to the past: if a book (has/have) stood the test of time, they say, it is a part of our culture worth preserving.

Kimberly and several other students in the class (opposes/oppose) the idea of a standardized high school curriculum. They argue that the content of such a curriculum is not easily determined in a multicultural society, especially in subjects such as sociology, history, and literature that (examines/examine) values and beliefs. Kimberly and other opponents of cultural literacy (believes/believe) that knowledge survives over time because a dominant culture preserves it. Kimberly (doesn't/don't) question the value of that knowledge, but she recognizes that the dominant culture over the years (neglects/neglect) to preserve and transmit knowledge that is important to less powerful cultures. The important factor in this debate (is/are) the students: each of them (deserves/deserve) attention and respect. Kimberly worries that plans to standardize cultural literacy (ignores/ignore) the cultures of too many students. She represents those in her class who (feels/feel) that a true cultural literacy program has to include knowledge from many cultures and that standardizing a multicultural curriculum may not be practical on any large scale.

EXERCISE 21−4

Look through a draft-in-progress for problems with subject-verb agreement, using the chart on pages 230–231.

EXERCISE 21−5

Subject-verb agreement causes occasional problems for nearly all writers, perhaps because the English language holds so many traps for us. An examination of when and why you fall into some of these traps will teach you at what points to be most alert.

Look through your past writings and analyze the cause of each subject-verb agreement error that you find. Which part or parts of the chart on pages 230–231 do you most need to keep in mind?

22

Make pronouns and antecedents agree.

A pronoun is a word that substitutes for a noun. (See 47b.) Many pronouns have antecedents, nouns or pronouns to which they refer. A pronoun and its antecedent agree when they are both singular or both plural.

SINGULAR   *Dr. Sarah Simms* finished *her* rounds.

PLURAL   The *doctors* finished *their* rounds.

ESL NOTE: The pronouns *he, his, she, her, it,* and *its* must agree in gender (masculine, feminine, or neuter) with their antecedents, not with the words they modify.

Jane visited *her* [not *his*] brother in Denver.

22a   Do not use plural pronouns to refer to singular antecedents.

Writers are frequently tempted to use plural pronouns to refer to two kinds of singular antecedents: indefinite pronouns and generic nouns.

Indefinite pronouns

Indefinite pronouns refer to nonspecific persons or things. Even though some of the following indefinite pronouns may seem to have plural meanings, treat them as singular in formal English.

any	each	everyone	none	someone
anybody	either	everything	no one	something
anyone	everybody	neither		

In class *everyone* performs at *his or her* [not *their*] fitness level.

When a plural pronoun refers mistakenly to a singular indefinite pronoun, you can usually choose one of three options for revision.

1. Replace the plural pronoun with *he or she* (or *his or her*).
2. Make the antecedent plural.
3. Rewrite the sentence so that no problem of agreement exists.

▶ When someone has been drinking, ~~they are~~ *he or she is* likely to speed.

▶ When ~~someone has~~ *drivers have* been drinking, they are likely to speed.

▶ ~~When someone~~ *A driver who* has been drinking/ ~~they are~~ *is* likely to speed.

Because the *he or she* construction is wordy, often the second or third revision strategy is more effective. Be aware that the traditional use of *he* (or *his*) to refer to persons of either sex is now widely considered sexist. (See 17f.)

Generic nouns

A generic noun represents a typical member of a group, such as a typical student, or any member of a group, such as any lawyer. Although generic nouns may seem to have plural meanings, they are singular.

Every *runner* must train rigorously if *he or she wants* [not *they want*] to excel.

When a plural pronoun refers mistakenly to a generic

noun, you will usually have the same three revision options as just mentioned for indefinite pronouns.

▶ A medical student must study hard if ~~they want~~ *he or she wants* to succeed.

▶ ~~A medical student~~ *Medical students* must study hard if they want to succeed.

▶ A medical student must study hard ~~if they want~~ to succeed.

22b   Treat collective nouns as singular unless the meaning is clearly plural.

Collective nouns such as *jury, committee, audience, crowd, class, troop, family, team,* and *couple* name a class or a group. Ordinarily the group functions as a unit, so the noun should be treated as singular; if the members of the group function as individuals, however, the noun should be treated as plural. (See also 21e.)

AS A UNIT   The *committee* granted *its* permission to build.

AS INDIVIDUALS   The *committee* put *their* signatures on the document.

▶ The jury has reached ~~their~~ *its* decision.

There is no reason to draw attention to the individual members of the jury, so *jury* should be treated as singular. Notice also that the writer treated the noun as singular when choosing the verb *has*, so for consistency the pronoun must be *its*.

▶ The audience shouted "Bravo" and stamped ~~its~~ *their* feet.

It is difficult to see how the audience as a unit can stamp *its* feet. The meaning here is clearly plural, requiring *their*.

22c Treat most compound antecedents connected by *and* as plural.

Joanne and John moved to the mountains, where *they* built a log cabin.

22d With compound antecedents connected by *or* or *nor* (or by *either . . . or* or *neither . . . nor*), make the pronoun agree with the nearer antecedent.

Either *Bruce* or *James* should receive first prize for *his* sculpture.

Neither the *mouse* nor the *rats* could find *their* way through the maze.

NOTE: If one of the antecedents is singular and the other plural, as in the second example, put the plural one last to avoid awkwardness.

EXERCISE 22 – 1

Edit the following sentences to eliminate problems with pronoun-antecedent agreement. Most of the sentences can be revised in more than one way, so experiment before choosing a solution. If a sentence is correct, write "correct" after it. Revisions of lettered sentences appear in the back of the book. Example:

> *Recruiters*
> ~~The recruiter~~ may tell the truth, but there is much that they
>   ∧
> choose not to tell.

a. Anyone who is taking the school bus to the volleyball game must bring in a permission slip signed by their parents.

b. The sophomore class elects its president tomorrow.

c. Late at night, I sometimes saw a priest or a brother entering the side door of the church, their faces silhouetted briefly in the moonlight.

d. A climatologist collects weather data from around the world. They then analyze the data and pass their analyses along to forecasters.

e. If you have anyone attending class who is still not on your roster, please send them to the registration office.

1. If a driver refuses to take a blood or breath test, he or she will have their licenses suspended for six months.

2. Why should we care about the timber wolf? One answer is that they have proven beneficial to humans by killing off weakened prey.

3. No one should be forced to sacrifice their prized possession — life — for someone else.

4. Everyone who enjoys freedom should recognize their indebtedness to the founders of our country.

5. The navy has much to offer any man or woman who knows what they want.

6. The committee plans to distribute copies of their proposal on Monday.

7. David lent his motorcycle to someone who allowed their friend to use it.

8. By the final curtain, ninety percent of the audience had voted with their feet.

9. A mountain climber must shift his or her emphasis from self-preservation to group survival. They must learn to rely completely on others.

10. A graduate student needs to be willing to take on a sizable debt unless they have wealthy families.

EXERCISE 22–2

Edit the following paragraphs for problems with pronoun-antecedent agreement. Choose an effective revision strategy that avoids sexist language. For examples, see the chart on page 185.

Reviewing your writing for problems with pronoun-antecedent agreement

First look for the most common trouble spots:

INDEFINITE PRONOUNS (SINGULAR) (22a)

any	each	everyone	none	someone
anybody	either	everything	no one	something
anyone	everybody	neither		

No one will see a salary increase until *he or she has* [not *they have*] been employed for two years.

GENERIC NOUNS (SINGULAR) (22a)

A generic noun names a typical person or thing (such as a typical teacher) or any person or thing (such as any employee of a company).

An adult panda must consume ninety pounds of bamboo if *it is* [not *they are*] to remain healthy.

COLLECTIVE NOUNS (SINGULAR UNLESS THE MEANING IS CLEARLY PLURAL) (22b)

audience	committee	couple	majority	team
class	crowd	family	minority	troop

The *committee* selected *its* [not *their*] new chairperson last night.

COMPOUND WORD GROUPS (SEE 22b, 22c)

Either *Steve or Larry* lost *his* [not *their*] notebook.

Pronoun-antecedent agreement (continued)

Choose an effective revision strategy that avoids sexist language.

Because many readers object to sexist language, avoid the use of *he, him,* and *his* as shorthand for *he or she, him or her,* and *his or hers.* Also try to be sparing in your use of *he or she* and *his or her,* since these expressions can become awkward, especially when repeated several times in a short passage. Where possible, seek out more graceful alternatives.

1. Use an occasional *he or she* (or *his or her*).

▶ In our office, everyone works at ~~their~~ his or her own pace.

2. Make the antecedent plural.

▶ ~~An employee~~ Employees on extended leave may continue their life insurance.

3. Recast the sentence.

▶ The amount of annual leave a federal worker may accrue depends on ~~their~~ length of service.

▶ ~~If a~~ A child ~~is~~ born to parents who are both schizo-phrenic/~~they have~~ has a high chance of being schizophrenic.

▶ A year later someone finally admitted ~~that they were~~ to being involved in the kidnapping.

▶ I was taught that no one who wanted to reach heaven could escape the fires of purgatory. ~~if they wanted to reach heaven.~~

John found himself surrounded by students who were returning to college after an absence of more than fifteen years, and they shared his nervousness. No one knew what changes they should expect. Because Alice and David had been in the same situation last year, Dean Shell asked each of them to share their experiences during an orientation workshop. Neither John nor the other older students allowed his schedule to interfere with the workshop.

David mentioned that the biggest surprise for him had been the extensive use of computers. Fifteen years ago, he recalled, a math student rarely did their homework on a computer. Now, he said, no one has to do their assignments without the help of a software program. David asked the audience if it remembered erasable bond paper and correction tape, and they groaned, recalling the frustration of typing term papers. Now, said David, a student can write their papers in the campus computer labs.

Alice said that a returning student would also be surprised when they saw how the course content had changed. Every department, she said, had found their own way of incorporating the work of women and minorities in their courses. And almost all the departments had pooled their resources to create interdisciplinary courses. A student shouldn't be surprised, Alice said, to find a novel assigned in their sociology class or an oral history project featured in their English class. A final surprise, Alice noted, is the extent to which writing is now emphasized across the curriculum—in the sciences, the social sciences, and even math.

After hearing David and Alice share their positive experience, the audience felt that many of its fears were unfounded, and they looked forward to the coming semesters.

EXERCISE 22-3

Look through a draft-in-progress for problems with pronoun-antecedent agreement, using the chart on pages 240–241. When revising problem sentences, avoid sexist language.

EXERCISE 22 – 4

Like subject-verb agreement, pronoun-antecedent agreement causes occasional problems for most writers. Look through your past writings and analyze the cause of each instance of faulty pronoun-antecedent agreement. Also take a look at your revision strategies and compare them with the suggestions on page 241. Have you usually selected the most effective method of revision?

23

Make pronoun references clear.

Pronouns substitute for nouns; they are a kind of shorthand. In a sentence like *After Andrew intercepted the ball, he kicked it as hard as he could,* the pronouns *he* and *it* substitute for the nouns *Andrew* and *ball.* The word a pronoun refers to is called its *antecedent.*

23a Avoid ambiguous or remote pronoun reference.

Ambiguous pronoun reference occurs when the pronoun could refer to two possible antecedents.

▶ *The pitcher broke when Gloria set it*
~~When Gloria set the pitcher~~ on the glass-topped table/. it
broke.

▶ Tom told James *"You have* ~~that he had~~ won the lottery.*"*

What broke — the table or the pitcher? Who won the lottery — Tom or James? The revisions eliminate the ambiguity.

Remote pronoun reference occurs when a pronoun is too far away from its antecedent for easy reading.

▶ After the court ordered my ex-husband to pay child support, he refused. Approximately eight months later, we were back in court. This time the court ordered him to make payments directly to the Support and Collections Unit, which would in turn pay me. For the first six months I received regular payments, but then they stopped. Again ~~he~~ *my ex-husband* was summoned to appear in court; he did not respond.

The pronoun *he* was too distant from its antecedent, *ex-husband*, which appeared several sentences earlier.

23b Generally, avoid broad reference of *this, that, which,* and *it.*

For clarity, the pronouns *this, that, which,* and *it* should ordinarily refer to specific antecedents rather than to whole ideas or sentences. When a pronoun's reference is needlessly broad, either replace the pronoun with a noun or supply an antecedent to which the pronoun clearly refers.

▶ More and more often, especially in large cities, we are finding ourselves victims of serious crimes. We learn to accept ~~this~~ *our fate* with minor gripes and groans.

For clarity the writer substituted a noun (*fate*) for the pronoun *this,* which referred broadly to the idea expressed in the preceding sentence.

▶ Romeo and Juliet were both too young to have acquired
a fact
much wisdom, which accounts for their rash actions.
        ∧

The writer added an antecedent (*fact*) that the pronoun *which* clearly refers to.

EXCEPTION: Many writers view broad reference as acceptable when the pronoun refers clearly to the sense of an entire clause.

> If you pick up a starving dog and make him prosperous, he will not bite you. This is the principal difference between a dog and a man.
> —Mark Twain

23c Do not use a pronoun to refer to an implied antecedent.

A pronoun must refer to a specific antecedent, not to a word that is implied but not present in the sentence.

the braids
▶ After braiding Ann's hair, Sue decorated ~~them~~ with ribbons.
                                           ∧

The pronoun *them* referred to Ann's braids (implied by the term *braiding*), but the word *braids* did not appear in the sentence.

Modifiers, such as possessives, cannot serve as antecedents. A modifier may strongly imply the noun that the pronoun might logically refer to, but it is not itself that noun.

Euripides
▶ In ~~Euripides'~~ *Medea*, ~~he~~ describes the plight of a woman
                              ∧
rejected by her husband.

The pronoun *he* cannot refer logically to the possessive modifier *Euripides'*. The revision substitutes the noun *Euripides* for the pronoun *he*, thereby eliminating the problem.

23d Avoid the indefinite use of *they, it,* and *you.*

Do not use the pronoun *they* to refer indefinitely to persons who have not been specifically mentioned. *They* should always refer to a specific antecedent.

▶ Sometimes a list of ways to save energy is included with the
      the gas company suggests
  gas bill. For example, ∧~~they suggest~~ setting a moderate

  temperature for the hot water heater.

The word *it* should not be used indefinitely in constructions such as "It is said on television. . . ." or "In the article it says that. . . ."

  The
▶ ~~In the~~ report ~~it~~ points out that lifting the ban on Compound
  ∧

  1080 would prove detrimental, possibly even fatal, to the

  bald eagle.

The pronoun *you* is appropriate when the writer is addressing the reader directly: *Once you have kneaded the dough, let it rise in a warm place for at least twenty-five minutes.* (See page 49.) Except in very informal contexts, however, the indefinite *you* (meaning "anyone in general") is inappropriate.

    one doesn't
▶ In Ethiopia ~~you don't~~ need much property to be considered
    ∧
  well-off.

If the pronoun *one* seems too stilted, the writer might recast the sentence: *In Ethiopia, a person doesn't need much property to be considered well-off.*

23e To refer to persons, use *who, whom,* or *whose,* not *that* or *which.*

In most contexts, use *who, whom,* or *whose* to refer to persons, *that* or *which* to refer to animals or things. Although *that* is occasionally used to refer to persons, it is more polite to use a form of *who. Which* is reserved only for animals or things, so it is impolite to use it to refer to persons.

▶ When he heard about my seven children, four of ~~which~~ *whom* lived

at home, Gill smiled and said, "I love children."

▶ Fans wondered how an out-of-shape old man ~~that~~ *who* walked

with a limp could play football.

NOTE: Occasionally *whose* may be used to refer to animals and things to avoid the awkward *of which* construction.

▶ It is a tree ~~the~~ name ~~of which~~ *whose* I have forgotten.

EXERCISE 23–1

Edit the following sentences to correct errors in pronoun reference. In some cases you will need to decide on an antecedent that the pronoun might logically refer to. Revisions of lettered sentences appear in the back of the book. Example:

Following the breakup of AT&T, many other companies

began to offer long-distance phone service. ~~This~~ *The competition* has led to

lower long-distance rates.

a. The detective removed the blood-stained shawl from the body and then photographed it.

b. In Professor Johnson's class, you are lucky to earn a C.

c. Satanism is a serious problem in our country. Their rites are grotesque perversions of many of Christianity's sacred rituals.

d. The Comanche braves' lifestyle was particularly violent; they gained respect for their skill as warriors.

e. All students can secure parking permits from the campus police office; they are open from 8 A.M. until 8 P.M.

1. The racetrack is well equipped for emergencies. They even have an ambulance at the track on racing days.

2. Many people believe that the polygraph test is highly reliable if you employ a licensed examiner.

3. We expected the concert to last for at least two hours. Since the average ticket sells for twenty dollars, this was not being unrealistic.

4. In Camilla's autobiography, she revealed the story behind her short stay in prison.

5. In the encyclopedia it states that male moths can smell female moths from several miles away.

6. When Aunt Harriet put the cake on the table, it collapsed.

7. Employees are beginning to take advantage of the company's athletic facilities. They offer squash and tennis courts, a small track, and several trampolines.

8. Be sure to visit Istanbul's bazaar, where they sell everything from Persian rugs to electronic calculators.

9. If an accountant makes errors regularly, it will cause him or her to be put on probation.

10. My favorite newscasters are those which reveal their point of view.

24

Use personal pronouns and nouns in the proper case.

The personal pronouns in the following chart change what is known as case form according to their grammatical function in a sentence. Pronouns functioning as subjects (or subject complements) appear in the *subjective* case; those functioning as objects appear in the *objective* case; and those showing ownership appear in the *possessive* case.

	SUBJECTIVE CASE	OBJECTIVE CASE	POSSESSIVE CASE
SINGULAR	I	me	my
	you	you	your
	he/she/it	him/her/it	his/her/its
PLURAL	we	us	our
	you	you	your
	they	them	their

Pronouns in the subjective and objective cases are frequently confused. Most of the rules in this section specify when to use one or the other of these cases (*I* or *me*, *he* or *him*, and so on). Rule 24g details a special use of pronouns and nouns in the possessive case.

24a Use the subjective case (*I, you, he, she, it, we, they*) for subjects and subject complements.

When personal pronouns are used as subjects, ordinarily your ear will tell you the correct pronoun. Problems sometimes arise, however, with compound word groups containing a pronoun, so it is not always safe to trust your ear.

▶ Joel ran away from home because his stepfather and ~~him~~ *he*

had quarreled.

His stepfather and he is the subject of the verb *had quarreled*. If we strip away the words *his stepfather and*, the correct pronoun becomes clear: *he had quarreled* (not *him had quarreled*).

When a pronoun is used as a subject complement (a word following a linking verb), your ear may mislead you, since the incorrect form is frequently heard in casual speech. (See subject complement, 48b.)

> *she.*
> ▶ Sandra confessed that the artist was ~~her.~~
>   ^

The pronoun *she* functions as a subject complement with the linking verb *was*. In formal, written English, subject complements must be in the subjective case. If your ear rejects *artist was she* as too stilted, try rewriting the sentence: *Sandra confessed that she was the artist.*

24b Use the objective case (*me, you, him, her, it, us, them*) for all objects.

When a personal pronoun is used as a direct object, an indirect object, or the object of a preposition, ordinarily your ear will lead you to the correct pronoun. When an object is compound, however, you may occasionally become confused.

> ▶ Janice was indignant when she realized that the salesclerk
>   *her.*
>   was insulting her mother and ~~she.~~
>   ^

Her mother and her is the direct object of the verb *was insulting.* Strip away the words *her mother and* to hear the correct pronoun: *was insulting her* (not *was insulting she*).

> *her*
> ▶ Father Minnorra gave Dorrie and ~~she~~ each a white flower.
>   ^

Dorrie and her is the indirect object of the verb *gave.* We would not say *gave she a white flower.*

> *me*
> ▶ Geoffrey went with my family and ~~I~~ to King's Dominion.
>   ^

Me is the object of the preposition *with.* We would not say *Geoffrey went with I.*

When in doubt about the correct pronoun, some writers try to avoid making the choice by using a reflexive pronoun such as *myself*. Such evasions are nonstandard, even though they are used by some educated persons.

▶ The Egyptian cab driver gave my husband and ~~myself~~ *me* some

good tips on traveling in North Africa.

My husband and me is the indirect object of the verb *gave*. For correct uses of *myself*, see the Glossary of Usage.

24c Put an appositive and the word to which it refers in the same case.

Appositives are noun phrases that rename nouns or pronouns. A pronoun in an appositive has the same function (usually subject or object) as the word(s) the appositive renames.

▶ At the drama festival, two actors, Christina and ~~me,~~ *I,* were

selected to do the last scene of *King Lear*.

The appositive *Christina and I* renames the subject, *actors*.

▶ The college interviewed only two applicants for the job,
Professor Stevens and ~~I.~~ *me.*

The appositive *Professor Stevens and me* renames the direct object *applicants*.

24d In elliptical constructions following *than* or *as*, choose the pronoun that expresses your meaning.

In an elliptical construction, words are omitted yet understood. When an elliptical construction follows a comparison beginning with *than* or *as*, your choice of a pronoun will depend on your intended meaning. Consider, for example, the difference in meaning between these sentences:

My husband likes football better than I.

My husband likes football better than me.

Finish each sentence mentally and its meaning becomes clear: *My husband likes football better than I [do]. My husband likes football better than [he likes] me.*

▶ Even though he is sometimes ridiculed by the other boys,
  they.
  Norman is much better off than ~~them.~~
                                    ∧

They is the subject of the verb *are*, which is understood: *Norman is much better off than they [are.]* If the correct English seems too formal, you can always add the verb.

                                                  her.
▶ We respected no other candidate as much as ~~she.~~
                                                  ∧

This sentence means that we respected no other candidate as much as *we respected her. Her* is the direct object of an understood verb.

24e When deciding whether *we* or *us* should precede a noun, choose the pronoun that would be appropriate if the noun were omitted.

  We
▶ ~~Us~~ tenants would rather fight than move.
  ∧

                                  us
▶ Management is short-changing ~~we~~ tenants.
                                  ∧

No one would say *Us would rather fight than move* or *Management is short-changing we.*

24f Use the objective case for subjects and objects of infinitives.

An infinitive is the word *to* followed by the base form of a verb. (See 49c.) Subjects of infinitives are an exception to the rule that subjects must be in the subjective case. Whenever an infinitive has a subject, it must be in the objective case. Objects of infinitives also are in the objective case.

▶ The crowd expected Chris and ~~I~~ *me* to defeat Tracy and ~~he~~ *him* in the doubles championship.

> *Chris and me* is the subject of the infinitive *to defeat; Tracy and him* is the direct object of the infinitive.

24g Use the possessive case to modify a gerund.

A pronoun that modifies a gerund or a gerund phrase should appear in the possessive case (*my, our, your, his/her/its, their*). A gerund is a verb form ending in *-ing* that functions as a noun. Gerunds frequently appear in phrases, in which case the whole gerund phrase functions as a noun. (See 49c.)

▶ My father always tolerated ~~us~~ *our* talking after the lights were out.

> The possessive pronoun *our* modifies the gerund *talking.*

Nouns as well as pronouns may modify gerunds. To form the possessive case of a noun, use an apostrophe and an *-s* (*a victim's rights*) or just an apostrophe (*victims' rights*). (See 36a.)

▶ We had to pay a fifty-dollar fine for ~~Brenda~~ driving without a
permit.

Brenda's (inserted above, with caret)

The possessive noun *Brenda's* modifies the gerund phrase *driving without a permit.*

Gerund phrases should not be confused with participial phrases, which function as adjectives, not as nouns: *We saw Brenda driving a yellow convertible.* Here *driving a yellow convertible* is a participial phrase modifying the noun *Brenda.* (See 49c.)

Sometimes the choice between the objective or the possessive case conveys a subtle difference in meaning:

> We watched *them* dancing.

> We watched *their* dancing.

In the first sentence the emphasis is on the people; *dancing* is a participle modifying the pronoun *them.* In the second sentence the emphasis is on the dancing; *dancing* is a gerund, and *their* is a possessive pronoun modifying the gerund.

NOTE: Do not use the possessive if it creates an awkward effect. Try to reword the sentence instead.

AWKWARD	The president agreed to the applications' being reviewed by a faculty committee.
REVISED	The president agreed that the applications could be reviewed by a faculty committee.
REVISED	The president agreed that a faculty committee could review the applications.

EXERCISE 24 – 1

Edit the following sentences to eliminate errors in case. If a sentence is correct, write "correct" after it. Answers to lettered sentences appear in the back of the book. Example:

Grandfather cuts down trees for neighbors much younger
         he.
than ~~him.~~
    ∧

a. My Ethiopian neighbor was puzzled by the dedication of we joggers.
b. Andrea whispered, "Who's there?" and Alfred replied softly that it was he.
c. Sue's husband is ten years older than her.
d. The winners, Julie and him, were unable to attend the awards ceremony.
e. My father always tolerated us whispering after the lights were out.

1. Doctors should take more seriously what us patients say about our treatment.
2. Grandfather said he would give anything to live nearer to Paulette and me.
3. Maxine did not do well on her medical boards because her and her tutor had spent the night before the exam worrying rather than reviewing.
4. A professional counselor advised the division chief that Marco, Fidelia, and myself should be allowed to apply for the opening.
5. Because of last night's fire, we are fed up with him drinking and smoking.
6. The governor granted David and I pardons on January 2, 1990.
7. The swirling cyclone caused he and his horse to race for shelter.
8. The four candidates — Paul, Erica, Tracy, and I — will participate in tonight's televised debate.
9. During the testimony the witness pointed directly at the defendant and announced that the thief was him.
10. When in Aruba, Marlena bought several shell paintings for Donelle and I.

Reviewing your writing for problems with pronoun case

Look for the most common trouble spots; where possible, apply a test for the correct pronoun.

COMPOUND WORD GROUPS (24a, 24b)

Test: Mentally strip away the rest of the compound word group.

> While diving for pearls, [Ikiko and] *she* found a treasure chest full of gold bars.

> The most traumatic experience for [her father and] *me* occurred long after her operation.

PRONOUN AFTER *IS, ARE, WAS,* OR *WERE* (24a)

In formal English, remember to use the subjective-case pronouns *I, he, she, we,* and *they* after the linking verbs *is, are, was,* and *were.*

> The panel was shocked to learn that the undercover agent was *she.*

APPOSITIVES (24c)

Test: Mentally strip away the word group that the appositive renames.

> [The chief strategists], Dr. Bell and *I,* could not agree on a plan.

> The company could afford to send only [one of two researchers], Dr. Davis or *me,* to Paris.

Pronoun case (continued)

PRONOUN AFTER *THAN* OR *AS* (24d)

Test: Mentally complete the sentence.

> The supervisor claimed that she was much more experienced than *I* [was].

> Gloria admitted that she liked Greg's twin better than [she liked] *him*.

WE OR *US* BEFORE A NOUN (24e)

Test: Mentally delete the noun.

> *We* [women] really have come a long way.

> Sadly, discrimination against *us* [women] occurs in most cultures.

PRONOUN BEFORE OR AFTER AN INFINITIVE (24f)

Remember that both subjects and objects of infinitives take the objective case.

> Ms. Wilson asked John and *me* to drive the senator and *her* to the airport.

PRONOUN OR NOUN BEFORE A GERUND (24g)

Remember to use the possessive case when a pronoun modifies a gerund.

> There is only a small chance of *his* bleeding excessively because of this procedure.

25

Use *who* and *whom* in the proper case.

The choice between *who* and *whom* (or *whoever* and *whom-ever*) occurs primarily in subordinate clauses and in questions. *Who* and *whoever*, subjective-case pronouns, are used for subjects and subject complements. *Whom* and *whomever*, objective-case pronouns, are used for objects. (For more about pronoun case, see 24.)

25a In subordinate clauses, use *who* and *whoever* for subjects or subject complements, *whom* and *whomever* for all objects.

When *who* and *whom* (or *whoever* and *whomever*) appear in subordinate clauses, their case is determined by their function *within the clause they introduce.* To choose the correct pronoun, you must isolate the subordinate clause and then decide how the pronoun functions within it. (See subordinate clauses, 49b.)

In the following two examples, the pronouns *who* and *whoever* function as the subjects of the clauses they introduce.

▶ The prize goes to the runner ~~whom~~ *who* collects the most points.

The subordinate clause is *who collects the most points.* The verb of the clause is *collects*, and its subject is *who*.

▶ He tells that story to ~~whomever~~ *whoever* will listen.

The writer selected the pronoun *whomever*, thinking that it was the object of the preposition *to*. However, the object of the preposition is the entire subordinate clause *whoever will listen*. The verb of the clause is *will listen*, and its subject is *whoever*.

Who occasionally functions as a subject complement in a subordinate clause. Subject complements occur with linking verbs (usually *be, am, is, are, was, were, being,* and *been*). (See 48b.)

▶ The receptionist knows ~~whom~~ *who* you are.

The subordinate clause is *who you are.* Its subject is *you*, and its subject complement is *who*.

When functioning as an object in a subordinate clause, *whom* (or *whomever*) appears out of order, before both the subject and the verb. To choose the correct pronoun, you must mentally restructure the clause.

▶ You will work with our senior industrial engineers, ~~who~~ *whom* you will meet later.

The subordinate clause is *whom you will meet later.* The subject of the clause is *you*, the verb is *will meet*, and *whom* is the direct object of the verb. This becomes clear if you mentally restructure the clause: *you will meet whom.*

When functioning as the object of a preposition in a subordinate clause, *whom* is often separated from its preposition.

▶ The tutor ~~who~~ *whom* I was assigned to was very supportive.

Whom is the object of the preposition *to*. That preposition can be moved in front of its object to make smoother reading: *The tutor to whom I was assigned was very supportive.*

NOTE: Inserted expressions such as *they know, I think,* and *she says* should be ignored in determining the case of a relative pronoun.

▶ All of the show-offs, bullies, and tough guys in school want
to take on a big guy ~~whom~~ *who* they know will not hurt them.

Who is the subject of *will hurt*, not the object of *know*.

25b In questions, use *who* and *whoever* for subjects, *whom* and *whomever* for all objects.

When *who* and *whom* (or *whoever* and *whomever*) are used to open questions, their case is determined by their function within the question. In the following example, *who* functions as the subject of the question.

▶ ~~Whom~~ *Who* is responsible for this dastardly deed?

When *whom* functions as the object of a verb or the object of a preposition in a question, it appears out of normal order. To choose the correct pronoun, you must mentally restructure the question.

▶ ~~Who~~ *Whom* did the committee select?

Whom is the direct object of the verb *did select*. To choose the correct pronoun, restructure the question: *The committee did select whom?*

▶ ~~Who~~ *Whom* did you enter into the contract with?

Whom is the object of the preposition *with*, as is clear if you restructure the question: *You did enter into the contract with whom?*

Reviewing your writing for problems with who *and* whom

Look for common trouble spots; where possible, apply a test for correct usage.

IN A SUBORDINATE CLAUSE

Isolate the subordinate clause. Then read its subject, verb, and any objects, restructuring the clause if necessary. Some writers find it helpful to substitute *he* for *who* and *him* for *whom*.

> Samuels hoped to become the business partner of (whoever/whomever) found the treasure.
>
> Test: . . . *whoever* found the treasure. [. . . *he* found the treasure.]
>
> Ada always seemed to be bestowing a favor on (whoever/ whomever) she worked for.
>
> Test: . . . she worked for *whomever*. [. . . she worked for *him*.]

IN A QUESTION

Read the subject, verb, and any objects, rearranging the sentence structure if necessary.

> (Who/Whom) conferred with Roosevelt and Stalin at Yalta in 1945?
>
> Test: *Who* conferred . . . ?
>
> (Who/Whom) did the committee nominate?
>
> Test: The committee did nominate *whom*?

USAGE NOTE: In spoken English *who* is frequently used to open a question even when it functions as an object: *Who did Joe replace?* Although some readers will accept such constructions in informal written English, it is safer to use the correct form *whom: Whom did Joe replace?*

EXERCISE 25 – 1

Edit the following sentences to eliminate errors in the use of *who* and *whom* (or *whoever* and *whomever*). If a sentence is correct, write "correct" after it. Answers to lettered sentences appear in the back of the book. Example:

> *whom*
> What is the name of the person ~~who~~ you are sponsoring for
>   ∧
> membership in the club?

a. In his first production of *Hamlet,* who did Laurence Olivier replace?

b. Who was Martin Luther King's mentor?

c. Datacall allows you to talk to whoever needs you no matter where you are in the building.

d. Some group leaders cannot handle the pressure; they give whomever makes the most noise most of their attention.

e. One of the women who Johnson hired became the most successful lawyer in the agency.

1. The shift supervisor will ask you to relieve whoever needs a break.

2. When medicine is scarce and expensive, physicians must give it to whomever has the best chance to survive.

3. Now that you have seen both fighters in action, who in your opinion will win the championship?

4. Mr. Barnes is the elementary school teacher who I recall most fondly.

5. Who was accused of receiving Mafia funds?

6. They will become business partners with whomever is willing to contribute to the company's coffers.
7. The only interstate travelers who get pulled over for speeding are the ones whom cannot afford a radar detector.
8. The elderly woman who I was asked to take care of was a clever, delightful companion.
9. The teacher often calls on whoever does not raise a hand.
10. Who should Howard see about the tickets?

EXERCISE 25–2

Edit the following paragraph to correct errors in case. (See 24 and 25, especially the charts on pages 256 and 261.)

After our freshman year, my friend Kim and me were trying to decide if we wanted to major in business administration. Dr. Bane, an economics professor who we had first semester, agreed to talk with Kim and I. At first, Kim did not seem as interested in a business career as I, but then Dr. Bane explained to us neophytes how many options are open to business graduates. Neither Kim nor myself had realized that the possibilities are so interesting. Dr. Bane told us about a recent graduate whom he felt was one of his most promising students: she owns and manages her own bookstore. Another recent graduate, who Dr. Bane almost flunked senior year, is a buyer for a chain of clothing stores. Dr. Bane was surprised at him becoming successful so soon, but he said there's a niche for everyone in business. Dr. Bane cautioned us with a story about another graduate who was interested only in whomever would pay her the most. "Money isn't everything," Dr. Bane said. "Your being well matched to your work is more important than earning large sums of money." He then invited us, both Kim and I, to his senior seminar in which students discuss their internships. When we thanked Dr. Bane for his advice, he told Kim and me that it probably would not be hard for we too to find our niche in business.

26

Choose adjectives and adverbs with care.

Adjectives ordinarily modify nouns or pronouns; occasionally they function as subject complements following linking verbs. Adverbs modify verbs, adjectives, or other adverbs. (See 47d and 47e.)

Many adverbs are formed by adding -*ly* to adjectives (*formal, formally; smooth, smoothly*). But don't assume that all words ending in -*ly* are adverbs or that all adverbs end in -*ly*. Some adjectives end in -*ly* (*lovely, friendly*) and some adverbs don't (*always, here, there*). When in doubt, consult a dictionary.

26a Use adverbs, not adjectives, to modify verbs, adjectives, and adverbs.

When adverbs modify verbs (or verbals), they nearly always answer the question When? Where? How? Why? Under what conditions? How often? or To what degree? When adverbs modify adjectives or other adverbs, they usually qualify or intensify the meaning of the word they modify. (See 47e.)

The incorrect use of adjectives in place of adverbs to modify verbs occurs primarily in casual or nonstandard speech.

▶ The arrangement worked out ~~perfect~~ for everyone.
                       perfectly

▶ We discovered that the patients hadn't been bathed ~~regular.~~
                                                regularly.

Perfect and *regular* are adjectives, so they should not be used to modify the verbs *worked* and *had been bathed*.

The incorrect use of the adjective *good* in place of the adverb *well* is especially common in casual and nonstandard speech.

▶ We were surprised to hear that Louise had done so ~~good~~ *well* on

the CPA exam.

> The adverb *well* (not the adjective *good*) should be used to modify the verb *had done*.

NOTE: The word *well* is an adjective when it means "healthy," "satisfactory," or "fortunate": *I am very well, thank you. All is well. It is just as well.*

Adjectives are sometimes used incorrectly to modify adjectives or adverbs.

▶ For a man eighty years old, Joe plays golf ~~real~~ *really* well.

▶ We were ~~awful~~ *awfully* sorry to hear about your uncle's death.

> Only adverbs can be used to modify adjectives or other adverbs. *Really* intensifies the meaning of the adverb *well*, and *awfully* intensifies the meaning of the adjective *sorry*. The writers could of course substitute other intensifiers: *very well*, for example, or *terribly sorry*.

ESL NOTE: Placement of adjectives and adverbs can be a tricky matter for second language speakers. See 31c.

26b Use adjectives, not adverbs, as complements.

Adjectives ordinarily precede nouns, but they can also function as subject complements or as object complements.

Subject complements

A subject complement follows a linking verb and completes the meaning of the subject. (See 48b.) When an adjective functions as a subject complement, it describes the subject.

Justice is *blind.*

Problems can arise with verbs such as *smell, taste, look,* and *feel,* which sometimes, but not always, function as linking verbs. If the word following one of these verbs describes the subject, use an adjective; if it modifies the verb, use an adverb.

ADJECTIVE The detective looked *cautious.*

ADVERB The detective looked *cautiously* for fingerprints.

The adjective *cautious* describes the detective; the adverb *cautiously* modifies the verb *looked.*

Linking verbs suggest states of being, not actions. Notice, for example, the different meanings of *looked* in the preceding examples. To look cautious suggests the state of being cautious; to look cautiously is to perform an action in a cautious way.

▶ The lilacs in our backyard smell especially ~~sweetly~~ this year.
      (sweet)

▶ Lori looked ~~well~~ in her new raincoat.
      (good)

The verbs *smell* and *looked* suggest states of being, not actions. Therefore, they should be followed by adjectives, not adverbs. (Contrast with action verbs: *We smelled the flowers. Lori looked for her raincoat.*)

ESL NOTE: Participles (such as *boring, bored*) used as subject complements can cause problems for second language speakers. See 31d.

Object complements

An object complement follows a direct object and completes its meaning. (See 48b.) When an adjective functions as an object complement, it describes the direct object.

> Sorrow makes us *wise.*

Object complements occur with verbs such as *call, consider, create, find, keep,* and *make.* When a modifier follows the direct object of one of these verbs, check to see whether it functions as an adjective describing the direct object or as an adverb modifying the verb.

ADJECTIVE   The referee called the plays *perfect.*

ADVERB   The referee called the plays *perfectly.*

The first sentence means that the referee considered the plays to be perfect; the second means that the referee did an excellent job of calling the plays.

▶ God created all men and women ~~equally.~~ *equal.*

> The adjective *equal* is an object complement describing the direct object *men and women.*

26c Use comparatives and superlatives with care.

Most adjectives and adverbs have three forms: the positive, the comparative, and the superlative.

POSITIVE	COMPARATIVE	SUPERLATIVE
soft	softer	softest
fast	faster	fastest
careful	more careful	most careful
bad	worse	worst
good	better	best

Comparative versus superlative

Use the comparative to compare two things, the superlative
to compare three or more.

▶ Which of these two brands of toothpaste is ~~best~~? *better*

▶ Though Shaw and Jackson are impressive, Hobbs is the
~~more~~ qualified of the three candidates running for mayor. *most*

Form of comparatives and superlatives

To form comparatives and superlatives of most one- and two-
syllable adjectives, use the endings *-er* and *-est: smooth,
smoother, smoothest; easy, easier, easiest.* With longer adjectives, use *more* and *most* (or *less* and *least* for downward
comparisons): *exciting, more exciting, most exciting; helpful,
less helpful, least helpful.*

Some one-syllable adverbs take the endings *-er* and *-est*
(*fast, faster, fastest*), but longer adverbs and all of those ending in *-ly* form the comparative and superlative with *more*
and *most* (or *less* and *least*).

The comparative and superlative forms of the following
adjectives and adverbs are irregular: *good, better, best; bad,
worse, worst; badly, worse, worst.*

▶ The Kirov was the ~~talentedest~~ ballet company we had ever *most talented*

seen.

▶ Lloyd's luck couldn't have been ~~worser~~ than David's. *worse*

Double comparatives or superlatives

Do not use double comparatives or superlatives. When you
have added *-er* or *-est* to an adjective or adverb, do not also
use *more* or *most* (or *less* or *least*).

▶ Of all her family, Julia is the ~~most~~ happiest about the move.

▶ That is the most ~~inanest~~ *inane* joke I have ever heard.

Absolute concepts

Avoid expressions such as *more straight, less perfect, very round,* and *most unique.* Either something is *unique* or it isn't. It is illogical to suggest that absolute concepts come in degrees.

▶ That is the most ~~unique~~ *unusual* wedding gown I have ever seen.

▶ The painting would have been even more ~~priceless~~ *valuable* had it been signed.

26d   Avoid double negatives.

Standard English allows two negatives only if a positive meaning is intended: *The orchestra was not unhappy with its performance.* Double negatives used to emphasize negation are nonstandard.

Negative modifiers such as *never, no,* and *not* should not be paired with other negative modifiers or with negative words such as *neither, none, no one, nobody,* and *nothing.*

▶ Management is not doing ~~nothing~~ *anything* to see that the trash is picked up.

▶ George won't ~~never~~ *ever* forget that day.

▶ I enjoy living alone because I don't have to answer to ~~nobody.~~ *anybody*

The double negatives *not . . . nothing, won't never,* and *don't . . . nobody* are nonstandard.

The modifiers *hardly*, *barely*, and *scarcely* are considered negatives in standard English, so they should not be used with negatives such as *not*, *no one*, or *never*.

▶ Maxine is so weak she ~~can't~~ *can* hardly climb stairs.

EXERCISE 26 – 1

Edit the following sentences to eliminate errors in the use of adjectives and adverbs. If a sentence is correct, write "correct" after it. Answers to lettered sentences appear in the back of the book. Example:

When I watched Carl run the 440 on Saturday, I was amazed at how ~~good~~ *well* he paced himself.

a. My mechanic showed me exactly where to wrap the wire firm around the muffler.
b. All of us on the team felt badly about our performance.
c. My mother thinks that Carmen is the most pleasant of the twins.
d. The vaulting box, commonly known as the horse, is the easiest of the four pieces of equipment to master.
e. Last Christmas was the most perfect day of my life.

1. When answering the phone, you should speak clearly and courteous.
2. Which restaurant do you think makes the better hamburger, McDonald's, Burger King, or Wendy's?
3. We wanted a hunting dog. We didn't care if he smelled badly, but we really did not want him to smell bad.
4. We were real surprised to hear that Uncle Bob had been nominated for a Nobel Prize.
5. The union contract may make all first-year teachers equal, but it does not make them equally effective.
6. The manager must see that the office runs smooth and efficient.
7. Professor Brown's public praise of my performance on the exam made me feel a little strangely.

8. Of all my relatives, Uncle Robert is the most cleverest.
9. The hall closet is so filled with ski equipment that the door won't hardly close.
10. Marcia performed very well at her Drama Club audition.

27

Choose standard English verb forms.

In nonstandard English, spoken by those who share a regional or cultural heritage, verb forms sometimes differ from those of standard English. In writing, use standard English verb forms unless you are quoting nonstandard speech or using nonstandard forms for literary effect. (See 17d.)

Except for the verb *be*, all verbs in English have five forms. The following chart lists the five forms and provides a sample sentence in which each might appear.

BASE FORM	Usually I (*walk, ride*).
PAST TENSE	Yesterday I (*walked, rode*).
PAST PARTICIPLE	I have (*walked, ridden*) many times before.
PRESENT PARTICIPLE	I am (*walking, riding*) right now.
-S FORM	He/she/it (*walks, rides*) regularly.

Both the past-tense and past-participle forms of regular verbs end in *-ed* (*walked, walked*). Irregular verbs form the past tense and past participle in other ways (*rode, ridden*).

The verb *be* has eight forms instead of the usual five: *be, am, is, are, was, were, being, been.*

27a Use the correct forms of irregular verbs.

For all regular verbs, the past-tense and past-participle forms are the same (ending in *-ed* or *-d*), so there is no danger of confusion. This is not true, however, for irregular verbs, such as the following.

BASE FORM	PAST TENSE	PAST PARTICIPLE
go	went	gone
fight	fought	fought
fly	flew	flown

You will find a list of irregular verbs beginning on page 273.

The past-tense form of a verb is used to express action that occurred entirely in the past.

> Last week Chris *went* to Harbor Island.

The past-participle form is used with a helping verb, either with *has, have,* or *had* to form one of the perfect tenses (see 28a) or with *be, am, is, are, was, were, being,* or *been* to form the passive voice (see 28c).

> Betty *has fought* for equal rights for women.

> Kate *was flown* to Bishop Hill to accept the award.

In nonstandard English speech, the past-tense and past-participle forms may differ from those of standard English, as in the following sentences.

> ► Yesterday we ~~seen~~ *saw* an unidentified flying object.

> ► The reality of the situation finally ~~sunk~~ *sank* in.

> The past-tense forms *saw* and *sank* are required.

▶ The driver had apparently ~~fell~~ *fallen* asleep at the wheel.

▶ The teacher asked Dwain if he had ~~did~~ *done* his homework.

Because of the helping verbs, the past-participle forms are required: *had fallen, had done.*

When in doubt about the standard English forms of irregular verbs, consult the following list or look up the base form of the verb in the dictionary, which also lists any irregular forms. (If no additional forms are listed in the dictionary, the verb is regular, not irregular.)

Common irregular verbs

BASE FORM	PAST TENSE	PAST PARTICIPLE
arise	arose	arisen
awake	awoke, awaked	awaked, awoke
be	was, were	been
beat	beat	beaten, beat
become	became	become
begin	began	begun
bend	bent	bent
bite	bit	bitten, bit
blow	blew	blown
break	broke	broken
bring	brought	brought
build	built	built
burst	burst	burst
catch	caught	caught
choose	chose	chosen
cling	clung	clung
come	came	come
cost	cost	cost
deal	dealt	dealt
dig	dug	dug
dive	dived, dove	dived
do	did	done

BASE FORM	PAST TENSE	PAST PARTICIPLE
drag	dragged	dragged
draw	drew	drawn
dream	dreamed, dreamt	dreamed, dreamt
drink	drank	drunk
drive	drove	driven
drown	drowned	drowned
eat	ate	eaten
fall	fell	fallen
fight	fought	fought
find	found	found
fly	flew	flown
forget	forgot	forgotten, forgot
freeze	froze	frozen
get	got	gotten, got
give	gave	given
go	went	gone
grow	grew	grown
hang (suspend)	hung	hung
hang (execute)	hanged	hanged
have	had	had
hear	heard	heard
hide	hid	hidden
hurt	hurt	hurt
keep	kept	kept
know	knew	known
lay (put)	laid	laid
lead	led	led
lend	lent	lent
let (allow)	let	let
lie (recline)	lay	lain
lose	lost	lost
make	made	made
prove	proved	proved, proven
read	read	read
ride	rode	ridden
ring	rang	rung
rise (get up)	rose	risen
run	ran	run
say	said	said

BASE FORM	PAST TENSE	PAST PARTICIPLE
see	saw	seen
send	sent	sent
set (place)	set	set
shake	shook	shaken
shoot	shot	shot
shrink	shrank	shrunk
sing	sang	sung
sink	sank	sunk
sit (be seated)	sat	sat
slay	slew	slain
sleep	slept	slept
speak	spoke	spoken
spin	spun	spun
spring	sprang	sprung
stand	stood	stood
steal	stole	stolen
sting	stung	stung
strike	struck	struck, stricken
swear	swore	sworn
swim	swam	swum
swing	swung	swung
take	took	taken
teach	taught	taught
throw	threw	thrown
wake	woke, waked	waked, woken
wear	wore	worn
wring	wrung	wrung
write	wrote	written

27b Distinguish among the forms of *lie* and *lay*.

Writers and speakers frequently confuse the various forms of *lie* (meaning to recline or rest on a surface) and *lay* (meaning to put or place something). *Lie* is an intransitive verb; it does not take a direct object: *The tax forms lie on the table.* The verb *lay* is transitive; it takes a direct object: *Please lay the tax forms on the coffee table.* (See 48b.)

In addition to confusing the meaning of *lie* and *lay*, writers and speakers are often unfamiliar with the standard English forms of these verbs.

BASE FORM	PAST TENSE	PAST PARTICIPLE	PRESENT PARTICIPLE
lie	lay	lain	lying
lay	laid	laid	laying

▶ Sue was so exhausted that she ~~laid~~ *lay* down for a nap.

The past-tense form of *lie* (to recline) is *lay.*

▶ The patient had ~~laid~~ *lain* in an uncomfortable position all night.

The past-participle form of *lie* (to recline) is *lain.*

▶ Mary ~~lay~~ *laid* the baby on my lap.

The past-tense form of *lay* (to place) is *laid.*

▶ My grandmother's letters were ~~laying~~ *lying* in the corner of the chest.

The present participle of *lie* (to rest on a surface) is *lying.*

EXERCISE 27–1

Edit the following sentences for problems with irregular verbs. If a sentence is correct, write "correct" after it. Answers to lettered sentences appear in the back of the book. Example:

Was it you I ~~seen~~ *saw* last night at the concert?

a. Noticing that my roommate was shivering and looking pale, I rung for the nurse.

b. When I get the urge to exercise, I lay down until it passes.

c. On our way to the airport we realized that Bob had forgotten to pick up our passports from the hotel.

d. The team of engineers watched in horror as the newly built dam bursted and flooded the small valley.

e. The young girl looked soulfully into her mother's eyes as she laid the wheezing puppy on its mat.

1. How many times have you swore to yourself, "I'll diet tomorrow, after one more piece of cheesecake"?

2. Laying there in a bed of wet leaves with mist falling lightly on my face, I could hear Linda call my name, but I never answered, not even to say I was alive.

3. My aunt may be poor, but she has always took care of her family.

4. When Sarah saw Mr. Johnson coming home from the corner store, she ran over to him to see if he had brung her some candy.

5. All parents were asked to send a mat for their children to lay on.

6. Lincoln took good care of his legal clients; the contracts he drew for the Illinois Central Railroad could never be broke.

7. Have you ever dreamed that you were falling from a cliff or flying through the air?

8. I locked my brakes, leaned the motorcycle to the left, and laid it down to keep from slamming into the fence.

9. In her junior year, Cindy run the 440-yard dash in 51.1 seconds.

10. Larry claimed that he had drank a bad soda, but Grandmother suspected the truth.

EXERCISE 27-2

Circle the correct form of each irregular verb in the following paragraphs.

We have (began/begun) writing in math class this semester, and it seems to me that in every class, Ms. Taylor, our instructor, asks me to read what I have (wrote/written). Before the semester (began/begun), I (swore/sworn) that I would study for every math class. The night before our third class, though, my good intentions and I (gone/went) to town with my roommates to find a party. Unprepared for math class the next day, I realized that my night of revelry had left my

mind (froze/frozen). When Ms. Taylor called on me, my heart
(sank/sunk): I was weak in math and weaker in writing. I just
(knew/known) my response was wrong. It was.

However, as the semester has progressed, I have (became/
become) more comfortable writing about math problems. One
reason is that I have (broke/broken) my roommates of their
bad habits, but Ms. Taylor has convinced me that other factors
have contributed too. She says that I learn more about math
if I have (wrote/written) about a problem, and I agree. Last
semester my math grade (fell/fallen) as the problems became
more difficult; this semester, because I have had to write about
the problems, my grade has (rose/risen) steadily.

At the start of every class, Ms. Taylor gives us a problem
to solve and asks us to explain in writing how we solved it and
why we (chose/chosen) the method we did. Even if a problem
has (drove/driven) me crazy, often the correct solution comes
to me when I analyze it in writing. Now I see that math is not
a series of complicated problems with mysterious answers that
are (hid/hidden) from me. The writing I have (did/done) in
math class has helped me understand mathematics, and I
think it has helped my writing too.

27c Use *-s* (or *-es*) endings on present-tense verbs that
have third-person singular subjects.

All singular nouns (*child, tree*) and the pronouns *he, she,*
and *it* are third-person singular; indefinite pronouns such as
everyone and *neither* are also third-person singular. When
the subject of a sentence is third-person singular, its verb
takes an *-s* or *-es* ending in the present tense. (See also 21.)

	SINGULAR		**PLURAL**	
FIRST PERSON	I	know	we	know
SECOND PERSON	you	know	you	know
THIRD PERSON	he/she/it	knows	they	know
	child	knows	parents	know
	everyone	knows		

In nonstandard speech, the *-s* ending required by standard English is sometimes omitted.

▶ Ellen taught him what he ~~know~~ *knows* about the paperwork in this agency.

▶ Sulfur dioxide ~~turn~~ *turns* leaves yellow, ~~dissolve~~ *dissolves* marble, and ~~eat~~ *eats* away iron and steel.

The subjects *he* and *sulfur dioxide* are third-person singular, so the verbs must end in *-s.*

CAUTION: Do not add the *-s* ending to the verb if the subject is not third-person singular.

The writers of the following sentences, knowing they sometimes dropped *-s* endings from verbs, overcorrected by adding the endings where they don't belong.

▶ I prepares program specifications and logic diagrams.

The writer mistakenly concluded that the *-s* ending belongs on present-tense verbs used with *all* singular subjects, not just *third-person* singular subjects. The pronoun *I* is first-person singular, so its verb does not require the *-s.*

▶ The dirt floors requires continual sweeping.

The writer mistakenly thought that the *-s* ending on the verb indicated plurality. The *-s* goes on present-tense verbs used with third-person *singular* subjects.

Has *versus* have

In the present tense, use *has* with third-person singular subjects; all other subjects require *have.*

	SINGULAR		**PLURAL**	
FIRST PERSON	I	have	we	have
SECOND PERSON	you	have	you	have
THIRD PERSON	he/she/it	has	they	have

In some dialects, *have* is used with all subjects. But standard English requires *has* for third-person singular subjects.

▶ This respected musician almost always ~~have~~ *has* a message to

convey in his work.

▶ As for the retirement income program, it ~~have~~ *has* finally been

established.

The subjects *musician* and *it* are third-person singular, so the verb should be *has* in each case.

CAUTION: Do not use *has* if the subject is not third-person singular. The writers of the following sentences were aware that they often wrote *have* when standard English requires *has*. Here they are using what appears to them to be the "more correct" form, but in an inappropriate context.

▶ My business law classes ~~has~~ *have* helped me to understand more

about contracts.

▶ I ~~has~~ *have* much to be thankful for.

The subjects of these sentences — *classes* and *I* — are third-person plural and first-person singular, so standard English requires *have*. *Has* is used with third-person singular subjects only.

Does *versus* do *and* doesn't *versus* don't

In the present tense, use *does* and *doesn't* with third-person singular subjects; all other subjects require *do* and *don't*.

	SINGULAR		**PLURAL**	
FIRST PERSON	I	do/don't	we	do/don't
SECOND PERSON	you	do/don't	you	do/don't
THIRD PERSON	he/she/it	does/doesn't	they	do/don't

The use of *don't* instead of the standard English *doesn't* is a feature of many dialects in the United States. Use of *do* for *does* is rarer.

▶ Grandfather really ~~don't~~ *doesn't* have a place to call home.

▶ ~~Do~~ *Does* she know the correct procedure for setting up the experiment?

Grandfather and *she* are third-person singular, so the verbs should be *doesn't* and *does.*

Am, is, *and* are; was *and* were

The verb *be* has three forms in the present tense (*am, is, are*) and two in the past tense (*was, were*). Use *am* and *was* with first-person singular subjects; use *is* and *was* with third-person singular subjects. With all other subjects, use *are* and *were*.

	SINGULAR		**PLURAL**	
FIRST PERSON	I	am/was	we	are/were
SECOND PERSON	you	are/were	you	are/were
THIRD PERSON	he/she/it	is/was	they	are/were

> Judy wanted to borrow Tim's notes, but she ~~were~~ too shy to
  ^was

  ask for them.

The subject *she* is third-person singular, so the verb should be
was.

27d Do not omit *-ed* endings on verbs.

Speakers who do not fully pronounce *-ed* endings sometimes
omit them unintentionally in writing. Failure to pronounce
-ed endings is common in many dialects and in informal
speech even in standard English. In the following frequently
used words and phrases, for example, the *-ed* ending is not
always fully pronounced.

advised	developed	prejudiced	stereotyped
asked	fixed	pronounced	used to
concerned	frightened	supposed to	

When a verb is regular, both the past tense and the past
participle are formed by adding *-ed* to the base form of the
verb. (See 27a.)

Past tense

Use an *-ed* or *-d* ending to express the past tense of regular
verbs. The past tense is used when the action occurred entirely in the past.

> Over the weekend, Ed ~~fix~~ his brother's skateboard and tuned
  ^fixed

  up his mother's 1955 Thunderbird.

> Last summer my counselor ~~advise~~ me to ask my chemistry
  ^advised

  instructor for help.

Past participles

Past participles are used in three ways: (1) following *have, has,* or *had* to form one of the perfect tenses; (2) following *be, am, is, are, was, were, being,* or *been* to form the passive voice; and (3) as adjectives modifying nouns or pronouns. The perfect tenses are listed on page 287, and the passive voice is discussed in 28c. For a discussion of participles functioning as adjectives, see 49c.

▶ Robin has ~~ask~~ me to go to California with her.
    asked

Has asked is present perfect tense (*have* or *has* followed by a past participle).

▶ Though it is not a new phenomenon, wife battery is ~~publicize~~ more frequently than before.
    publicized

Is publicized is a verb in the passive voice (a form of *be* followed by a past participle).

▶ All aerobics classes end in a cool-down period to stretch ~~tighten~~ muscles.
    tightened

The past participle *tightened* functions as an adjective modifying the noun *muscles.*

27e Do not omit needed verbs.

Although standard English allows some linking verbs and helping verbs to be contracted, at least in informal contexts, it does not allow them to be omitted.

Linking verbs, used to link subjects to subject complements, are frequently a form of *be: be, am, is, are, was, were, being, been.* (See 48b.) Some of these forms may be contracted (*I'm, she's, we're*), but they should not be omitted altogether.

▶ When we~~,~~ out there in the evening, we often hear the ^ *are*

    helicopters circling above.

▶ Alvin a man who can defend himself. ^ *is*

Helping verbs, used with main verbs, include forms of *be, do,* and *have* or the words *can, will, shall, could, would, should, may, might,* and *must.* (See 47c.) Some helping verbs may be contracted (*he's leaving, we'll celebrate, they've been told*), but they should not be omitted altogether.

▶ We been in Chicago since last Thursday. ^ *have*

▶ Do you know someone who be good for the job? ^ *would*

EXERCISE 27–3

Edit the following sentences for problems with *-s* and *-ed* verb forms and for omitted verbs. If a sentence is correct, write "correct" after it. Answers to lettered sentences appear in the back of the book. Example:

    The psychologist ~~have~~ so many problems in her own life that ^ *has*
    she ~~don't~~ know how to advise anyone else. ^ *doesn't*

a. I love to watch Anthony as he leaps off the balance beam and lands lightly on his feet.
b. The police are use to helping lost tourists.
c. The whooping crane have been an endangered species since the late 1930s.

d. We often don't know whether he angry or just joking.
e. Staggered working hours have reduce traffic jams and save motorists many gallons of gas.

1. Even though Maria is in her late twenties, her mother treat her like a child.
2. Have there ever been a time in your life when you were too depressed to get out of bed?
3. Many people in my hometown have been ask to help with the rally.
4. Today a modern school building covers most of the old grounds.
5. Chris didn't know about Marlo's death because he never listens. He always talking.
6. That line of poetry can be express more dramatically.
7. Our four children plays one or two instruments each.
8. The ball was pass from one player to the other so fast that even the TV crew miss some of the exchanges.
9. Do he have enough energy to hold down two jobs while going to night school?
10. How would you feel if your mother or a love one had been a victim of a crime like this?

28

Use verbs in the appropriate tense, mood, and voice.

28a Choose the appropriate verb tense.

Tenses indicate the time of an action in relation to the time of the speaking or writing about that action.

The most common problem with tenses — shifting confusingly from one tense to another — is discussed in 13. Other problems with tenses are detailed in this section, after the following survey of tenses.

Survey of tenses

English has three simple tenses (past, present, and future) and three perfect tenses (present perfect, past perfect, and future perfect). In addition, there is a progressive form of each of these six tenses.

SIMPLE TENSES The *simple present tense* is used primarily to describe habitual actions (Jane *walks* to work) or to refer to actions occurring at the time of speaking (I *see* a cardinal in our maple tree). It is also used to state facts or general truths and to describe fictional events in a literary work (see page 288). The present tense may even be used to express future actions that are to occur at some specified time (The semester *begins* tomorrow). The *simple past tense* is used for actions completed entirely in the past (Yesterday Jane *walked* to work). The *simple future tense* is used for actions that will occur in the future (Tomorrow Jane *will walk* to work) or for actions that are predictable, given certain causes (Meat *will spoil* if not properly refrigerated).

In the following chart, the simple tenses are given for the regular verb *walk*, the irregular verb *ride*, and the highly irregular verb *be*.

SIMPLE PRESENT

SINGULAR		PLURAL	
I	walk, ride, am	we	walk, ride, are
you	walk, ride, are	you	walk, ride, are
he/she/it	walks, rides, is	they	walk, ride, are

SIMPLE PAST

SINGULAR		PLURAL	
I	walked, rode, was	we	walked, rode, were
you	walked, rode, were	you	walked, rode, were
he/she/it	walked, rode, was	they	walked, rode, were

SIMPLE FUTURE
I, you, he/she/it, we, they   will walk, ride, be

PERFECT TENSES   More complex time relations are indicated by the perfect tenses (which consist of a form of *have* plus the past participle). The *present perfect tense* is used for an action that began in the past and is still going on in the present (Jane *has walked* to work for years) or an action that began in the past and is finished by the time of speaking or writing (Jane *has stopped* walking to work). The *past perfect tense* is used for an action already completed by the time of another past action (Jane hailed a cab after she *had walked* several blocks in the rain) or for an action already completed at some specific past time (By 8:30, Jane *had walked* two miles). (See also page 289.) The *future perfect tense* is used for an action that will be completed before or by a certain future time (Jane *will have left* Troy by the time Jo arrives).

PRESENT PERFECT

I, you, we, they	have walked, ridden, been
he/she/it	has walked, ridden, been

PAST PERFECT

I, you, he/she/it, we, they	had walked, ridden, been

FUTURE PERFECT

I, you, he/she/it, we, they	will have walked, ridden, been

PROGRESSIVE FORMS   The simple and perfect tenses already discussed have progressive forms that describe actions in progress. The *present progressive* form is used for actions currently in progress (Jane *is writing* a letter) or for future actions that are to occur at some specified time (Jane *is leaving* for Chicago on Monday). The *past progressive* is used for past actions in progress (Jane *was writing* a letter last night). The *future progressive* is used for future actions in progress (Jane *will be traveling* next week).

PRESENT PROGRESSIVE

I	am walking, riding, being
he/she/it	is walking, riding, being
you, we, they	are walking, riding, being

PAST PROGRESSIVE

| I, he/she/it | was walking, riding, being |
| you, we, they | were walking, riding, being |

FUTURE PROGRESSIVE

| I, you, he/she/it, we, they | will be walking, riding, being |

Like the simple tenses, the perfect tenses have progressive forms. The perfect progressive forms express the length of time an action is, was, or will be in progress. Jane *has been walking* to work for five years (*present perfect progressive*). Jane *had been walking* to work before she was mugged (*past perfect progressive*). Jane *will have been walking* to work for five years by the end of this month (*future perfect progressive*).

PRESENT PERFECT PROGRESSIVE

| I, you, we, they | have been walking, riding, being |
| he/she/it | has been walking, riding, being |

PAST PERFECT PROGRESSIVE

| I, you, he/she/it, we, they | had been walking, riding, being |

FUTURE PERFECT PROGRESSIVE

| I, you, he/she/it, we, they | will have been walking, riding, being |

ESL NOTE: The progressive forms are not normally used with mental activity verbs such as *believe*. See 29a.

Special uses of the present tense

Use the present tense when writing about literature or when expressing general truths.

When writing about a work of literature, you may be tempted to use the past tense. The convention, however, is to describe fictional events in the present tense. (See also 13b.)

▶ In Masuji Ibuse's *Black Rain,* a child ~~reached~~ for a
   reaches

pomegranate in his mother's garden, and a moment later

he ~~was~~ *is* dead, killed by the blast of the atomic bomb.

Scientific principles or general truths should appear in the present tense, unless such principles have been disproved.

▶ Galileo taught that the earth ~~revolved~~ *revolves* around the sun.

Since Galileo's teaching has not been discredited, the verb should be in the present tense. The following sentence, however, is acceptable: *Ptolemy taught that the sun revolved around the earth.*

The past perfect tense

The past perfect tense consists of a past participle preceded by *had* (*had worked, had gone*). (See page 287.) This tense is used for an action already completed by the time of another past action or for an action already completed at some specific past time.

Everyone *had spoken* by the time I arrived.

Everyone *had spoken* by 10:00 A.M.

Writers sometimes use the simple past tense when they should use the past perfect.

▶ We built our cabin high on a pine knoll, forty feet above an abandoned quarry that ~~was~~ *had been* flooded in 1920 to create a lake.

The building of the cabin and the flooding of the quarry both occurred in the past, but the flooding was completed before the time of building.

▶ By the time we arrived at the party, the guest of honor ˄*had* left.

The past perfect tense is needed because the action of leaving was completed at a specific past time (by the time we arrived).

Some writers tend to overuse the past perfect tense. Do not use the past perfect if two past actions occurred at the same time.

▶ When we arrived in Paris, Pauline ~~had~~ met us at the train

station.

Sequence of tenses with infinitives and participles

An infinitive is the base form of a verb preceded by *to*. (See 49c.) Use the present infinitive to show action at the same time as or later than the action of the verb in the sentence.

▶ The club had hoped to ~~have~~ *raise* ~~raised~~ a thousand dollars by ˄

April 1.

The action expressed in the infinitive (*to raise*) occurred later than the action of the sentence's verb (*had hoped*).

Use the perfect form of an infinitive (*to have* followed by the past participle) for an action occurring earlier than that of the verb in the sentence.

▶ David would like to ~~join~~ *have joined* the Green Berets, but he did not ˄

pass the physical.

The liking occurs in the present; the joining would have occurred in the past.

The tense of a participle is also governed by the tense of the sentence's verb. Use the present participle (ending in *-ing*) for an action occurring at the same time as that of the sentence's verb.

> Hiking the Appalachian Trail in early spring, we spotted many wildflowers.

Use the past participle (such as *given* or *helped*) or the present perfect participle (*having* plus the past participle) for an action occurring before that of the verb.

> *Discovered* off the coast of Florida, the *Atocha* yielded many treasures.

> *Having worked* her way through college, Melanie graduated debt-free.

28b Use the subjunctive mood in the few contexts that require it.

There are three moods in English: the *indicative*, used for facts, opinions, and questions; the *imperative*, used for orders or advice; and the *subjunctive*, used in certain contexts to express wishes, requests, or conditions contrary to fact. Of these moods, only the subjunctive causes problems for writers.

Forms of the subjunctive

In the subjunctive mood, present-tense verbs do not change form to indicate the number and person of the subject (see 21). Instead, the subjunctive uses the base form of the verb (*be, drive, employ*) with all subjects.

> It is important that you *be* [not *are*] prepared for the interview.

> We asked that she *drive* [not *drives*] more slowly.

Also, in the subjunctive mood, there is only one past-tense form of *be: were* (never *was*).

If I *were* [not *was*] you, I'd proceed more cautiously.

Uses of the subjunctive

The subjunctive mood appears only in a few contexts: in contrary-to-fact clauses beginning with *if* or expressing a wish; in *that* clauses following verbs such as *ask, insist, recommend, request,* and *suggest;* and in certain set expressions.

IN CONTRARY-TO-FACT CLAUSES BEGINNING WITH *IF* When a subordinate clause beginning with *if* expresses a condition contrary to fact, use the subjunctive mood.

▶ If I ~~was~~ a member of Congress, I would vote for that bill.
   were

▶ We could be less cautious if Jake ~~was~~ more trustworthy.
   were

The verbs in these sentences express conditions that do not exist: The writer is not a member of Congress, and Jake is not trustworthy.

Do not use the subjunctive mood in *if* clauses expressing conditions that exist or may exist.

If Dana *wins* the contest, she will leave for Barcelona in June.

IN CONTRARY-TO-FACT CLAUSES EXPRESSING A WISH In formal English the subjunctive is used in clauses expressing a wish or desire; in informal speech, however, the indicative is more common.

FORMAL   I wish that Dr. Kurtinitis *were* my professor.

INFORMAL   I wish that Dr. Kurtinitis *was* my professor.

IN *THAT* CLAUSES FOLLOWING VERBS SUCH AS *ASK, INSIST, RECOMMEND, REQUEST,* AND *SUGGEST* Because requests have not yet become reality, they are expressed in the subjunctive mood.

▶ Professor Moore insists that her students ~~are~~ *be* on time.
                                    ∧

▶ We recommend that Lambert ~~files~~ *file* form 1050 soon.
                          ∧

IN CERTAIN SET EXPRESSIONS The subjunctive mood, once more widely used in English, remains in certain set expressions: *Be* that as it may, as it *were, come* rain or shine, far *be* it from me, and so on.

EXERCISE 28 – 1

Edit the following sentences to eliminate errors in verb tense or mood. If a sentence is correct, write "correct" after it. Answers to lettered sentences appear in the back of the book. Example:

After the path ~~was~~ *had been* plowed, we were able to walk through the
                   ∧
park.

a. The fire was thought to have been started around nine o'clock.
b. Watson and Crick discovered the mechanism that controlled inheritance in all life: the workings of the DNA molecule.
c. Marion would write more if she wasn't distracted by a house full of children.
d. Sharon told me that she went to the meeting the day before.
e. Ken recommended that John remain on the beginners' slope for at least a week.

1. Dad called in the morning and said that he took Mom to the hospital around midnight.
2. They had planned to have adopted a girl, but they got twin boys.
3. If I were in better health, I would enjoy competing in the dance marathon.

4. As soon as my aunt applied for the position of assistant pastor, the post was filled by an inexperienced seminary graduate who had been so hastily snatched that his mortarboard was still in midair.

5. Sheila knew that Bruce would have preferred to have double-dated, but she really wanted to be alone with him.

6. Don Quixote, in Cervantes' novel, was an idealist ill suited for life in the real world.

7. On arrival at the police station, Cindy pulled Tom out of the car, and he had fallen face down on the ground.

8. I would like to have been on the *Mayflower* but not to have lived through that first winter.

9. On the very day that Alex signed up for the marines, his girlfriend had joined the navy.

10. Hearing the screams and wondering whether Chuck had had an accident, I ran to the garage.

28c Prefer the active voice.

Transitive verbs (verbs that take a direct object) appear in either the active or the passive voice. (See 48c.) In the active voice, the subject of the sentence does the action; in the passive, the subject receives the action. Although both voices are grammatically correct, the active voice is usually more effective because it is simpler, more direct, and less wordy.

ACTIVE The committee *reached* a decision.

PASSIVE A decision *was reached* by the committee.

To transform a sentence from the passive to the active voice, make the actor the subject of the sentence.

▶ For the opening flag ceremony, ~~a dance was choreographed by~~
choreographed a dance
Mr. Martins to the song "Two Hundred Years and Still a Baby."

The revision emphasizes Mr. Martins by making him the subject.

► We did not take down the
~~The~~ Christmas decorations ~~were not taken down~~ until
Valentine's Day.

Very often the actor does not even appear in a passive-voice
sentence. To turn such a sentence into the active voice, the
writer must decide on an appropriate subject, depending on
the context.

The passive voice is appropriate if you wish to emphasize
the receiver of the action or to minimize the importance of
the doer.

> **APPROPRIATE** Many native Hawaiians *are forced* to leave
> **PASSIVE** their beautiful beaches to make room for
> hotels and condominiums.
>
> **APPROPRIATE** As the time for harvest approaches, the
> **PASSIVE** tobacco plants *are sprayed* with a chemical
> to retard the growth of suckers.

The writer of the first sentence wished to emphasize the re-
ceivers of the action, Hawaiians. The writer of the second
sentence wished to focus on the tobacco plants, not on the
people spraying them.

EXERCISE 28–2

Change the following sentences from the passive to the active voice.
You may need to invent an actor to be the subject in the active voice.
Revisions of lettered sentences appear in the back of the book.
Example:

We
~~It was~~ learned from the test that our son was reading on the
second-grade level.

a. The results were reported by the research assistant.
b. Not enough discretion is used by parents in deciding which television programs their children may watch.
c. As the patient undressed, scars were seen on his back, stomach, and thighs. We suspected child abuse.
d. It was noted right away that the taxi driver had been exposed to Americans because he knew all the latest slang.
e. The buttons were replaced, the hems were lengthened or shortened, and all of the costumes were cleaned and pressed.

1. All of my friends were invited to the party by my mother.
2. No loyalty at all was shown by the dog to his owner, who had mistreated him.
3. It can be concluded that a college education provides a significant economic advantage.
4. The new car was purchased without serious thought about how she would make the monthly payments.
5. Home equity loans were explained to me by the assistant manager.

EXERCISE 28 – 3

In the following paragraphs, the italicized passive verbs are less effective than active verbs would be. Replace each italicized passive verb with an active verb. Be prepared to discuss why the remaining passive verbs (printed in brackets) are appropriate.

Although Professor Whist works as a consultant for several corporations that manufacture electrical generating equipment, he [is known and respected] by environmentalists as an advocate for the preservation of natural resources. Professor Whist feels that his influence *can be used* to affect corporate decisions concerning the environment. The environment *is protected* to some extent by many corporations, but when someone with Professor Whist's reputation *is hired* by them, their public image *is improved* too.

Although Professor Whist [is besieged] by many groups for his expertise, he continues to teach. For part of every class a discussion *is led* about how the environment *is affected* by everyday decisions of big corporations as well as ordinary people. Each semester, for example, students learn that electricity [is produced] by a very inefficient process, with only about 35 percent of the potential energy in coal, oil, or uranium converting directly into electricity. Students also learn that simple steps *can be taken* at home to conserve every type of energy that *is used*. Professor Whist believes that he can make a difference, and his conviction *is demonstrated* by his personal example in the conference room and in the classroom.

Editing for ESL Problems

Part VI is intended for speakers of English as a second language (ESL). It surveys rules that native speakers have mastered simply because they grew up speaking the language.

29

Be alert to special problems with verbs.

Both native and nonnative speakers of English encounter the following problems with verbs, which are treated elsewhere in this handbook:

> problems with subject-verb agreement (21),
>
> misuse of verb forms (27),
>
> problems with tense, mood, and voice (28).

This section focuses on features of the English verb system that cause special problems for second language speakers.

29a   Match helping verbs and main verbs appropriately.

Only certain combinations of helping verbs and main verbs make sense in English. The correct combinations are discussed in this section, after the following review of helping verbs and main verbs.

Review of helping verbs and main verbs

Helping verbs always appear before main verbs. (See 47c.)

> HV   MV   HV   MV
> We *will leave* for the picnic at noon. *Do* you *want* a ride?

There are twenty-three helping verbs in English. Nine of them, called *modals,* function only as helping verbs. The others — forms of *do, have,* and *be* — function either as helping or as main verbs.

> **HELPING VERBS**
>
> *Modals:* can, could, may, might, must, shall, should, will, would
>
> *Forms of* do: do, does, did
>
> *Forms of* have: have, has, had
>
> *Forms of* be: be, am, is, are, was, were, being, been

Every main verb has five forms (except *be,* which has eight forms). The following list shows these forms for the regular verb *help* and the irregular verb *give.* (See 27a for a list of common irregular verbs.)

BASE FORM	help, give
PAST TENSE	helped, gave
PAST PARTICIPLE	helped, given
PRESENT PARTICIPLE	helping, giving
-S FORM	helps, gives

Modal + base form

After the modals *can, could, may, might, must, shall, should, will,* and *would,* use the base form of the verb.

can help	can give	shall help	shall give
could help	could give	should help	should give
may help	may give	will help	will give
might help	might give	would help	would give
must help	must give		

▶ My cousin will send~~s~~ us photographs from her wedding.

       speak
▶ We could ~~spoke~~ Spanish when we were young.
        ∧

Do, does, *or* did + *base form*

After helping verbs that are a form of *do*, use the base form
of the verb.

do help	do give
does help	does give
did help	did give

The helping verbs *do*, *does*, and *did* are used in three ways:
(1) to express a negative meaning with the adverbs *not* or
never, (2) to ask a question, and (3) to emphasize a main verb
used in a positive sense.

▶ Taking an aspirin does not help~~ing~~ the pain.

        buy
▶ Did Janice ~~bought~~ the gift for Katherine?
       ∧

   hope
▶ We do ~~hoping~~ that you will come to the party.
   ∧

Have, has, *or* had + *past participle*

After helping verbs that are a form of *have*, use the past participle to form one of the perfect tenses. (See 28a.) Past participles usually end in *-ed*, *-d*, *-en*, *-n*, or *-t*. (See 27a.)

have helped	have given
has helped	has given
had helped	had given

                                     offered
▶ On cold nights many churches in the city have ~~offer~~ shelter
                                                 ∧

to the homeless.

▶ My friend An-Mei has not ~~speaking~~ *spoken* Chinese since she was a

young girl.

Form of be + present participle (progressive tenses)

After the helping verbs *be, am, is, are, was, were,* or *been,*
use a present participle to form one of the progressive tenses.
The progressive tenses express a continuing action. (See
28a.)

HELPING VERBS	PRESENT PARTICIPLE
am, is, are	helping, giving
was, were	helping, giving
can, could be	helping, giving
may, might, must be	helping, giving
shall, should be	helping, giving
will, would be	helping, giving
has, have, had been	helping, giving
can, could have been	helping, giving
may, might, must have been	helping, giving
shall, should have been	helping, giving
will, would have been	helping, giving

▶ Carlos is ~~build~~ *building* his house on a cliff overlooking the ocean.

▶ Uncle Roy was ~~driven~~ *driving* a brand new red Corvette.

In the progressive tenses, notice that the helping verbs *be*
and *been* must be preceded by other helping verbs.

▶ Anna *has* been studying English for two years.

CAUTION: Certain verbs are not normally used in the progressive sense in English. In general, these verbs express a state
of being or mental activity, not a dynamic action. Common

examples are *appear, believe, belong, contain, have, hear, know, like, need, see, seem, taste, think, understand,* and *want.*

▶ I ~~am~~ ~~wanting~~ to see August Wilson's *Fences* at Arena Stage.

Some of these verbs, however, have special uses in which progressive forms are normal (*We are thinking about going to the Bahamas*). You will need to make a note of exceptions as you encounter them.

Form of be + *past participle* (*passive voice*)

After the helping verbs *be, am, is, are, was, were, being,* or *been,* use a past participle to form the passive voice. When a sentence is written in the passive voice, the subject receives the action instead of doing it (*Melissa was given a jade ring by her grandmother*). (See 48c and 28c.)

HELPING VERBS	PAST PARTICIPLE
am, is, are	helped, given
was, were	helped, given
am, is, are being	helped, given
was, were being	helped, given
can, could be	helped, given
may, might, must be	helped, given
shall, should be	helped, given
will, would be	helped, given
can, could have been	helped, given
may, might, must have been	helped, given
shall, should have been	helped, given
will, would have been	helped, given

▶ *Bleak House* was ~~write~~ *written* by Charles Dickens.

▶ Nancy was ~~chose~~ *chosen* to go on a secret assignment in Africa.

CAUTION: Intransitive verbs, those that cannot take a direct object, may not be used to form the passive voice. (See transitive and intransitive verbs, 48b.)

▶ The earthquake ~~was~~ occurred last Wednesday.

EXERCISE 29–1

Revise any sentences in which helping and main verbs do not match. You may need to look at the list of irregular verbs in 27a to determine the correct form of some irregular verbs. Answers to lettered sentences appear in the back of the book. Example:

Maureen should find~~s~~ an apartment closer to campus.

a. We will making this a better country.
b. There is nothing in the world that TV has not touch on.
c. Did you understood my question?
d. A hard wind was blown while we were climbing the mountain.
e. The child's innocent world has been taking away from him.

1. Children are expose at an early age to certain aspects of adult life.
2. The student can't concentrated on his lessons.
3. Can you told me the time?
4. I have ate Thai food only once before.
5. Sandra says that she doesn't wants any help.

29b Become familiar with verbs that may be followed by gerunds or infinitives.

A gerund is a verb form that ends in -*ing* and is used as a noun: *sleeping, dreaming.* (See 49c.) An infinitive is the base form of the verb preceded by the word *to: to sleep, to dream.* The word *to* is not a preposition in this use but an infinitive marker. (See 49c.)

A few verbs may be followed by either a gerund or an infinitive; others may be followed by a gerund but not by an infinitive; still others may be followed by an infinitive (either directly or with a noun or pronoun intervening) but not by a gerund.

Verb + gerund or infinitive

These commonly used verbs may be followed by a gerund or an infinitive, with little or no difference in meaning:

begin	continue	like	start
can't stand	hate	love	

I love *skiing*.   I love *to ski*.

With a few verbs, however, the choice of a gerund or infinitive changes the meaning dramatically:

forget	remember	stop	try

She stopped *speaking* to Lucia. [She no longer spoke to Lucia.]

She stopped *to speak* to Lucia. [She paused so that she could speak to Lucia.]

Verb + gerund

These verbs may be followed by a gerund but not by an infinitive:

admit	discuss	imagine	put off	risk
appreciate	enjoy	miss	quit	suggest
avoid	escape	postpone	recall	tolerate
deny	finish	practice	resist	

Have you finished *decorating* [not *to decorate*] the tree?

Bill enjoys *playing* [not *to play*] the piano.

Verb + infinitive

These verbs may be followed by an infinitive but not by a gerund:

agree	decide	manage	pretend	wait
ask	expect	mean	promise	want
beg	have	offer	refuse	wish
claim	hope	plan		

We plan *to visit* [not *visiting*] the Yucatán next week.

Jill has offered *to water* [not *watering*] the plants while we are away.

Verb + noun (or pronoun) + infinitive

With certain verbs in the active voice, a noun or pronoun must come between the verb and the infinitive that follows it. The noun or pronoun usually names a person who is affected by the action.

advise	command	have	persuade	tell
allow	convince	instruct	remind	warn
cause	encourage	order	require	

The dean encourages *you to apply* for the scholarship.

The class asked *Luis to tell* the story of his escape.

A few verbs may be followed either by an infinitive directly or by an infinitive preceded by a noun or pronoun.

ask	expect	need	want	would like

We asked *to speak* to the congregation.

We asked *Rabbi Abrams to speak* to our congregation.

Verb + noun or pronoun + unmarked infinitive

An unmarked infinitive is an infinitive without *to*. A few verbs may be followed by a noun or pronoun and an unmarked (but not a marked) infinitive.

> have ("cause") let ("allow") make ("force")

> Absence makes *the heart grow* [not *to grow*] fonder.

> Please let *me pay* [not *to pay*] for the tickets.

EXERCISE 29–2

Form sentences by adding gerund or infinitive constructions to the following sentence openings. In some cases, more than one kind of construction may be possible. Possible sentences for lettered items appear in the back of the book. Example:

Please remind *your sister to call me.*
　　　　　　　λ

a. I enjoy
b. Will you help Samantha
c. The team hopes
d. Tom and his brothers miss
e. The babysitter let

1. Pollen makes
2. The club president asked
3. Next summer we plan
4. Waverly intends
5. Please stop

29c Become familiar with commonly used two-word verbs.

Many verbs in English consist of a verb followed by a preposition or adverb known as a *particle*. (See 47c.) A two-word verb (also known as a *phrasal verb*) often expresses an idiomatic meaning that cannot be understood literally. Consider the verbs in the following sentences, for example.

> We *ran across* Professor Magnotto on the way to the bookstore.

> Calvin *dropped in* on his adviser this morning.

> At the last minute, Lucinda *called* the wedding *off*.

As you probably know, *ran across* means "encountered," *dropped in* means "paid an unexpected visit," and *called off* means "canceled." When you were first learning English, however, these two-word verbs must have suggested strange meanings.

Some two-word verbs are intransitive; they do not take direct objects. (See 48b.)

> This morning I *got up* at dawn.

Transitive two-word verbs (those that take direct objects) have particles that are either separable or inseparable. Separable particles may be separated from the verb by the direct object.

> Lucinda *called* the wedding *off*.

When the direct object is a noun, a separable particle may also follow the verb immediately:

> At the last minute, Lucinda *called off* the wedding.

When the direct object is a pronoun, however, the particle must be separated from the verb.

> Why was there no wedding? Lucinda *called* it *off* [not *called off it*].

Inseparable particles must follow the verb immediately. A direct object cannot come between the verb and the particle.

The police will *look into* the matter [not *look* the matter *into*].

NOTE: Not all prepositions or adverbs following verbs are particles. The phrase *looked at*, for example, is a verb and a preposition. A preposition following a verb can be moved in a question or a clause: *At what did James look? The house at which James looked was too small.* Particles, by contrast, cannot be moved. We cannot ask, for example, *"Up what did James look?"* Nor can we say, "The information *up* which James *looked* was interesting." We can be sure, therefore, that *look up* is a two-word verb.

The following list includes common two-word verbs. If a particle can be separated from the verb by a direct object, a pronoun is shown between the verb and the particle: *ask (someone) out.* When in doubt about the meaning of a two-word verb, consult the dictionary.

COMMON TWO-WORD VERBS

ask (someone) out
break down
burn (something) down
burn down
burn (something) up
burn up
bring (something or
   someone) up
call (something) off
call (someone) up
clean (something) up
clean up
come across
cut (something) up
do (something) over

drop in (on someone)
drop (someone or
   something) off
drop out (of something)
fill (something) out
fill (something) up
get along (with someone)
get away (with something)
get up
give (something) away
give (something) back
give in
give up
go out (with someone)
go over (something)

COMMON TWO-WORD VERBS

grow up
hand (something) in
hand (something) out
hang (something) up
help out
help (someone) out
keep on (doing something)
keep up (with someone or
  something)
leave (something) out
look into (something)
look (something) over
look (something) up
make (something) up
pick (something) out
pick (someone) up
pick (something) up
play around
point (something) out
put (something) away
put (something) back
put (something) off
put (something) on
put (something) out
put (something) together
put up (with someone or
  something)
quiet down
run across (someone or
  something)
run out (of something)

run into (someone or
  something)
see (someone) off
shut (something) off
speak to (someone)
speak up
stay away (from someone or
  something)
stay up
take care of (someone or
  something)
take off
take (something) off
take (someone) out
take (something) over
think (something) over
throw (something) away
throw (something) out
try (something) on
try (something) out
turn (something) down
turn (something) on
turn up
wake up
wake (someone) up
wear out
wrap (something) up

EXERCISE 29–3

From the list of two-word verbs, choose ten verbs, preferably ones
whose meaning you are not sure of. First look the verbs up in the
dictionary; then use each verb in a sentence of your own.

30

Use the articles *a, an,* and *the* appropriately.

Except for occasional difficulty in choosing between *a* and *an,* native speakers of English encounter few problems with articles. To speakers whose native language is not English, however, articles can prove troublesome, for the rules governing their use are surprisingly complex. This section summarizes those rules.

The definite article *the* and the indefinite articles *a* and *an* signal that a noun is about to appear. The noun may follow the article immediately or modifiers may intervene (see 47a and 47d):

> *the candidate, the* exceptionally well qualified *candidate*
> *a sunset, a* spectacular *sunset*
> *an apple, an* appetizing *apple*

A is used before a consonant sound: *a banana, a tree, a picture, a hand, a happy child. An* is used before a vowel sound: *an eggplant, an occasion, an uncle, an hour, an honorable person.* Notice that words beginning with *h* can have either a consonant sound (*hand, happy*) or a vowel sound (*hour, honorable*). (See also the Glossary of Usage.)

Articles are not the only words used to mark nouns. Other noun markers include possessive nouns (*Helen's*), numbers, and the following pronouns: *my, your, his, her, its, our, their, whose, this, that, these, those, all, any, each, either, every, few, many, more, most, much, neither, several, some.*

Usually an article is not used with another noun marker. Common exceptions include expressions such as *a few, the most,* and *all the.*

30a Use *a* (or *an*) with singular count nouns whose specific identity is not known to the reader.

Count nouns refer to persons, places, or things that can be counted: *one girl, two girls; one city, three cities; one apple, four apples.* Noncount nouns refer to entities or abstractions that cannot be counted: *water, steel, air, furniture, patience, knowledge.* It is important to remember that noncount nouns vary from language to language. To see what nouns English categorizes as noncount nouns, refer to the list on page 314.

If the specific identity of a singular count noun is not known to the reader — perhaps because it is being mentioned for the first time, perhaps because its specific identity is unknown even to the writer — the noun should be preceded by *a* or *an* unless it has been preceded by another noun marker. *A* (or *an*) usually means "one among many" but can also mean "any one."

▶ Mary Beth arrived in ∧*a* limousine.

▶ We are looking for ∧*an* apartment close to the lake.

30b Do not use *a* (or *an*) with plural nouns or with noncount nouns.

Because *a* (or *an*) has a singular meaning, it is never used to mark a plural noun.

▶ As a child I earned money by delivering ⁄*a* newspapers.

A (or *an*) is not used to mark noncount nouns, such as *sugar, gold, honesty,* or *jewelry.*

▶ Claudia asked her mother for ~~an~~ advice.

If you want to express an amount of something designated by a noncount noun, you can often add a count noun in front of it: *a quart of milk, a piece of furniture, a bar of soap*.

▶ Mother asked us to pick up a _∧ sugar at the corner store.

pound of

NOTE: A few noncount nouns may also be used as count nouns: *Bill loves chocolate; Bill offered me a chocolate*.

COMMONLY USED NONCOUNT NOUNS

Food and drink: bacon, beef, beer, bread, broccoli, butter, cabbage, candy, cauliflower, celery, cereal, cheese, chicken, chocolate, coffee, corn, cream, fish, flour, fruit, ice cream, lettuce, meat, milk, oil, pasta, rice, salt, spinach, sugar, tea, water, wine, yogurt

Nonfood substances: air, cement, coal, dirt, gasoline, gold, paper, petroleum, plastic, rain, silver, snow, soap, steel, wood, wool

Abstract nouns: advice, anger, beauty, confidence, courage, employment, fun, happiness, health, honesty, information, intelligence, knowledge, love, poverty, satisfaction, truth, wealth

Other: biology (and other areas of study), clothing, equipment, furniture, homework, jewelry, luggage, lumber, machinery, mail, money, news, poetry, pollution, research, scenery, traffic, transportation, violence, weather, work

30c Use *the* with most nouns whose specific identity is known to the reader.

The definite article *the* is used with most nouns whose iden-tity is known to the reader. (For exceptions, see 30d.) Usually the identity will be clear to the reader for one of the following reasons:

1. The noun has been previously mentioned.
2. A phrase or clause following the noun restricts its identity.
3. A superlative such as *best* or *most intelligent* makes the noun's identity specific.
4. The noun describes a unique person, place, or thing.
5. The context or situation makes the noun's identity clear.

▶ A truck loaded with dynamite cut in front of our van. When
the
⋏truck skidded a few seconds later, we almost plowed into it.

The noun *truck* is preceded by *A* when it is first mentioned. When the noun is mentioned again, it is preceded by *the* since readers now know the specific truck being discussed.

the
▶ Bob warned me that gun on the top shelf of the cupboard
⋏
was loaded.

The phrase *on the top shelf of the cupboard* identifies the specific gun.

the
▶ Our petite daughter dated tallest boy in her class.
⋏

The superlative *tallest* restricts the identity of the noun *boy*.

the
▶ During an eclipse, one should not look directly at sun.
⋏

There is only one sun in our solar system, so its identity is clear.

the
▶ Please don't slam door when you leave.
⋏
Both the speaker and the listener know which door is meant.

30d Do not use *the* with plural or noncount nouns meaning "all" or "in general"; do not use *the* with most proper nouns.

When a plural or a noncount noun means "all" or "in general," it is not marked with *the.*

▶ ~~The~~ ᖴountains are an expensive element of landscape design.

▶ In some parts of the world, ~~the~~ rice is preferred to all other

grains.

Although there are many exceptions, as a rule *the* is not used with proper nouns. Do not use *the* with names of persons (Jessica Webner), names of streets, cities, and states (Prospect Street, Detroit, Idaho), names of continents and most countries (Europe, South America, Costa Rica, India), and the proper names of most lakes and single mountains (Lake Geneva, Mount Everest).

Plural proper nouns such as *the United States, the Great Lakes,* and *the Alps* are exceptions.

EXERCISE 30–1

Articles have been omitted from the following story, adapted from *Zen Flesh, Zen Bones,* compiled by Paul Reps. Insert the articles *a, an,* and *the* where English requires them and be prepared to explain the reasons for your choices.

Moon Cannot Be Stolen

Ryokan, who was Zen master, lived simple life in little hut at foot of mountain. One evening thief visited hut only to discover there was nothing in it to steal.

Ryokan returned and caught him. "You may have come long way to visit me," he told prowler, "and you should not return empty-handed. Please take my clothes as gift." Thief was bewildered. He took Ryokan's clothes and slunk away. Ryokan sat naked, watching moon. "Poor fellow," he mused, "I wish I could give him this beautiful moon."

31

Be aware of other potential trouble spots.

31a Do not omit subjects, expletives, or verbs.

English requires a subject for all sentences except imperatives, in which the subject *you* is understood (*Give to the poor*). (See 48a.) If your native language allows the omission of an explicit subject in other sentences or clauses, be especially alert to this requirement in English.

▶ *I have*
~~Have~~ a large collection of baseball cards.
∧

▶ If *you* fly nonstop, *you* can reach Santiago in eight hours.
∧   ∧

When the subject has been moved from its normal position before the verb, English sometimes requires an expletive (*there* or *it*) at the beginning of the sentence or clause. (See 48c.) Except for questions, sentences in English cannot begin with *is, are, was,* or *were.*

▶ *There are*
~~Are~~ two drugstores on Main Street.
∧

The subject *drugstores* follows the verb *are*, so the expletive *There* is needed at the beginning of the sentence.

It is
▶ ~~Is~~ healthy to eat fruit rather than candy.
∧

The subject *to eat fruit rather than candy* follows the verb *Is,* so the expletive *It* is needed at the beginning of the sentence.

NOTE: The word *it* is also used to open a sentence describing the weather. In such cases, *it* functions as the subject of the sentence.

It is very hot in Saudi Arabia.

Some languages allow the omission of the verb when the meaning is clear without it; English does not.

is
▶ Jim exceptionally intelligent.
∧

31b Do not repeat an object or adverb in an adjective clause; do not repeat the subject of a sentence.

In some languages an object or an adverb is repeated later in the adjective clause in which it appears; in English such repetitions are not allowed. Adjective clauses begin with relative pronouns (*who, whom, whose, which, that*) or relative adverbs (*when, where*), and these words always serve a grammatical function within the clauses they introduce. (See 49b.) Another word in the clause cannot also serve that same grammatical function.

When a relative pronoun functions as the object of a verb or the object of a preposition, do not add another word with the same function later in the clause.

▶ The puppy ran after the car that we were riding in ~~it~~.

The relative pronoun *that* is the object of the preposition *in,* so the object *it* is not allowed.

Like a relative pronoun, a relative adverb should not be echoed later in its clause.

▶ The place where I work ~~there~~ is one hour from the city.

The adverb *there* should not echo the relative adverb *where.*

English does not allow the repetition of the subject of a sentence, even when a clause comes between the subject and the verb.

▶ The car that had been stolen ~~it~~ was found.

The pronoun *it* repeats the subject *car.*

EXERCISE 31 – 1

In the following sentences, add needed subjects, expletives, or verbs, and delete any repeated subjects, objects, or adverbs. Answers to lettered sentences appear in the back of the book. Example:

Nancy is the woman whom I talked to ~~her~~ last week.

a. Is easy to learn how to operate our computers.
b. My grandfather very old-fashioned.
c. The prime minister she is the most popular leader in my country.
d. Pavel hasn't heard from the cousin that he wrote to her last month.
e. Are many skyscrapers in New York City.

1. Henri and Nicole they are good friends.
2. Is important to study the grammar of English.
3. The neighbor we trusted he was a thief.
4. I don't use the subway because am afraid.
5. Archeologists have excavated the city where the old Persian kings are buried there.

31c Place adjectives and adverbs with care.

Adjectives modify nouns or pronouns; adverbs modify verbs, adjectives, or other adverbs (see 47d and 47e). Both native and nonnative speakers encounter problems in the use of adjectives and adverbs (see 26). For nonnative speakers, the placement of adjectives and adverbs can also be troublesome.

Placement of adjectives

No doubt you have already learned that in English adjectives usually precede the nouns they modify and that they may also appear following linking verbs. (See 26b and 48b.)

Janine wore a *new* necklace. Janine's necklace was *new*.

When adjectives pile up in front of a noun, however, you may sometimes have difficulty arranging them. English is quite particular about the order of cumulative adjectives, those not separated by commas. (See 32d.)

> Janine was wearing a *beautiful antique silver* necklace [not *silver antique beautiful* necklace].

The chart on page 321 shows the order in which cumulative adjectives ordinarily appear in front of the noun they modify. This list is just a general guide; don't be surprised when you encounter exceptions.

NOTE: Long strings of cumulative adjectives tend to be awkward. As a rule, use no more than two or three of them between the article (or other noun marker) and the noun modified. Here are several examples:

a beautiful old pine table   Susan's large round painting
two enormous French urns   some small blue medicine
an exotic purple jungle flower   bottles

Usual order of cumulative adjectives

ARTICLE OR OTHER NOUN MARKER

a, an, the, her, Joe's, two, many, some

EVALUATIVE WORD

attractive, dedicated, delicious, ugly, disgusting

SIZE

large, enormous, small, little

LENGTH OR SHAPE

long, short, round, square

AGE

new, old, young, antique

COLOR

yellow, blue, crimson

NATIONALITY

French, Scandinavian, Vietnamese

RELIGION

Catholic, Protestant, Jewish, Muslim

MATERIAL

silver, walnut, wool, marble

NOUN/ADJECTIVE

tree (as in *tree house*), kitchen (as in *kitchen table*)

THE NOUN MODIFIED

house, sweater, bicycle, bread, woman, priest

Placement of adverbs

Adverbs modifying verbs appear in various positions: at the beginning or end of the sentence, before or after the verb, or between a helping verb and its main verb.

> *Slowly*, we drove along the rain-slick road.

> Mother wrapped the gift *carefully*.

> Martin *always* wins our tennis matches.

> Christina is *rarely* late for our lunch dates.

> My daughter has *often* spoken of you.

An adverb may not, however, be placed between a verb and its direct object.

▶ Mother wrapped ~~carefully~~ the gift. *carefully.*

> The adverb *carefully* may be placed at the beginning or at the end of this sentence or before the verb. It cannot appear after the verb because the verb is followed by the direct object *the gift*.

EXERCISE 31–2

Using the chart on page 321, arrange the following modifiers and nouns in their proper order. Answers to lettered items appear in the back of the book. Example:

> *two new French racing bicycles*
> **new, French, two, bicycles, racing**

  a. woman, young, an, Vietnamese, attractive
  b. dedicated, a, priest, Catholic
  c. old, her, sweater, blue, wool
  d. delicious, Joe's, Scandinavian, bread
  e. many, cages, bird, antique, beautiful

1. round, two, marble, tables, large
2. several, yellow, tulips, miniature
3. a, sports, classic, car
4. courtyard, a, square, small, brick
5. charming, restaurants, Italian, several

31d Distinguish between present participles and past participles used as adjectives.

Both present and past participles may be used as adjectives. The present participle always ends in *-ing*. Past participles usually end in *-ed*, *-d*, *-en*, *-n*, or *-t*. (See 27a.)

PRESENT PARTICIPLES   confusing, speaking

PAST PARTICIPLES   confused, spoken

Participles used as adjectives can precede the nouns they modify; they can also follow linking verbs, in which case they will describe the subject of the sentence. (See 48b.)

It was a *depressing* movie. Jim was a *depressed* young man.

The essay was *confusing*. The student was *confused*.

A present participle should describe a person or thing causing or stimulating an experience; a past participle should describe a person or thing undergoing an experience.

The lecturer was *boring* [not *bored*].

The audience was *bored* [not *boring*].

In the first example, the lecturer is causing boredom, not experiencing it. In the second example, the audience is experiencing boredom, not causing it.

The participles that cause the most trouble for nonnative speakers are those describing mental states:

annoying / annoyed	exhausting / exhausted
boring / bored	fascinating / fascinated
confusing / confused	frightening / frightened
depressing / depressed	satisfying / satisfied
exciting / excited	surprising / surprised

When you come across these words in your drafts, check to see that you have used them correctly.

EXERCISE 31 – 3

Edit the following sentences for proper use of present and past participles. Do not change correct sentences. Answers to lettered sentences appear in the back of the book. Example:

excited
Danielle and Monica were very ~~exciting~~ to be going to a
Broadway show for the first time.

a. My mother was annoying at me for coming home late.
b. The noise in the hall was distracted to me.
c. After the overnight trip to Washington, Samuel was exhausted.
d. The violence in recent movies is often disgusted.
e. I have never seen anyone as surprised as Mona when she walked through the door and we turned on the lights.

1. Megan worked on her art project for eight hours but still she was not satisfying.
2. That blackout was the most frightened experience I've ever had.
3. I couldn't concentrate on my homework because I was distracted.
4. Psalm 23 is one of the most uplifting pieces of writing I've ever read.
5. The exhibit on the La Brea tar pits was fascinated.

PART VII

Editing for Punctuation

32

The comma

The comma, like all forms of punctuation, was invented to help readers. Without it, sentence parts can collide into one another unexpectedly, causing misreadings.

CONFUSING   If you cook Elmer will do the dishes.

CONFUSING   While we were eating a rattlesnake approached our campsite.

Add commas in the logical places (after *cook* and *eating*), and suddenly all is clear. No longer is Elmer being cooked, the rattlesnake being eaten.

Various rules have evolved to prevent such misreadings and to speed readers along through complex grammatical structures. Those rules are detailed in this section.

32a Use a comma before a coordinating conjunction joining independent clauses.

When a coordinating conjunction connects two or more independent clauses — word groups that might have been punctuated as separate sentences — a comma must precede it. There are seven coordinating conjunctions in English: *and, but, or, nor, for, so,* and *yet.*

▶ Nearly everyone has heard of love at first sight, but I fell in

love at first dance.

Together the comma and the coordinating conjunction *but* signal that one independent clause has come to a close and that another is about to begin.

CAUTION: As a rule, do *not* use a comma to separate coordinate word groups that are not independent clauses. See 33a.

▶ A good money manager controls expenses/ and invests

surplus dollars to meet future needs.

The word group following *and* is not an independent clause; it is the second half of a compound predicate.

32b Use a comma after an introductory clause or phrase.

See 34b

The most common introductory word groups are clauses and phrases functioning as adverbs. Such word groups usually tell when, where, how, why, or under what conditions the main action of the sentence occurred. See 49a, 49b, and 49c. *p. 457*

▶ Near a small stream at the bottom of the canyon, we

discovered an abandoned shelter.

The comma is a useful signal that the introductory phrase is over and that the main part of the sentence is about to begin.

▶ When Irwin was ready to eat, his cat jumped onto the table.

Without the comma, readers may have Irwin eating his cat. The comma signals that *his cat* is the subject of a new clause, not part of the introductory one.

EXCEPTION: The comma may be omitted after a short adverb clause or phrase if there is no danger of misreading.

In no time we were at 2,800 feet.

Sentences also frequently begin with phrases describing the noun or pronoun immediately following them. The comma tells readers that they are about to learn the identity of the person or thing described; therefore, the comma is usually required even when the phrase is short. See 49c.

▶ **Knowing that he couldn't outrun a car,Sy took to the fields.**

▶ **Excited about the move,Alice and Don began packing their books.**

The commas tell readers that they are about to hear the nouns described: *Sy* in the first sentence, *Alice and Don* in the second.

NOTE: Other introductory word groups include transitional expressions and absolute phrases. See 32f.

EXERCISE 32 – 1

Add or delete commas where necessary in the following sentences. If a sentence is correct, write "correct" after it. Answers to lettered sentences appear in the back of the book. Example:

Because it rained all Labor Day,our picnic was rather soggy.

a. Carla didn't know whether to punish the boy for lying or praise him for being so clever.
b. The man at the next table complained loudly and the waiter stomped off in disgust.
c. Instead of eating half a cake or two dozen cookies I now grab a banana or an orange.
d. Nursing is physically, and mentally demanding, yet the pay is low.
e. After I won the hundred-yard dash I found a bench in the park and collapsed.

1. After everyone had eaten Lu and George cut the cake.
2. He pushed the car beyond the toll gate and poured a bucket of water on the smoking hood.

3. Lighting the area like a second moon the helicopter circled the scene.
4. While one of the robbers tied Laureen to a chair, and gagged her with an apron, the other emptied the contents of the safe into a knapsack.
5. Many musicians of Bach's time played several instruments, but few mastered them as early or played with as much expression as Bach.

32c Use a comma between all items in a series.

When three or more items are presented in a series, those items should be separated from one another with commas. Items in a series may be single words, phrases, or clauses.

> At Dominique's one can order fillet of rattlesnake, bison burgers, or pickled eel.

Although some writers view the comma between the last two items as optional, most experts advise using the comma because its omission can result in ambiguity or misreading.

▶ Uncle willed me all of his property, houses ˄ and warehouses.

Did Uncle will his property *and* houses *and* warehouses — or simply his property, consisting of houses and warehouses? If the former meaning is intended, a comma is necessary to prevent ambiguity.

▶ The activities include a search for lost treasure, dubious

financial dealings, much discussion of ancient heresies ˄ and

midnight orgies.

Without the comma, the people seem to be discussing orgies, not participating in them. The comma makes it clear that *midnight orgies* is a separate item in the series.

32d Use a comma between coordinate adjectives not
joined by *and.* Do not use a comma between cumulative
adjectives.

When two or more adjectives each modify a noun separately,
they are coordinate.

> Mother has become a *strong, confident, independent* woman.

Adjectives are coordinate if they can be joined with *and*
(strong *and* confident *and* independent) or if they can be
scrambled (an *independent, strong, confident* woman).

Adjectives that do not modify the noun separately are
cumulative.

> *Three large gray* shapes moved slowly toward us.

Beginning with the adjective closest to the noun *shapes,*
these modifiers lean on one another, piggyback style, with
each modifying a larger word group. *Gray* modifies *shapes,*
large modifies *gray shapes,* and *three* modifies *large gray
shapes.* Cumulative adjectives cannot be joined with *and*
(three *and* large *and* gray shapes). Nor can they be scrambled
(*gray three large* shapes).

COORDINATE ADJECTIVES

▶ Robert is a warm, gentle, affectionate father.

The adjectives *warm, gentle,* and *affectionate* modify *father*
separately. They can be connected with *and* (warm *and* gentle
and affectionate), and they can be scrambled (an *affectionate,
warm, gentle* father).

CUMULATIVE ADJECTIVES

▶ Ira ordered a rich / chocolate / layer cake.

Ira didn't order a cake that was rich and chocolate and layer: He ordered a *layer cake* that was *chocolate*, a *chocolate layer cake* that was *rich*. These cumulative adjectives cannot be scrambled: a *layer chocolate rich* cake.

EXERCISE 32–2

Add or delete commas where necessary in the following sentences. If a sentence is correct, write "correct" after it. Answers to lettered sentences appear in the back of the book. Example:

> We gathered our essentials, took off for the great outdoors,
>
> and ignored the fact that it was Friday the 13th.

a. She wore a black silk cape, a rhinestone collar, satin gloves and high tops.

b. I called the fire department, ran downstairs to warn my neighbors, and discovered that they had set the fire on purpose.

c. City Café is noted for its spicy vegetarian dishes and its friendly efficient service.

d. Juan walked through the room with casual elegant grace.

e. My cat's pupils had constricted to small black shining dots.

1. My brother and I found a dead garter snake, picked it up and placed it on Miss Eunice's doorstep.

2. For breakfast the children ordered cornflakes, English muffins with peanut butter and cherry Cokes.

3. With a little ingenuity and a few spices, a good cook can create an appealing variety of nutritious, low-cost meals.

4. Mark was clad in a luminous orange rain suit and a brilliant white helmet.

5. Anne Frank and thousands like her were forced to hide in attics, cellars and secret rooms in an effort to save their lives.

32e Use commas to set off nonrestrictive elements. Do not use commas to set off restrictive elements.

Word groups describing nouns or pronouns (adjective clauses, adjective phrases, and appositives) are restrictive or nonrestrictive. A *restrictive* element defines or limits the meaning of the word it modifies and is therefore essential to the meaning of the sentence. Because it contains essential information, a restrictive element is not set off with commas.

RESTRICTIVE   For camp the children needed clothes *that were washable.*

If you remove a restrictive element from a sentence, the meaning changes significantly, becoming more general than you intended. The writer of the example sentence does not mean that the children needed clothes in general. The intended meaning is more limited: the children needed *washable* clothes.

A *nonrestrictive* element describes a noun or pronoun whose meaning has already been clearly defined or limited. Because it contains nonessential or parenthetical information, a nonrestrictive element is set off with commas.

NONRESTRICTIVE   For camp the children needed sturdy shoes, *which were expensive.*

If you remove a nonrestrictive element from a sentence, the meaning does not change dramatically. Some meaning is lost, to be sure, but the defining characteristics of the person or thing described remain the same as before. The children needed *sturdy shoes,* and these happened to be expensive.

Word groups describing proper nouns are nearly always nonrestrictive: The Illinois River, *which flows through our town,* has reached flood stage. Word groups modifying indefinite pronouns such as *everyone* and *something* are nearly always restrictive: Joe whispered something *that we could not hear.*

Often it is difficult to tell whether a word group is restrictive or nonrestrictive without seeing it in context and considering your meaning. Should you write "The dessert made with fresh raspberries was delicious" or "The dessert, made with fresh raspberries, was delicious"? That depends. If the phrase *made with fresh raspberries* tells readers which of two or more desserts you're referring to, you should omit the commas. If the phrase merely adds information about the one dessert served with the meal, you should use the commas.

Adjective clauses

Adjective clauses are patterned like sentences, containing subjects and verbs, but they function within sentences as modifiers of nouns or pronouns. They always follow the word they modify, usually immediately. Adjective clauses begin with a relative pronoun (*who, whom, whose, which, that*) or with a relative adverb (*where, when*).

Nonrestrictive adjective clauses are set off with commas; restrictive adjective clauses are not.

NONRESTRICTIVE CLAUSE

▶ Ed's country house, which is located on thirteen acres, was completely furnished with bats in the rafters and mice in the kitchen.

The clause *which is located on thirteen acres* does not restrict the meaning of *Ed's country house*, so the information is non-essential.

RESTRICTIVE CLAUSE

▶ An office manager for a corporation/that had government contracts/asked her supervisor whether she could reprimand her co-workers for smoking.

Because the adjective clause *that had government contracts* identifies the corporation, the information is essential.

NOTE: Use *that* with restrictive clauses only. Many writers prefer to use *which* with nonrestrictive clauses only, but usage varies. See the Glossary of Usage.

Phrases functioning as adjectives

Prepositional or verbal phrases functioning as adjectives may be restrictive or nonrestrictive. Nonrestrictive phrases are set off with commas; restrictive phrases are not.

NONRESTRICTIVE PHRASE

▶ The helicopter, with its 100,000-candlepower spotlight

illuminating the area, circled above.

The *with* phrase is nonessential because its purpose is not to specify which of two or more helicopters is being discussed.

RESTRICTIVE PHRASE

▶ One corner of the attic was filled with newspapers/ dating

from the turn of the century.

Dating from the turn of the century restricts the meaning of *newspapers*, so the comma should be omitted.

Appositives

An appositive is a noun or noun phrase that renames a nearby noun. Nonrestrictive appositives are set off with commas; restrictive appositives are not.

NONRESTRICTIVE APPOSITIVE

▶ Norman Mailer's first novel, *The Naked and the Dead,* was a

best-seller.

The term *first* restricts the meaning to one novel, so the appositive *The Naked and the Dead* is nonrestrictive.

RESTRICTIVE APPOSITIVE

▶ The song/ "Fire It Up/ " was blasted out of amplifiers ten

feet tall.

Once they've read *song*, readers still don't know precisely which song the writer means. The appositive following *song* restricts its meaning.

EXERCISE 32 – 3

Add or delete commas where necessary in the following sentences. If a sentence is correct, write "correct" after it. Answers to lettered sentences appear in the back of the book. Example:

> My youngest sister, who plays left wing on the team, now
>
> lives at The Sands , a beach house near Los Angeles.

a. We encountered no problems until we reached Cripple Creek where the trail forked.

b. The Scott Pack which is a twenty-five-pound steel bottle of air is designed to be worn on a firefighter's back.

c. The woman running for the council seat in the fifth district had a long history of community service.

d. Shakespeare's tragedy, *King Lear*,/ was given a splendid performance by the actor,/ Laurence Olivier.

e. It was a dreary barn of a place located in an even drearier section of town.

1. I had the pleasure of talking to a woman who had just returned from India where she had lived for ten years.

2. Greg's cousin, Albert, lives in Huntington Beach. [*Greg has more than one cousin.*]

3. The gentleman waiting for a prescription is Mr. Riley.

4. *Where the Wild Things Are*, the 1964 Caldecott Medal winner, is my nephew's favorite book.

5. Going on an archeological dig which has always been an ambition of mine seems out of the question this year.

32f Use commas to set off transitional and parenthetical expressions, absolute phrases, and elements expressing contrast.

Transitional expressions

Transitional expressions serve as bridges between sentences or parts of sentences. They include conjunctive adverbs such as *however*, *therefore*, and *moreover* and transitional phrases such as *for example*, *as a matter of fact*, and *in other words*. (For more complete lists, see 34b.)

When a transitional expression appears at the beginning of a sentence or in the middle of an independent clause, it is usually set off with commas.

▶ As a matter of fact ⌄ American football was established by fans who wanted to play a more organized game of rugby.

▶ The prospective babysitter looked very promising; she was busy ⌄ however ⌄ throughout January.

When a transitional expression appears between independent clauses in a compound sentence, it is preceded by a semicolon and is usually followed by a comma. (See 34b.)

▶ Alex did not understand the assignment; moreover ⌄ he was confused about its due date.

▶ Natural foods are not always salt free; for example ⌄ celery and watercress contain more sodium than most people would imagine.

EXCEPTION: If a transitional expression blends smoothly with the rest of the sentence, calling for little or no pause in reading, it does not need to be set off with a comma. Expressions such as *also, at least, certainly, consequently, indeed, of course, moreover, no doubt, perhaps, then,* and *therefore* do not always call for a pause.

> Bill's typewriter is broken; *therefore* you will need to borrow Sue's.

NOTE: The conjunctive adverb *however* always calls for a pause, but it should not be confused with *however* meaning "no matter how," which does not: *However hard Bill tried, he could not match his previous record.*

Parenthetical expressions

Expressions that are distinctly parenthetical should be set off with commas. Providing supplemental comments or information, they interrupt the flow of a sentence or appear as afterthoughts.

▶ Evolution ‚as far as we know‚ doesn't work this way.

▶ The bass weighed about twelve pounds‚ give or take a few

ounces.

Absolute phrases

An absolute phrase, which modifies the whole sentence, usually consists of a noun followed by a participle or participial phrase. (See 49e.) Absolute phrases may appear at the beginning or at the end of a sentence. Wherever they appear, they should be set off with commas.

▶ Her tennis game at last perfected‚ Chris won the cup.

▶ Brian was forced to rely on public transportation, his car

having been wrecked the week before.

In the first example, the absolute phrase appears at the beginning of the sentence; in the second example, it appears at the end.

CAUTION: Do not insert a comma between the noun and participle of an absolute construction.

▶ The next day/ being a school day, we turned down the

invitation.

Contrasted elements

Sharp contrasts beginning with words such as *not, never,* or *unlike* are set off with commas.

▶ Celia, unlike Robert, had no loathing for dance contests.

▶ Jane talks to me as an adult and friend, not as her little

sister.

32g   Use commas to set off nouns of direct address, the words *yes* and *no*, interrogative tags, and mild interjections.

▶ Forgive us, Dr. Spock, for reprimanding Jason.

▶ Yes, the loan will probably be approved.

▶ The film was faithful to the book, wasn't it?

▶ Well, cases like these are difficult to decide.
    ∧

32h Use commas with expressions such as *he said* to set off direct quotations. (See also 37f.)

▶ Naturalist Arthur Cleveland Bent remarked, "In part the
    ∧
peregrine declined unnoticed because it is not adorable."

▶ "Convictions are more dangerous foes of truth than lies,"
                                                          ∧
wrote philosopher Friedrich Nietzsche.

32i Use commas with dates, addresses, titles, and numbers.

Dates

In dates, the year is set off from the rest of the sentence with a pair of commas.

▶ On December 12, 1890, orders were sent out for the arrest
                   ∧   ∧
of Sitting Bull.

EXCEPTIONS: Commas are not needed if the date is inverted or if only the month and year are given.

The recycling plan goes into effect on 15 April 1992.

January 1990 was an extremely cold month.

Addresses

The elements of an address or place name are followed by commas. A zip code, however, is not preceded by a comma.

▶ John Lennon was born in Liverpool, England, in 1940.

▶ Please send the package to Greg Tarvin at 708 Spring Street,

Washington, Illinois 61571.

Titles

If a title follows a name, separate it from the rest of the sentence with a pair of commas.

▶ Sandra Barnes, M.D., has been appointed to the board of

directors.

Numbers

In numbers more than four digits long, use commas to separate the numbers into groups of three, starting from the right. In numbers four digits long, a comma is optional.

        3,500 [*or* 3500]
      100,000
    5,000,000

EXCEPTIONS: Do not use commas in street numbers, zip codes, telephone numbers, or years.

32j Use a comma to prevent confusion.

In certain contexts, a comma is necessary to prevent confusion. If the writer has omitted a word or phrase, for example, a comma may be needed to signal the omission.

▶ To err is human; to forgive, divine.

If the same word appears twice in a row in the same sentence, a comma may be needed for ease of reading.

▶ All of the catastrophes that we had feared might happen, happened.

Sometimes a comma is needed to prevent readers from grouping words in ways that do not match the writer's intention.

▶ Patients who can, walk up and down the halls several times a day.

EXERCISE 32 — 4: Major uses of the comma

This exercise covers the major uses of the comma listed in the chart on page 342. Add or delete commas where necessary; do not change correct sentences. Answers to lettered sentences appear in the back of the book. Example:

Although we invited him to the party, Gerald decided to spend another late night in the computer room.

a. The whiskey stills which were run mostly by farmers and fishermen were about twenty miles from the nearest town.
b. At the sound of a starting pistol the horses surged forward toward the first obstacle, a sharp incline three feet high.
c. Each morning the seventy-year-old woman cleans the barn, shovels manure and spreads clean hay around the milking stalls.
d. The students of Highpoint are required to wear dull green, polyester pleated skirts.
e. You will be unable to answer all the clients' questions or solve all their problems but you may turn to the directory when difficult issues arise.

Major uses of the comma

BEFORE A COORDINATING CONJUNCTION JOINING INDEPENDENT CLAUSES (32a)

No grand idea was ever born in a conference, but a lot of foolish ideas have died there.   — F. Scott Fitzgerald

AFTER AN INTRODUCTORY CLAUSE OR PHRASE (32b)

If thought corrupts language, language can also corrupt thought.   — George Orwell

BETWEEN ALL ITEMS IN A SERIES (32c)

All the things I really like to do are either immoral, illegal, or fattening.   — Alexander Woollcott

BETWEEN COORDINATE ADJECTIVES (32d)

There is a mighty big difference between good, sound reasons and reasons that sound good.   — Burton Hillis

TO SET OFF NONRESTRICTIVE ELEMENTS (32e)

Silence, which will save me from shame, will also deprive me of fame.   — Igor Stravinsky

1. Many Americans prefer Japanese cars which are generally more reliable and a better value than domestic automobiles.
2. Janice's costume was completed with bright red, snakeskin sandals.
3. Siddhartha decided to leave his worldly possessions behind and live in the forest by a beautiful river.
4. The lawyer fully explained the contract, but we weren't certain we understood all of its implications.
5. While hunting with a relative Greg was accidentally shot in the back.
6. Magic Johnson, who was the highest scorer in the game became the National Basketball Association's Most Valuable Player.
7. Aunt Betsy was an impossible demanding guest.
8. The French Mirage, the fastest airplane in the Colombian air force, was an astonishing machine to fly.
9. After being juggled among a dentist, a periodontist and an oral surgeon during the last two years, I have learned to appreciate my teeth.
10. As the summer slowly passed and we came to terms with Mike's death we visited the grave site less frequently.

EXERCISE 32 – 5: All uses of the comma

Add or delete commas where necessary in the following sentences; do not change correct sentences. Answers to lettered sentences appear in the back of the book. Example:

> "Yes ‚Virginia, there is a Santa Claus," said the editor.
> ∧

a. On January 29, 1990 we finally received Ms. Gilroy's reply to our letter of November 16 1989.
b. The coach having bawled us out thoroughly, we left the locker room with his last harsh words ringing in our ears.
c. Good technique does not guarantee however, that the power you develop will be sufficient for Kyok Pa competition.
d. We bought a home in Upper Marlboro where my husband worked as a mail carrier.
e. Please make the check payable to David Kerr D.D.S., not David Kerr M.D.

1. Mr. Mundy was born on July 22, 1939 in Arkansas, where his family had lived for four generations.
2. It has been reported that the Republican who suggested Eisenhower as a presidential candidate meant Milton not Ike.
3. Thermography, most experts agree, was safer than early forms of mammography.
4. We pulled into the first apartment complex we saw, and slowly patrolled the parking lots.
5. On Christmas morning, the children wildly excited about their gifts forgot their promise not to wake their parents.
6. I found Bill, my pet piranha, belly up in the tank one day his body floating listlessly in the water.
7. We wondered how our overweight grandmother could have been the pretty bride in the picture, but we kept our wonderings to ourselves.
8. "The last flight" she said with a sigh "went out five minutes before I arrived at the airport."
9. The Rio Grande, the border between Texas and Mexico lay before us. It was a sluggish mud-filled meandering stream that gave off an odor akin to sewage.
10. Julia lives in Sawbridgeworth, Hertfordshire England for most of the year.

33

Unnecessary commas

Many common misuses of the comma result from an incomplete understanding of the major comma rules presented in 32. In particular, writers frequently form misconceptions about rules 32a—e, either extending the rules inappropriately or misinterpreting them. Such misconceptions can lead to the errors described in 33a—e; rules 33f—h list other common misuses of the comma.

33a Do not use a comma between compound elements that are not independent clauses.

Though a comma should be used before a coordinating conjunction joining independent clauses (see 32a), this rule should not be extended to other compound word groups.

▶ Jake still doesn't realize that his illness is serious/and that

he will have to alter his diet to improve.

> *And* links two subordinate clauses, each beginning with *that.*

▶ The director led the cast members to their positions/and

gave an inspiring last-minute pep talk.

> *And* links the two parts of a compound predicate: *led . . . and gave.*

33b Do not use a comma after a phrase that begins an inverted sentence.

Though a comma belongs after most introductory phrases (see 32b), it does not belong after phrases that begin an inverted sentence. In an inverted sentence, the subject follows the verb, and a phrase that ordinarily would follow the verb is moved to the beginning.

▶ At the bottom of the sound/ lies a ship laden with treasure.

33c Do not use a comma before the first or after the last item in a series.

Though commas are required between items in a series (32c), do not place them either before or after the whole series.

▶ Other causes of asthmatic attacks are/stress, change in

temperature, humidity, and cold air.

▶ Ironically, this job that appears so glamorous, carefree, and

easy/carries a high degree of responsibility.

33d Do not use a comma between cumulative
adjectives, between an adjective and a noun, or between
an adverb and an adjective.

Commas are required between coordinate adjectives (those
that can be separated with *and*), but they do not belong between cumulative adjectives (those that cannot be separated
with *and*). (For a full discussion, see 32d.)

▶ In the corner of the closet we found an old/maroon hatbox

from Sears.

A comma should never be used to separate an adjective
from the noun that follows it.

▶ It was a senseless, dangerous/mission.

Nor should a comma be used to separate an adverb from
an adjective that follows it.

▶ The Hurst Home is unsuitable as a mental facility for

severely/disturbed youths.

33e Do not use commas to set off restrictive or mildly parenthetical elements.

Restrictive elements are adjectival modifiers or appositives that restrict the meaning of the nouns they follow. Because they are essential to the meaning of the sentence, they are not set off with commas. (For a full discussion of both restrictive and nonrestrictive elements, see 32e.)

▶ Drivers/ who think they own the road/ make cycling a

dangerous sport.

The modifier *who think they own the road* identifies the exact group of drivers the sentence is about. Putting commas around this modifier falsely suggests that all drivers think they own the road.

▶ Margaret Mead's book/ *Coming of Age in Samoa/* stirred up

considerable controversy when it was published.

Since Margaret Mead wrote more than one book, the appositive contains information that is essential to the meaning of the sentence.

Although commas should be used with distinctly parenthetical expressions (see 32f), do not use them to set off elements that are only mildly parenthetical.

▶ As long as patients are treated in a professional yet

compassionate manner, most/ eventually/ learn to deal with

their illness.

33f Do not use a comma to set off a concluding adverbial clause that is essential to the meaning of the sentence.

When adverb clauses introduce a sentence, they are nearly always followed by a comma (see 32b). When they conclude a sentence, however, they are not set off by commas if their content is essential to the meaning of the earlier part of the sentence. Adverb clauses beginning with *after, as soon as, before, because, if, since, unless, until,* and *when* are usually essential.

▶ Don't visit Paris at the height of the tourist season̷ unless

you have booked hotel reservations.

The *unless* clause is essential. Without it, the meaning of the sentence would be broader than the writer intended.

When a concluding adverb clause is nonessential, it should be preceded by a comma. Clauses beginning with *although, even though, though,* and *whereas* are usually nonessential.

The lecture seemed to last only a short time, although the clock said it had gone on for more than an hour.

33g Do not use a comma to separate the subject from the verb or the verb from its object or complement.

A sentence should flow from subject to verb to object without unnecessary pauses. Commas may appear between these major sentence elements only when a specific rule calls for them.

▶ Abiding by the 55-mile-per-hour speed limit╱ can save

considerable gasoline.

The gerund phrase *Abiding by the 55-mile-per-hour speed limit* is the subject of the verb *can save*, and it should not be separated from that verb. In fact, a comma here would lead to misreading, for readers would expect a sentence opening with a participial phrase, such as *Abiding by the 55-mile-per-hour speed limit, we can save considerable gasoline.*

▶ Fran explained to Mr. Dospril╱ that she was busy and would

have to see him later.

The *that* clause is the direct object of the verb *explained.* The writer has mistakenly used a comma to separate the verb from its object.

33h Avoid other common misuses of the comma.

Do not use a comma in the following situations.

AFTER A COORDINATING CONJUNCTION (*AND, BUT, OR, NOR, FOR, SO, YET*)

▶ Occasionally soap operas are taped, but╱ more often they are

being performed as they are telecast.

AFTER *SUCH AS* OR *LIKE*

▶ Many shade-loving plants, such as╱ begonias, impatiens, and

coleus, can add color to a shady garden.

BEFORE *THAN*

▶ Touring Crete was more thrilling for us/than visiting the Greek islands frequented by the jet set.

BEFORE A PARENTHESIS

▶ At MCI Sylvia began at the bottom/(with only three and a half walls and a swivel chair), but within five years she had been promoted to supervisor.

TO SET OFF AN INDIRECT (REPORTED) QUOTATION

▶ Samuel Goldwyn once said/that a verbal contract isn't worth the paper it's written on.

WITH A QUESTION MARK OR AN EXCLAMATION POINT

▶ "Why don't you try it?/" she coaxed. "You can't do any worse than the rest of us."

EXERCISE 33 – 1

Delete commas where necessary in the following sentences. If a sentence is correct, write "correct" after it. Answers to lettered sentences appear in the back of the book. Example:

Loretta Lynn has paved the way for artists such as/Reba

McEntire and the Judds.

a. We'd rather spend our money on blue-chip stocks, than speculate on porkbellies.

b. Being prepared for the worst, is one way to escape disappointment.

c. When he heard the groans, he opened the door, and ran out.

d. My father said, that he would move to California, if I would agree to transfer to UCLA.

e. I quickly accepted the fact that I was, literally, in third-class quarters.

1. Ms. Smith's favorite is the youngest brother, Timmy.

2. He wore a thick, black, wool coat over army fatigues.

3. Often public figures, (Michael Jackson is a good example) go to great lengths to guard their private lives.

4. She loved early spring flowers such as, crocuses, daffodils, forsythia, and irises.

5. Students, who sign up for Children's Literature and expect an easy A, have usually revised their expectations by the end of the first week.

6. Mesquite, the hardest of the softwoods, grows primarily in the Southwest.

7. Dougherty says that the record for arrests would have been better, if he had not pulled the officers away from their regular duties to assist the homicide division.

8. The kitchen was covered with black soot, that had been deposited by the woodburning stove, which stood in the middle of the room.

9. Captain Edward Spurlock observed, that the vast majority of crimes in our city are committed by repeat offenders.

10. Sharecroppers are given a free house, but they pay for everything else.

34

The semicolon

The semicolon is used between major sentence elements of equal grammatical rank.

34a Use a semicolon between closely related independent clauses not joined by a coordinating conjunction.

When related independent clauses appear in one sentence, they are ordinarily linked with a comma and a coordinating conjunction (*and, but, or, nor, for, so, yet*). The coordinating conjunction signals the relation between the clauses. If the clauses are closely related and the relation is clear without a conjunction, they may be linked with a semicolon instead.

> Injustice is relatively easy to bear; what stings is justice.
> — H. L. Mencken

> Wit has truth in it; wisecracking is simply calisthenics with words.   — Dorothy Parker

> When I was a boy, I was told that anybody could become President; I'm beginning to believe it.   — Clarence Darrow

A semicolon must be used whenever a coordinating conjunction has been omitted between independent clauses. To use merely a comma creates an error known as a comma splice. (See 20.)

▶ Some of the inmates were young and strung out on drugs/**;** others looked as if they might kill at any moment.

▶ Grandmother's basement had walls of Mississippi clay/**;** to me it looked like a dungeon.

CAUTION: Do not overuse the semicolon as a means of revising comma splices. For other revision strategies, see 20a, 20c, and 20d.

34b Use a semicolon between independent clauses linked with a conjunctive adverb or transitional phrase.

The following conjunctive adverbs and transitional phrases frequently link independent clauses appearing in one sentence.

CONJUNCTIVE ADVERBS
accordingly, also, anyway, besides, certainly, consequently, conversely, finally, furthermore, hence, however, incidentally, indeed, instead, likewise, meanwhile, moreover, nevertheless, next, nonetheless, otherwise, similarly, specifically, still, subsequently, then, therefore, thus

TRANSITIONAL PHRASES
after all, as a matter of fact, as a result, at any rate, at the same time, even so, for example, for instance, in addition, in conclusion, in fact, in other words, in the first place, on the contrary, on the other hand

When a conjunctive adverb or transitional phrase appears between independent clauses, it is preceded by a semicolon and usually followed by a comma.

▶ I learned all the rules and regulations/; however, I never really learned to control the ball. ∧

When a conjunctive adverb or transitional phrase appears in the middle or at the end of the second independent clause, the semicolon goes *between the clauses.*

Most singers gain fame through hard work and dedication; Evita, however, found other means.

Conjunctive adverbs and transitional phrases should not be confused with the coordinating conjunctions *and, but, or, nor, for, so,* and *yet,* which are preceded by a comma when they link independent clauses. (See 20.)

34c Use a semicolon between items in a series containing internal punctuation.

▶ Classic science fiction sagas are *Star Trek,* with Mr. Spock and his large pointed ears/;*Battlestar Galactica,* with its Cylon Raiders/;and *Star Wars,* with Han Solo, Luke Skywalker, and Darth Vader.

Without the semicolons, the reader would have to sort out the major groupings, distinguishing between important and less important pauses according to the logic of the sentence. By inserting semicolons at the major breaks, the writer does this work for the reader.

34d Avoid common misuses of the semicolon.

1. Do not use a semicolon to separate a subordinate clause or an appositive phrase from the rest of the sentence. The semicolon should be used only between elements of equal grammatical rank.

▶ Unless you brush your teeth within ten or fifteen minutes after eating/,brushing does almost no good.

The *Unless* clause is subordinate. Introductory subordinate clauses are usually followed by a comma (32b), never by a semicolon.

▶ Another delicious dish is the chef's special ; a roasted duck
^

rubbed with spices and stuffed with french fried potatoes.

The appositive phrase at the end of the sentence describes the
chef's special. Commas are used to separate most appositive
phrases from the words they describe. (See 32e.)

2. Do not use a semicolon to introduce a list. Use a colon
or a dash instead. (See 35a and 39a.)

▶ Over the past twenty years, James Taylor has worked with

many fine artists ; Carly Simon, Carole King, Joni Mitchell,
^

Simon and Garfunkel, Stevie Wonder, and Linda Ronstadt.

3. As a rule, do not use a semicolon between independent
clauses when those clauses have been joined with a coordinating conjunction (*and, but, or, nor, for, so, yet*).

▶ Twenty-eight of the applicants had college degrees ; but
^

most of them were clearly unqualified for the position.

EXCEPTIONS: If at least one of the independent clauses contains internal punctuation, a writer may choose to use a
semicolon even though the clauses are joined with a coordinating conjunction.

As a vehicle [the model T] was hard-working, commonplace,
and heroic; and it often seemed to transmit those qualities to
the person who rode in it.   — E. B. White

Although a comma would also be correct in this sentence, the
semicolon is more effective, for it indicates the relative
weights of the pauses.

Occasionally, a semicolon may be used to emphasize a sharp contrast or a firm distinction between clauses joined with a coordinating conjunction.

> We hate some persons because we do not know them; and we will not know them because we hate them.
>
> — Charles Caleb Colton

EXERCISE 34 – 1

Add commas or semicolons where needed in the following well-known quotations. If a sentence is correct, write "correct" after it. Answers to lettered sentences appear in the back of the book. Example:

If an animal does something, we call it instinct; if we do the same thing, we call it intelligence.   — **Will Cuppy**

a. If fifty million people say a foolish thing it is still a foolish thing.
     — Anatole France

b. No amount of experimentation can ever prove me right a single experiment can prove me wrong.   — Albert Einstein

c. Don't talk about yourself it will be done when you leave.
     — Wilson Mizner

d. The only sensible ends of literature are first the pleasurable toil of writing second the gratification of one's family and friends and lastly the solid cash.   — Nathaniel Hawthorne

e. All animals are equal but some animals are more equal than others.   — George Orwell

1. Everyone is a genius at least once a year a real genius has his [or her] original ideas closer together.   — G. C. Lichtenberg

2. When choosing between two evils I always like to try the one I've never tried before.   — Mae West

3. I don't know who my grandfather was I am much more concerned to know what his grandson will be.   — Abraham Lincoln

4. America is a country that doesn't know where it is going but is determined to set a speed record getting there.
     — Lawrence J. Peter

5. I've been rich and I've been poor; rich is better.
     — Sophie Tucker

EXERCISE 34–2

Edit the following sentences to correct errors in the use of the comma and the semicolon. If a sentence is correct, write "correct" after it. Answers to lettered sentences appear in the back of the book. Example:

> Love is blind ; envy has its eyes wide open.

a. For some, happiness comes all in one satisfying, glowing piece; others, by patching together little bits of it, manage to salvage enough to keep warm.

b. America has been called a country of pragmatists; although the American devotion to ideals is legendary.

c. The first requirement is honesty, everything else follows.

d. I am not fond of opera, I must admit; however, that I was greatly moved by *Les Misérables.*

e. Delegates to the convention came from Basel, Switzerland, Waikiki, Hawaii, Nome, Alaska, and Pretoria, South Africa.

1. When she entered the room, everyone quit discussing the incident; until she had finished her errand and left.

2. Martin Luther King, Jr., who forged the nonviolent civil rights movement in the United States, had not intended to be a preacher; initially, he had planned to become a lawyer.

3. Severe, unremitting pain is a ravaging force; especially when the patient tries to hide it from others.

4. I entered this class feeling jittery and incapable, I leave feeling poised and confident.

5. Our physical education teacher always matched the punishment to the crime, for example, for talking during class, I had to write a five-hundred-word essay entitled "The Glories of Silence."

35

The colon

The colon is used primarily to call attention to the words that follow it.

35a Use a colon after an independent clause to direct attention to a list, an appositive, or a quotation.

A LIST
The daily routine should include at least the following: twenty knee bends, fifty sit-ups, fifteen leg lifts, and five minutes of running in place.

To bring law and order to the fish tank, I had several alternatives: I could separate the villain from the victim, I could destroy the evil one, or I could hire a watchdog.

AN APPOSITIVE
My roommate is guilty of two of the seven deadly sins: gluttony and sloth.

A QUOTATION
Consider the words of John F. Kennedy: "Ask not what your country can do for you; ask what you can do for your country."

For other ways of introducing quotations, see 37e.

35b Use a colon between independent clauses if the second summarizes or explains the first.

Faith is like love: It cannot be forced.

NOTE: When an independent clause follows a colon, it may begin with a lowercase or a capital letter.

35c Use a colon after the salutation in a formal letter, to indicate hours and minutes, to show proportions, between a title and subtitle, and between city and publisher in bibliographic entries.

Dear Sir or Madam:

5:30 P.M. (or p.m.)

The ratio of women to men was 2:1.

The Glory of Hera: Greek Mythology and the Greek Family

Boston: Bedford, 1990

NOTE: In biblical references, a colon is ordinarily used between chapter and verse (Luke 2:14). The Modern Language Association recommends a period instead (Luke 2.14).

35d Avoid common misuses of the colon.

A colon must be preceded by a full independent clause. Therefore, avoid using it in the following situations.

**BETWEEN A VERB AND ITS OBJECT
OR COMPLEMENT**

▶ Some important vitamins found in vegetables are⫽ vitamin A, thiamine, niacin, and vitamin C.

BETWEEN A PREPOSITION AND ITS OBJECT

▶ The areas to be painted consisted of⫽ three gable ends, trim work, sixteen windows, and a front and back porch.

AFTER *SUCH AS, INCLUDING,* OR *FOR EXAMPLE*

▶ The trees on our campus include many fine Japanese specimens such as⫽ black pines, ginkgos, weeping cherries, and cutleaf maples.

EXERCISE 35–1

Edit the following sentences to correct errors in the use of the comma, the semicolon, or the colon. If a sentence is correct, write "correct" after it. Answers to lettered sentences appear in the back of the book. Example:

> Smiling confidently, the young man stated his major goal in
>
> life|: to be secretary of agriculture before he was thirty.
>   ∧

a. The second and most memorable week of survival school consisted of five stages: orientation; long treks; POW camp; escape and evasion; and return to civilization.

b. Among the canceled classes were: calculus, physics, advanced biology, and English 101.

c. His only desires were for vengeance; vengeance for his father's death, vengeance for his mother's loss of eyesight, vengeance for his own lost youth.

d. For example: when a student in private school is caught with drugs, he or she is immediately expelled.

e. In the introduction to his wife's book on gardening, E. B. White describes her writing process: "The editor in her fought the writer every inch of the way; the struggle was felt all through the house. She would write eight or ten words, then draw her gun and shoot them down."

1. The patient survived for one reason, the medics got to her in time.

2. While traveling through France, Helen visited: the Loire Valley, Chartres, the Louvre, and the McDonald's stand at the foot of the Eiffel Tower.

3. I'm from Missouri you must show me.

4. Historian Robert Kee looks to the past for the source of the political troubles in Ireland: "If blame is to be apportioned for today's situation in Northern Ireland, it should be laid not at the door of men today but of history.

5. Dean Summerfelt had several projects to complete before leaving for vacation; hiring a data-processing instructor, completing a report on curriculum revision, and defending the departmental budget at the annual budget hearing.

36

The apostrophe

36a Use an apostrophe to indicate that a noun is possessive.

Possessive nouns usually indicate ownership, as in *Tim's hat* or *the lawyer's desk*. Frequently, however, ownership is only loosely implied: *the tree's roots, a day's work*. If you are not sure whether a noun is possessive, try turning it into an *of* phrase: *the roots of the tree, the work of a day*.

When to add -'s

1. If the noun does not end in -*s*, add -'*s*.

Roy managed to climb out on the *driver's* side.

Thank you for refunding the *children's* money.

2. If the noun is singular and ends in -*s*, add -'*s*.

Lois's sister spent last year in India.

EXCEPTION: If pronunciation would be awkward with the added -'*s*, some writers use only the apostrophe. Either use is acceptable.

Euripides' plays are among my favorites.

When to add only an apostrophe

If the noun is plural and ends in -*s*, add only an apostrophe.

Both *diplomats'* briefcases were stolen.

Joint possession

To show joint possession, use *-'s* or (*-s'*) with the last noun only; to show individual possession, make all nouns possessive.

> Have you seen *Joyce and Greg's* new camper?

> *John's and Marie's* expectations of marriage couldn't have been more different.

In the first sentence, Joyce and Greg jointly own one camper. In the second sentence, John and Marie individually have different expectations.

Compound nouns

If a noun is compound, use *-'s* (or *-s'*) with the last element.

> My father-in-law's sculpture won first place.

36b Use an apostrophe and *-s* to indicate that an indefinite pronoun is possessive.

Indefinite pronouns refer to no specific person or thing: *everyone, someone, no one, something.* (See 47b.)

> *Someone's* raincoat has been left behind.

> This diet will improve almost *anyone's* health.

36c Use an apostrophe to mark omissions in contractions and numbers.

In contractions the apostrophe takes the place of missing letters.

It's a shame that Frank *can't* go on the tour.

It's stands for *it is*, *can't* for *cannot*.

The apostrophe is also used to mark the omission of the first two digits of a year (the class of '85) or years (the '60s generation).

We'll never forget the blizzard of '78.

36d Use an apostrophe and -s to pluralize numbers mentioned as numbers, letters mentioned as letters, words mentioned as words, and abbreviations.

Peggy skated nearly perfect figure 8's.

The bleachers in our section were marked with large red *J*'s.

We've heard enough *maybe*'s.

You must ask to see their I.D.'s.

Notice that the *-s* is not italicized when used with an italicized number, letter, or word.

EXCEPTION: An *-s* alone is often added to the years in a decade: *the 1980s*.

36e Avoid common misuses of the apostrophe.

1. Do not use an apostrophe with nouns that are not possessive.

▶ Some ~~outpatient's~~ *outpatients* are given special parking permits.

2. Do not use an apostrophe in the possessive pronouns *its*, *whose*, *his*, *hers*, *ours*, *yours*, and *theirs*.

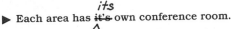

> *its*
> ▶ Each area has ~~it's~~ own conference room.
> ⌃

It's means *it is*. The possessive pronoun *its* contains no apostrophe, despite the fact that it is possessive.

> *whose*
> ▶ This course was taught by a professional florist ~~who's~~
> ⌃
>
> technique was oriental.

Who's means *who is*. The possessive pronoun is *whose*.

EXERCISE 36 – 1

Edit the following sentences to correct errors in the use of the apostrophe. If a sentence is correct, write "correct" after it. Answers to lettered sentences appear in the back of the book. Example:

> *Jack's.*
> Marietta lived above the only bar in town, Smiling ~~Jacks.~~
> ⌃

a. In a democracy anyones vote counts as much as mine.
b. He received two A's, three B's, and a C.
c. The puppy's favorite activity was chasing it's tail.
d. After we bought J.J. the latest style pants and shirts, he decided that last years faded, ragged jeans were perfect for all occasions.
e. A crocodiles' life span is about thirteen years.

1. The snow does'nt rise any higher than the horses' fetlocks. [*more than one horse*]
2. For a bus driver, complaints, fare disputes, and robberies are all part of a days work.
3. Each day the menu features a different European countries' dish.
4. We cleared four years accumulation of trash out of the attic; its amazing how much junk can pile up.
5. Booties are placed on the sled dogs feet to protect them from sharp rocks and ice. [*more than one dog*]
6. Sue and Ann went to a party for a friend of theirs'.

7. Three teenage son's can devour about as much food as four full-grown field hands. The only difference is that they dont do half as much work.
8. Ethiopians's meals were served on fermented bread.
9. Luck is an important element in a rock musicians career.
10. My sister-in-law's quilts are being shown at the Fendrick Gallery.

37

Quotation marks

37a Use quotation marks to enclose direct quotations.

Direct quotations of a person's words, whether spoken or written, must be in quotation marks.

> In a husky voice Muhammad Ali bragged, "My opponent will be on the floor in round four. He'll take a dive in round five. In round nine he'll be all mine."

> "A foolish consistency is the hobgoblin of little minds," wrote Ralph Waldo Emerson.

CAUTION: Do not use quotation marks around indirect quotations. An indirect quotation reports someone's ideas without using that person's exact words.

> Ralph Waldo Emerson believed that senseless consistency is the mark of a small mind.

NOTE: In dialogue, begin a new paragraph to mark a change in speaker.

"Mom, his name is Willie, not William. A thousand times I've told you, it's *Willie*."

"Willie is a derivative of William, Lester. Surely his birth certificate doesn't have Willie on it, and I like calling people by their proper names."

"Yes, it does, ma'am. My mother named me Willie K. Mason."   — Gloria Naylor

If a single speaker utters more than one paragraph, introduce each paragraph with quotation marks, but do not use closing quotation marks until the end of the speech.

37b Set off long quotations of prose or poetry by indenting.

When a quotation of prose runs to more than four typed lines, set if off by indenting ten spaces from the left margin. Quotation marks are not required because the indented format tells readers that the quotation is taken word for word from a source. Long quotations are ordinarily introduced by a sentence ending with a colon.

James Horan, after making an exhaustive study of the historical record, evaluates Billy the Kid like this:

The portrait that emerges of [the Kid] from the thousands of pages of affidavits, reports, trial transcripts, his letters, and his testimony is neither the mythical Robin Hood nor the stereotyped adenoidal moron and pathological killer. Rather Billy appears as a disturbed, lonely young man, honest, loyal to his friends, dedicated to his beliefs, and betrayed by our institutions and the corrupt, ambitious, and compromising politicians of his time. (158)

The number in parentheses is a citation handled according to the Modern Language Association style. (See 54a.)

NOTE: When you quote two or more paragraphs from the source, indent the first line of each paragraph an additional three spaces.

When a quotation from poetry runs more than three lines, set it off from the text by indenting ten spaces from the left margin. Use no quotation marks unless they appear in the poem itself.

> Although many anthologizers "modernize" her punctuation, Emily Dickinson relied heavily on dashes, using them, perhaps, as a musical device. Here, for example, is the original version of the opening stanza from "The Snake":
>
>> A narrow Fellow in the Grass
>> Occasionally rides —
>> You may have met Him — did you not
>> His notice sudden is —

37c Use single quotation marks to enclose a quotation within a quotation.

> According to Paul Eliott, Eskimo hunters "chant an ancient magic song to the seal they are after: 'Beast of the sea! Come and place yourself before me in the early morning!' "

37d Use quotation marks around the titles of short works: newspaper and magazine articles, poems, short stories, songs, episodes of television and radio programs, and chapters or subdivisions of books.

> Katherine Mansfield's "The Garden Party" provoked a lively discussion in our short-story class last night.

NOTE: Titles of books, plays, and films and names of magazines and newspapers are put in italics or underlined. See 42a.

37e Quotation marks may be used to set off words used as words.

Although words used as words are ordinarily underlined, to indicate italics (see 42d), quotation marks are also acceptable. Just be sure to follow consistent practice throughout a paper.

> The words "flaunt" and "flout" are frequently confused.

> The words *flaunt* and *flout* are frequently confused.

37f Use punctuation with quotation marks according to convention.

This section describes the conventions used by American publishers in placing various marks of punctuation inside or outside quotation marks. It also explains how to punctuate when introducing quoted material.

Periods and commas

Always place periods and commas inside quotation marks.

> "This is a stick-up," said the well-dressed young couple. "We want all your money."

This rule applies to single quotation marks as well as double quotation marks. (See 37c.) It also applies to all uses of quotation marks: for quoted material, for titles of works, and for words used as words.

EXCEPTION: In the Modern Language Association's style of parenthetical in-text citations (see 54a), the period follows the citation in parentheses:

James M. McPherson acknowledges that the Whigs "were not averse to extending the blessings of American liberty, even to Mexicans and Indians" (48).

Colons and semicolons

Put colons and semicolons outside quotation marks.

> Harold wrote, "I regret that I am unable to attend the fundraiser for AIDS research"; his letter, however, came with a substantial contribution.

Question marks and exclamation points

Put question marks and exclamation points inside quotation marks unless they apply to the whole sentence.

> Contrary to tradition, bedtime at my house is marked by "Mommy, can I tell you a story now?"

> Have you heard the old proverb "Do not climb the hill until you reach it"?

In the first sentence, the question mark applies only to the quoted question. In the second sentence, the question mark applies to the whole sentence.

Introducing quoted material

After a word group introducing a quotation, choose a colon, a comma, or no punctuation at all, whichever is appropriate in context.

If a quotation has been formally introduced with a full independent clause — not just explanatory words such as *he said* or *she remarked* — a colon is appropriate.

> Freuchen points out that the diet is not as monotonous as it may seem: "When you have meat and meat, and meat again, you learn to distinguish between the different parts of an animal."

If a quotation is introduced with or followed by explanatory words such as *he said* or *she remarked*, a comma is needed.

> Robert Frost said, "You can be a little ungrammatical if you come from the right part of the country."

> "You can be a little ungrammatical if you come from the right part of the country," Robert Frost said.

If a quotation appears at the beginning of a sentence, set if off with a comma unless the quotation ends with a question mark or an exclamation point.

> "We shot them like dogs," boasted Davy Crockett, who was among Jackson's troops.

> "What is it?" I asked, bracing myself.

If a quoted sentence is interrupted by explanatory words, use commas to set off the explanatory words.

> "A great many people think they are thinking," wrote William James, "when they are merely rearranging their prejudices."

If two whole sentences from the same source are interrupted by explanatory words, use a comma before the explanatory words and a period after them.

> "I was a flop as a daily reporter," admitted E. B. White. "Every piece had to be a masterpiece — and before you knew it, Tuesday was Wednesday."

When a quotation is blended into the writer's own sentence, either a comma or no punctuation is appropriate, depending on the way in which the quotation fits into the sentence structure.

> The future champion could, as he put it, "float like a butterfly and sting like a bee."

Charles Hudson noted that the prisoners escaped "by squeezing through a tiny window eighteen feet above the floor of their cell."

37g Avoid common misuses of quotation marks.

1. Do not use quotation marks to draw attention to familiar slang, to disown trite expressions, or to justify an attempt at humor.

▶ Between Thanksgiving and Super Bowl Sunday, many

American wives become ~~"~~football widows.~~"~~

2. Do not use quotation marks around indirect quotations. (See 37a.)

3. Do not use quotation marks around the title of your own essay.

EXERCISE 37–1

Add or delete quotation marks as needed and make any other necessary changes in punctuation in the following sentences. If a sentence is correct, write "correct" after it. Answers to lettered sentences appear in the back of the book. Example:

Bill Cosby once said, "I don't know the key to success, but the key to failure is trying to please everyone."

a. Fire and Ice is one of Robert Frost's most famous poems.
b. As Emerson wrote in 1849, I hate quotations. Tell me what you know.
c. Joggers have to run up the hills and then back down, but bicyclers, once they reach the top of a hill, get a "free ride" back down.
d. "Ladies and gentlemen," said the emcee, "I am happy to present our guest speaker.

e. Historians Segal and Stineback tell us that the English settlers considered these epidemics "the hand of God making room for His followers in the "New World"."

1. The dispatcher's voice cut through the still night air: "Scout 41, robbery in progress, alley rear of 58th and Blaine.

2. For the body to turn sugar into glucose, other nutrients in the body must be used. Sugar "steals" these other nutrients from the body.

3. Kara looked hopelessly around the small locked room. "If only I were a flea," she thought, "I could get out of here."

4. My skiing instructor promised us that "we would all be ready for the intermediate slope in one week."

5. After the movie Vicki said, "The reviewer called this flick "trash of the first order." I guess you can't believe everything you read."

6. Some critics believe that when Hamlet says "To be, or not to be, that is the question," he knows that others are hidden in the room watching him.

7. Who said, "I have sworn upon the altar of God eternal hostility against every form of tyranny"?

8. As David Anable has written: "The time is approaching when we will be able to select the news we want to read from a pocket computer."

9. "Could one define the word 'red,' " asks Wittgenstein, "by pointing to something that was *not red*?"

10. One of my favorite poems is Langston Hughes's 'Mother to Son.'

38

End punctuation

38a The period

1. Use a period to end all sentences except direct questions or genuine exclamations.

Everyone knows that a period should be used to end most sentences. The only problems that arise concern the choice between a period and a question mark or between a period and an exclamation point.

If a sentence reports a question instead of asking it directly, it should end with a period, not a question mark.

> Celia asked whether the picnic would be canceled.

If a declarative or an imperative sentence is not a genuine exclamation, it should end with a period, not an exclamation point.

> After years of working her way through school, Pat finally graduated with high honors.

> Fill out the travel form in triplicate and then send it to the main office.

2. Use periods in abbreviations according to convention. A period is conventionally used in abbreviations such as the following:

Mr.	B.A.	B.C.	i.e.	A.M. (or a.m.)
Mrs.	M.A.	B.C.E.	e.g.	P.M. (or p.m.)
Ms.	Ph.D.	A.D.	etc.	
Dr.	R.N.	C.E.		

A period is not used with U.S. Postal Service abbreviations for states: MD, TX, CA.

Ordinarily a period is not used in abbreviations of organization names:

NATO	UNESCO	AFL-CIO	FCC
TVA	IRS	SEC	IBM
USA	NAACP	PUSH	FTC
(or U.S.A.)	UCLA	NBA	NIH

Usage varies, however. When in doubt, consult a dictionary, a style manual, or a publication by the agency in question. Even the yellow pages can help.

NOTE: If a sentence ends with a period marking an abbreviation, do not add a second period.

38b The question mark

1. Use a question mark after a direct question.
Obviously a direct question should be followed by a question mark.

What is the horsepower of a 747 engine?

If a polite request is written in the form of a question, it too is usually followed by a question mark.

Would you please send me your catalog of lilies?

CAUTION: Do not use a question mark after an indirect question (one that is reported rather than asked directly). Use a period instead.

He asked me who was teaching the mythology course.

2. Questions in a series may be followed by question marks even when they are not complete sentences:

We wondered where Calamity had hidden this time. Under the sink? Behind the furnace? On top of the bookcase?

38c The exclamation point

1. Use an exclamation point after a word group or sentence that expresses exceptional feeling or deserves special emphasis.

The medic shook me and kept yelling, "He's dead! He's dead! Can't you see that?"

2. Do not overuse the exclamation point.

▶ In the fisherman's memory the fish lives on, increasing in
length and weight with each passing year, until at last it is
big enough to shade a fishing boat/.

This sentence doesn't need to be pumped up with an exclamation point. It is emphatic enough without it.

▶ Whenever I see Martina lunging forward to put away an
overhead smash, it might as well be me/. She does it just the
way that I would!

The first exclamation point should be deleted so that the second one will have more force.

EXERCISE 38 – 1

Add appropriate end punctuation in the following paragraph.

Although I am generally rational, I am superstitious I
never walk under ladders or put shoes on the table If I spill the
salt, I go into frenzied calisthenics picking up the grains and
tossing them over my left shoulder As a result of these curious
activities, I've always wondered whether knowing the roots of
superstitions would quell my irrational responses Superstition
has it, for example, that one should never place a hat on the
bed This superstition arises from a time when head lice were
quite common and placing a guest's hat on the bed stood a
good chance of spreading lice through the host's bed Doesn't
this make good sense And doesn't it stand to reason that if I
know that my guests don't have lice I shouldn't care where
their hats go Of course it does It is fair to ask, then, whether I
have changed my ways and place hats on beds Are you kidding
I wouldn't put a hat on a bed if my life depended on it

39

Other punctuation marks: the dash, parentheses, brackets, the ellipsis mark, the slash

39a The dash

When typing, use two hyphens to form a dash (--). Do not put spaces before or after the dash.

1. Use dashes to set off parenthetical material that deserves emphasis.

> Everything that went wrong — from the peeping Tom at her window to my head-on collision — was blamed on our move.

2. Use dashes to set off appositives that contain commas.

An appositive is a noun or noun phrase that renames a nearby noun. Ordinarily most appositives are set off with commas (32e), but when the appositive contains commas, a pair of dashes helps readers see the relative importance of all the pauses.

> In my hometown the basic needs of people — food, clothing, and shelter — are less costly than in Los Angeles.

3. Use a dash to prepare for a list, a restatement, an amplification, or a dramatic shift in tone or thought.

> Along the wall are the bulk liquids — sesame seed oil, honey, safflower oil, and that half-liquid "peanuts only" peanut butter.

> Consider the amount of sugar in the average person's diet — 104 pounds per year, 90 percent more than that consumed by our ancestors.

Everywhere we looked there were little kids — a box of Cracker Jacks in one hand and mommy or daddy's sleeve in the other.

Kiere took a few steps back, came running full speed, kicked a mighty kick — and missed the ball.

In the first two examples, the writer could also use a colon. (See 35a.) The colon is more formal than the dash, and not quite as dramatic.

4. Do not overuse the dash.

Unless there is a specific reason for using the dash, avoid it. Unnecessary dashes create a choppy effect.

▶ Seeing that our young people learn to use computers as instructional tools / for information retrieval / makes good sense. Herding them / sheeplike / into computer technology does not.

39b Parentheses

1. Use parentheses to enclose supplemental material, minor digressions, and afterthoughts.

After taking her temperature, pulse, and blood pressure (routine vital signs), the nurse made Becky as comfortable as possible.

The weights James was first able to move (not lift, mind you) were measured in ounces.

2. Use parentheses to enclose letters or numbers labeling items in a series.

Regulations stipulated that only the following equipment could be used on the survival mission: (1) a knife, (2) thirty feet of parachute line, (3) a book of matches, (4) two ponchos, (5) an *E* tool, and (6) a signal flare.

3. Do not overuse parentheses.

Rough drafts are likely to contain more afterthoughts than necessary. As writers head into a sentence, they often think of additional details, occasionally working them in as best they can with parentheses. Usually such sentences should be revised so that the additional details no longer seem to be afterthoughts.

▶ Tucker's Restaurant serves homestyle breakfasts with fresh
    warm
    eggs, ∧buttered toast ⸝(which is still warm), sausage, bacon,

    waffles, pancakes, and even kippers.

                                    from ten to fifty million
▶ Researchers have said that ∧ten million (estimates run as

    high as fifty million) Americans have hypoglycemia.

39c   Brackets

Use brackets to enclose any words or phrases that you have inserted into an otherwise word-for-word quotation.

> *Audubon* reports that "if there are not enough young to balance deaths, the end of the species [California condor] is inevitable."

The sentence quoted from the *Audubon* article did not contain the words *California condor* (since the context made clear what species was meant), so the writer in this example needed to add the name in brackets.

The Latin word *sic* in brackets indicates that an error in a quoted sentence appears in the original source.

> According to the review, Suzanne Farrell's performance was brilliant, "exceding [*sic*] the expectations of even her most loyal fans."

Do not overuse *sic,* however, since calling attention to others' mistakes can appear snobbish. The preceding quotation, for example, might have been paraphrased instead: *According to the review, even Suzanne Farrell's most loyal fans were surprised by the brilliance of her performance.*

39d The ellipsis mark

The ellipsis mark consists of three spaced periods. Use an ellipsis mark to indicate that you have deleted words from an otherwise word-for-word quotation.

> Reuben reports that "when the amount of cholesterol circulating in the blood rises over . . . 300 milligrams per 100, the chances of a heart attack increase dramatically."

If you delete a full sentence or more in the middle of a quoted passage, use a period before the three ellipsis dots.

> "Most of our efforts," writes Dave Erikson, "are directed toward saving the bald eagle's wintering habitat along the Mississippi River. . . . It's important that the wintering birds have a place to roost, where they can get out of the cold wind and be undisturbed by man."

CAUTION: Do not use the ellipsis mark at the beginning of a quotation; do not use it at the end of a quotation unless you have cut some words from the final sentence quoted. (See also 53.)

In quoted poetry, use a full line of dots to indicate that you have dropped a line or more from the poem:

> Had we but world enough, and time,
> This coyness, lady, were no crime.
>
> .   .   .   .
>
> But at my back I always hear
> Time's wingèd chariot hurrying near;   — Andrew Marvell

The ellipsis mark may also be used to mark a hesitation or interruption in speech or to suggest unfinished thoughts.

> Before falling into a coma, the victim whispered,
> "It was a man with a tatoo on his. . . ."

39e The slash

Use the slash to separate two or three lines of poetry that have been run in to your text. Add a space both before and after the slash.

> In the opening lines of "Jordan," George Herbert pokes gentle fun at popular poems of his time: "Who says that fictions only and false hair / Become a verse? Is there in truth no beauty?"

More than three lines of poetry should be handled as an indented quotation. See 37b.

The slash may occasionally be used to separate options such as *pass/fail* and *producer/director.* Do not use a space before or after the slash.

> Roger Sommers, the play's producer/director, announced a change in casting.

Be sparing, however, in this use of the slash. In particular, avoid use of *and/or, he/she,* and *his/her.*

EXERCISE 39 – 1

Edit the following sentences for punctuation problems, focusing especially on appropriate use of the dash, parentheses, brackets, ellipsis mark, and slash. If a sentence is correct, write "correct" after it. Answers to lettered sentences appear in the back of the book. Example:

Social insects/—bees, for example/—are able to communicate quite complicated messages to their fellows.

a. We lived in Iowa (Davenport, to be specific) during the early years of our marriage.
b. Every night — after her jazzercise class — Elizabeth bragged about how invigorated she felt, but she always looked exhausted.
c. *Infoworld* reports that "customers without any particular aptitude for computers can easily learn to use it [the Bay Area Teleguide] through simple, three-step instructions located at the booth."
d. Cancer — a disease that strikes without regard to age, race, or religion and causes dread in the most stalwart person, had struck my family.
e. The class stood, faced the flag, placed hands over hearts, and raced through "I pledge allegiance — liberty and justice for all" in less than sixty seconds.

1. Of the three basic schools of detective fiction, the tea-and-crumpet, the hardboiled detective, and the police procedural, I find the quaint, civilized quality of the tea-and-crumpet school the most appealing.
2. In *Lifeboat,* Alfred Hitchcock appears (some say without his knowledge) in a newspaper advertisement for weight loss.
3. There are three points of etiquette in poker: 1. always allow someone to cut the cards, 2. don't forget to ante up, and 3. never stack your chips.
4. "April is the cruelest month . . . ," wrote T. S. Eliot, but we all know that February holds that honor.
5. The old Valentine verse we used to chant said it all: "Roses are red, / violets are blue, / sugar is sweet, / and so are you."

EXERCISE 39 – 2: Review

Punctuate the following letter.

> 27 Latches Lane
> Missoula Missouri 55432
> April 16 1990

Dear Rosalie

I have to tell you about the accident We were driving home at around 5 30 PM of course wed be on the Schuylkill Expressway at rush hour when a tan Cutlass smashed us in the rear Luckily we all had our seatbelts fastened Dr Schabbles who was in the back seat and my husband Bob complained of whiplash but really we got off with hardly a scratch

The mother and daughter in the Cutlass however werent as fortunate They ended up with surgical collars and Ace bandages but their car certainly fared better than ours

The driver of the third car involved in the accident confused everyone Although her car was in the front of the line she kept saying I hit the tan car I hit the tan car We didnt understand until she told us that a fourth car had hit her in the rear and had pushed her ahead of all the rest Can you imagine how frustrated we were when we found out that this man the one who had started it all had left the scene of the accident You were the last car in line someone said No you were we answered The policeman had to reconstruct the disaster from the hopeless babble of eight witnesses

Its uncanny Out of 34800 cars on the expressway on April 14 the police keep count you know our car had to be the one in front of that monstrous tan Cutlass

Well I just wanted to send you a report I hope your days are less thrilling than mine

> Yours
>
> Marie

PART VIII

Editing for Mechanics

40

Abbreviations

40a Use standard abbreviations for titles immediately
before and after proper names.

TITLES BEFORE PROPER NAMES	TITLES AFTER PROPER NAMES
Mr. Ralph Meyer	William Albert, Sr.
Ms. Nancy Linehan	Thomas Hines, Jr.
Mrs. Edward Horn	Anita Lor, Ph.D.
Dr. Margaret Simmons	Robert Simkowski, M.D.
the Rev. John Stone	William Lyons, M.A.
St. Joan of Arc	Margaret Chin, LL.D.
Prof. James Russo	Polly Stein, D.D.S.

Do not abbreviate a title if it is not used with a proper name.

▶ My history ~~prof.~~ was an expert on America's use of the
professor

atomic bomb in World War II.

Avoid redundant titles such as *Dr. Susan Hasselquist,
M.D.* Choose one title or the other: *Dr. Susan Hasselquist* or
Susan Hasselquist, M.D.

40b Use commonly accepted abbreviations for the
names of organizations, corporations, and countries.

Familiar abbreviations, often written without periods, are acceptable:

CIA, FBI, AFL-CIO, NAACP   USA, USSR
IBM, UPI, CBS   (or U.S.A., U.S.S.R.)

While in Washington the schoolchildren toured the FBI.

The YMCA has opened a new gym close to my office.

NOTE: When using an unfamiliar abbreviation (such as CBE for Council of Biology Editors) throughout a paper, write the full name followed by the abbreviation in parentheses at the first mention of the name. Then use the abbreviation throughout the rest of the paper.

40c Use the following commonly accepted abbreviations: B.C., A.D., A.M. (or a.m.), P.M. (or p.m.), $, No. (or no.).

40 B.C.	4:00 A.M.
40 B.C.E.	$100
A.D. 44	No. 12
C.E. 44	

NOTE: Use the abbreviations No. and $ only with specific numbers and amounts. Otherwise, write out the words.

▶ There were an odd ~~no.~~ *number* of seats in the room.

40d Be sparing in your use of Latin abbreviations.

Latin abbreviations are acceptable in footnotes and bibliographies and in informal writing for comments in parentheses.

cf. (Latin *confer,* "compare")
e.g. (Latin *exempli gratia,* "for example")
et al. (Latin *et alii,* "and others")
etc. (Latin *et cetera,* "and so forth")
i.e. (Latin *id est,* "that is")
N.B. (Latin *nota bene,* "note well")

Harold Simms et al., *The Race for Space*

She hated the slice-and-dice genre of horror movies (e.g., *Happy Birthday to Me, Psycho, Friday the 13th*).

In formal writing use the appropriate English phrases.

▶ Many obsolete laws remain on the books, ~~e.g.~~ *for example,* a law in Vermont forbidding an unmarried man and woman to sit closer than six inches apart on a park bench.

40e Avoid inappropriate abbreviations.

In formal writing, abbreviations for the following are not commonly accepted: personal names, units of measurement, days of the week, holidays, months, courses of study, divisions of written works, states and countries (except in addresses and except Washington, D.C.). Do not abbreviate *Company* and *Incorporated* unless their abbreviated forms are part of an official name.

PERSONAL NAME   Charles (not Chas.)

UNITS OF MEASUREMENT   pound (not lb.)

DAYS OF THE WEEK   Monday through Friday (not Mon. through Fri.)

HOLIDAYS   Christmas (not Xmas)

MONTHS   January, February, March (not Jan., Feb., Mar.)

COURSES OF STUDY   political science, psychology (not poli. sci., psych.)

DIVISIONS OF WRITTEN WORKS   chapter, page (not ch., p.)

STATES AND COUNTRIES   Massachusetts, New York (not MA or Mass., NY or N.Y.)

PARTS OF A BUSINESS NAME   Adams Lighting Company (not Adams Lighting Co.); Fletcher and Brothers, Incorporated (not Fletcher and Bros., Inc.)

▶ Eliza promised to buy me one ~~lb.~~ *pound* of Godiva chocolate for my birthday, which was last ~~Fri.~~ *Friday.*

EXERCISE 40 – 1

Edit the following sentences to correct errors in abbreviations. If a sentence is correct, write "correct" after it. Answers to lettered sentences appear in the back of the book. Example:

This year ~~Xmas~~ *Christmas* will fall on a ~~Fri.~~ *Friday.*

a. Marlon Mansard, a reporter for CBS, received a congressional citation for his work in Lebanon.
b. My grandmother told me that of all the subjects she studied, she found econ. the most challenging.
c. The Rev. Martin Luther King, Sr., spoke eloquently about his son's work against segregation in the South.
d. The first discovery of America was definitely not in 1492 A.D.
e. Turning to p. 195, Marion realized that she had finally reached the end of ch. 22.

1. Many girls fall prey to a cult worship of great entertainers — e.g., in my generation, girls worshiped the Beatles.
2. Three interns were selected to assist the chief surgeon, Dr. Paul Hunter, M.D., in the hospital's first heart-lung transplant.
3. Some historians think that the New Testament was completed by A.D. 100.
4. My soc. prof. spends most of his lecture time talking about political science.
5. Distinctions between the CIA and the FBI may not seem important, but they are.

41

Numbers

41a Spell out numbers of one or two words or those that begin a sentence. Use figures for numbers that require more than two words to spell out.

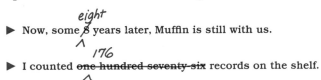

► Now, some ~~8~~ years later, Muffin is still with us.
    eight

► I counted ~~one hundred seventy-six~~ records on the shelf.
    176

If a sentence begins with a number, spell out the number or rewrite the sentence.

► ~~150~~ children in our program need expensive dental
    One hundred fifty
treatment.

> Rewriting the sentence will also correct the error and may be less awkward if the number is long: *In our program are 150 children who need expensive dental treatment.*

EXCEPTIONS: In technical and some business writing, figures are preferred even when spellings would be brief, but usage varies.

When several numbers appear in the same passage, many writers choose consistency rather than strict adherence to the rule.

When one number immediately follows another, spell out one and use figures for the other: three 100-meter events, 125 four-poster beds.

41b Generally, figures are acceptable for dates, addresses, percentages, fractions, decimals, scores, statistics and other numerical results, exact amounts of money, divisions of books and plays, pages, identification numbers, and the time.

DATES July 4, 1776, 56 B.C., A.D. 30

ADDRESSES 77 Latches Lane, 519 West 42nd Street

PERCENTAGES 55 percent (or 55%)

FRACTIONS, DECIMALS ½, 0.047

SCORES 7 to 3, 21–18

STATISTICS average age 37, average weight 180

SURVEYS 4 out of 5

EXACT AMOUNTS OF MONEY $105.37, $106,000

DIVISIONS OF BOOKS volume 3, chapter 4, page 189

DIVISIONS OF PLAYS Act III, scene iii (or Act 3, scene 3)

IDENTIFICATION NUMBERS serial number 10988675

TIME OF DAY 4:00 P.M., 1:30 A.M.

▶ Several doctors put up ~~two hundred fifty-five thousand dollars~~ $255,000 ∧ for the construction of a golf course.

▶ Though I was working on a ~~nineteen thirty-nine~~ 1939 ∧ sewing machine, my costume turned out well.

NOTE: When not using A.M. or P.M., write out the time in words (*four o'clock in the afternoon, twelve noon, seven in the morning*).

EXERCISE 41–1

Edit the following sentences to correct errors in the use of numbers. If a sentence is correct, write "correct" after it. Answers to lettered sentences appear in the back of the book. Example:

$3.06

By the end of the evening Brandon had only ~~three dollars~~ ^
~~and six cents~~ left.

a. We have ordered 4 azaleas, 3 rhododendrons, and 2 mountain laurels for the back area of the garden.
b. The president of Vivelle Cotton announced that all shifts would report back to work at the Augusta plant on June 6, 1990.
c. The score was tied at 5–5 when the momentum shifted and carried the Standards to a decisive 12–5 win.
d. We ordered three four-door sedans for company executives.
e. In nineteen eighty-nine, only one hundred and two male high school students in our state planned to make a career of teaching.

1. One of my favorite scenes in Shakespeare is the property division scene in Act I of *King Lear.*
2. The president's plane will arrive in Houston at 6:30 P.M.
3. 90 of the firm's employees signed up for the insurance program.
4. After her 5th marriage ended in divorce, Melinda decided to give up her quest for the perfect husband.
5. With 6 students and 2 teachers, the class had a 3:1 student-teacher ratio.

42

Italics (underlining)

In handwritten or typed papers, <u>underlining</u> represents *italics,* a slanting typeface used in printed material.

42a Underline the titles of books, plays, films, long poems, long musical compositions, works of visual art, magazines, newspapers, pamphlets, and radio and television programs.

TITLES OF BOOKS *The Great Gatsby, The Color Purple, A Distant Mirror*

PLAYS *Julius Caesar, Death of a Salesman, A Raisin in the Sun*

FILMS *Lethal Weapon, Bagdad Café, Last Year at Marienbad*

LONG POEMS T. S. Eliot's *The Waste Land,* Milton's *Paradise Lost*

LONG MUSICAL COMPOSITIONS Handel's *Messiah,* Gershwin's *Porgy and Bess*

WORKS OF VISUAL ART Rodin's *The Thinker,* da Vinci's *The Last Supper*

MAGAZINES *Time, Scientific American*

NEWSPAPERS the *New York Times,* the *Boston Globe,* the *San Francisco Chronicle*

PAMPHLETS Thomas Paine's *Common Sense*

TELEVISION PROGRAMS *Inside Washington, A Different World*

The titles of other works, such as short stories, essays, songs, and short poems, are enclosed in quotation marks. (See 37d.)

NOTE: Do not underline the Bible or the titles of books in the Bible (Genesis, not *Genesis*); the titles of legal documents (the Constitution, not *Constitution*); or the titles of your own papers.

42b   Underline the names of spacecraft, aircraft, ships, and trains.

Challenger, Spirit of St. Louis, Queen Elizabeth II, Silver Streak

▶ The success of the Soviet's <u>Sputnik</u> galvanized the U.S.

space program.

42c   Underline foreign words used in an English sentence.

▶ Although Joe's method seemed to be successful, I decided to

establish my own <u>modus operandi</u>.

EXCEPTION: Do not underline foreign words that have become part of the English language — "laissez-faire," "fait accompli," "habeus corpus," and "per diem," for example.

42d   Underline words mentioned as words, letters mentioned as letters, and numbers mentioned as numbers.

▶ Tim assured us that the howling probably came from his

bloodhound, Hill Billy, but his <u>probably</u> stuck in our minds.

▶ Sarah called her father by his given name, Johnny, but she

was unable to pronounce <u>J</u>.

▶ A big <u>3</u> was painted on the door.

NOTE: Quotation marks may be used instead of underlining to set off words mentioned as words. (See 37e.)

42e Avoid excessive underlining for emphasis.

Underlining to emphasize words or ideas is distracting and should be used sparingly.

▶ Tennis is a sport that has become an ~~addiction~~.

EXERCISE 42−1

Edit the following sentences to correct errors in the use of italics. If a sentence is correct, write "correct" after it. Answers to lettered sentences appear in the back of the book. Example:

Leaves of Grass by Walt Whitman was quite controversial

when it was published a century ago.

a. Howard Hughes commissioned the Spruce Goose, a beautifully built but thoroughly impractical wooden aircraft.
b. Pulaski was so *exhausted* he could barely lift his foot the six inches to the elevator floor.
c. Even though it is almost always hot in Mexico in the summer, you can usually find a cool spot on one of the park benches in the town's zócalo.
d. I will never forget the way he whispered the word *finished.*
e. One of my favorite novels is George Eliot's "Middlemarch."

1. Bernard watched as Eileen stood transfixed in front of Vermeer's Head of a Young Girl.
2. The preacher was partial to quotations from Exodus.
3. I learned the Latin term ad infinitum from an old nursery rhyme about fleas: "Great fleas have little fleas upon their back to bite 'em, / Little fleas have lesser fleas and so on ad infinitum."

4. Redford and Newman in the movie "The Sting" were amateurs compared with the seventeen-year-old con artist who lives at our house.

5. I find it impossible to remember the second *l* in *llama*.

43

Spelling

You learned to spell from repeated experience with words in both reading and writing, but especially writing. Words have a look, a sound, and even a feel to them as the hand moves across the page. As you proofread, you can probably tell if a word doesn't look quite right. In such cases, the solution is obvious: Look up the word in the dictionary.

A word processor equipped with a spelling checker is a useful alternative to a dictionary, but only up to a point. A spelling checker will not tell you how to spell words not listed in its dictionary; nor will it help you catch words commonly confused, such as *accept* and *except,* or common typographical errors, such as *own* for *won.* You will still need to proofread, and for some words you may need to turn to the dictionary.

43a Become familiar with your dictionary.

A good desk dictionary — such as *The American Heritage Dictionary of the English Language, The Random House College Dictionary,* or *Webster's New Collegiate Dictionary* or *New World Dictionary of the American Language* — is an indispensable writer's aid. By reading or at least skimming your dictionary's guide to its use, which usually appears at the front of the book, you will discover many new reasons for turning to the dictionary for help.

A sample dictionary entry, taken from *The American Heritage Dictionary*, appears below. Labels show where various kinds of information about a word can be found in that dictionary.

Spelling, word division, pronunciation

The main entry (*pre·vent* in the sample entry) shows the correct spelling of the word. When there are two correct spellings of a word (*preventable, preventible*), both are given, with the preferred spelling usually appearing first.

The main entry also shows how the word is divided into syllables. The dot between *pre* and *vent* separates the word's

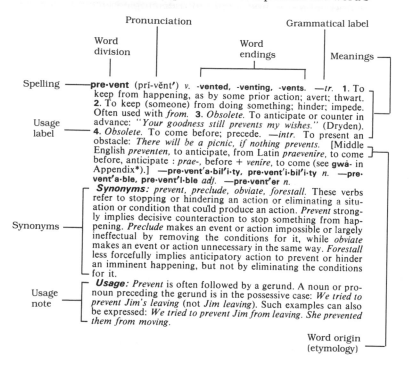

Pronunciation

Grammatical label

Word division

Word endings

Meanings

Spelling —— **pre·vent** (prĭ-vĕnt′) *v.* **-vented, -venting, -vents.** —*tr.* **1.** To keep from happening, as by some prior action; avert; thwart. **2.** To keep (someone) from doing something; hinder; impede. Often used with *from.* **3.** *Obsolete.* To anticipate or counter in advance: "*Your goodness still prevents my wishes.*" (Dryden). **4.** *Obsolete.* To come before; precede. —*intr.* To present an obstacle: *There will be a picnic, if nothing prevents.* [Middle English *preventen,* to anticipate, from Latin *praevenire,* to come before, anticipate : *prae-,* before + *venire,* to come (see gwā- in Appendix*).] —**pre·vent′a·bil′i·ty, pre·vent′i·bil′i·ty** *n.* —**pre·vent′a·ble, pre·vent′i·ble** *adj.* —**pre·vent′er** *n.*

Usage label

Synonyms —— **Synonyms:** *prevent, preclude, obviate, forestall.* These verbs refer to stopping or hindering an action or eliminating a situation or condition that could produce an action. *Prevent* strongly implies decisive counteraction to stop something from happening. *Preclude* makes an event or action impossible or largely ineffectual by removing the conditions for it, while *obviate* makes an event or action unnecessary in the same way. *Forestall* less forcefully implies anticipatory action to prevent or hinder an imminent happening, but not by eliminating the conditions for it.

Usage note —— **Usage:** *Prevent* is often followed by a gerund. A noun or pronoun preceding the gerund is in the possessive case: *We tried to prevent Jim's leaving* (not *Jim leaving*). Such examples can also be expressed: *We tried to prevent Jim from leaving. She prevented them from moving.*

Word origin (etymology)

two syllables. When a word is compound, the main entry shows how to write it: as one word (*crossroad*), as a hyphenated word (*cross-stitch*), or as two words (*cross section*).

The word's pronunciation is given just after the main entry. The accents indicate which syllables are stressed; the other marks are explained in the dictionary's pronunciation key. In some dictionaries this key appears at the bottom of every page or every other page.

Word endings and grammatical labels

When a word takes endings to indicate grammatical functions (called *inflections*), the endings are listed in boldface, as with -*vented*, -*venting*, and -*vents* in the sample entry.

Labels for the parts of speech and for other grammatical terms are abbreviated. The most commonly used abbreviations are these:

n.	noun	adj.	adjective
pl.	plural	adv.	adverb
sing.	singular	pron.	pronoun
v.	verb	prep.	preposition
tr.	transitive verb	conj.	conjunction
intr.	intransitive verb	interj.	interjection

Meanings, word origin, synonyms, and antonyms

Each meaning for the word is given a number. Occasionally a word's use is illustrated in a quoted sentence, as with the sentence by Dryden in the sample entry.

The origin of the word, called its *etymology*, appears in brackets after the list of meanings (in some dictionaries it appears before the meanings).

Synonyms, words similar in meaning to the main entry, are frequently listed. In the sample entry, the dictionary draws distinctions in meaning among the various synonyms. Antonyms, which do not appear in the sample entry, are words having a meaning opposite from that of the main entry.

Usage

Usage labels indicate when, where, or under what conditions a particular meaning for a word is appropriately used. Common labels are *informal* (or *colloquial*), *slang, nonstandard, dialect, obsolete, archaic, poetic,* and *British*. In the sample entry, two meanings of *prevent* are labeled *obsolete* because they are no longer in use.

Dictionaries sometimes include usage notes as well. In the sample entry, the dictionary offers advice on a grammatical problem that sometimes arises following the verb *prevent*. Such advice is based on the opinions of many experts and on actual usage in current magazines, newspapers, and books.

43b Discriminate between words that sound alike but have different meanings.

Pronunciation can be a useful guide to spelling, but don't rely too heavily on it. As you know by now, words are not always spelled as they sound, especially in English. Think of the different sounds for *-ough* in the following words: *rough, thorough, through, slough*. Other sets of words that cause spelling troubles are homophones, words sounding alike or nearly alike but having different meanings and spellings.

HOMOPHONES (WORDS WITH SIMILAR PRONUNCIATION AND DIFFERENT MEANINGS)

accept (to receive)
except (to take or leave out)

advice (n., opinion about what to do for a problem; counsel)
advise (v., to offer advice)

affect (v., to exert an influence)
effect (n., result; v., to accomplish)

allusion (an indirect reference)
illusion (a false perception of reality)

all ready (prepared)
already (by this time)

altar (n., a structure on which religious ceremonies are held)
alter (v., to change)

altogether (entirely)
all together (gathered; everything in one place)

always (every time, forever)
all ways (every way)

ascent (a climb)
assent (agreement)

bare (v., to reveal; adj., naked, unadorned)
bear (v., to carry, to put up with; n., an animal)

board (a flat piece of wood)
bored (uninterested, weary)

brake (n., something used to stop movement; v., to stop
  movement)
break (v., to split or smash into pieces; n., a split or opening;
  a pause or interval)

breath (n., air inhaled and exhaled)
breathe (v., to inhale and exhale air)

buy (to purchase)
by (near)

capital (seat of government)
capitol (building in which a legislative body meets)

choose (to select)
chose (past tense of *choose*)

cite (to quote)
sight (vision)
site (position, place)

coarse (of ordinary or inferior quality)
course (path or policy chosen)

complement (n., something that completes; v., to complete)
compliment (n., praise; v., to praise)

conscience (sense of right and wrong)
conscious (awake, aware)

council (n., a group that consults, advises, or governs)
counsel (v., to advise; n., advice)

descent (the act of going down)
dissent (disagreement)

desert (v., to withdraw from; n., uninhabited and arid land)
dessert (sweet course at the end of a meal)

discreet (prudent, tactful)
discrete (constituting a separate entity)

elicit (to draw or bring out)
illicit (illegal)

eminent (famous, respected)
immanent (indwelling, inherent)
imminent (ready to take place)

fair (adj., lovely, light-colored, just; n., a market or
   exhibition)
fare (v., to get along; n., money for transportation; food or
   drink)

forth (forward)
fourth (referring to the number four)

gorilla (a large ape)
guerrilla (a member of an independent military force)

hear (to sense by the ear)
here (this place)

heard (past tense of *hear*)
herd (a group of animals)

hole (hollow place)
whole (entire, unhurt)

its (of or belonging to it)
it's (contraction for *it is*)

know (to be aware of)
no (opposite of *yes*)

lead (n., metal)
led (past tense of the verb *lead*)

lessen (to make less)
lesson (something learned)

loose (free, not securely attached)
lose (to fail to keep, to be deprived of)

maybe (adv., perhaps)
may be (v., might be)

moral (adj., distinguishing between right and wrong)
morale (n., spirit or attitude of a group)

pair (set of two)
pare (to trim)
pear (a fruit)

passed (past tense of the verb *pass*)
past (belonging to a former time)

patience (calm endurance)
patients (a doctor's clients)

peace (a state of calm; a time without war)
piece (a part)

personal (private; intimate)
personnel (a body of employees)

plain (adj., simple, unadorned; n., a level area of land)
plane (aircraft; a flat surface)

precede (to come before)
proceed (to go forward)

presence (attendance)
presents (gifts)

principal (adj., most important; n., a person who has
    authority)
principle (a general or fundamental truth)

quiet (silent, calm)
quite (very)

rain (water falling in drops)
reign (to rule)
rein (restraining influence; a strap attached to an animal for
    control)

raise (to lift)
raze (to destroy, to lay level with the ground)

right (proper or just; correct; opposite of *left*)
rite (a ritual)
write (to put words on paper)

road (a street or path)
rode (past tense of *ride*)

scene (a place of action; part of a play)
seen (past participle of the verb *see*)

stationary (standing still)
stationery (writing paper)

straight (free from curves, bends, or angles)
strait (narrow space or passage)

taught (past tense of *teach*)
taut (tight)

than (besides)
then (at that time; next)

their (belonging to them)
they're (contraction of *they are*)
there (that place or position)

through (by means of; finished; into or out of)
threw (past tense of *throw*)
thorough (careful or complete)

to (prep., toward)
too (also, excessively)
two (one more than one in number)

waist (midsection)
waste (v., to squander; n., something that is discarded)

weak (feeble, not strong)
week (seven days)

weather (state of the atmosphere)
whether (indicating a choice between alternatives)

who's (contraction of *who is*)
whose (possessive of *who*)

your (possessive of *you*)
you're (contraction of *you are*)
yore (time long past)

43c Become familiar with the major spelling rules.

1. Use *i* before *e* except after *c* or when sounded like the letter *a,* as in *neighbor* and *weigh.*

i **BEFORE** *e*	relieve, believe, sieve, frieze
e **BEFORE** *i*	receive, deceive, sleigh, freight, eight
EXCEPTIONS	seize, either, weird, height, foreign, leisure

2. Generally, drop a final silent *e* when adding a suffix that begins with a vowel. Keep the final *e* if the suffix begins with a consonant.

desire, desiring; remove, removable

achieve, achievement; care, careful

Words such as *argument, truly,* and *changeable* are exceptions.

3. When adding *-s* or *-ed* to words ending in *y,* ordinarily change *y* to *i* when the *y* is preceded by a consonant but not when it is preceded by a vowel.

comedy, comedies; dry, dried

monkey, monkeys; play, played

With proper names ending in *y,* however, do not change the *y* to *i* even if it is preceded by a consonant: *Dougherty, the Doughertys.*

4. If a final consonant is preceded by a single vowel *and* the consonant ends a one-syllable word or a stressed syllable, double the consonant when adding a suffix beginning with a vowel.

bet, betting; commit, committed; occur, occurrence

5. Add *-s* to form the plural of most nouns; add *-es* to singular nouns ending in *-s, -sh, -ch,* and *-x.*

table, tables; paper, papers

church, churches; dish, dishes

Ordinarily add *-s* to nouns ending in *-o* when the *o* is preceded by a vowel. Add *-es* when it is preceded by a consonant.

radio, radios; video, videos

hero, heroes; tomato, tomatoes

To form the plural of a hyphenated compound word, add the -*s* to the chief word even if it does not appear at the end.

mother-in-law, mothers-in-law

NOTE: English words derived from other languages such as Latin or French sometimes form the plural as they would in their original language.

medium, media; criterion, criteria; chateau, chateaux

ESL NOTE: Spelling may vary slightly among English-speaking countries. This can prove particularly confusing for ESL students, who may have learned British or Canadian English. Following is a list of some common words spelled differently in American and British English. Consult a dictionary for others.

AMERICAN	BRITISH
cancel<u>ed</u>, travel<u>ed</u>	cancel<u>led</u>, travel<u>led</u>
colo<u>r</u>, hum<u>or</u>	col<u>ou</u>r, hum<u>ou</u>r
jud<u>g</u>ment	jud<u>ge</u>ment
che<u>ck</u>	che<u>que</u>
reali<u>z</u>e, apolo<u>g</u>ize	reali<u>s</u>e, apolo<u>gis</u>e
defen<u>s</u>e	defen<u>c</u>e
an<u>e</u>mia, an<u>e</u>sthetic	an<u>ae</u>mia, an<u>ae</u>sthetic
theate<u>r</u>, cente<u>r</u>	theat<u>re</u>, cent<u>re</u>
f<u>e</u>tus	f<u>oe</u>tus
m<u>o</u>ld, sm<u>o</u>lder	m<u>ou</u>ld, sm<u>ou</u>lder
civili<u>z</u>ation	civili<u>s</u>ation
conne<u>ct</u>ion, infle<u>ct</u>ion	conne<u>x</u>ion, infle<u>x</u>ion
li<u>c</u>orice	li<u>qu</u>orice

43d Be alert to the following commonly misspelled words.

absence	accessible	accommodate	accuracy
acceptable	accidentally	accumulate	accustomed

achieve
acknowledge
acquaintance
acquire
across
actually
address
admission
adolescence
adolescent
advice
affected
affectionately
against
aggravate
aggressive
allotted
all right
almost
although
altogether
amateur
analysis
analyze
annihilate
announcement
annual
answer
apparent
appearance
appreciate
appropriate
approximately
arctic
argument
arising
arithmetic
arrangement
arrest
ascend

assassination
association
atheist
athlete
attendance
audience
average
bargain
basically
bazaar
beginning
belief
believe
beneficial
benefited
benefiting
bizarre
breath
breathe
brilliant
Britain
bureau
bureaucracy
busily
business
cafeteria
calculator
calendar
calf, calves
candidate
category
ceiling
cemetery
changeable
characteristic
chief
chocolate
choose
chosen
column

coming
commercial
commission
commitment
committed
committee
competent
competition
competitive
completely
concede
conceivable
concentrate
condemn
conferred
confidence
conqueror
conscience
conscientious
conscious
consistent
continuous
controlled
controversial
convenience
convenient
courageous
courteous
criticism
criticize
cruelty
curiosity
curious
dealt
deceive
decide
decision
definitely
dependent
descendant

describe
description
desirable
despair
desperate
develop
dictionary
difference
different
dining
disagree
disappear
disappoint
disapprove
disastrous
discipline
discussion
disease
dissatisfied
divide
dormitory
ecstasy
efficiency
eighth
either
elaborately
eligible
eliminate
embarrass
eminent
emphasize
entirely
entrance
environment
equivalent
especially
evidently
exaggerate
exceed
excellent

excitement
exhaust
existence
experience
experiment
explanation
extraordinary
extremely
familiar
fascinate
favorite
February
finally
financially
foreign
foresee
forty
forward
fourth
friend
fulfill
gauge
generally
government
governor
grammar
grief
guarantee
guard
guidance
half, halves
happily
harass
height
heroes
hindrance
humorous
hungry
hypocrisy

hypocrite
ideally
ignorant
illogical
illiterate
imaginary
imagination
imagine
imitation
immediately
immense
incidentally
incredible
indefinitely
independent
indispensable
inevitable
infinite
influential
initiate
innocuous
insistent
intelligence
interest
interference
interesting
interpret
irrelevant
irresistible
irritated
joyous
judgment
knives
knowledge
laboratory
lavender
legitimate
leisure
library

license
lightning
literature
loneliness
loose
lose
lying
magazine
maintenance
manageable
maneuver
marriage
marriageable
mathematics
meant
medicine
miniature
minutes
mischievous
missile
mortgage
muscle
mysterious
necessary
neither
nickel
niece
ninety
ninth
noticeable
noticing
nuclear
nuisance
numerous
obstacle
occasion
occasionally
occur
occurred

occurrence
official
omission
omitted
opponent
opportunity
opposite
optimism
optimistic
originally
outrageous
paid
pamphlet
parallel
paralleled
particularly
pastime
peaceable
peculiar
perceive
performance
permanent
permissible
perseverance
persistence
personnel
perspiration
phenomenon
physical
picnicking
planning
playwright
pleasant
poison
politician
politics
possession
possibly
potatoes

practically
prairie
precede
precedence
preference
preferred
prejudice
preparation
prevalent
primitive
privilege
probably
procedure
proceed
professor
prominent
pronunciation
psychology
publicly
purpose
pursue
pursuing
quantity
questionnaire
quiet
quite
quizzes
realistically
realize
receipt
receive
recognize
recommend
reference
referred
referring
regard
religion
religious

remembrance
repetition
resemblance
restaurant
rhythm
rhythmical
ridiculous
roommate
safety
sandwich
scarcity
schedule
science
secretary
seize
self, selves
separate
sergeant
several
shelf, shelves
sheriff
shining
siege
significance
similar
sincerely
skiing
soliloquy
sophomore
specialty
specimen
speech
sponsor
stopping
strength
strenuous
strict
strictly
stubbornness

studying
subtly
succeed
successful
succession
sufficient
summary
superintendent
supersede
suppress
surely
surprise
susceptible
suspicious
technical
technique
temperature
tendency
than
thief, thieves
their
then
therefore
thorough
through
together
tomorrow
tragedy
transferred
tremendous
tries
truly
Tuesday
twelfth
tyranny
unanimous
unconscious
undoubtedly
unnecessarily

unnecessary
until
usage
usually
vacuum
valuable
various
vegetable
vengeance
vicious
villain
violence
visible
weather
Wednesday
weird
wherever
whether
wholly
wives
woman,
  women
worshiped
writing
written

EXERCISE 43 – 1

Ask a friend or classmate to dictate the following paragraph to you. When you have transcribed it, check your version with this one. Note any words that you misspelled and practice writing them correctly.

The members of a faculty committee that recommends changes in course requirements invited several students to meet with them. In their invitation, the members emphasized that even though they would ask specific questions, they especially wanted the students to discuss their experience in various courses and to offer suggestions for changes. The students who were chosen represented a variety of academic interests, and the committee particularly selected students who were in their first year and in their last year. In his separate interview with the committee, John, who is graduating in May, questioned whether it was necessary to take so many courses that were apparently unrelated to his business major. He acknowledged that the requirement for some courses outside his major was legitimate; however, he believed that more thorough preparation for his specialty, international finance, would have been appropriate. John was worried because the job market had become so competitive, and he did not feel that he had benefited from some of the courses he had taken outside the business school. John apologized for being so negative, and he praised the committee for its willingness to listen to the opinions of students.

EXERCISE 43 – 2

The following paragraphs have been run through a spell checker on a computer. Proofread them carefully, editing the spelling and typographical errors that remain.

Later, John wrote a letter to the faculty committee, describing the kinds of classes that had had the greatest affect on him. John's letter impressed the committee, because he was able to site specific professors and specific teaching method. He started his letter very candidly: "Even though your professors, I must say that the best learning experiences I had did not involve the professor, accept as a resource or as a guide." John explained that he achieved more when he was actively involved in the class then when he sat and listened to the professor lecturing an asking questions.

John praised one professor in particular, an imminent psychologist and author. "When Professor Howell past control to the class," wrote John, "we took this as a complement. We had all assumed that being subjected to lengthy, boring lectures was a fundamental principal in higher education, but Professor Howell proved us wrong." In his letter, John went one to describe how the class was taught. Professor Howell asked each student to give reports, and she regularly had small groups discuss material or solve specific problems and report to the class. She participated in the class, to, but students had more access to her as she circulated though the room to answer questions or to challenge students to think in different ways. John closed his letter with further praise for Professor Howell and for teachers like her, saying, "Their what I'll remember most about my educational experiences in college."

44

The hyphen

44a Consult the dictionary to determine how to treat a compound word.

The dictionary will tell you whether to treat a compound word as a hyphenated compound (*water-repellent*), one word (*waterproof*), or two words (*water table*). If the compound word is not in the dictionary, treat it as two words.

▶ The prosecutor chose not to cross—examine any witnesses.
                                              ∧

▶ Grandma kept a small note⌢book in her apron pocket.

▶ Alice walked through the looking⁄glass into a backward

world.

44b   Use a hyphen to connect two or more words
functioning together as an adjective before a noun.

▶ Mrs. Douglas gave Mary a seashell and some newspaper‿

wrapped fish to take home to her mother.

▶ Priscilla Hobbes is not yet a well‿ known candidate.

Newspaper-wrapped and *well-known* are adjectives used before
the nouns *fish* and *candidate.*

Generally, do not use a hyphen when such compounds
follow the noun.

▶ After our television campaign, Priscilla Hobbes will be well⁄

known.

Do not use a hyphen to connect *-ly* adverbs to the words
they modify.

▶ A slowly⁄moving truck tied up traffic.

NOTE: In a series, hyphens are suspended.

Do you prefer first-, second-, or third-class tickets?

44c Hyphenate the written form of fractions and of compound numbers from twenty-one to ninety-nine.

▶ One‑fourth of my income goes to pay off the national debt.

44d Use a hyphen with the prefixes *all-*, *ex-* (meaning "former"), and *self-* and with the suffix *-elect.*

▶ The charity is funneling more money into self‑help projects.

▶ Anne King is our club's president‑elect.

44e A hyphen is used in some words to avoid ambiguity or to separate awkward double or triple letters.

Without the hyphen there would be no way to distinguish between words such as *re-creation* and *recreation.*

Bicycling in the country is my favorite recreation.

The film was praised for its astonishing re-creation of nineteenth-century London.

Hyphens are sometimes used to separate awkward double or triple letters in compound words (*anti-intellectual, cross-stitch*). Always check a dictionary for the standard form of the word.

44f If a word must be divided at the end of a line, divide it correctly.

1. Divide words between syllables.

▶ When I returned from overseas, I didn't ~~reco~~ recognize
~~gnize~~ one face on the magazine covers.

2. Never divide one-syllable words.

▶ He didn't have the courage or the ~~stren~~ strength
~~gth~~ to open the door.

3. Never divide a word so that a single letter stands alone at the end of a line or fewer than three letters begin a line.

▶ She'll bring her brother with her when she comes ~~a~~ again.
~~gain.~~

▶ As audience to *The Mousetrap*, Hamlet is a ~~watch~~ watcher
~~er~~ watching watchers.

4. When dividing a compound word at the end of a line, either make the break between the words that form the compound or put the whole word on the next line.

▶ My niece is determined to become a long-~~dis~~ distance
~~tance~~ runner when she grows up.

EXERCISE 44–1

Edit the following sentences to correct errors in hyphenation. If a sentence is correct, write "correct" after it. Answers to lettered sentences appear in the back of the book. Example:

Zola's first readers were scandalized by his slice‿of‿life
novels.

a. Gold is the seventy-ninth element in the periodic table.
b. The quietly-purring cat cleaned first one paw and then the other
   before curling up under the stove.
c. Many states are adopting laws that limit property taxes for homeowners.
d. Your dog is well-known in our neighborhood.
e. He did fifty push-ups in two minutes and then collapsed.

1. We knew we were driving too fast when our tires skidded over
   the rain slick surface.
2. Many people protested when the drinking age was lowered from
   twenty-one to twenty.
3. Instead of an old Victorian, we settled for a modern split-lev-
   el surrounded by maples.
4. One-quarter of the class signed up for the debate on U.S. foreign
   aid to Latin America.
5. At the end of *Macbeth*, the hero feels himself profoundly a-
   lone.

45

Capital letters

In addition to the following rules, a good dictionary can often
tell you when to use capital letters.

45a Capitalize proper nouns and words derived from them; do not capitalize common nouns.

Proper nouns are the names of specific persons, places, and
things. All other nouns are common nouns. The following

types of words are usually capitalized: names for the deity, religions, religious followers, sacred books; words of family relationship used as names; particular places; nationalities and their languages, races, tribes; educational institutions, departments, degrees, particular courses; government departments, organizations, political parties; and historical movements, periods, events, documents.

PROPER NOUNS	**COMMON NOUNS**
God (used as a name)	a god
Book of Jeremiah	a book
Grandmother Bishop	my grandmother
Father (used as a name)	my father
Lake Superior	a picturesque lake
the Capital Center	a center for advanced studies
the South	a southern state
Japan, a Japanese garden	an ornamental garden
University of Wisconsin	a good university
Geology 101	geology
Environmental Protection Agency	a federal agency
Phi Kappa Psi	a fraternity
a Democrat	an independent
the Enlightenment	the eighteenth century
the Declaration of Independence	a treaty

Months, holidays, and days of the week are treated as proper nouns; the seasons and numbers of the days of the month are not.

Our academic year begins on a Tuesday in early September, right after Labor Day.

My mother's birthday is in early summer, on the thirteenth of June.

Names of school subjects are capitalized only if they are

names of languages. Names of particular courses are capitalized.

> This semester Austin is taking math, geography, geology, French, and English.

> Professor Anderson offers Modern American Fiction 501 to graduate students.

CAUTION: Do not capitalize common nouns to make them seem important: *Our company is currently hiring computer programmers* (not *Company, Computer Programmers*).

45b Capitalize titles of persons when used as part of a proper name but usually not when used alone.

> Professor Margaret Barnes; Dr. Harold Stevens; John Scott Williams, Jr.; Anne Tilton, LL.D.

> District Attorney Marshall was reprimanded for badgering the witness.

> The district attorney was elected for a two-year term.

Usage varies when the title of an important public figure is used alone: *The president* (or *President*) *vetoed the bill.*

45c Capitalize the first, last, and all major words in titles and subtitles of works such as books, articles, and songs.

In both titles and subtitles, major words such as nouns, verbs, adjectives, and adverbs should be capitalized. Minor words such as articles, prepositions, and coordinating conjunctions are not capitalized unless they are the first or last word of a title or subtitle. Capitalize the second part of a hyphenated term in a title if it is a major word but not if it is a minor word.

> *The Country of the Pointed Firs*
> *The Impossible Theater: A Manifesto*
> *The F-Plan Diet*

Capitalize chapter titles and the titles of other major divisions of a work following the same guidelines used for titles of complete works.

> "Work and Play" in Santayana's *The Nature of Beauty*

45d Capitalize the first word of a sentence.

> When lightning struck the house, the chimney collapsed.

Capitalize the first word in every line of poetry unless the poet uses a different convention.

> When I consider everything that grows
> Holds in perfection but a little moment   — *Shakespeare*

> it was the week   that
> i felt the city's narrow breezes rush about
> me   — *Don L. Lee*

45e Capitalize the first word of a quoted sentence unless it is blended into the sentence that introduces it.

> In *Time* magazine Robert Hughes writes, "There are only about sixty Watteau paintings on whose authenticity all experts agree."

> Russell Baker has written that in our country "it is sport that is the opiate of the masses."

If a quoted sentence is interrupted by explanatory words, do not capitalize the first word after the interruption. (See 37f.)

"If you wanted to go out," he said sharply, "you should have told me."

45f Do not capitalize the first word after a colon unless it begins an independent clause, in which case capitalization is optional.

Most of the bar's patrons can be divided into two groups: the occasional after-work socializers and the nothing-to-go-home-to regulars.

This we are forced to conclude: the [*or* The] federal government is needed to protect the rights of minorities.

45g Capitalize abbreviations for departments and agencies of government, other organizations, and corporations; capitalize trade names and the call letters of radio and television stations.

EPA, FBI, OPEC, IBM, Xerox, WCRB, KNBC-TV

EXERCISE 45 – 1

Edit the following sentences to correct errors in capitalization. If a sentence is correct, write "correct" after it. Answers to lettered sentences appear in the back of the book. Example:

On our trip to the West we visited the *G*rand *C*anyon and the *G*reat *S*alt *D*esert.

a. District attorney Johnson was disgusted when the jurors turned in a verdict of not guilty after only one hour of deliberation.

b. My mother has begun to research the history of her indian ancestors in North Carolina.
c. W. C. Fields's epitaph reads, "On the whole, I'd rather be in Philadelphia."
d. Refugees from central America are finding it more and more difficult to cross the rio Grande into the United States.
e. I want to take Environmental Biology 103, one other Biology course, and one English course.

1. "Forbidding people things they like or think they might enjoy," contends Gore Vidal, "Only makes them want those things all the more."
2. If someone were to approach me looking for the secret to running a good bar, I suppose I'd offer the following advice: Get your customers to pour out their ideas at a greater rate than you pour out the liquor.
3. Does your Aunt still preach in local churches whenever she's asked?
4. Historians have described Robert E. Lee as the aristocratic south personified.
5. My brother is a Doctor and my sister-in-law is an Attorney.

46

Manuscript preparation

By following standard guidelines in preparing manuscripts, a writer fulfills the reader's expectations about how a paper should look. Decisions about where to put the title, where to number the pages, and how much margin to leave become easier for the writer, and the paper is more legible for the reader. If your instructor provides formal guidelines, follow them; otherwise, use the guidelines given in this section, which are based on advice given in the *MLA Handbook for Writers of Research Papers*, 3rd edition, (New York: Modern Language Association, 1988).

Materials

For a typed essay use 8½″ × 11″, 20-pound typing paper, not onionskin. A self-correcting typewriter or word processor will allow you to eliminate errors completely, but if you don't have access to such a typewriter or a word processor, use white correction fluid. Some instructors will accept a line through the mistake with the correction neatly written or typed above. Use a caret (∧) to indicate where the correction should be inserted.

For an essay typed on a word processor, make sure that the print quality and the paper quality meet your instructor's standards. If the paper emerges from the printer in a continuous sheet, separate the pages, remove the feeder strips from the sides of the paper, and assemble the pages in order.

Before you consider submitting a handwritten essay, be sure that your instructor will accept work that is not typewritten. Use 8½″ × 11″ wide-ruled white paper, and write in blue or black ink on one side of the paper only. Do not use legal-size paper or sheets torn from a notebook. Obviously you should make your handwriting as clear as possible; if your handwriting is difficult to read, make an effort to type the essay or have it typed.

Title and identification

College essays normally do not require a separate title page. Unless instructed otherwise, against the left margin about one inch from the top of the paper, place on separate lines your name, the instructor's name, the course name and number, and the date. Double-space between lines.

Double-space after the heading and center the title of the essay in the width of the page. Capitalize the first and last words of the title and all other words except articles, prepositions, and coordinating conjunctions (see 45c). If there is a subtitle, separate it from the title with a colon and follow the capitalization rules for titles. Do not underline your title or put it in quotation marks, and do not use a period after it.

If you decide to use a title page, center the title and all elements of identification. Place the title about one-third down the page. About an inch below the title, write "By" followed by your name. About an inch below your name on separate lines, write the course name and number, your instructor's name, and the date; double-space between lines.

Margins, spacing, and indentation

Leave margins of at least one inch but no more than an inch and a half at the top, bottom, and sides of the page.

Double-space between lines in a typewritten essay and indent the first line of each paragraph five spaces from the left margin.

For quotations of longer than four typed lines of prose or longer than three lines of verse, indent each line ten spaces from the left margin. Double-space between the body of the paper and the quotation, and double-space the lines of the quotation.

Pagination

Number all pages at the upper right corner, one-half inch below the top edge. (If you have a separate title page, the title page is uncounted and unnumbered.) Use arabic numerals (1, 2, 3, and so on). Do not put a period after the number and do not enclose the number in parentheses.

Punctuation and typing

In typing the essay, leave one space after words, commas, and semicolons and between the dots in ellipses. Leave two spaces after periods, question marks, and exclamation points. Usage is divided concerning spacing after a colon. Many authorities recommend two spaces, but the *MLA Handbook* recommends one space.

To form a dash, type two hyphens with no space between them. Do not put a space on either side of a dash.

Documentation

If in your essay you draw on written sources, you will need to document those sources according to a consistent system. (See 54 and 55.)

Proofreading

Misspelled words, incorrect hyphenation, and errors in grammar and punctuation detract from the overall effect of an essay; if there are too many of these errors, readers will lose patience. Your ideas deserve clear and correct expression. Proofread the final draft of the paper and then proofread it again.

PART IX

Grammar Basics

47

Parts of speech

Traditional grammar recognizes eight parts of speech: noun, pronoun, verb, adjective, adverb, preposition, conjunction, and interjection. Many words can function as more than one part of speech. For example, depending on its use in a sentence, the word *paint* can be a noun (*The paint is wet*) or a verb (*Please paint the ceiling next*).

A quick-reference chart of the parts of speech appears on pages 436–438.

47a Nouns

As most schoolchildren can attest, a noun is the name of a person, place, or thing.

> The *cat* in *gloves* catches no *mice.*

In addition to the traditional definition of a noun, grammarians describe a noun as follows:

the kind of word that is often marked with an article (*a spoon, an apple, the newspaper*);

the kind of word that can be made plural (*one cat, two cats*) or possessive (*the cat's paw*);

the kind of word that when derived from another word typically takes one of these endings: play*er*, just*ice*, happi*ness*, divis*ion*, guid*ance*, refer*ence*, pave*ment*, child*hood*, king*dom*, agen*cy*, tour*ist*, sincer*ity*, censor*ship*;

the kind of word that can fill one of these positions in a sentence: subject, direct object, indirect object, subject complement, object complement, object of the preposition. (See 48a and 48b.)

Nouns, in other words, may be identified as much by their form and function as by their meaning.

Nouns sometimes function as adjectives modifying other nouns. Because of their dual function, nouns used in this manner may be called *noun/adjectives.*

You can't make a *silk* purse out of a *sow's* ear.

Nouns are classified for a variety of purposes. When capitalization is the issue, we speak of *proper* versus *common nouns* (see 45a). If the problem is one of word choice, we may speak of *concrete* versus *abstract nouns* (see 18b). The distinction between *count nouns* and *noncount nouns* is useful primarily for nonnative speakers of English (see 30a, b). The term *collective noun* refers to a set of nouns that may cause problems with subject-verb or pronoun-antecedent agreement (see 21e and 22b).

EXERCISE 47 – 1

Underline the nouns (and noun/adjectives) in the following sentences. Answers to lettered sentences appear in the back of the book. Example:

Pride is at the bottom of all great mistakes.

a. Clothe an idea in words, and it loses its freedom of movement.
b. Idle hands are the devil's workshop.
c. Our national flower is the concrete cloverleaf.
d. The ultimate censorship is the flick of the dial.
e. Figures won't lie, but liars will figure.

1. Conservatism is the worship of dead revolutions.
2. The winds and the waves are always on the side of the ablest navigators.
3. Problems are opportunities in work clothes.

4. A scalded dog fears even cold water.
5. Prejudice is the child of ignorance.

47b Pronouns

There are thousands of nouns, and new ones come into the language every year. This is not true of pronouns, which number about one hundred and are extremely resistant to change. Most of the pronouns in English are listed in this section.

A pronoun is a word used for a noun. Usually the pronoun substitutes for a specific noun, known as its *antecedent.*

When the *wheel* squeaks, *it* is greased.

Although most pronouns function as substitutes for nouns, some can function as adjectives modifying nouns.

This hanging will surely be a lesson to me.

Because they have the form of a pronoun and the function of an adjective, such pronouns may be called *pronoun/adjectives.*

Pronouns are classified as personal, possessive, intensive and reflexive, relative, interrogative, demonstrative, indefinite, and reciprocal.

PERSONAL PRONOUNS Personal pronouns refer to specific persons or things. They are singular or plural in form, and they always function as noun equivalents.

Singular: I, me, you, she, her, he, him, it
Plural: we, us, you, they, them

POSSESSIVE PRONOUNS Possessive pronouns indicate ownership. Like personal pronouns, they are singular or plural in form.

Singular: my, mine, your, yours, her, hers, his, its
Plural: our, ours, your, yours, their, theirs

Some of these possessive pronouns function as adjectives modifying nouns: *my, your, his, her, its, our, their.*

INTENSIVE AND REFLEXIVE PRONOUNS Intensive pronouns emphasize a noun or another pronoun (The congresswoman *herself* met us at the door). Reflexive pronouns, which have the same form as intensive pronouns, name a receiver of an action identical with the doer of the action (Paula cut *herself*). Intensive and reflexive pronouns are singular or plural in form.

Singular: myself, yourself, himself, herself, itself
Plural: ourselves, yourselves, themselves

RELATIVE PRONOUNS Relative pronouns introduce subordinate clauses functioning as adjectives (The man *who robbed us* was never caught.) In addition to introducing the clause, the relative pronoun, in this case *who,* points back to the noun or pronoun that the clause modifies (*man*). (See 49b.)

who, whom, whose, which, that

Some grammarians also treat *whichever, whoever, whomever, what,* and *whatever* as relative pronouns. These words introduce noun clauses; they do not point back to a noun or pronoun. (See 49b.)

INTERROGATIVE PRONOUNS Interrogative pronouns introduce questions (*Who* is expected to win the election?).

who, whom, whose, which, what

DEMONSTRATIVE PRONOUNS Demonstrative pronouns identify or point to nouns. Frequently they function as adjectives (*This* chair is my favorite), but they may also function as noun equivalents (*This* is my favorite chair).

> this, that, these, those

INDEFINITE PRONOUNS Indefinite pronouns refer to nonspecific persons or things. Most are always singular (*everyone, each, none*); some are always plural (*all, both*); a few may be singular or plural (see 21d). Most indefinite pronouns function as noun equivalents (*Something* is burning), but some can also function as adjectives (*All* campers must check in at the lodge).

all	anything	everyone	nobody	several
another	both	everything	none	some
any	each	few	no one	somebody
anybody	either	many	nothing	someone
anyone	everybody	neither	one	something

RECIPROCAL PRONOUNS Reciprocal pronouns refer to individual parts of a plural antecedent (By turns, we helped *each other* through college).

> each other, one another

EXERCISE 47–2

Underline the pronouns (and pronoun/adjectives) in the following sentences. Answers to lettered sentences appear in the back of the book. Example:

> Beware of persons <u>who</u> are praised by <u>everyone</u>.

a. Every society honors its live conformists and its dead troublemakers.
b. Watch the faces of those who bow low.

c. I have written some poetry that I myself don't understand.
d. A skeptic is a person who would ask God for his I.D.
e. No one can be hanged for thinking.

1. Doctors can bury their mistakes, but architects can only advise their clients to plant vines.
2. Nothing is interesting if you are not interested.
3. We will never have friends if we expect to find them without fault.
4. If a man bites a dog, that is news.
5. Anyone who serves God for money will serve the devil for better wages.

47c Verbs

The verb of a sentence usually expresses action (*jump, think*) or being (*is, become*). It is composed of a main verb possibly preceded by one or more helping verbs:

> **MV**
> The best fish *swim* near the bottom.

> **HV   MV**
> A marriage *is* not *built* in a day.

> **HV HV   MV**
> Even God *has been defended* with nonsense.

Notice that words can intervene between the helping and the main verb (*is* not *built*).

There are twenty-three helping verbs in English. Nine of them, called *modals*, function only as helping verbs, never as main verbs:

can	shall	could	may	must
will	should	would	might	

The others may function either as helping verbs or as main verbs:

> have, has, had
> do, does, did
> be, am, is, are, was, were, being, been

The main verb of a sentence is always the kind of word that would change form if put into these test sentences:

BASE FORM	Usually I (*walk, ride*).
PAST TENSE	Yesterday I (*walked, rode*).
PAST PARTICIPLE	I have (*walked, ridden*) many times before.
PRESENT PARTICIPLE	I am (*walking, riding*) right now.
-S FORM	He/she/it (*walks, rides*) regularly.

If a word doesn't change form when slipped into these test sentences, you can be certain that it is not a main verb. For example, the noun *revolution*, though it may seem to suggest an action, can never function as a main verb. Just try to make it behave like one (*Today I revolution . . . Yesterday I revolutioned . . .*) and you'll see why.

When both the past-tense and the past-participle forms of a verb end in *-ed*, the verb is regular (*walked, walked*). Otherwise, the verb is irregular (*rode, ridden*). (See 27a.)

The verb *be* is highly irregular, having eight forms instead of the usual five: the base form *be*, the present-tense forms *am*, *is*, and *are*, the past-tense forms *was* and *were*, the present participle *being*, and the past participle *been*.

Helping verbs combine with the various forms of main verbs to create tenses. For a survey of tenses, see 28a.

NOTE: Some verbs are followed by words that look like prepositions but are so closely associated with the verb that they are a part of its meaning. These words are known as *particles*.

Common verb-particle combinations include *bring up, call off, drop off, give in, look up, run into,* and *take off.*

> A lot of parents *pack up* their troubles and *send* them *off* to camp.

ESL NOTE: Particles can cause problems for speakers of English as a second language. See 29c.

EXERCISE 47–3

Underline the verbs in the following sentences, including helping verbs and particles. Answers to lettered sentences appear in the back of the book. Example:

> <u>Throw</u> a lucky man into the sea, and he <u>will emerge</u> with a
>
> fish in his mouth.

a. Great persons have not commonly been great scholars.
b. Without the spice of guilt, can sin be fully savored?
c. One arrow does not bring down two birds.
d. Birds of a feather flock together.
e. Don't scald your tongue in other people's broth.

1. The king can do no wrong.
2. The road to ruin is always kept in good repair.
3. Love your neighbor, but don't pull down the hedge.
4. Life can only be understood backward, but it must be lived forward.
5. He has every attribute of a dog except loyalty.

47d Adjectives

An adjective is a word used to modify, or describe, a noun or pronoun. An adjective usually answers one of these questions: Which one? What kind of? How many?

the *lame* elephant [Which elephant?]

rare, valuable, old stamps [What kind of stamps?]

sixteen candles [How many candles?]

Grammarians also define adjectives according to their form and their typical position in a sentence, as follows:

the kind of word that usually comes before a noun in a noun phrase (a *frisky* puppy, an *amiable young* man);

the kind of word that can follow a linking verb and describe the subject (the ship was *unsinkable*; talk is *cheap*) (see 48b);

the kind of word that when derived from another part of speech typically takes one of these endings: wonder*ful*, courte*ous*, luck*y*, fool*ish*, pleasur*able*, colon*ial*, defen*sible*, urg*ent*, help*less*, disgust*ing*, friend*ly*, spectacul*ar*, secret*ive*.

The definite article *the* and the indefinite articles *a* and *an* are also classified as adjectives.

Some possessive, demonstrative, and indefinite pronouns can function as adjectives. (See 47b.)

47e Adverbs

An adverb is a word used to modify, or qualify, a verb (or verbal), an adjective, or another adverb. It usually answers one of these questions: When? Where? How? Why? Under what conditions? To what degree?

Pull *gently* at a weak rope. [Pull how?]

Read the best books *first*. [Read when?]

Adverbs that modify a verb are also defined according to their form and their typical position in a sentence, as follows:

the kind of word that can appear nearly anywhere in a sentence and is often movable (he *sometimes* jogged after work; *sometimes* he jogged after work);

the kind of word that when derived from an adjective typically takes an *-ly* ending (nice, nice*ly*; profound, profound*ly*).

Adverbs modifying adjectives or other adverbs usually intensify or limit the intensity of the word they modify.

Be *extremely* good, and you will be *very* lonesome.

Adverbs modifying adjectives and other adverbs are not movable. We can't say "Be good *extremely*" or "*Extremely* be good."

The negators *not* and *never* are classified as adverbs. A word such as *cannot* contains the helping verb *can* and the adverb *not*. A contraction such as *can't* contains the helping verb *can* and a contracted form of the adverb *not*.

NOTE: Adverbs can also modify prepositions (Helen left *just* before midnight), prepositional phrases (The budget is *barely* on target), subordinate clauses (We will try to attend, *especially* if you will be there), or whole sentences (*Certainly* Joe did not intend to insult you).

EXERCISE 47 – 4

Underline the adjectives and circle the adverbs in the following sentences. If a word is a pronoun in form but an adjective in function, treat it as an adjective. Also, treat the articles *a, an,* and *the* as adjectives. Answers to lettered sentences appear in the back of the book. Example:

A little sincerity is a dangerous thing, and a great deal of it

is (absolutely) fatal.

a. Little strokes fell great oaks.

b. The American public is wonderfully tolerant.
c. You cannot spoil a rotten egg.
d. Hope is a very thin diet.
e. Sleep faster. We need the pillows.

1. We cannot be too careful in the choice of our enemies.
2. A wild goose never laid a tame egg.
3. Money will buy a pretty good dog, but it will not buy the wag of its tail.
4. Loquacious people seldom have much sense.
5. An old quarrel can be easily revived.

47f Prepositions

A preposition is a word placed before a noun or pronoun to form a phrase modifying another word in the sentence. The prepositional phrase nearly always functions as an adjective or as an adverb.

The road *to hell* is usually paved *with good intentions.*

To hell functions as an adjective, modifying the noun *road; with good intentions* functions as an adverb, modifying the verb *is paved.*

Prepositional phrases functioning as adjectives usually answer one of the adjective questions: Which one? What kind of? And they nearly always appear immediately following the word they modify. (See 49a.)

Prepositional phrases functioning as adverbs usually answer one of the adverb questions: When? Where? How? Why? Under what conditions? To what degree? Prepositional phrases modifying verbs may appear nearly anywhere in the sentence, and they are often movable.

There are a limited number of prepositions in English. The most common ones are included in the following list.

about	across	against	among	as
above	after	along	around	at

before	despite	next	regarding	underneath
behind	down	of	respecting	unlike
below	during	off	round	until
beside	except	on	since	unto
besides	for	onto	than	up
between	from	opposite	through	upon
beyond	in	out	throughout	with
but	inside	outside	till	without
by	into	over	to	
concerning	like	past	toward	
considering	near	plus	under	

Some prepositions are more than one word long. *Along with, as well as, in addition to,* and *next to* are common examples.

47g Conjunctions

Conjunctions join words, phrases, or clauses, and they indicate the relation between the elements joined.

A coordinating conjunction is used to connect grammatically equal elements. The coordinating conjunctions are *and, but, or, nor, for, so,* and *yet.*

> Poverty is the parent of revolution *and* crime.

> Admire a little ship, *but* put your cargo in a big one.

In the first sentence, *and* connects two nouns; in the second, *but* connects two independent clauses.

Correlative conjunctions come in pairs: *either . . . or; neither . . . nor; not only . . . but also; whether . . . or; both . . . and.* Like coordinating conjunctions, they connect grammatically equal elements.

> *Either* Jack Sprat *or* his wife could eat no fat.

A subordinating conjunction introduces a subordinate clause and indicates its relation to the rest of the sentence.

Parts of speech

A **NOUN** names a person, place, thing, or idea.

> N   N N
> *Repetition* does not transform a *lie* into *truth*.

A **PRONOUN** substitutes for a noun.

>   PN PN   PN
> When the gods wish to punish *us, they* heed *our* prayers.

> *Personal pronouns:* I, me, you, he, him, she, her, it, we, us, they, them

> *Possessive pronouns:* my, mine, your, yours, her, hers, his, its, our, ours, their, theirs

> *Intensive and reflexive pronouns:* myself, yourself, himself, herself, itself, ourselves, themselves

> *Relative pronouns:* that, which, who, whom, whose (*also* what, whatever, whichever, whoever, whomever)

> *Interrogative pronouns:* who, whom, whose, which, what

> *Demonstrative pronouns:* this, that, these, those

> *Indefinite pronouns:* all, another, any, anybody, anyone, anything, both, each, either, everybody, everyone, everything, few, many, neither, nobody, none, no one, nothing, one, several, some, somebody, someone, something

> *Reciprocal pronouns:* each other, one another

A **HELPING VERB** comes before a main verb.

> *Modals:* can, could, may, might, must, shall, should, will, would

> *Forms of* be: be, am, is, are, was, were, being, been

Parts of speech (continued)

Forms of have: have, has, had

Forms of do: do, does, did

(The forms of *be, have,* and *do* may also function as main verbs.)

A **MAIN VERB** asserts action, being, or state of being.

> MV   HV   MV
> Charity *begins* at home but *should* not *end* there.

A main verb will always change form when put into these positions in sentences:

Usually I _____ .	(walk, ride)
Yesterday I _____ .	(walked, rode)
I have _____ many times before.	(walked, ridden)
I am _____ right now.	(walking, riding)
He _____ regularly.	(walks, rides)

There are eight forms of the highly irregular verb *be:* be, am, is, are, was, were, being, been.

An **ADJECTIVE** modifies a noun or pronoun, usually answering one of these questions: Which one? What kind of? How many? The articles *a, an,* and *the* are also adjectives.

> ADJ   ADJ
> *Useless* laws weaken *necessary* ones.

An **ADVERB** modifies a verb, adjective, or adverb, usually answering one of these questions: When? Where? Why? How? Under what conditions? To what degree?

> ADV   ADV
> People think *too historically.*

Parts of speech (continued)

A **PREPOSITION** indicates the relationship between the noun or pronoun that follows it and another word in the sentence.

A journey *of* a thousand miles begins *with* a single step.

Common prepositions: about, above, across, after, against, along, among, around, as, at, before, behind, below, beside, besides, between, beyond, but, by, concerning, considering, despite, down, during, except, for, from, in, inside, into, like, near, next, of, off, on, onto, opposite, out, outside, over, past, plus, regarding, respecting, round, since, than, through, throughout, till, to, toward, under, underneath, unlike, until, unto, up, upon, with, without

A **CONJUNCTION** connects words or word groups.

Coordinating conjunctions: and, but, or, nor, for, so, yet

Subordinating conjunctions: after, although, as, as if, because, before, even though, how, if, in order that, rather than, since, so that, than, that, though, unless, until, when, where, whether, while, why

Correlative conjunctions: either . . . or, neither . . . nor, not only . . . but also, both . . . and, whether . . . or

Conjunctive adverbs: accordingly, also, anyway, besides, certainly, consequently, conversely, finally, furthermore, hence, however, incidentally, indeed, instead, likewise, meanwhile, moreover, nevertheless, next, nonetheless, otherwise, similarly, specifically, still, subsequently, then, therefore, thus

An **INTERJECTION** expresses surprise or emotion. (Oh! Wow! Hey! Hooray!)

(See 49b.) The most common subordinating conjunctions are *after, although, as, as if, because, before, even though, if, in order that, rather than, since, so that, than, that, though, unless, until, when, where, whether,* and *while.*

If triangles had a god, it would have three sides.

A conjunctive adverb may be used with a semicolon to connect independent clauses; it usually serves as a transition between the clauses. The most common conjunctive adverbs are *consequently, finally, furthermore, however, moreover, nevertheless, similarly, then, therefore,* and *thus.*

When we want to murder a tiger, we call it sport; *however,* when the tiger wants to murder us, we call it ferocity.

47h Interjections

An interjection is a word used to express surprise or emotion (*Oh! Hey! Wow!*).

48

Sentence patterns

Most English sentences flow from subject to verb to any objects or complements. The vast majority of sentences conform to one of these five patterns:

subject / verb / subject complement

subject / verb / direct object

subject / verb / indirect object / direct object

subject / verb / direct object / object complement

subject / verb

Adverbial modifiers (single words, phrases, or clauses) may be added to any of these patterns, and they may appear nearly anywhere — at the beginning, the middle, or the end.

Predicate is the grammatical term given to the verb plus its objects, complements, and adverbial modifiers.

For a quick-reference chart of sentence patterns, see page 447.

48a Subjects

The subject of a sentence names who or what the sentence is about. The *complete subject* is usually composed of a *simple subject,* always a noun or pronoun, plus any words or word groups modifying the simple subject. To find the complete subject, ask Who? or What?, insert the verb, and finish the question. The answer is the complete subject.

┌── COMPLETE SUBJECT ──┐
The purity of a revolution usually lasts about two weeks.

Who or what lasts about two weeks? *The purity of a revolution.*

┌───── COMPLETE SUBJECT ─────┐
Historical books that contain no lies are extremely tedious.

Who or what are extremely tedious? *Historical books that contain no lies.*

COMPLETE SUBJECT
┌────┐
In every country the sun rises in the morning.

Who or what rises in the morning? *The sun.* Notice that *In every country the sun* is not a sensible answer to the question. *In every country* is a prepositional phrase modifying the verb *rises.* Since sentences frequently open with such modifiers, it is not safe to assume that the subject must always appear first in a sentence.

To find the simple subject, strip away all modifiers in the complete subject. This includes single-word modifiers such as *the* and *historical*, phrases such as *of a revolution*, and subordinate clauses such as *that contain no lies*.

┌ **SS** ┐
The purity of a revolution usually lasts about two weeks.

┌**SS**┐
Historical books that contain no lies are extremely tedious.

┌**SS**┐
In every country *the sun* rises in the morning.

A sentence may have a compound subject containing two or more simple subjects joined with a coordinating conjunction such as *and, but,* or *or*.

┌ **SS** ┐   ┌ **SS** ┐
Much industry and little conscience make us rich.

Occasionally a verb's subject is understood but not present in the sentence. In imperative sentences, which give advice or commands, the subject is understood to be *you*.

[*You*] Hitch your wagon to a star.

Although the subject ordinarily comes before the verb, occasionally it does not. When a sentence begins with *there is* or *there are* (or *there was* or *there were*), the subject follows the verb. The word *there* is an expletive in such constructions, an empty word serving merely to get the sentence started.

┌ **SS** ┐
There is *no substitute for victory*.

Occasionally a writer will invert a sentence for effect.

┌─ **ss** ─┐
Happy is *the nation that has no history.*

Happy is an adjective, so it cannot be the subject. Turn this sentence around and its structure becomes obvious: *The nation that has no history is happy.*

In questions, the subject frequently appears in an unusual position, sandwiched between parts of the verb.

┌**ss**┐
Do *married men* make the best husbands?

Turn the question into a statement, and the words will appear in their usual order: *Married men do make the best husbands.* (*Do make* is the verb.)

EXERCISE 48 – 1

In the following sentences, underline the complete subject and write *ss* above the simple subject(s). If the subject is an understood *you*, insert it in parentheses. Answers to lettered sentences appear in the back of the book. Example:

ss
A little inaccuracy sometimes saves many explanations.

a. A spoiled child never loves its mother.
b. To some lawyers, all facts are created equal.
c. Speak softly and carry a big stick.
d. There is nothing permanent except change.
e. Does hope really spring eternal in the human breast?

1. Habit is overcome by habit.
2. The gardens of kindness never fade.
3. The dog with the bone is always in danger.
4. Fools and their money are soon parted.
5. There is honor among thieves.

48b Verbs, objects, and complements

Section 47c explains how to find the verb of a sentence, which consists of a main verb possibly preceded by one or more helping verbs. A sentence's verb is classified as linking, transitive, or intransitive, depending on the kinds of objects or complements the verb can (or cannot) take.

Linking verbs and subject complements

Linking verbs link the subject to a subject complement, a word or word group that completes the meaning of the subject by renaming or describing it. If the subject complement renames the subject, it is a noun or noun equivalent (sometimes called a *predicate noun*).

┌─────────────── s ───────────────┐ ┌─ v ─┐ ┌─ sc ─┐
The handwriting on the wall may be a forgery.

If the subject complement describes the subject, it is an adjective or adjective equivalent (sometimes called a *predicate adjective*).

   s   v sc
Love is blind.

Whenever they appear as main verbs (rather than helping verbs), the forms of *be* — *be, am, is, are, was, were, being, been* — usually function as linking verbs. In the preceding examples, for instance, the main verbs are *be* and *is*.

Verbs such as *appear, become, feel, grow, look, make, seem, smell, sound,* and *taste* are sometimes linking, depending on the sense of the sentence.

┌─ s ─┐ ┌─ v ─┐ ┌─ sc ─┐
At the touch of love, everyone becomes a poet.

```
     ┌──── S ────┐        ┌─V─┐ ┌SC┐
At first sight, original art often looks ugly.
```

When you suspect that a verb such as *becomes* or *looks* is linking, check to see if the word or words following it rename or describe the subject. In the sample sentences, *a poet* renames *everyone* and *ugly* describes *art*.

Transitive verbs and direct objects

A transitive verb takes a direct object, a word or word group that names a receiver of the action.

```
┌──────── S ────────┐ ┌── V ──┐ ┌──────────── DO ────────────┐
The little snake studies the ways of the big serpent.
```

In such sentences, the subject and verb alone will seem incomplete. Once we have read "The little snake studies," for example, we want to know the rest: The little snake studies what? The answer to the question What? (or Whom?) is the complete direct object: *the ways of the big serpent.* The simple direct object is always a noun or pronoun, in this case *ways.* To find it, simply strip away all modifiers.

Transitive verbs usually appear in the active voice, with the subject doing the action and a direct object receiving the action. Active-voice sentences can be transformed into the passive voice, with the subject receiving the action instead. See 48c.

Transitive verbs, indirect objects, and direct objects

The direct object of a transitive verb is sometimes preceded by an indirect object, a noun or pronoun telling to whom or for whom the action of the sentence is done.

```
 S    V   IO  ┌DO┐       S ┌── V ──┐  IO  ┌─ DO ─┐
You show me a hero, and I will write you a tragedy.
```

The simple indirect object is always a noun or pronoun. To test for an indirect object, insert the word *to* or *for* before the word or word group in question. If the sentence makes sense, the word or word group is an indirect object.

> You show [to] me a hero, and I will write [for] you a tragedy.

An indirect object may be turned into a prepositional phrase using *to* or *for: You show a hero to me, and I will write a tragedy for you.*

Only certain transitive verbs take indirect objects. Common examples are *give, ask, bring, find, get, hand, lend, offer, pay, pour, promise, read, send, show, teach, tell, throw,* and *write.*

Transitive verbs, direct objects, and object complements

The direct object of a transitive verb is sometimes followed by an object complement, a word or word group that completes the direct object's meaning by renaming or describing it.

> ┌─ **S** ─┐   ┌**V**┐ ┌─**DO**─┐ ┌───────── **OC** ─────────┐
> People now call a spade an agricultural implement.

> ┌**S**┐ ┌**V**┐ ┌─── **DO** ───┐ ┌**OC**┐
> Love makes all hard hearts gentle.

When the object complement renames the direct object, it is a noun or pronoun (such as *implement*). When it describes the direct object, it is an adjective (such as *gentle*).

Intransitive verbs

Intransitive verbs take no objects or complements. Their pattern is always subject/verb.

```
      S    V
```
Money talks.

```
┌──── S ────┐   ┌ V ┐
```
Revolutions never go backward.

Nothing receives the actions of talking and going in these sentences, so the verbs are intransitive. Notice that such verbs may or may not be followed by adverbial modifiers. In the second sentence, *backward* is an adverb modifying *go*.

NOTE: The dictionary will tell you whether a verb is transitive or intransitive. Some verbs have both transitive and intransitive functions.

TRANSITIVE   Sandra flew her Cessna over the canyon.

INTRANSITIVE   A bald eagle flew overhead.

In the first example, *flew* has a direct object that receives the action: *her Cessna*. In the second example, the verb is followed by an adverb (*overhead*), not by a direct object.

EXERCISE 48–2

Label the subject complements, direct objects, indirect objects, and object complements in the following sentences. If an object or complement consists of more than one word, bracket and label all of it. Answers to lettered sentences appear in the back of the book. Example:

```
                DO  ┌─OC─┐
```
All work and no play make Jack a dull boy.

a. Victory has a hundred fathers, but defeat is an orphan.
b. No one tests the depth of a river with both feet.
c. Lock your door and keep your neighbors honest.
d. Not every day can be a feast of lanterns.
e. Lizzie Borden gave her father forty whacks.

Sentence patterns

Subject / linking verb / subject complement

  ┌———— s ————┐ v ┌———sc———┐
Advertising is legalized lying. [*Legalized lying* renames *advertising.*]

  ┌————— s —————┐ v ┌— sc—┐
Great intellects are skeptical. [*Skeptical* describes *great intellects.*]

Subject / transitive verb / direct object

  ┌— s —┐ ┌———— v ————┐ ┌DO ┐
A stumble may prevent a fall.

Subject / transitive verb / indirect object / direct object

  s   v   IO ┌——DO——┐
Fate gives us our relatives.

Subject / transitive verb / direct object / object complement

  ┌— s —┐ ┌—v —┐DO   OC
Our fears do make us traitors. [*Traitors* renames *us.*]

  ┌—s—┐   v   ┌—DO—┐   OC
The pot calls the kettle black. [*Black* describes *the kettle.*]

Subject / intransitive verb

  s   v
Time flies.

1. Good medicine always tastes bitter.
2. Ask me no questions, and I will tell you no lies.
3. The mob has many heads but no brains.
4. Some folk want their luck buttered.
5. Prejudice is the child of ignorance.

48c Pattern variations

Although most sentences follow one of the five patterns in the chart on page 447, variations of these patterns commonly occur in questions, commands, sentences with delayed subjects, and passive transformations.

Questions and commands

Questions are sometimes patterned in normal word order, with the subject preceding the verb.

> S ⌐—V—⌐
> Who will take the first step?

Just as frequently, however, the pattern of a question is inverted, with the subject appearing between the helping and main verbs or after the verb.

> **HV S MV**
> Will you take the first step?

> V ⌐——— S ———⌐
> Why is the first step so difficult?

In commands, the subject of the sentence is an understood *you*.

> [You] Keep your mouth shut and your eyes open.

Sentences with delayed subjects

Writers sometimes choose to delay the subject of a sentence to achieve a special effect such as suspense or humor.

                                        v ┌──── **s** ────┐
Behind the phony tinsel of Hollywood lies the real tinsel.

The subject of the sentence is also delayed in sentences opening with the expletives *there* or *it*. When used as expletives, the words *there* and *it* have no strict grammatical function; they serve merely to get the sentence started.

        v ┌─────────────── **s** ───────────────┐
There are many paths to the top of the mountain.

        v   ┌──────── **s** ────────┐
It is not good to wake a sleeping lion.

The subject in the second example is an infinitive phrase. (See 49c.)

Passive transformations

Transitive verbs, those that can take direct objects, usually appear in the active voice. In the active voice, the subject does the action and a direct object receives the action.

                                s   **v** ┌──── **DO** ────┐
ACTIVE   The early *bird* sometimes *catches the early worm.*

Sentences in the active voice may be transformed into the passive voice, with the subject receiving the action instead.

                ┌──── **s** ────┐**HV**   **v**
PASSIVE   *The early worm is* sometimes *caught* by the early
               bird.

What was once the direct object (*the early worm*) has become the subject in the passive-voice transformation, and the original subject appears in a prepositional phrase beginning with *by*. The *by* phrase is frequently omitted in passive-voice constructions.

> **PASSIVE** The early worm is sometimes caught.

Verbs in the passive voice can be identified by their form alone. The main verb is always a past participle, such as *caught* (see 47c), preceded by a form of *be* (*be, am, is, are, was, were, being, been*): *is caught.* Sometimes adverbs intervene (*is* sometimes *caught*).

For a review of the uses of the passive voice, see 28c.

49

Subordinate word groups

Subordinate word groups include prepositional phrases, subordinate clauses, verbal phrases, appositives, and absolutes. Not all of these word groups are subordinate in quite the same way. Some are subordinate because they are modifiers; others function as noun equivalents, not as modifiers.

49a Prepositional phrases

A prepositional phrase begins with a preposition such as *at, by, for, from, in, of, on, to,* or *with* (see 47f) and usually ends with a noun or noun equivalent: *on the table, for him, with great fanfare.* The noun or noun equivalent is known as the *object of the preposition.*

Prepositional phrases function either as adjectives modifying a noun or pronoun or as adverbs modifying a verb, an adjective, or another adverb. When functioning as an adjective, a prepositional phrase nearly always appears immediately following the noun or pronoun it modifies:

Variety is the spice *of life.*

Adjective phrases usually answer one or both of the questions Which one? and What kind of? If we ask Which spice? or What kind of spice? we get a sensible answer: the spice *of life.*

Adverbial prepositional phrases that modify the verb can appear nearly anywhere in a sentence.

Do not judge a tree *by its bark.*

Tyranny will *in time* lead to revolution.

To the ant, a few drops of rain are a flood.

Adverbial word groups usually answer one of these questions: When? Where? How? Why? Under what conditions?

Do not judge a tree *how? By its bark.*

Tyranny will lead to revolution *when? In time.*

A few drops of rain are a flood *under what conditions? To the ant.*

If a prepositional phrase is movable, you can be certain that it is adverbial; adjectival prepositional phrases are wedded to the words they modify. At least some of the time, adverbials can be moved to other positions in the sentence.

By their fruits you shall know them.

You shall know them *by their fruits.*

NOTE: In questions and subordinate clauses, a preposition may appear after its object.

What are you afraid *of?*

We avoided the clerk *whom* John had warned us *about.*

EXERCISE 49 – 1

Underline the prepositional phrases in the following sentences. Be prepared to explain the function of each phrase. Answers to lettered sentences appear in the back of the book. Example:

You can tell the ideals of a nation by its advertising.

[Adjective phrase modifying ideals; adverbial phrase modifying can tell.]

a. Laughter is a tranquilizer with no side effects.
b. One misfortune always carries another on its back.
c. The love of money is the root of all evil.
d. Wall Street begins in a graveyard and ends in a river.
e. You can stroke people with words.

1. A pleasant companion reduces the length of the journey.
2. A society of sheep produces a government of wolves.
3. Some people feel with their heads and think with their hearts.
4. In love and war, all is fair.
5. He leaped from the frying pan into the fire.

49b Subordinate clauses

Subordinate clauses are patterned like sentences, having subjects and verbs and sometimes objects or complements. But they function within sentences as adjectives, adverbs, or nouns. They cannot stand alone as complete sentences.

 A subordinate clause usually begins with a subordinating conjunction or a relative pronoun.

SUBORDINATING CONJUNCTIONS

after	before	rather than	though	where
although	even though	since	unless	whether
as	if	so that	until	while
as if	how	than	when	why
because	in order that	that		

RELATIVE PRONOUNS

that	who	whom	whose	whatever
which	whoever	whomever	what	

The chart on page 457 classifies these words according to the kinds of clauses (adjective, adverb, or noun) they introduce.

Adjective clauses

Like other word groups functioning as adjectives, adjective clauses modify nouns or pronouns. An adjective clause nearly always appears immediately following the noun or pronoun it modifies.

The arrow *that has left the bow* never returns.

Relatives are persons *who live too near and die too seldom.*

To test whether a subordinate clause functions as an adjective, ask the adjective questions: Which one? What kind of? The answer should make sense. Which arrow? The arrow *that has left the bow.* What kind of persons? Persons *who live too near and die too seldom.*

Most adjective clauses begin with a relative pronoun (*who, whom, whose, which,* or *that*), which marks them as grammatically subordinate. In addition to introducing the clause, the relative pronoun points back to the noun that the clause modifies.

The fur *that warms a monarch* once warmed a bear.

Relative pronouns are sometimes "understood."

> The things [*that*] we know best are the things [*that*] we haven't been taught.

Occasionally an adjective clause is introduced by a relative adverb, usually *when, where,* or *why.*

> Home is the place *where you slip in the bathtub and break your neck.*

The parts of an adjective clause are often arranged as in sentences (subject/verb/object or complement).

>   S   V   DO
> We often forgive the people *who bore us.*

Frequently, however, the object or complement appears first, violating the normal order of subject/verb/object.

>   DO   S   V
> We rarely forgive those *whom we bore.*

To determine the subject of a clause, ask Who? or What? and insert the verb. Don't be surprised if the answer is an echo, as in the first adjective clause above: Who bore us? *Who.* To find any objects or complements, read the subject and the verb and then ask Who? Whom? or What? Again, be prepared for a possible echo, as in the second adjective clause: We bore whom? *Whom.*

Adverb clauses

Adverb clauses usually modify verbs, in which case they may appear nearly anywhere in a sentence — at the beginning, at the end, or somewhere in the middle. Like other adverbial word groups, they tell when, where, why, under what conditions, or to what degree an action occurred or a situation existed.

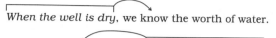

When the well is dry, we know the worth of water.

Venice would be a fine city *if it were only drained.*

When do we know the worth of water? *When the well is dry.* Under what conditions would Venice be a fine city? *If it were only drained.*

Unlike adjective clauses, adverb clauses are frequently movable. In the preceding example sentences, for instance, the adverb clauses can be moved without affecting the meaning of the sentences.

We know the worth of water *when the well is dry.*

If it were only drained, Venice would be a fine city.

When an adverb clause modifies an adjective or an adverb, it is not movable; it must appear next to the word it modifies. In the following examples the *because* clause modifies the adjective *angry,* and the *than* clause modifies the adverb *faster.*

Angry *because the mayor had not kept his promises,* we worked for his defeat.

Joan can run faster *than I can bicycle.*

Adverb clauses always begin with a subordinating conjunction (see the chart on p. 457 for a list). Subordinating conjunctions introduce clauses and express their relation to the rest of the sentence.

Adverb clauses are sometimes elliptical, with some of their words being "understood."

When [it is] *painted,* the room will look larger.

Noun clauses

Because they do not function as modifiers, noun clauses are not subordinate in the same sense as are adjective and adverb clauses. They are called subordinate only because they cannot stand alone: They must function within another sentence pattern, always as nouns.

A noun clause functions just like a single-word noun, usually as a subject, subject complement, direct object, or object of a preposition.

    ⌐——————— **S** ———————⌐

Whoever gossips to you will gossip of you.

    ⌐——————— **DO** ———————⌐

We never forget *that we buried the hatchet.*

A noun clause usually begins with a relative pronoun (*that, which, who, whoever, whomever, whose, what, whatever*) or with one of the following subordinating conjunctions: *how, when, where, whether, why.* The subordinating word may or may not play a significant role in the clause. In the preceding example sentences, *whoever* is the subject of its clause, but *that* does not perform a function in its clause.

As with adjective clauses, the parts of a noun clause may appear out of their normal order (subject/verb/object).

        DO   **S**   **V**

Talent is *what you possess.*

The parts of a noun clause may also appear in their normal order.

        S   **V**   **DO**

Genius is *what possesses you.*

Words that introduce subordinate clauses

WORDS INTRODUCING ADVERB CLAUSES (SUBORDINATING CONJUNCTIONS)

Subordinating conjunctions: after, although, as, as if, because, before, even though, if, in order that, rather than, since, so that, than, that, though, unless, until, when, where, whether, while

WORDS INTRODUCING ADJECTIVE CLAUSES (RELATIVE PRONOUNS AND RELATIVE ADVERBS)

Relative pronouns: that, which, who, whom, whose

Relative adverbs: when, where, why

WORDS INTRODUCING NOUN CLAUSES (RELATIVE PRONOUNS AND SUBORDINATING CONJUNCTIONS*)

Relative pronouns: that, who, whoever, whom, whomever, whose, what, whatever, which, whichever

Subordinating conjunctions: how, if, when, whenever, where, wherever, whether, why

*Some grammarians use other terms to describe the words that introduce noun clauses.

EXERCISE 49−2

Underline the subordinate clauses in the following sentences. Be prepared to explain the function of each clause. Answers to lettered sentences appear in the back of the book. Example:

> When the insects take over the world, we hope that they will
>
> remember our picnics with gratitude. *[Adverb clause*
>
> *modifying hope; noun clause used as direct object.]*

a. Though you live near a forest, do not waste firewood.
b. The gods help those who help themselves.
c. What is written without effort is read without pleasure.
d. The dog that trots finds the bone.
e. A fraud is not perfect unless it is practiced on clever persons.

1. What history teaches us is that we have never learned anything from it.
2. Dig a well before you are thirsty.
3. Whoever named it necking was a poor judge of anatomy.
4. If you were born lucky, even your rooster will lay eggs.
5. He gave her a look that you could have poured on a waffle.

49c Verbal phrases

A verbal is a verb form that does not function as the verb of a clause. Verbals include infinitives (the word *to* plus the base form of the verb), present participles (the *-ing* form of the verb), and past participles (the verb form usually ending in *-d*, *-ed*, *-n*, *-en*, or *-t*). (See 27a and 47c.)

INFINITIVE	PRESENT PARTICIPLE	PAST PARTICIPLE
to dream	dreaming	dreamed
to choose	choosing	chosen
to build	building	built
to grow	growing	grown

Instead of functioning as the verb of a clause, a verbal or a verbal phrase functions as an adjective, a noun, or an adverb.

ADJECTIVE   *Stolen* grapes are especially sweet.

NOUN   Continual *dripping* wears away a stone.

ADVERB   Were we born *to suffer*?

Verbals can take objects, complements, and modifiers to form verbal phrases; the phrases usually lack subjects.

Living well is the best revenge.

Governments exist *to protect the rights of minorities*.

The verbal *Living* is followed by an adverb modifier, *well*; the verbal *to protect* is followed by a direct object, *the rights of minorities*.

Like single-word verbals, verbal phrases function as adjectives, nouns, or adverbs. In the sentences just given, for example, *living well* functions as a noun used as the subject of the sentence, and *to protect the rights of minorities* functions as an adverb, answering the question Why?

Verbal phrases are ordinarily classified as participles, gerunds, and infinitives. This classification is based partly on form (whether the verbal is a present participle, a past participle, or an infinitive) and partly on function (whether the whole phrase functions as an adjective, a noun, or an adverb).

Participial phrases

Participial phrases always function as adjectives. Their verbals are either present participles, always ending in *-ing*, or past participles, frequently ending in *-d*, *-ed*, *-n*, *-en*, or *-t* (see 27a).

Participial phrases frequently appear immediately following the noun or pronoun they modify.

Congress shall make no law *abridging the freedom of speech or of the press.*

Truth *kept in the dark* will never save the world.

Unlike other adjectival word groups, however, which must always follow the noun or pronoun they modify, participial phrases are often movable. They can precede the word they modify.

Being a philosopher, I have a problem for every solution.

They may also appear at some distance from the word they modify.

History is something that never happened, *written by someone who wasn't there.*

Gerund phrases

Gerund phrases are built around present participles (verb forms ending in *-ing*), and they always function as nouns: usually as subjects, subject complements, direct objects, or objects of a preposition.

s
Justifying a fault doubles it.

sc
The secret of education is *respecting the pupil.*

do
Kleptomaniacs can't help *helping themselves.*

```
         ┌──────OBJ OF PREP──────┐
```
The hen is an egg's way of *producing another egg.*

Infinitive phrases

Infinitive phrases, always constructed around *to* plus the base form of the verb (*to call, to drink*), can function as nouns, as adjectives, or as adverbs.

When functioning as a noun, an infinitive phrase may appear in almost any noun slot in a sentence, usually as a subject, subject complement, or direct object.

```
┌──────── S ────────┐
```
To side with truth is noble.

```
           ┌──────────── DO ─────────────┐
```
Never try *to leap a chasm in two jumps.*

Infinitive phrases functioning as adjectives usually appear immediately following the noun or pronoun they modify.

We do not have the right *to abandon the poor.*

The infinitive phrase modifies the noun *right*. Which right? *The right to abandon the poor.*

Adverbial infinitive phrases usually qualify the meaning of the verb, telling when, where, how, why, under what conditions, or to what degree an action occurred.

He cut off his nose *to spite his face.*

Why did he cut off his nose? *To spite his face.*

NOTE: In some constructions, the infinitive is unmarked; in other words, the *to* does not appear: *No one can make you* [*to*] *feel inferior without your consent.*

EXERCISE 49–3

Underline the verbal phrases in the following sentences. Be prepared to explain the function of each phrase. Answers to lettered sentences appear in the back of the book. Example:

Fate tried to conceal him by naming him Smith. *[Infinitive phrase used as direct object; gerund phrase used as object of the preposition by.]*

  a. The best substitute for experience is being sixteen.
  b. Concealing a disease is no way to cure it.
  c. To help a friend is to give ourselves pleasure.
  d. Beware of Greeks bearing gifts.
  e. Every genius is considerably helped by being dead.

  1. The thing generally raised on city land is taxes.
  2. Do not use a hatchet to remove a fly from your friend's forehead.
  3. He has the gall of a shoplifter returning an item for a refund.
  4. Do you want to be a writer? Then write.
  5. Being weak, foxes are distinguished by superior tact.

49d Appositive phrases

Though strictly speaking they are not subordinate word groups, appositive phrases function somewhat as adjectives do, to describe nouns or pronouns. Instead of modifying nouns or pronouns, however, appositive phrases rename them. In form they are nouns or noun equivalents.

Appositives are said to be "in apposition" to the nouns or pronouns they rename.

> Politicians, *acrobats at heart*, can sit on a fence and yet keep both ears to the ground.

Acrobats at heart is in apposition to the noun *politicians*.

49e Absolute phrases

An absolute phrase modifies a whole clause or sentence, not just one word, and it may appear nearly anywhere in the sentence. It consists of a noun or noun equivalent usually followed by a participial phrase.

> *His words dipped in honey,* the senator mesmerized the crowd.

> The senator, *his words dipped in honey,* mesmerized the crowd.

> The senator mesmerized the crowd, *his words dipped in honey.*

50

Sentence types

Sentences are classified in two ways: according to their structure (simple, compound, complex, and compound-complex) and according to their purpose (declarative, imperative, interrogative, and exclamatory).

50a Sentence structures

Depending on the number and types of clauses they contain, sentences are classified as simple, compound, complex, or compound-complex.

Clauses come in two varieties: independent and subordinate. An *independent clause* is a full sentence pattern that does not function within another sentence pattern: It contains a subject and verb plus any objects, complements, and modifiers of that verb, and it either stands alone or could stand alone. A *subordinate clause* is a full sentence pattern that functions within a sentence as an adjective, an adverb, or a noun but that cannot stand alone as a complete sentence. (See 49b.)

Simple sentences

A simple sentence is one independent clause with no subordinate clauses.

┌─────────── **INDEPENDENT CLAUSE** ───────────┐
Without music, life would be a mistake.

This sentence contains a subject (*life*), a verb (*would be*), a complement (*a mistake*), and an adverbial modifier (*Without music*).

A simple sentence may contain compound elements — a compound subject, verb, or object, for example — but it does not contain more than one full sentence pattern. The following sentence is simple because its two verbs (*enters* and *spreads*) share a subject (*Evil*).

┌─────────── **INDEPENDENT CLAUSE** ───────────┐
Evil enters like a needle and spreads like an oak.

Compound sentences

A compound sentence is composed of two or more independent clauses with no subordinate clauses. The independent clauses are usually joined with a comma and a coordinating conjunction (*and, but, or, nor, for, so, yet*) or with a semicolon. (See 8.)

┌─**INDEPENDENT CLAUSE**─┐   ┌──────**INDEPENDENT CLAUSE**──────┐
One arrow is easily broken, but you can't break a bundle of ten.

┌─────── **INDEPENDENT CLAUSE** ────────┐ ┌─ **INDEPENDENT** ──
We are born brave, trusting, and greedy; most of us have
─**CLAUSE** ───────┐
remained greedy.

Complex sentences

A complex sentence is composed of one independent clause
with one or more subordinate clauses. (See 49b.)

SUBORDINATE
┌─── **CLAUSE** ───┐
ADJECTIVE   They that sow in tears shall reap in joy.

┌**SUBORDINATE CLAUSE**┐
ADVERB   If you scatter thorns, don't go barefoot.

┌──────── **SUBORDINATE CLAUSE** ────────┐
NOUN   What the scientists have in their briefcases is
terrifying.

Compound-complex sentences

A compound-complex sentence contains at least two independent clauses and at least one subordinate clause. The following sentence contains two full sentence patterns that can
stand alone.

┌**INDEPENDENT CLAUSE**┐   ┌──**INDEPENDENT CLAUSE**──┐
Tell me what you eat, and I will tell you what you are.

And each independent clause contains a subordinate clause,
making the sentence both compound and complex.

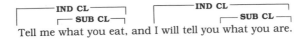

Tell me what you eat, and I will tell you what you are.

50b Sentence purposes

Writers use declarative sentences to make statements, imperative sentences to issue requests or commands, interrogative sentences to ask questions, and exclamatory sentences to make exclamations.

DECLARATIVE	The echo always has the last word.
IMPERATIVE	Love your neighbor.
INTERROGATIVE	Are second thoughts always wisest?
EXCLAMATORY	I want to wash the flag, not burn it!

EXERCISE 50–1

Identify the following sentences as simple, compound, complex, or compound-complex. Be prepared to identify the subordinate clauses and classify them according to their function: adjective, adverb, or noun. (See 49b.) Answers to lettered sentences appear in the back of the book. Example:

My folks didn't come over on the Mayflower; they were there

to meet the boat. *compound*

a. The poet is a liar who always speaks the truth.
b. Before marriage, keep your eyes wide open; afterward, keep them half shut.
c. The frog in the well knows nothing of the ocean.
d. If you don't go to other people's funerals, they won't go to yours.
e. People who sleep like a baby usually don't have one.

1. We often give our enemies the means for our own destruction.
2. Those who write clearly have readers; those who write obscurely have commentators.
3. The impersonal hand of government can never replace the helping hand of a neighbor.
4. Human action can be modified to some extent, but human nature cannot be changed.
5. When an elephant is in trouble, even a frog will kick him.

PART X

Research Guide

51

Conducting research

College research assignments are an opportunity for you to contribute to an intellectual inquiry or debate. Most college assignments ask you to pose a question worth exploring, to read widely in search of possible answers, to interpret what you read, to draw reasoned conclusions, and to support those conclusions with valid and well-documented evidence. Such assignments may at first seem overwhelming, but if you pose a question that intrigues you and approach it like a detective, with genuine curiosity, you will soon learn how rewarding doing research can be.

Admittedly, the process takes time: time for researching and time for drafting, revising, and documenting the paper in the style recommended by your instructor (see 54 or 55). Before beginning a research project, you should set a realistic schedule of deadlines. For example, before she began researching the sample research paper that appears on pages 544–580, Karen Shaw constructed the following schedule. She received her assignment on October 1, and the due date was November 1.

SCHEDULE	**FINISHED BY**
1. Take the college's library tour.	October 2
2. Choose a topic and plan a search strategy.	4
3. Locate sources; make bibliography cards.	8
4. Read and take notes.	15
5. Decide on a tentative thesis and outline.	17
6. Draft the paper.	22
7. Visit the writing center to get help with ideas for revision.	24
8. Revise the paper.	25
9. Prepare a list of works cited.	26
10. Type and proofread the final draft.	27

Notice that Shaw built some extra time into her schedule to allow for unexpected delays. Although the due date for the paper was November 1, her schedule called for completing the paper by October 27.

51a Pose possible questions worth exploring.

Working within the guidelines of your assignment, jot down a few questions that seem worth researching. Here, for example, are some preliminary questions jotted down by students who were asked to write about a significant political or scholarly issue:

Should the use of lie detectors be banned?

Is musical therapy just a fashionable fraud? Or does it show some promise as a treatment for physical and psychological problems?

How serious is the problem of computer crime, and what can companies do to increase security?

What was Marcus Garvey's contribution to the fight for racial equality?

What are the hazards of fad diets?

In what kinds of medical cases is euthanasia justified?

What does a woman need to know about breast cancer treatment in the 1990s?

Is the Bureau of Indian Affairs helping or harming Indian children?

If you have trouble coming up with a list of questions, you can browse through certain library references for ideas. For example, *Hot Topics* lists recent articles on controversial social issues and current events, and *Editorial Research Reports* contains digests of recent articles and editorials on contemporary issues. You can discover other possible lines of inquiry by skimming through current magazines such as *Newsweek, Harper's, Science News,* and *Smithsonian* or by consulting specialized periodicals in the field. Scholarly controversies encountered in college courses are yet another potential source of ideas; ask your professors for suggestions.

Once you have come up with a list of possible questions, choose the question that intrigues you the most and do a bit of preliminary research to see where your line of inquiry might lead. If it seems to be leading to a dead end — maybe because you can't find a variety of sources on the subject or because the information is too technical for you to understand — turn to another question on your list, which may prove more promising.

Once you have settled on a question that looks promising, check to see if it is too broad, given the length of the paper you plan to write. If you suspect it is — and most writers' initial questions are — look for ways to narrow your focus as you begin researching.

Narrowing your focus

Even before you visit the library, you may be able to limit the scope of your investigation. For instance, if initially you asked "Should the use of lie detectors be banned?" you might restrict your inquiry to the use of lie detectors *by private employers.* Or if at first you asked "What are the hazards of fad diets?" you might narrow your focus to the hazards of *liquid* diets. (Also see the chart on p. 7.)

Once inside the library, you will discover a number of ways to narrow your topic. For many topics, you can read encyclopedia articles or scan the headings and subheadings in the library's catalog (or in the *Library of Congress Subject Headings;* see pp. 481–483), to get a sense of your topic's natural subdivisions. For current topics, check the subheadings and titles in periodical indexes such as the *Magazine Index Plus* or *Readers' Guide to Periodical Literature* (see pp. 484–486) or consult the pamphlet file. Without reading a single article, you can narrow your focus drastically just by skimming subheadings and titles.

As you begin reading books and articles and become more knowledgeable, you may be able to restrict your focus even further and at the same time decide what approach you will take in your paper — or even decide on a tentative main point. The main point of your paper, known as a *thesis*, will be an answer to the central question that you finally decide to pose. (See 53a.)

51b Become familiar with your library.

If you have not already done so, explore your library to find out what it's like. Most libraries provide maps and handouts that describe their services; many conduct orientation programs or have cassette walking tours or slide-cassette shows.

As you explore your library, seek out answers to at least the following questions:

- Are the stacks (the shelves on which books are stored) open or closed? In other words, can you go to the books directly, or must you request them at a desk?

- Are some books, periodicals, and reference materials located in special rooms or even special buildings?

- Is there a traditional card catalog in rows of drawers, or are the library's holdings cataloged on microfiche or microfilm or on a computer? Where is the catalog located?

- Where is the reference section?

- Where are the periodical indexes?

- How and where are periodicals stored? If some periodicals are on microfilm or microfiche, where are the machines for reading them? Do some of these machines print copies as well?

— Does the library own films, videotapes, filmstrips, records, or floppy disks, and where are they cataloged?

— Is there a computer search service? (At some libraries you can buy time on a computer to search one or more of the hundreds of computer databases available.)

As you get to know your library, don't forget the library staff. Librarians are information specialists who can save you time by helping you define what you are looking for and then telling you where to find it. Librarians, especially those in college and university libraries, are educators. Feel free to tell them about your information needs, not just to ask where to find the encyclopedias.

51c   Follow a search strategy.

A search strategy is a systematic plan for tracking down source materials. To create a search strategy, you'll need to ask yourself two questions:

What kinds of source materials should I consult?

In what order should I consult them?

A good search strategy usually moves from general reference works such as encyclopedias to specific books (located through the card or computer catalog) and specific magazine and newspaper articles (located through periodical indexes). But be prepared to modify this strategy in light of your topic, your library resources, your level of expertise, and the amount of time you are able to spend researching.

To research the topic of apes and language, Karen Shaw, whose paper appears on pages 544–580, decided to begin with books. Because she was working in a relatively small library, she suspected she might need to request books from neighboring libraries, which would take some time. She began, then, by checking out a few books and ordering others through interlibrary loans. She held off on reading the books, though, because she didn't have time to read them all cover to cover. Before she could read selectively, she needed an overview of her subject.

For an overview Shaw might have turned to a specialized encyclopedia, but because her topic was fairly current, she decided to try magazines instead. Her librarian recommended *Magazine Index Plus* as the fastest way to locate magazine articles on her topic.

After reading several magazine articles, Shaw became intrigued by the differing opinions of two key researchers, Herbert Terrace and Francine Patterson. With the Terrace-Patterson controversy in mind, she took another look at the books she had collected. She decided that two books, one by Terrace and another by Patterson, were worth reading in their entirety; as for the others, only certain chapters dealt with the key issues raised by Terrace and Patterson, so Shaw focused primarily on those chapters. Because Shaw had planned her search strategy carefully, most of her reading was relevant to her final approach to the topic.

As you survey the possible sources of information listed on the following pages, try to develop an organized search strategy appropriate to your topic. Remember that if you run into problems, a reference librarian will be glad to help.

Reference works

Often you'll want to begin by reading background information in a general encyclopedia, a specialized encyclopedia, or a biographical reference. Later in your research, you may need to turn to other reference works such as atlases, almanacs, or unabridged dictionaries.

GENERAL ENCYCLOPEDIAS Articles in general encyclopedias introduce the topic to you, give you a sense of how broad or narrow it is, and often end with a bibliography of books for further reading. Here is a brief list of general encyclopedias frequently used on the college level.

> *Academic American Encyclopedia.* 21 vols. 1988. Yearbooks.
> *Collier's Encyclopedia.* 24 vols. 1988.
> *Encyclopedia Americana.* 30 vols. New printing yearly.
>   Yearbooks.
> *The New Encyclopaedia Britannica.* 32 vols. 1990. In three
>   parts: *Propaedia*, a one-volume "Outline of Knowledge";
>   twelve-volume *Micropaedia* with brief entries; seventeen-
>   volume *Macropaedia* with long articles and bibliogra-
>   phies. Two-volume index. Yearbooks.

Although general encyclopedias are a good place to begin your research, do not rely too heavily on them in your finished paper. No doubt you will find more specific information later during your search.

SPECIALIZED ENCYCLOPEDIAS For topics that fall within a particular academic discipline, turn to a specialized ency-clopedia for an overview. As you read, look for areas in which experts take different positions or in which trends, attitudes, beliefs, or circumstances are changing; your finished paper could demonstrate your support for one of the positions or explain the causes or effects of the changes.

Following is a list of specialized encyclopedias covering a number of disciplines.

> *The Dance Encyclopedia.* 1978.
> *Encyclopedia of Anthropology.* 1976.
> *Encyclopedia of Banking and Finance.* 1983.
> *The Encyclopedia of Biological Sciences.* 1981.
> *Encyclopedia of Computers and Data Processing.* 1978.
> *Encyclopedia of Crime and Justice.* 4 vols. 1983.
> *The Encyclopedia of Management.* 1982.
> *The Encyclopedia of Philosophy.* 8 vols. 1973.
> *Encyclopedia of Psychology.* 4 vols. 1984.
> *Encyclopedia of World Architecture.* 1982.
> *Encyclopedia of World Art.* 16 vols. 1959–68. Supplement 1983.

An Encyclopedia of World History. 1972.
Encyclopedia of World Literature in the 20th Century. 4 vols.
   1981–86.
Grzimek's Animal Life Encyclopedia. 13 vols. 1972–75.
Harvard Guide to American History. 2 vols. 1974.
International Encyclopedia of the Social Sciences. 8 vols.
   plus supplement. 1977.
McGraw-Hill Dictionary of Modern Economics. 1984.
McGraw-Hill Encyclopedia of Science and Technology. 20
   vols. 1987.
McGraw-Hill Encyclopedia of World Drama. 5 vols. 1984.
The New Grove Dictionary of Music and Musicians. 20 vols.
   1981.
The Oxford Companion to American Literature. 1983.
The Oxford Companion to English Literature. 1987.
Reference Encyclopedia of the American Indian. 1990.
Short Story Index: 1900–1949. 1956. Supplements through
   1978.

BIOGRAPHICAL REFERENCES If your subject is a person,
a good place to begin is with a biographical reference such as
one of the following.

Biography Index. 1946–.
Contemporary Authors. 1972–.
Current Biography. 1940–.
Dictionary of American Biography. 17 vols. plus supplements.
   1927–84.
Dictionary of Literary Biography. 38 vols. plus supplements.
   1978.
McGraw-Hill Encyclopedia of World Biography. 16 vols. 1989.
Notable American Women, 1607–1950. 1974. Supplement:
   Notable American Women: The Modern Period. 1980.
Webster's New Biographical Dictionary. 1988.
Who's Who in America. 1899–.

ATLASES An atlas is a bound collection of maps. For current topics, make sure that you are working with an up-to-
date atlas. For historical topics, consult an atlas covering the

particular period. Following is a brief list of commonly used atlases.

National Geographic Atlas of the World. 1981.
Rand McNally Cosmopolitan World Atlas. 1984.
Rand McNally Historical Atlas of the World. 1981.
The New York Times Atlas of the World. 1983.

ALMANACS AND YEARBOOKS Almanacs and yearbooks are annual publications that record information about a year, often in the form of lists, charts, and tables. The information covers a range of subjects such as politics, world events, sports, economics, and even the weather. Here is a brief list of almanacs and yearbooks.

Americana Annual. 1923–.
Britannica Book of the Year. 1938–.
Facts on File. 1941–,
Statistical Abstract of the United States. 1878–.
World Almanac and Book of Facts. 1868–.

UNABRIDGED DICTIONARIES An unabridged dictionary such as one of the following is more comprehensive than an ordinary college or desk dictionary.

The Oxford English Dictionary. 2nd ed. 20 vols. plus supplements. 1989.
The Random House Dictionary of the English Language. 2nd ed., unabridged, 1987.
Webster's Third New International Dictionary. 1986.

Books

Your library may have a card catalog, a microform catalog, a computer catalog, or some combination of these. The card catalog files information about books on cards arranged alphabetically in drawers, and the microform catalog reprints the cards on microfilm or microfiche. The computer catalog allows you to call up the information using a keyboard.

THE CARD CATALOG The card catalog lists books alphabetically in three ways: by author's name, by the title of the book, and by subject. The cards in the catalog look like the example below, though the top line might list an author or title instead of the subject.

If you know what to look for on the card, you can immediately select or reject a book, and you can use the "tracings" (lists of related headings) to lead you to more books. Keep the following points in mind as you look through the catalog for books most relevant to your topic.

Check the date to see when the book was published. For some topics, only the most recent books may be useful.

Check to see if the book has an index (for easy reference) and a bibliography (to suggest more books).

Check the tracings, lists of other places to look in the card catalog.

WHAT THE CARD CATALOG TELLS YOU

Subject heading

Author and dates of birth and death

Call number

Title

City, publisher, copyright date

CHIMPANZEES--PSYCHOLOGY.

QL 737 .P96 D47

Desmond, Adrian J., 1947–
The ape's reflexion / Adrian J. Desmond. New York : Dial Press/J. Wade, c1979.
288 p., [12] leaves of plates : ill. ; 24 cm.

Contains a bibliography and index

Includes index.
Bibliography: p. [245]-247.

Number of pages, illustrations, size

Tracings

1.Chimpanzees--Psychology.
2.Chimpanzees--Behavior. 3.Gorillas--Psychology. 4.Gorillas--Behavior.
5.Mammals--Psychology. 6.Mammals--Behavior. I.T.

RG80-5068
QL737.P96D47

79-13480
156/.3

Technical data useful to library

If the book looks useful, write down on a bibliography card the call number, author, title, and publishing information — details that you will need later when constructing your list of works cited (see 54). If you just want to look at the book — to decide whether to use it — write down at least the call number and the title so that you can locate the book on the shelf.

If books on a subject are not listed under the first or second heading you try, consult the *Library of Congress Subject Headings* (discussed later in this section).

THE MICROFORM CATALOG   In some libraries, catalogs are presented on rolls of microfilm or on microfiche, 4" × 6" pieces of film. The microfilm or microfiche is viewed on a machine called a *reader.* Some readers allow you to print a copy of the titles that appear on the screen, saving you the trouble of handcopying (and the possibility of miscopying) the information.

THE COMPUTER CATALOG   Like a card catalog or microform catalog, a computer catalog contains bibliographic information about a library's holdings, filed alphabetically under authors, titles, and key words relating to subjects. The advantage of a computer catalog is that the user is able to conduct a search more quickly and efficiently, as a variety of information is instantly accessible from the central database. Some computer catalogs save you even more time by printing the bibliographic information for you.

Computer catalog systems vary from library to library, but most are user friendly, and a reference librarian will be available to help you if you get stuck. To begin, follow the instructions on the terminal's menu display. Usually, you will enter a simple command, such as "find author Melville, Herman" or "a = Melville, Herman." The computer will then display a list of books under that author heading. You will select a particular entry, and the terminal will then display detailed

WHAT THE COMPUTER CATALOG TELLS YOU

```
COMMAND?
 HU SHORT DISPLAY  page 1 of 1      Item 1 of 14 retrieved by your search:
FIND AU PATTERSON F
-----------------------------------------------------------HOLLIS: AEK5177
       AUTHOR: Patterson, Francine.
        TITLE: The education of Koko / Francine Patterson and Eugene Linden.
      EDITION: 1st ed.
    PUB. INFO: New York : Holt, Rinehart and Winston, c1981.
  DESCRIPTION: xiv, 224 p. : ill. ; 24 cm.

     SUBJECTS: *S1 Gorillas--Psychology.
               *S2 Human-animal communication.
               *S3 Sign language.

     LOCATION: Gutman Education: QL737.P96 P37
```

bibliographic information for that work. An example of what you might see on the screen is shown above.

Searching by subject involves the use of key words, which prompt the computer to retrieve relevant information from its memory. The reference *The Library of Congress Subject Headings (LCSH)* contains a list of key words used in cataloging books and is a good starting point for subject searches. After consulting *LCSH*, for instance, you might realize that the key word "old age" would generate a list of holdings far too long, so you might begin your search with the subheading "gerontology" instead. Some computer catalogs allow you to restrict your search by using more than one key word. For example, you might call up all publications on gerontology issued in 1990 by entering a command such as "find: gerontology//yr = 1990." Learn how your library's system works, and use it; the computer catalog is a major step forward in information technology.

THE LIBRARY OF CONGRESS SUBJECT HEADINGS The headings under which you are likely to find books listed in the library's catalog are contained in *The Library of Congress Subject Headings.* It consists of two large volumes usually placed near the catalog. The headings are also likely to be similar to those used in magazine and newspaper indexes.

Because the library's catalog does not always list books under the most obvious headings, the *LCSH* is an extremely useful reference tool. If you are interested in researching senior citizens, for example, you would be frustrated by going directly to the card catalog and discovering nothing under "senior citizens." But by looking up "senior citizens" in

WHAT THE LCSH TELLS YOU

Primary headings and call numbers used by Library of Congress for this subject	**Old age** *(Charities, HV1451-1493; Ethics, BJ1691; Physiology, QP86)*
sa = see also	*sa* Ability, Influence of age on Aged Aged, Killing of the Aging Centenarians Geriatrics Longevity Middle age Old age assistance Old age pensions Retirement
x = subject heading *not* used by Library of Congress	*x* Senescence
xx = see also these broader headings	*xx* Adulthood Age Death—Causes Gerontology Life Life (Biology) Longevity Middle age Physiology
Subdivisions of a subject; dash indicates they are always combined with a primary subject	— Diseases 　*See* Geriatrics — Periodicals 　*See* Aged—Periodicals — Psychological aspects 　*See* Aged—Psychology — Research 　*x* Aged—Research
This entry redirects you to another subject heading	Old age and employment 　*See* Aged—Employment

LCSH, you would be referred to "aged," which covers two entire pages with subheadings. By looking up just one heading, "old age," you would learn that twenty-three different subheadings are used for books on the subject (see the example on page 482). From that one look into *LCSH,* you might also be able to restrict your topic. For example, you might limit your investigation to a pyschological aspect of growing old, to a disease that afflicts the elderly, or to employment opportunities after retirement.

OTHER INDEXES TO BOOKS *Books in Print* and *Paperbound Books in Print* list books by author, title, subject, and publisher; *Cumulative Book Index* lists books by author and subject. These indexes are available in print form and on CD-ROM (compact disc–read-only memory), a database accessed by a computer terminal and keyboard.

You may also want to consult bibliographies, which are lists of books on specific topics. These are filed by author and subject in the library's catalog.

Periodicals

Periodicals are publications issued at regular intervals, such as magazines, newspapers, and scholarly or technical journals. Articles in periodicals are useful reference tools because they often contain more up-to-date information than books and because they usually discuss in detail a specific aspect of a subject.

To track down useful articles, consult a magazine index, a newspaper index, or one of the many specialized indexes to scholarly or technical journals. Most libraries provide, in a conspicuous spot close to these indexes, a list of the periodicals they own. This list, sometimes called the "serials catalog," usually tells you the form in which the periodical has been preserved: on microfilm, on microfiche, in bound volumes, or in unbound files. It also tells you which years of the periodical the library owns. You will save yourself time if you check the periodicals list as you use the index. If your library doesn't have the periodical in which an article appears, there is no need to make a note of its name unless you plan to visit another library or obtain the periodical through interlibrary loan.

MAGAZINE AND NEWSPAPER INDEXES Magazine indexes list articles in general-interest magazines such as *Time*, *Popular Mechanics*, *Science*, and *Fortune* as well as scholarly and professional journals. Newspaper indexes list articles in major newspapers such as the *New York Times*, the *Washington Post*, and the *Christian Science Monitor*. Some indexes are in book form; others are stored as databases in a computer.

The latter indexes use a type of computer technology called CD-ROM (for compact disc–read-only memory), in which information is stored on compact discs and accessed through a computer terminal. By typing key words into the terminal, researchers can quickly search for references related to their topic from among the thousands of sources stored in the database. A bibliographic citation appears on the screen; sometimes the full text of an article is available either to read on the screen or to print out. InfoTrac is one computer system that offers a number of magazine and newspaper indexes in database form (your library may offer one or more of the InfoTrac databases; see the following list).

A sample entry from the most widely used magazine print index, *The Readers' Guide to Periodical Literature*, and a sample printout of an entry from an InfoTrac database are shown on page 485. The following is a list of the most useful indexes of both sorts.

> *Readers' Guide to Periodical Literature*. 1900–. A print index to articles in nearly 200 general-interest magazines, cataloged annually by author and subject. Paperback supplements are issued monthly or semimonthly for the current year. (Also available on CD-ROM from 1983 to the present.)

WHAT THE READERS' GUIDE TELLS YOU

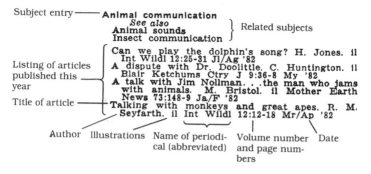

Subject entry —— **Animal communication**
See also
Animal sounds } Related subjects
Insect communication

Listing of articles published this year

Title of article

Can we play the dolphin's song? H. Jones. il Int Wildl 12:25-31 Jl/Ag '82
A dispute with Dr. Doolittle. C. Huntington. il Blair Ketchums Ctry J 9:36-8 My '82
A talk with Jim Nollman...the man who jams with animals. M. Bristol. il Mother Earth News 73:148-9 Ja/F '82
Talking with monkeys and great apes. R. M. Seyfarth. il Int Wildl 12:12-18 Mr/Ap '82

Author Illustrations Name of periodi- Volume number Date
cal (abbreviated) and page num-
bers

WHAT A COMPUTER INDEX TELLS YOU

General Periodicals Index-A

HUMAN-ANIMAL COMMUNICATION
-research

Kanzi extends his speech reach.... (language use by chimpanzee) by Bruce Bower   v134   Science News
Aug 27   '88   p140(1)
46D0013

New York Times Index. 1913–. An annual print index to all the articles printed in the *New York Times.* The index contains a brief summary of each news story and is an excellent source of condensed topical information. Other major newspapers — the *Washington Post,* the *Christian Science Monitor,* the *Wall Street Journal,* the *Times* (London) — publish similar indexes.

General Periodicals Index (InfoTrac). The most comprehensive computer index offered by the InfoTrac system, this indexes articles from 1,100 general-interest and scholarly publications in the humanities, sciences, social sciences, business, and current affairs. Updated monthly.

Magazine Index Plus (InfoTrac). An index of articles from more than 400 popular magazines for the past four years plus the last two months of the *New York Times.* Updated monthly.

     National Newspaper Index (InfoTrac). An index of articles
        from five newspapers for the past three to four years: the
        New York Times, the *Christian Science Monitor*, the *Wall
        Street Journal*, the *Washington Post*, and the *Los Angeles
        Times*. Updated monthly.

     Academic Index (InfoTrac). An index of research articles for
        the past three or four years in the humanities, sciences,
        social sciences, and current events from nearly 400
        scholarly and general-interest journals plus articles for the
        past six months from the *New York Times*. Updated
        monthly.

     NewsBank. A computer index of articles in more than 450
        newspapers.

    SPECIALIZED DATABASES In addition to magazine and
newspaper databases, your library may have more specialized
CD-ROM databases that index articles from scholarly publications in specific fields such as education, psychology, and
medicine. Some libraries have more than one such database
accessed from one computer system (such as the SilverPlatter
system). At some libraries, you can perform your own database search; at others, a librarian does the searching. Often
you must pay for the search or are allowed only a specific time
on the computer, so it is important to conduct the search
efficiently. In these types of databases, the researcher types a
key word and is presented with numerous entries giving complete bibliographic data as well as an abstract of the content
of each article. (Most CD-ROM databases contain entries dating back to the early 1980s.) Some of the most common specialized databases are the following. (A sample printout of an
entry from the ERIC database appears on page 487.)

    ERIC (Educational Resources Information Center). A database
        indexing bibliographic citations from 750 journals in
        education. The ERIC database is itself a network of
        sixteen clearinghouses, each specializing in a separate
        subject area.

WHAT A SPECIALIZED DATABASE TELLS YOU

```
SilverPlatter 1.6                    ERIC (1/83 - 6/90)
                                                        4 of 6
AN: EJ295275
AU: Fouts,-Roger-S.; And-Others
TI: Sign Language Conversational Interaction between Chimpanzees.
PY: 1984
JN: Sign-Language-Studies; n42 p1-12 Spr 1984
DT: Reports - Research (143)
LA: English
DE: Communication-Skills; Language-Acquisition; Language-
 Research; Play-; Social-Cognition
DE: *American-Sign-Language; *Animal-Behavior; *Manual-
 Communication; *Nonverbal-Communication
ID: *Chimpanzees-
IS: CIJJUN84
AB: Systematic sampling was done of signing between five home-
 reared chimpanzees who had had 4-7 years of complete immersion
 in integrating their signing interaction into their nonverbal
 communication. Eight-eight percent of all signs reported fell
 into the social categories of reassurance, social interaction,
 and play. (SL)
CH: FL
FI: EJ
DTN: 143
```

> PsycLIT. A database containing summaries of professional
> articles in psychology and related fields from 1,300
> journals in twenty-seven languages and fifty countries.
> Sociofile. A database containing abstracts of professional
> articles in sociology and related disciplines from 1,600
> journals in thirty languages and fifty-five countries as well
> from *Dissertation Abstracts International*.

Other academic disciplines have their own databases. A librarian can tell you whether your library subscribes to these
or other specialized databases.

SPECIALIZED PERIODICAL INDEXES   To locate articles in
technical and scholarly journals such as *Computer World* and
Communication Quarterly, you may need to turn to a specialized index. You can find specialized indexes easily in the
library's catalog. In the subject file of the card catalog, look

for cards giving the subheadings "Abstracts" and "Periodicals and Indexes" (for example, "Biology — Periodicals and Indexes"). In a subject search in the computer catalog, include the term "periodicals" or "indexes" as a subheading with the key word. The catalog entry will provide the title and call number for an index, usually with REF as the top line, indicating that you will find it in the reference section. The librarian also can help you locate specialized indexes.

Following is a list of specialized indexes covering a variety of academic disciplines. (Many of these are also available on CD-ROM.)

Applied Science and Technology Index. 1958–. Formerly *Industrial Arts Index*, 1913–57.

Art Index. 1929–.

Biological Abstracts. 1926–.

Biological and Agricultural Index. 1964–. Formerly *Agricultural Index*, 1916–64.

Business Periodicals Index. 1958–. Formerly *Industrial Arts Index*, 1913–57.

Central Index to Journals of Education. 1969–.

Education Index. 1929–.

Engineering Index. 1884–.

General Science Index. 1978–.

Historical Abstracts. 1955–.

Humanities Index, 1974–. Formerly *International Index to Periodicals*, 1907–65, and *Social Sciences and Humanities Index*, 1965–74.

MLA International Bibliography of Books and Articles in the Modern Languages and Literature. 1921–.

Monthly Catalog of United States Government Publications. 1895–.

Music Index. 1949–.

Philosopher's Index. 1967–.

Public Affairs Information Service Bulletin. 1915–.

Psychological Abstracts. 1927–.

Social Sciences Index. 1974–. Formerly *International Index*, 1907–65, and *Social Sciences and Humanities Index*, 1965–74.

Other library sources

A library's holdings are not limited to reference works, books, and periodicals. Your library may have pamphlets, usually located in a large file cabinet known as the *vertical file*, or rare and unpublished manuscripts in a special collection. Holdings might also include records, tapes, and compact discs; films, filmstrips, and videos; drawings, paintings, engravings, and slides.

If your research topic is especially complex or unusual, you may need greater resources than your library offers. In such cases, talk to a librarian about interlibrary loan, a process in which one library borrows materials from another. This procedure can take several weeks, so be sure to plan ahead.

Sources beyond the library

For some topics, you may want to look beyond the library for information. Many organizations, both public and private, willingly mail literature in response to a phone call or a letter. Consider also the possibility of learning more about your subject through interviews or through experiments that you conduct yourself.

Interviews can often shed new light on a topic. Look for experts who have firsthand knowledge of the subject or for individuals whose personal experience provides an enlightening perspective on your topic. Look too for sources with alternative or underrepresented viewpoints to balance the perspectives of conventional authorities.

When asking for an interview, be clear about who you are, what the purpose of the interview is, whether you plan to tape it, and approximately how long it will take. If you succeed in getting an appointment, plan for the interview by writing down a series of questions and arranging them in a logical order. Try to avoid questions with yes or no answers or those that encourage vague rambling; instead, phrase your questions to elicit facts, anecdotes, and opinions that will add a meaningful dimension to your paper.

Accuracy is important in an interview. If you cannot tape the interview, take careful notes, and if a point is unclear, ask your subject to explain it. When quoting your source in your paper, you should of course be as accurate and as fair as possible. For instance, if you interviewed a record store owner about the popularity of a particular rap group and she told you, "Their records don't sell as well as two or three other groups' recordings," it would be misrepresenting your source to write, "Their records don't sell well."

For some topics you may want to supplement others' research with your own experiments. Most academic disciplines have specific guidelines for conducting experiments and reporting results; if you are unsure of the appropriate method in your discipline, consult a style manual (see 55c) or ask your instructor.

52

Reading sources and taking notes

52a Read selectively; maintain a working bibliography.

Even after you have narrowed your focus, your search for useful research materials may supply you with many more books and articles than you have time to read, so you will need to be selective.

As you consult the library's catalog and its periodical indexes, take down bibliographic information only for sources that seem promising (see pp. 492–493 for the exact information to take down). Be alert for clues that indicate whether a book or article is worth tracking down. Here are some questions to guide you as you make your choices.

DECIDING WHETHER TO TRACK DOWN A SOURCE

— How relevant to your research question is the work's title?

— How recent is the source? For current topics, some books or articles may be outdated.

— How long is the source? A very short article may be too general to be helpful.

— Is the source available in your library? When working with a periodical index, check to see if your library has the magazine, journal, or newspaper containing the article that looks promising.

— In what form is the work available? Many articles are available only on microfilm or microfiche, which must read on a machine — sometimes a time-consuming process.

Once you have tracked down a source, preview it quickly to see how much of your attention, if any, it is worth. Techniques for previewing a book and an article are a bit different.

PREVIEWING A BOOK

— Glance through the table of contents, keeping your research question in mind.

— Skim the preface in search of a statement of the author's purposes.

— Using the index, look up a few key words related to your research question.

— If a chapter seems useful, read its opening and closing paragraphs and skim any headings.

— Consider the author's style, level, and tone. Does the style invite further reading? Is the level appropriate (neither above nor below your ability to comprehend)? Does the tone suggest a balanced approach?

— If the author's credentials are given on the cover or dust jacket, how relevant are they to the book and your research question?

PREVIEWING AN ARTICLE

— For magazine and journal articles, look for a statement of purpose in the opening paragraphs; look for a possible summary in the closing paragraph.

— For newspaper articles, focus on the headline and the opening sentences, known as the *lead*.

— Skim any headings and take a look at any charts, graphs, diagrams, or illustrations that might indicate the article's focus and scope.

Maintaining a working bibliography

Keep a record of any sources that you decide to consult. You will need this record, called a working bibliography, when you compile the list of works cited that will appear at the end of your paper. (See p. 578 for an example.) This list of works cited will almost certainly be shorter than your working bibliography, since it will include only the sources that you actually cite in your paper.

You may record bibliographic information about sources in a notebook or on separate 3″ × 5″ cards. The advantage of 3″ × 5″ cards is that you can easily arrange them in alphabetical order when you type the list of works cited, which appears at the end of your paper. (If you have used a computer catalog or index that prints bibliographic information for you, you can use the printouts as your working bibliography.) For books, you will need the following bibliographic information:

Call number

All authors; any editors or translators

Title and subtitle

Edition (if not the first)

Publishing information: city, publishing company, and date

For periodical articles you need this information:

All authors of the article

Title and subtitle of the article

Title of the magazine, journal, or newspaper

Date and page numbers

Volume and issue numbers, if relevant

NOTE: For the exact bibliographic form to be used in the final paper, see 54b.

SAMPLE BIBLIOGRAPHY CARD FOR A BOOK

QL776.D38 1978

Davis, Flora. _Eloquent Animals: A Study in Animal Communication: How Chimps Lie, Whales Sing and Slime Molds Pass the Message Along._ New York: Coward, McCann & Geoghegan, 1978.

SAMPLE BIBLIOGRAPHY CARD FOR A PERIODICAL

Seyfarth, Robert M. "Talking with Monkeys and Great Apes." *International Wildlife* Mar./Apr. 1982: 12-18.

52b Read with a critical eye.

When you read critically, you are not necessarily judging an author's work harshly; you are simply examining its assumptions, assessing its evidence, and weighing its conclusions.

Distinguishing between primary and secondary sources

As you begin assessing the evidence in a text, consider whether you are reading a primary or a secondary source. Primary sources are original documents such as speeches, diaries, novels, legislative bills, laboratory studies, field research reports, or eyewitness accounts. Secondary sources are commentaries on primary sources.

A primary source for Karen Shaw, whose research paper appears beginning on page 544, was an article by Allen and Beatrice Gardner reporting their experiments with the chimpanzee Washoe. Shaw also consulted Flora Davis's book

Eloquent Animals, a secondary source that reports on the studies of the Gardners and other researchers.

Although a primary source is not necessarily more reliable than a secondary source, it has the advantage of being a firsthand account. Naturally, you can better evaluate what a secondary source says if you have first read the primary source and are familiar with it.

Assessing the author's argument

In nearly all subjects worth writing about, there is some element of argument, so don't be surprised to encounter experts who disagree. When you encounter areas of disagreement, you will want to read your sources' arguments with special care, testing them with your own critical intelligence. Questions such as the following can help you weigh the strengths and weaknesses of each author's argument.

— What is the author's central claim or thesis?

— How does the author support this claim — with relevant and sufficient evidence or with just a few anecdotes or emotional examples?

— Are any of the author's assumptions questionable?

— Does the author consider opposing arguments and refute them persuasively? (See pp. 611–612.)

— Are there any reasons to be suspicious of the author's motives or to question his or her objectivity?

52c As you read, take notes systematically. Avoid unintentional plagiarism.

Systematic notes about your reading will make it clear to you later, as you are drafting your paper, just which words and phrases belong to your sources and which are your own. This is a crucial matter, for if any language from your sources finds its way into your final draft without quotation marks and proper documentation, you will be guilty of plagiarism, a serious academic offense. (See 53d.)

You can take notes in a variety of ways, as long as they are accurate, but the following suggestions may help you make the most efficient use of your time. Have nearby a stack of blank, white cards ($4'' \times 6''$ is customary). Write one note on each card so you can shuffle and reshuffle the cards in different orders later as you experiment with the organization of your paper. Put the last name of the author of your source in the upper right corner of the card, and put a subject label in the upper left corner. If you have read enough to form a preliminary outline, use the subdivisions of the outline as subject headings on your cards.

Next decide the most helpful way to preserve the information in a particular source: summarizing, paraphrasing, quoting word for word, or writing personal comments. As you take notes, be sure to include exact page references next to the information, since you will need the page numbers later if you use the information in your paper.

Note cards that summarize

Summarizing is the best kind of preliminary note taking because it is the fastest. A summary condenses information, perhaps capsulizing a chapter in a short paragraph or a paragraph in a single sentence. A summary should be written in your own words; if you use apt phrases from the source, put them in quotation marks.

Here is a passage from an original source read by Karen Shaw in researching her essay on apes and language. Following the passage is Shaw's note card summarizing it.

ORIGINAL SOURCE

Public and scientific interest in the question of apes' ability to use language first soared some 15 years ago when Washoe, a chimpanzee raised like a human child by R. Allen Gardner and

SUMMARY

Types of languages   Eckholm, "Pygmy"

The ape experiments began about 20 years ago with Washoe, who learned sign language. In later experiments some apes learned to communicate using plastic chips or symbols on a keyboard. (p. B7)

Beatrice Gardner of the University of Nevada, learned to make hand signs for many words and even seemed to be making short sentences.

Since then researchers have taught many chimpanzees and a few gorillas and orangutans to "talk" using the sign language of deaf humans, plastic chips or, like Kanzi, keyboard symbols. Washoe, Sarah, a chimpanzee trained by David Premack of the University of Pennsylvania, and Koko, a gorilla trained by the psychologist Francine Patterson, became media stars.   — Eckholm, "Pygmy," p. B7

Note cards that paraphrase

Like a summary, a paraphrase is written in your own words; but whereas a summary reports significant information in fewer words than the source, a paraphrase retells the information in roughly the same number of words. If you retain occasional choice phrases from the source, put quotation marks around them so that you'll know later which phrases are your own.

You will discover that it is amazingly easy to borrow too much language from a source as you paraphrase. Do not allow this to happen. You are guilty of plagiarism if you half-copy the author's sentences — either by mixing the author's well-chosen phrases with your own without quotation marks or by plugging your synonyms into the author's sentence structure. (For examples of this kind of plagiarism, see 53d.)

To prevent unintentional borrowing, resist the temptation to look at the source while you are paraphrasing. Keep the source close by — to check for accuracy — but don't try to paraphrase with the source's sentences in front of you. You should also follow this advice while drafting your paper. (See the chart on pp. 514–515.)

As you read the note card below, which paraphrases the first paragraph of Shaw's original source (see pp. 496–497), notice that the language is significantly different from that in the original. Working with this note card, Shaw was in no danger of unintentional plagiarism.

PARAPHRASE

Washoe   Eckholm, "Pygmy"

A chimpanzee named Washoe, trained
20 years ago by U. of Nevada professors
R. Allen and Beatrice Gardner, learned
words in the sign language of the deaf
and may even have created short
sentences. (p. B7)

Note cards that quote

A quotation consists of the exact words from a source. On your note cards, put all quoted material in quotation marks; do not trust yourself to remember later which words, phrases, and passages you have quoted and which are your own. When you quote, be sure to copy the words of your source exactly, including punctuation and capitalization.

Quotations should be reserved for special purposes: to use a writer's especially vivid or expressive wording, to allow an expert to explain a complex matter clearly, or to let critics of an opinion object in their own words. If you find yourself quoting a great deal in your notes, you are probably wasting time, because your final essay should not contain excessive quotations. (See 53e.)

Below is an example of a note card containing a quotation from Shaw's original source (p. 496).

QUOTATION

> Washoe   Eckholm, "Pygmy"
>
> Washoe, trained by R. Allen and Beatrice Gardner, "learned to make hand signs for many words and even seemed to be making short sentences."
> (p. B7)

Personal note cards

At unexpected moments in your reading, you will experience the lucky accidents typical of the creative process: flashes of insight, connections with other reading, sharp questions, a more restricted topic, ways to set up the arguments of two opposing positions, a vivid scenario. Write these inspirations down before you forget them. An example of such a note card appears below.

PERSONAL COMMENT

> *Types of training*
> *Washoe (and I think Koko) were raised almost like children, not in a laboratory setting. Does the setting affect the apes' performance? What about scientific objectivity?*

Alternatives to note cards

Not every researcher uses note cards. For short research projects, some writers prefer to photocopy important material and underline or highlight key ideas, sometimes color coding the highlighted passages to reflect subdivisions of the topic. In the margins they write personal comments or cross-references to other sources. Photocopying has the obvious advantage of saving time and labor. For extensive research projects, however, the technique is of limited value since there is no way of physically sorting the highlighted passages into separate batches of information.

A second alternative to note cards, the use of computer software, overcomes this disadvantage. With the appropriate software, you can type notes as you read, coding them to reflect the divisions of your outline. You can then print the notes in sorted batches. For example, Karen Shaw might have printed one batch of notes on the apes' sign language vocabularies, another on their creative uses of language, another on their mastery of grammar, and so on.

Although software programs can be time savers, their advantages should not be oversold. Any style of note taking demands that you read carefully, analyze what you read, and record information with care.

53

Writing the research paper

53a Form a tentative thesis and construct a preliminary outline.

A look through your note cards will probably suggest many ways to focus and organize your material. Before you begin writing, you should decide on a tentative thesis and construct a preliminary outline or you will flounder among the possibilities. Remain flexible, however, because you may need to revise your approach later. Writing about a subject is a way of learning about it; as you write, your understanding of your subject will almost certainly deepen.

Forming a tentative thesis

A thesis is a sentence asserting the main point of your essay (see 2b). If you are writing on a clearly argumentative topic, such as some aspect of the problem of nuclear waste, your thesis should state your informed opinion: that seabed disposal is not as safe as has been claimed, for example, or that because of politics and economics certain states have become dumping grounds for nuclear waste. You should avoid writing a paper that reports information for no apparent purpose. Few instructors want to read a paper that simply lists and describes the methods for disposing of nuclear waste. Most instructors want their students to take a stand.

Even if your subject is not so obviously controversial as nuclear waste, you can still assert a thesis. Nearly all subjects worth writing about contain some element of controversy; that is why scholars so often engage in polite — and sometimes not so polite — arguments. In researching the topic of apes and language, Karen Shaw, whose paper appears on pages 544–580, encountered a number of scholarly arguments. Early in her reading Shaw was impressed with the views of Francine Patterson, trainer of the gorilla Koko, who makes fairly dramatic claims about the linguistic abilities of apes. Later, after reading H. S. Terrace's criticisms of the ape language experiments, Shaw nearly reversed her earlier view. Finally, as she looked at all the arguments more closely, Shaw reached a conclusion: Patterson was right in insisting that the apes had used language spontaneously and creatively (despite Terrace's arguments to the contrary); Terrace was right in claiming that the apes' mastery of grammar has not yet been proved. For the exact wording of Shaw's final thesis, see her outline on pages 546–547.

Constructing a preliminary outline

Before committing yourself to a detailed outline, experiment with alternatives. Shuffle and reshuffle your note cards to get a feeling for the possibilities. With your tentative thesis in mind, plan a way to arrange your material in stages through a convincing argument. Rather than dividing your subject into static subdivisions, see the main body of your paper as a line of thought that moves step by step. What should be presented and analyzed first? Second? What is the most important evidence to save for the end?

Keep your preliminary outline as simple as possible, and construct it one step at a time. Put the thesis at the top and list your major points, leaving plenty of space between each one so that you can add minor ideas later. In her preliminary outline, Karen Shaw listed two major points in support of her thesis: first, that the apes have demonstrated significant language skills; second, that those skills apparently do not extend to grammar. You might of course have more than two major points supporting your thesis, but you should rarely have more than five. If your list grows too long, you are probably not making enough connections among ideas or you may need to narrow your topic.

Once you have decided on the thesis and the major points in support of the thesis, fill in the second level of organization by listing ideas supporting the major points. This is probably as much as you should attempt in a preliminary outline; a simple plan will be easier to adjust later as you gain new insights about your topic while writing the paper.

Many instructors require a formal outline with the final paper. For advice on constructing a formal outline, see 1d; for the final version of Karen Shaw's formal outline, see pages 546–547.

53b Draft the paper in your own voice.

With a restricted thesis, a preliminary outline, and stacks of note cards, you are ready to write a first draft. Keep it rough and keep it moving. Don't let your wish for perfect sentences stall you at this stage. First write down your ideas and their supporting details; polish your sentences later. Writing rapidly usually produces a more natural, individual voice and helps you avoid echoing the language of your sources.

A chatty, breezy voice is usually not welcome in academic papers, but neither is a stuffy, pretentious style or a timid, unsure one. If you believe in your main point and are interested in your subject, try to communicate that sense of conviction. Some writers find that they convey their tone more intensely if they imagine as they write that they are talking to a group of people or explaining their ideas to a television interviewer. To sound natural, Karen Shaw pretended that she was the guest lecturer in a psychology class.

Many researchers find that writing only from their outlines (rather than directly from their note cards) allows them to write in their own voices without mimicking the style of their sources. In writing their first draft, they refer to their note cards only for direct quotations and specific statistics. Other writers prefer to work more closely with their note cards, consulting them frequently as they write. Whichever method you use, make sure that your sentences are written in your own words, not half-copied from your sources. (See 53d.)

Writing an introduction

In a research paper that refers to many other writers, it is especially important to establish your own voice in the introduction. Your opening paragraphs introduce you as well as your ideas to the reader.

One or two paragraphs are usually enough introduction for most papers in undergraduate courses. Most readers don't want a great deal of background; they want you to get right to the point.

Readers are accustomed to seeing the thesis statement — a one-sentence summary of the main point of the essay — at the beginning or at the end of the introduction. The advantage of beginning with the thesis is that readers can immediately grasp your purpose. The advantage of delaying the thesis is that you can provide a context for your point. You may first want to establish the importance of your topic, then review various attitudes toward it, and finally point to your view in your thesis statement.

In addition to stating the thesis and showing its importance, an introduction should hook readers. (See 2b.) Sometimes you can connect your topic to something recently in the news or bring your readers up to date about changing ideas. Other strategies are to present a puzzling problem or to open with a startling statistic. Karen Shaw's paper (pp. 544–580) begins with a series of vivid examples leading up to her thesis.

53c As you write, document sources using a consistent system such as the MLA style of in-text citation. (See 54a for important details.)

In a research paper, you will be drawing on the work of other writers, and you must document their contributions. Documentation is required when you quote from a source, when you summarize or paraphrase a source, and when you borrow facts and ideas from a source (except for common knowledge). (See also 53d.)

The various academic disciplines use their own editorial styles for documenting sources. Most English professors prefer the Modern Language Association's system of in-text citations. Here, very briefly, is how an MLA in-text citation usually works:

1. The source is introduced by a signal phrase that names its author.
2. The source is followed by a page number in parentheses.
3. At the end of the paper, a list of works cited (arranged alphabetically according to the authors' last names) gives complete publishing information about the source.

SAMPLE IN-TEXT CITATION

According to Eugene Linden, some psychologists
have adopted the oddly unscientific attitude that
"the idea of the language capacity of apes is so
preposterous that it should not be investigated at
all" (11).

SAMPLE ENTRY IN THE LIST OF WORKS CITED

Linden, Eugene. <u>Silent Partners: The Legacy of the
Ape Language Experiments</u>. New York: Random,
1986.

Handling an MLA citation is not always this simple. For
a detailed discussion of possible variations, see 54a. Section
54 is easy to find because its pages have a vertical band in
color.

If your instructor has asked you to use footnotes (also
acceptable to MLA) or the American Psychological Association
(APA) style of in-text citation, consult 55, where you will also
find a list of style manuals used in various disciplines.

53d Do not plagiarize: Document all quotations and borrowed ideas; avoid paraphrases that closely resemble your sources.

Your research paper is a collaboration between you and your
sources. To be fair and ethical, you must acknowledge your
borrowing of another writer's ideas and words by documenting the source, as explained in 53c. To borrow without proper
documentation is a form of dishonesty known as plagiarism.
(See also 52c.)

The academic, business, and legal communities take plagiarism very seriously. Universities have been known to withdraw graduate degrees from students who have plagiarized.

Professional writers sue for (and often get) thousands of dollars when they discover that someone has plagiarized their work.

Two different acts are considered plagiarism: (1) borrowing someone's ideas, information, or language without documenting the source and (2) documenting the source but paraphrasing the source's language too closely, without using quotation marks to indicate that words and phrases have been borrowed.

Documenting quotations and borrowed ideas

You must of course document all direct quotations. You must also document any ideas borrowed from a source: paraphrases of sentences, summaries of paragraphs or chapters, statistics and little-known facts, and tables, graphs, or diagrams.

The only exception is common knowledge — information that your readers could find in any number of general sources because it is commonly known. For example, the current population of the United States is common knowledge in such fields as sociology and economics; Freud's theory of the unconscious is common knowledge in the field of psychology.

As a rule, when you have seen certain information repeatedly in your reading, you don't need to document it. However, when information has appeared in only one or two sources or when it is controversial, you should document it. If a topic is new to you and you are not sure what is considered common knowledge or what is a matter of controversy, ask someone with expertise. When in doubt, document the source.

Avoiding close paraphrases

Close paraphrases are the most common form of plagiarism because if a researcher is sloppy at the note-taking stage, unacceptable borrowings can occur unintentionally (see 52c). When you paraphrase, it is not enough to name the source; you must restate the source's meaning completely in your own words. The following is an example of plagiarizing an author's wording even though the source is cited.

ORIGINAL VERSION
If the existence of a signing ape was unsettling for linguists, it was also startling news for animal behaviorists.
— Davis, *Eloquent Animals*, p. 26

UNACCEPTABLE BORROWING OF WORDS AND PHRASES
The existence of a signing ape unsettled linguists and startled animal behaviorists (Davis 26).

Notice that the phrase "the existence of a signing ape" has been lifted from the source without quotation marks. Notice, too, that "unsettled linguists and startled animal behaviorists" closely resembles the wording of the source.

It is also plagiarism to borrow the source's sentence structure but to substitute your own synonyms, even though the source is cited, as illustrated here.

UNACCEPTABLE BORROWING OF STRUCTURE
If the presence of a sign-language-using chimp was disturbing for scientists studying language, it was also surprising to scientists studying animal behavior (Davis 26).

To avoid plagiarizing an author's wording, close the book, write from memory, and then open the book to check for accuracy. (See also 52c.) This technique prevents you from being captivated by the words on the page; it encourages you to write naturally, in your own voice, without plagiarizing. These two paraphrases were written with the book closed.

ACCEPTABLE PARAPHRASES
According to Flora Davis, linguists and animal behaviorists were unprepared for the news that a chimp could communicate with its trainers through sign language (26).

When they learned of an ape's ability to use sign language, both linguists and animal behaviorists were taken by surprise (Davis 26).

53e Limit quotations and integrate them as smoothly as possible.

It is tempting to insert many long quotations in your paper and to use your own words only for connecting passages. This is an especially strong temptation if you feel that the authors of your sources are better writers than you are. But do not quote excessively. Long series of quotations give readers the impression that you cannot think for yourself.

Use direct quotations only when the source is particularly clear or expressive or when it is important to let the debaters of an issue explain their positions in their own words. Except for this infrequent need for direct quotations, use your own words to summarize and paraphrase your sources and to explain your own ideas.

Integrating quotations

Integrate quotations smoothly enough for readers to move from your words to the words of a source without feeling a jolt. Avoid dropping quotations into the text without warning; instead, provide clear signal phrases, usually including the author's name, to prepare readers for the quotation.

DROPPED QUOTATION

Although the bald eagle is still listed as an endangered species, its ever-increasing population is very encouraging. "The bald eagle seems to have stabilized its population, at the very least, almost everywhere" (Sheppard 96).

QUOTATION WITH SIGNAL PHRASE

Although the bald eagle is still listed as an endangered species, its ever-increasing population

is very encouraging. According to ornithologist
Jay Sheppard, "The bald eagle seems to have stabilized its population, at the very least, almost
everywhere" (96).

To avoid monotony, try to vary your signal phrases. The
following models suggest a range of possibilities:

. In the words of researcher Herbert Terrace, " . . . "

As Flora Davis has noted, " . . . "

The Gardners, Washoe's trainers, point out that " . . . "

" . . . ," claims linguist Noam Chomsky.

Psychologist H. S. Terrace offers an odd argument for this
view: " . . . "

Terrace answers these objections with the following analysis:
" . . . "

When your signal phrase includes a verb, choose one that
is appropriate in the context. Is your source arguing a point,
making an observation, reporting a fact, drawing a conclusion, refuting an argument, or stating a belief? By choosing
an appropriate verb, such as one on the following list, you
can make your source's stance clear.

acknowledges	comments	endorses	reasons
adds	compares	grants	refutes
admits	confirms	illustrates	rejects
agrees	contends	implies	reports
argues	declares	insists	responds
asserts	denies	notes	suggests
believes	disputes	observes	thinks
claims	emphasizes	points out	writes

It is not always necessary to quote full sentences from a
source. At times you may wish to borrow only a phrase or to

weave part of a source's sentence into your own sentence
structure:

> Brian Millsap claims that the banning of DDT in
> 1972 was "the major turning point" leading to the
> eagles' comeback (2).

> The ultrasonography machine takes approximately
> 250 views of each breast, step by step.   Mary
> Spletter likens the process to "examining an en-
> tire loaf of bread, one slice at a time" (40).

Handling long quotations

When you quote more than four typed lines, set off the quotation by indenting it ten spaces from the left margin. Use
the normal right margin and do not single-space. This format
displays your source's words more obviously than a set of
widely separated quotation marks.

Long quotations should be introduced by an informative
sentence, usually followed by a colon. Quotation marks are
unnecessary because the indented format tells readers that
the words are taken directly from the source.

> Desmond describes how Washoe tried signing to the
> other apes when the Gardners returned her to an
> ape colony in Oklahoma:

> > One particularly memorable day, a snake
> > spread terror through the castaways on
> > the ape island, and all but one fled in
> > panic.   This male sat absorbed, staring
> > intently at the serpent.   Then Washoe
> > was seen running over signing to him
> > "come, hurry up." (42)

Reviewing your use of quotations

AVOIDING PLAGIARISM; BEING ACCURATE

1. Have you placed each quotation in quotation marks (except long quotations that have been set off from the text)? To use another writer's words as if they were your own is a form of dishonesty known as plagiarism. (See 53d.)
2. Is each quotation word-for-word accurate? If you added a word, did you place it in brackets? If you deleted part of the quotation, did you use an ellipsis mark? (See 53e.)
3. Have you documented each quotation with a combination of a signal phrase and a parenthetical citation? (See numbers 4 and 5.)

DOCUMENTING QUOTATIONS

4. Have you introduced each quotation with a clear signal phrase? Usually the signal phrase should name the author. Here are some examples of commonly used signal phrases:

   According to Jane Doe, " . . . "

   In the words of researcher Jane Doe, " . . . "

   As biologist Jane Does puts it, " . . . "

   Jane Doe points out that " . . . "

Quotations (continued)

argues that " . . . "

admits that " . . . "

has concluded that " . . . "

reports that " . . ."

writes that " . . . "

stated in an interview that " . . . "

" . . .," remarks Jane Doe, " . . . "

" . . .," claims attorney Jane Doe.

Jane Doe offers an intriguing argument for this view: " . . . "

Jane Doe's language is biased. Consider, for example, the following passage: " . . . "

5. Have you placed a parenthetical citation after each quotation? As a rule, if the author has been named in the signal phrase, only a page number goes in the parentheses. (See 54a.)

```
Flora Davis reports that a chimp at the

Yerkes Primate Research Center "has combined

words into new sentences that she was never

taught" (67).
```

Reviewing your use of summaries and paraphrases

AVOIDING PLAGIARISM

1. Did you write summaries and paraphrases from memory, without looking at the source as you wrote? (If not, you may have borrowed too much language from the source. See number 2.) Did you then reread the source to check for accuracy?

2. Are you certain you have not borrowed too much language from your sources? It is plagiarism to borrow strings of words without putting them in quotation marks or to borrow sentence structures and simply plug in synonyms. (For examples of plagiarism, see p. 508.)

3. Have you documented each summary and paraphrase (except for common knowledge) with a citation? (See number 4.)

DOCUMENTING SUMMARIES AND PARAPHRASES

4. Have you introduced most summaries and paraphrases with a clear signal phrase and followed them with a page number in parentheses? The signal phrase lets readers know where the summarized or paraphrased material begins. In the following example, the signal phrase is underlined.

CITATION PRECEDED BY SIGNAL PHRASE

In spite of claims made for Washoe, Koko, and

others, however, there is still skepticism

about whether the apes really learn signs or
whether they merely imitate or respond to the cues
of their trainers. Psychologist H. S. Terrace,
the chief trainer of a chimp named Nim, is one of
the most formidable of the skeptics because he was
once a believer. <u>Ultimately Terrace concluded
that</u> most of Nim's, Washoe's, and Koko's signs
were responses to deliberate or nondeliberate cues
by trainers immediately before the ape signed
(899).

NOTE: If readers will understand from the context precisely
what information comes from the source, the signal phrase
may be omitted. In such cases, put the name of the author in
the parentheses along with the page number.

CITATION WITH NAME OF AUTHOR IN PARENTHESES

One of the most dramatic instances of one ape
signing to another occurred in 1976, when
Washoe had a baby. Though the baby chimp
lived for only a few hours, Washoe signed to
it before it died (Davis 42).

Notice that at the end of a block quotation the parenthetical citation goes outside the final period.

Using the ellipsis mark and brackets

Two useful marks of punctuation, the ellipsis mark and brackets, allow you to keep quoted material to a minimum and to integrate it smoothly into your text.

THE ELLIPSIS MARK   To condense a quoted passage, you can use the ellipsis mark (three periods, with spaces between) to indicate that you have omitted words. What remains must be grammatically complete.

```
In a recent New York Times article, Erik Eckholm

reports that "a 4-year-old pygmy chimpanzee . . .

has demonstrated what scientists say are the most

humanlike linguistic skills ever documented in

another animal" (A1).
```

The writer has omitted the words *at a research center near Atlanta,* which appeared in the original.

On the rare occasions when you want to omit a full sentence or more, use a period before the three ellipsis dots.

```
According to Wade, the horse Clever Hans "could

apparently count by tapping out numbers with his

hoof. . . .  Clever Hans owes his celebrity to his

master's innocence.  Von Osten sincerely believed

he had taught Hans to solve arithmetical problems"

(1349).
```

Ordinarily, do not use an ellipsis mark at the beginning or at the end of a quotation. Your readers will understand that the quoted material is taken from a longer passage, so such ellipsis marks are not necessary. The only exception occurs when words at the end of the final quoted sentence have been dropped.

Obviously you should not use an ellipsis mark to distort the meaning of your source.

BRACKETS Brackets (square parentheses) allow you to insert words of your own into quoted material. You can insert words in brackets to explain a confusing reference or to keep a sentence grammatical in your context.

```
Robert Seyfarth reports that "Premack [a scientist

at the University of Pennsylvania] taught a seven-

year-old chimpanzee, Sarah, that the word for

'apple' was a small, plastic triangle" (13).
```

If your typewriter has no brackets, ink them in by hand.

53f Revise the paper.

When you are revising any paper, it is a good idea to concentrate first on the larger elements of writing — content, focus, organization, paragraphing, and coherence — and then to turn to matters of style and correctness. With the research paper, this strategy is especially important because reviewing your use of sources requires considerable attention to detail.

The following checklist will help you review your draft for issues other than your use of sources. To review your use of sources (quotations, summaries, and paraphrases), consult the charts on pages 512–515.

CONTENT, FOCUS, AND ORGANIZATION

— Is your topic restricted?
— Is your thesis or purpose clearly stated in the introduction?
— Does the body of the paper support the thesis with

appropriate evidence such as facts, statistics, reasons, and expert testimony?

— Can readers follow the organization? Are the ideas effectively arranged?

PARAGRAPHING AND COHERENCE

— Does each paragraph have a clear topic sentence stating a central idea related to the thesis?

— Does each paragraph fully support its topic sentence?

— Do the paragraphs read smoothly? Can readers move from one paragraph to another without feeling lost?

STYLE AND CORRECTNESS

— Are the sentences clear, emphatic, and varied?

— Is your style formal without being inflated?

— Is the paper free of errors in grammar, punctuation, and mechanics?

Once you have revised and edited your draft, type the final copy according to your instructor's guidelines and proofread it carefully. Then only one task remains: compiling the list of works cited.

53g Prepare a list of works cited.

On a separate page at the end of your paper you must provide a list of the works you have cited in your paper. The purpose of this list is to acknowledge your sources and to help your readers track down a source should they be interested in doing so.

Rules for preparing the list of works cited are quite strict, and they are complex. Fortunately, however, there is no need to memorize these rules. If you are using the MLA style of documentation, consult 54b; if you are using APA style, consult 55a.

54

Using the MLA system for documenting sources

The various academic disciplines use their own editorial styles for citing sources and for listing the works that have been cited. The style described in this section is that of the Modern Language Association (MLA), contained in the *MLA Handbook for Writers of Research Papers* (3rd ed., 1988), which recommends that citations be given in the text of the paper rather than in footnotes or endnotes. If your instructor prefers footnotes or endnotes (also acceptable to MLA) or the American Psychological Association (APA) style of in-text citation, consult 55, where you will also find a list of style manuals used in various disciplines.

54a MLA in-text citations

The MLA's in-text citations are made with a combination of signal phrases and parenthetical references. A signal phrase indicates that something taken from a source (such as a quotation, summary, or paraphrase) is about to be used; usually the signal phrase includes the author's name. The parenthetical reference includes at least a page number.

Citations in parentheses should be as concise as possible but complete enough so that readers can find the source in the list of works cited at the end of the paper, where works are listed alphabetically by authors' last names. The following models illustrate the form for the MLA style of citation.

Directory to the MLA system

NOTE: For a sample paper documented with the MLA system, see pages 544–580.

AUTHOR NAMED IN A SIGNAL PHRASE   Ordinarily, you should introduce the material being cited with a signal phrase that includes the author's name. In addition to preparing readers for the source, the signal phrase allows you to keep the parenthetical citation brief.

```
Flora Davis reports that a chimp at the Yerkes

Primate Research Center "has combined words into

new sentences that she was never taught" (67).
```

The signal phrase — "Flora Davis reports" — provides the name of the author; the parenthetical citation gives the page number where the quoted sentence may be found. By looking up the author's last name in the list of works cited, readers will find complete information about the work's title, publisher, and date of publication.

AUTHOR NOT NAMED IN A SIGNAL PHRASE   If the signal phrase does not include the author's name (or if there is no signal phrase), the author's last name must appear in parentheses along with the page number.

```
Although the baby chimp lived only a few hours,

Washoe signed to it before it died (Davis 42).
```

Use no punctuation between the name and the page number.

TWO OR MORE WORKS BY THE SAME AUTHOR   If your list of works cited includes two or more works by the same author, include the title of the work either in the signal phrase or in abbreviated form in the parenthetical reference.

```
In Eloquent Animals, Flora Davis reports that a

chimp at the Yerkes Primate Research Center "has

combined words into sentences that she was never

taught" (67).
```

> Flora Davis reports that a chimp at the Yerkes
> Primate Research Center "has combined words into
> sentences that she was never taught" (<u>Eloquent</u> 67).

In the rare case when both the author and a short title must be given in parentheses, the citation should appear as follows:

> Although the baby chimpanzee lived only for a few
> hours, Washoe signed to it before it died (Davis,
> <u>Eloquent</u> 42).

TWO OR THREE AUTHORS If your source has two or three authors, name them in the signal phrase or include them in the parenthetical reference.

> Patterson and Linden agree that the gorilla Koko
> acquired language more slowly than a normal speak-
> ing child (83-90).

FOUR OR MORE AUTHORS If your source has four or more authors, include only the first author's name followed by "et al." (Latin for "and others") in the signal phrase or in the parenthetical reference.

> The study was extended for two years, and only
> after results were duplicated on both coasts did
> the authors publish their results (Doe et al. 137).

CORPORATE AUTHOR Either name the corporate author in the signal phrase or include a shortened version in the parentheses.

> The Internal Revenue Service warns businesses that
> deductions for "lavish and extravagant entertain-
> ment" are not allowed (43).

UNKNOWN AUTHOR   If the author is not given, either use the complete title in a signal phrase or use a short form of the title in the parentheses.

> The UFO reported by the crew of a Japan Air Lines
>
> flight remains a mystery. Radar tapes did not
>
> confirm the presence of another craft ("Strange
>
> Encounter" 26).

AUTHORS WITH THE SAME LAST NAME   If your list of works cited includes works by two or more authors with the same last name, include the first name of the author you are citing in the signal phrase or parenthetical reference.

> Both Lucy and Koko have been reported to lie
>
> (Adrian Desmond 201).

> Adrian Desmond has reported that Lucy was clever
>
> enough to see through the lies of her trainers
>
> (102).

A MULTIVOLUME WORK   If your paper cites more than one volume of a multivolume work, indicate in the parentheses the volume you are referring to, followed by a colon.

> Terman's studies of gifted children reveal a pat-
>
> tern of accelerated language acquisition (2: 279).

If your paper cites only one volume of a multivolume work, you will include the volume number in the list of works cited at the end of the paper and will not need to include it in the parentheses.

A NOVEL, A PLAY, OR A POEM   In citing literary sources, include information that will enable readers to find the passage in various editions of the work. For a novel, put the page number first and then indicate the part or chapter in which the passage can be found.

> Fitzgerald's narrator captures Gatsby in a moment
> of isolation: "A sudden emptiness seemed to flow
> now from the windows and the great doors, endowing
> with complete isolation the figure of the host"
> (56; ch. 3).

For a verse play, list the act, scene, and line numbers, separated by periods. Use arabic numerals unless your instructor prefers roman numerals.

> In his famous advice to the players, Hamlet de-
> fines the purpose of theater, "whose end, both at
> the first and now, was and is, to hold, as 'twere,
> the mirror up to nature" (3.2.21-23).

For a poem, cite the part (if there are a number of parts) and the line numbers, separated by periods.

> When Homer's Odysseus came to the hall of Circe,
> he found his men "mild / in her soft spell, fed on
> her drug of evil" (10.209-11).

✓ **INDIRECT SOURCE** When a writer's or speaker's quoted words appear in a source written by someone else, begin the citation with the abbreviation "qtd. in."

> "We only used seven signs in his presence," says
> Fouts. "All of his signs were learned from the
> other chimps at the laboratory" (qtd. in Toner
> 24).

AN ENTIRE WORK   To cite an entire work, use the author's name in a signal phrase or a parenthetical reference.

> Patterson and Linden provide convincing evidence
>
> for the speech-making abilities of nonhuman pri-
>
> mates.

TWO OR MORE WORKS   To cite more than one source to document a particular point, separate the citations with a semicolon.

> With intensive training, the apes in this study
>
> learned more than 200 signs or signals (Desmond
>
> 229; Linden 173).

Multiple citations can be distracting to readers, however, so the technique should not be overused. If you want to alert readers to several sources that discuss a particular topic, consider using an information note instead (discussed next).

MLA information notes

Researchers who use the MLA system of parenthetical documentation may also use information notes for one of two purposes:

1. to provide additional material that might interrupt the flow of the paper yet is important enough to include;
2. to refer readers to sources not included in the list of works cited.

Information notes may be either footnotes or endnotes. Footnotes appear at the foot of the page; endnotes appear at the end of the paper, just before the list of works cited. For either style, the notes are numbered consecutively throughout the paper. The text of the paper contains a raised arabic numeral that corresponds to the number of the note.

TEXT

```
The apes' achievements cannot be explained away as
the simple results of conditioning or unconscious
cueing by trainers.¹
```

NOTE

```
    ¹ For a discussion of the cueing of animals,
see Wade 1349-51.
```

Information notes should not be confused with notes used as an alternative to parenthetical documentation (see 55b).

54b   MLA list of works cited

A list of works cited, which appears at the end of your research paper, gives publishing information for each of the sources you have cited in the paper. Start on a new page and title your list "Works Cited." Then, working from your bibliography cards (see 52a), list in alphabetical order all the sources that you have cited in the paper. Unless your instructor asks for them, sources not actually cited in the paper should not be given in this list, even if you may have read them.

Alphabetize the list by the last names of the authors (or editors); if a work has no author or editor, alphabetize by the first word of the title other than *a, an,* or *the.*

Do not indent the first line of each bibliography entry, but indent any additional lines five spaces. This technique highlights the names by which the list has been alphabetized (see, for example, the list of works cited at the end of Karen Shaw's paper on p. 578).

The following models illustrate the form that the Modern Language Association (MLA) recommends for bibliographic entries.

Books

✓   **BASIC FORMAT FOR A BOOK**   For most books, arrange the information into three units, each followed by a period: (1) the author's name, last name first; (2) the title and subtitle, underlined; and (3) the place of publication, the publisher, and the date.

    Davis, Flora. <u>Eloquent Animals: A Study in Animal</u>
        <u>Communication</u>. New York: Coward, 1978.

The information is taken from the title page of the book and from the reverse side of the title page (the copyright page), not from the outside cover. The complete name of the publisher (in this case Coward, McCann & Geoghegan, Inc.) need not be given. You may use a short form as long as it is easily identifiable; omit terms such as *Press, Inc.,* and *Co.* except when naming university presses such as Harvard UP. The date to use in your bibliographic entry is the most recent copyright date.

TWO OR THREE AUTHORS   Name the authors in the order in which they are presented on the title page; reverse the name of only the first author.

    Fisher, Roger, and William Ury. <u>Getting to Yes</u>:
        <u>Negotiating Agreement without Giving In</u>.
        Boston: Houghton, 1981.

The names of three authors are separated by commas.

    Kagan, Donald, Steven Ozment, and Frank M. Turner.
        <u>The Western Heritage since 1300</u>. New York:
        Macmillan, 1987.

FOUR OR MORE AUTHORS   Cite only the first author, name reversed, followed by "et al." (Latin for "and others").

Curtin, Philip, et al. <u>African History</u>. Boston:

  Little, 1978.

EDITORS An entry for an editor is similar to that for an author except that the name is followed by a comma and the abbreviation "ed." for "editor." If there is more than one editor, use the abbreviation "eds." for "editors."

Lenneberg, Eric H., and Elizabeth Lenneberg,

  eds. <u>Foundations of Language Development</u>.

  New York: Academic, 1975.

AUTHOR WITH AN EDITOR Begin with the author and title, followed by the name of the editor. In this case the abbreviation "Ed." means "edited by," so it is the same for one or multiple editors.

Shakespeare, William. <u>The Tragedy of Macbeth</u>.

  Ed. Louis B. Wright and Virginia A. Lamar.

  New York: Washington Square, 1959.

TRANSLATION List the entry under the name of the author, not the translator. After the title, write "Trans." (for "translated by") and the name of the translator.

Tolstoy, Leo. <u>Anna Karenina</u>. Trans. Constance

  Garnett. Indianapolis: Bobbs, 1978.

CORPORATE AUTHOR List the entry under the name of the corporate author, even if it is also the name of the publisher.

Maryland Commission for Women. <u>How to Translate

  Volunteer Skills into Employment Credentials</u>.

  Baltimore: MD Commission for Women, 1979.

UNKNOWN AUTHOR Begin with the title. Alphabetize the entry by the first word of the title other than *a, an,* or *the.*

The Times Atlas of the World. 5th ed. New York:

New York Times, 1975.

TWO OR MORE WORKS BY THE SAME AUTHOR If your list of works cited includes two or more works by the same author, use the author's name only for the first entry. For subsequent entries use three hyphens followed by a period. The three hyphens must stand for exactly the same name or names as in the preceding entry. List the titles in alphabetical order.

Davis, Flora. Eloquent Animals: A Study in Animal

Communication. New York: Coward, 1978.

---. Inside Intuition: What We Know about Nonver-

bal Communication. New York: McGraw, 1973.

EDITION OTHER THAN THE FIRST If you are citing an edition other than the first, include the number of the edition after the title: 2nd ed., 3rd ed., and so on.

Spatt, Brenda. Writing from Sources. 3rd ed.

New York: St. Martin's, 1991.

MULTIVOLUME WORK Include the number of volumes before the city and publisher, using the abbreviation "vols."

Graves, Robert. The Greek Myths. 2 vols. New

York: Braziller, 1967.

If your paper cites only one of the volumes, write the volume number before the city and publisher and write the total number of volumes in the work after the date.

Graves, Robert.   The Greek Myths.   Vol. 2.   New

York: Braziller, 1967.   2 vols.

ENCYCLOPEDIA OR DICTIONARY   Articles in well-known dictionaries and encyclopedias are handled in abbreviated form. Simply list the author of the article (if there is one), the title of the article, the title of the reference work, and the date of the edition.

Frankel, Mark S.   "Human Experimentation: Social

and Professional Control."   Encyclopedia of

Bioethics.   1978 ed.

Volume and page numbers are not necessary because the entries are arranged alphabetically and therefore are easy to locate.

If a reference work is not well known, provide full publishing information as well.

✓ **SELECTION IN AN ANTHOLOGY**   Present the information in this order, with each item followed by a period: author of the selection; title of the selection; title of the anthology; editor of the anthology, preceded by "Ed."; city, publisher, and date; page numbers on which the selection appears.

Abrams, M. H.   "English Romanticism: The Spirit of

the Age."   Romanticism Reconsidered.   Ed.

Northrop Frye.   New York: Columbia UP, 1963.

63–88.

If an anthology gives the original publishing information for a selection and if your instructor prefers that you use it, cite that information first. Follow with the words "Rpt. in," the title, editor, and publishing information for the anthology, and the page numbers in the anthology on which the selection appears.

```
Gilman, Richard.  "Arden's Unsteady Ground."  Tu-

     lane Drama Review 11.2 (1966): 54-62.  Rpt.

     in Modern British Dramatists.  Ed. John

     Russell Brown.  Englewood Cliffs: Spectrum-

     Prentice, 1968.  104-16.
```

TWO OR MORE SELECTIONS FROM THE SAME ANTHOLOGY
Provide a separate entry for the anthology with complete publication information.

```
King, Woodie, and Ron Milner, eds.  Black Drama

     Anthology.  New York: Columbia UP, 1972.
```

Then include entries for each selection from the anthology by author and title of the selection with a cross-reference to the anthology. The cross-reference should include the last name of the editor of the anthology and the page numbers in the anthology on which the selection appears.

```
Baraka, Imamu Amiri [LeRoi Jones].  Bloodrites.

     King and Milner 25-31.

Hughes, Langston.  Mother and Child.  King and

     Milner 399-405.
```

FOREWORD, INTRODUCTION, PREFACE, OR AFTERWORD   If in your paper you quote from one of these elements, begin with the name of the writer of that element. Then identify the element being cited, neither underlined nor in quotation marks, followed by the title of the complete book, the book's author, and the book's editor, if any. After the publishing information, give the page numbers on which the foreword, introduction, preface, or afterword appears.

Van Vechten, Carl. Introduction. <u>Last Operas and
Plays</u>. By Gertrude Stein. Ed. Van Vechten.
New York: Vintage-Random, 1975. vii-xix.

BOOK WITH A TITLE WITHIN ITS TITLE If the book title
contains a title normally underlined, neither underline the
internal title nor place it in quotation marks.

Abbott, Keith. <u>Downstream from</u> Trout Fishing in
America<u>: A Memoir of Richard Brautigan</u>.
Santa Barbara: Capra, 1989.

If the title within the title is normally enclosed within quotation marks, retain the quotation marks and underline the
entire title.

Faulkner, Dewey R. <u>Twentieth Century Interpretations of "The Pardoner's Tale."</u> Englewood
Cliffs: Spectrum-Prentice, 1973.

BOOK IN A SERIES Before the publishing information,
cite the series name as it appears on the title page followed
by the series number, if any.

Holmes, Oliver Wendell. <u>The Autocrat of the
Breakfast-Table</u>. Everyman's Library 66.
London: Dent, 1970.

REPUBLISHED BOOK After the title of the book, cite the
original publication date followed by the current publishing
information. If the republished book contains new material,
such as an introduction or afterword, include that information after the original date.

Dreiser, Theodore. <u>Sister Carrie</u>. 1900. Introd.
Alfred Kazin. New York: Penguin, 1981.

PUBLISHER'S IMPRINT   If a book was published by a division (or imprint) of a publishing company, cite the name of the imprint followed by a hyphen and the publisher's name. An imprint name usually precedes the publisher's name on the title page.

```
Oates, Joyce Carol.    (Woman) Writer: Occasions and

     Opportunities.    New York: Abrahams-Dutton,

     1988.
```

Articles in periodicals

ARTICLE IN A MONTHLY MAGAZINE   In addition to the author, the title of the article, and the title of the magazine, list the month and year and the page numbers on which the article appears. Abbreviate the names of months except May, June, and July.

```
Lorenz, Wanda L.    "Problem Areas in Accounting for

     Income Taxes."    The Practical Accountant Feb.

     1984: 69-77.
```

If the article had appeared on pages 69–71 and 89–95, you would write "69 + " (not "69–95").

ARTICLE IN A WEEKLY MAGAZINE   Handle articles in weekly (or biweekly) magazines as you do those for monthly magazines, but give the exact date of the issue, not just the month and year.

```
Clark, Matt.    "Medicine: A Brave New World."

     Newsweek 5 Mar. 1984: 64-70.
```

ARTICLE IN A JOURNAL PAGINATED BY VOLUME   Many professional journals continue page numbers throughout the year instead of beginning each issue with page 1; at the end of the year, all of the issues are collected in a volume. Interested readers need only the volume number, the year, and the page numbers to find an article.

Otto, Mary L. "Child Abuse: Group Treatment for

Parents." Personnel and Guidance Journal 62

(1984): 336-38.

ARTICLE IN A JOURNAL PAGINATED BY ISSUE If each issue of the journal begins with page 1, you need to indicate the number of the issue. Simply place a period after the number of the volume, followed by the number of the issue.

Nichols, Randall G. "Word Processing and Basic

Writers." Journal of Basic Writing 5.2

(1986): 81-97.

ARTICLE IN A DAILY NEWSPAPER Begin with the author, if there is one, followed by the title of the article. Next give the name of the newspaper, the date, the section letter or number, and the page number.

Diehl, Jackson. "Exodus of Soviet Jews May Alter

Israel's Fate." Washington Post 10 June

1990: A1+.

If the section is marked with a number rather than a letter, handle the entry as follows:

"Market Leaks: Illegal Insider Trading Seems to Be

on Rise; Ethical Issues Muddled." Wall

Street Journal 2 Mar. 1984, sec. 1: 1.

If an edition of the newspaper is specified on the masthead, name the edition after the date and before the page reference: eastern ed., late ed., natl. ed., and so on.

UNSIGNED ARTICLE IN A NEWSPAPER OR MAGAZINE   Use the same form you would use for an article in a newspaper or a weekly or monthly magazine, but begin with the article title.

"When Ballots Turn toward Mecca." <u>U.S. News and</u>

   <u>World Report</u> 25 June 1990: 17-18.

EDITORIAL IN A NEWSPAPER   Cite an editorial as you would an unsigned article, adding the word "Editorial" after the title.

"A Farm-Water Utility." Editorial. <u>Miami Herald</u>

   19 June 1990: 10A.

LETTER TO THE EDITOR   Cite the writer's name, followed by the word "Letter" and the publishing information for the newspaper or magazine in which the letter appears.

Daley, Dan, and Sheila Daley. Letter. <u>Commonweal</u>

   15 June 1990: 370.

BOOK REVIEW   Cite first the reviewer's name and the title of the review, if any, followed by the words "Rev. of" and the title and author of the work reviewed. Add the publishing information for the publication in which the review appears.

Donoghue, Denis. "A Worldly Philosopher." Rev.

   of <u>The Examined Life</u>, by Robert Nozick.

   <u>Wilson Quarterly</u> 14.2 (1990): 92-94.

Other sources

GOVERNMENT PUBLICATION   Treat the government agency as the author, giving the name of the government followed by the name of the agency.

United States. Internal Revenue Service. <u>Tax</u>

> Guide for Small Business. Publication 334.
> Washington: GPO, 1983.

PAMPHLET   Cite a pamphlet as you would a book.

> United States. Dept. of the Interior. National
> Park Service. Ford's Theatre and the House
> Where Lincoln Died. Washington: GPO, 1989.

PUBLISHED DISSERTATION   Cite a published dissertation as you would a book, underlining the title and giving the place of publication, the publisher, and the year of publication. After the title, add the word "Diss.," the institution name, and the year the dissertation was written.

> Healey, Robert F. Eleusinian Sacrifices in the
> Athenian Law Code. Diss. Harvard U, 1961.
> New York: Garland, 1990.

UNPUBLISHED DISSERTATION   Begin with the author's name, followed by the dissertation title in quotation marks, the word "Diss.," the name of the institution, and the year.

> Fedorko, Kathy Anne. "Edith Wharton's Haunted
> House: The Gothic in Her Fiction." Diss.
> Rutgers U, 1987.

ABSTRACT OF A DISSERTATION   Give the author's name, the dissertation title in quotation marks, and the abbreviation *DA* or *DAI* (for *Dissertation Abstracts* or *Dissertation Abstracts International*), followed by the volume number, date, and page number. Add the name of the institution at the end.

> Berkman, Anne Elizabeth. "The Quest for Authen-
> ticity: The Novels of Toni Morrison." DAI 48
> (1988): 2059A. Columbia U.

PUBLISHED PROCEEDINGS OF A CONFERENCE   Cite published conference proceedings as you would a book, adding information about the conference after the title.

```
Howell, Benita J., ed.  Cultural Heritage Conser-
     vation in the American South.  Proc. of
     Southern Anthropological Society.  Tampa,
     1988.  Athens: U of Georgia P, 1990.
```

WORK OF ART   Cite the artist's name, followed by the title of the artwork, usually underlined, and the institution and city in which the artwork can be found.

```
Cassatt, Mary.  At the Opera.  Museum of Fine
     Arts, Boston.
```

PERSONAL LETTER   To cite a letter you have received, begin with the writer's name and add the phrase "Letter to the author," followed by the date.

```
Flynn, Samantha.  Letter to the author.  18 June
     1990.
```

LECTURE OR PUBLIC ADDRESS   Cite the speaker's name, followed by the title of the lecture (if any) in quotation marks, the organization sponsoring the lecture, the location, and date.

```
Lederer, Richard.  "Brave New Words."  Columbia
     Scholastic Press Association 66th Annual Con-
     vention.  New York, 21 Mar. 1990.
```

PERSONAL INTERVIEW   To cite an interview that you conducted, begin with the name of the person interviewed. Then write "Personal interview," followed by the date of the interview.

Shaw, Lloyd.   Personal interview.   21 Mar. 1987.

PUBLISHED INTERVIEW   Cite the name of the person interviewed, followed by the word "Interview" and the publication in which the interview was printed. If the interview has a title, put the title in quotation marks after the interviewee's name and do not use the word "Interview." If the interview was broadcast on radio or television, give the title of the program, underlined, after the word "Interview," followed by identifying information about the broadcast.

Francis, Dick.   Interview.   The Writer July 1990:

 9-10.

Holm, Celeste.   Interview.   Fresh Air.   Natl. Pub-

 lic Radio.   WBUR, Boston.   28 June 1990.

COMPUTER SOFTWARE   Begin with the author of the program (if known), the title of the program, underlined, and the words "Computer software." Then name the distributor and the year of publication. At the end of the entry you may add other pertinent information, such as the computer for which the program is designed or the form of the program.

Childpace.   Computer software.   Computerose, 1984.

 Commodore 64, disk.

MATERIAL FROM INFORMATION SERVICE OR DATABASE
Cite the material as you would any other material, including all publishing information. At the end of the citation add the name of the service (such as ERIC, for Educational Resources Information Center) and the number the service assigns to the material.

Horn, Pamela.   "The Victorian Governess."   History

 of Education 18 (1989): 333-44.   ERIC EJ 401

 533.

FILM   Begin with the title and the director, and end with the distributor and the year, separated by a comma. After the name of the director, include other information if you wish, such as the name of lead actors.

> <u>North by Northwest</u>. Dir. Alfred Hitchcock. With
>
> Cary Grant and Eva Marie Saint. MGM, 1959.

TELEVISION PROGRAM   List the information about the program in this order: the title of the episode (if any), in quotation marks; the title of the program, underlined; the writer ("By"), director ("Dir."), narrator ("Narr."), producer ("Prod."), or main actors ("With"), if relevant; the network; the local station on which you saw the program; the city; and the date the program was broadcast.

> "Mr. Sears' Catalogue." <u>The American Experience</u>.
>
> Narr. David McCullough. PBS. WGBH, Boston.
>
> 7 Aug. 1990.

LIVE PERFORMANCE OF A PLAY   Begin with the title of the play, followed by the author. Then include specific information about the live performance: the director, the major actors, the theater company and its location, and the date of the performance.

> <u>Mother Courage</u>. By Bertolt Brecht. Dir. Timothy
>
> Mayer. With Linda Hunt. Boston Shakespeare
>
> Company Theater, Boston. 20 Jan. 1984.

RECORDING   Begin with the composer (or author, if the recording is spoken), followed by the title of the piece. Next list pertinent artists (for instance, the conductor, the pianist, or the reader). End with the company label, the catalog number, and the date.

Handel, George Frederick. <u>Messiah</u>. With

Elizabeth Harwood, Janet Baker, Paul Esswood,

Robert Tear, and Raimund Herincz. Cond.

Charles Mackerras. English Chamber Orch. and

the Ambrosian Singers. Angel, R 67-2682,

1967.

CARTOON Begin with the cartoonist's name, the title of the cartoon (if it has one) in quotation marks, the word "Cartoon," and the publishing information for the publication in which the cartoon appears.

Watterson, Bill. "Calvin and Hobbes." Cartoon.

<u>Orlando Sentinel</u> 18 June 1990, Florida ed.:

C6.

MAP OR CHART Cite a map or chart as you would a book with an unknown author. Underline the title of the map or chart and add the word "Map" or "Chart" following the title.

<u>Southeastern States</u>. Map. Falls Church, VA: AAA,

1990.

SAMPLE RESEARCH PAPER
(WITH MLA DOCUMENTATION)

On the following pages is a sample research paper, written by Karen Shaw, a student in a first-semester composition class. Shaw's paper is documented with the MLA style of in-text citations and list of works cited.

Numbered comments on the pages opposite Shaw's paper draw your attention to features of special interest. (A corresponding number appears in the margins of the paper.) Here is a directory of those numbered comments:

TITLE PAGE, OUTLINE, FORMAT

1. Title page format
2. Outline
3. Title
4. Paper format

COMPOSITION PRINCIPLES

5. Opening paragraph
8. Thesis
9. Importance of statistics and other specific evidence
14. Addressing opposing arguments
18. Use of summary as a transition
19. Effective use of evidence
22. Use of anecdotal evidence
23. Importance of topic sentences
24. Echoing the thesis as a transition
25. Use of definition
26. Use of long quotations
27. A balanced approach
29. An open-minded approach
31. Revision
32. Conclusion

HANDLING SOURCE MATERIAL; CITATIONS

INFORMATION NOTES

BIBLIOGRAPHIC FORMAT

Somewhere Between the Word and the Sentence:
The Great Apes and the Acquisition of Language

1

By Karen Shaw

English 101, Section 30

Dr. Barshay

November 1, 1990

1. *Title page format.* Shaw uses a separate title page. She types the title about one-third down the page. One inch below the title Shaw types *By* and then her name, and one inch below that she types the name and section number of the course, her instructor's name, and the date. Each item is on a separate line, and the lines are double-spaced. All the information is centered between the left and right margins.

Pages 546–547

2. *Outline.* Shaw begins the outline with her thesis, the main point of the paper: Shaw's outline is presented in standard form, with roman numerals for the major categories, capital letters indented for the next level, and arabic numerals indented further for the third level (see 1d).

   Shaw decided that a sentence outline was necessary to reflect the complexity of the ideas in her paper. She keeps the sentences as parallel and as simple as possible to make the relationships between and among ideas clear.

   The second page of the outline is numbered with a small roman numeral *ii*. The first page is left unnumbered.

Outline

Thesis: The great apes resemble humans in lan-   2
guage abilities more than researchers
once believed, but it is as yet unknown
to what extent apes can combine symbols
in grammatical patterns.

I. The great apes have demonstrated
significant language skills.

A. Apes have acquired large vocabularies
in sign language and in a language of
symbols.

B. Despite charges that they are merely
responding to their trainers' cues,
apes have used language spontaneously.

1. They have performed well in experiments that eliminate the possibility of cueing.

2. They initiate conversations with
other apes.

3. They can learn signs and symbols
from one another.

C. Apes appear to use their language
skills creatively.

1. They have invented creative names.

Shaw ii

      2.   There is some evidence that they
           lie, joke, and swear.

    D. Apparently apes begin to conceptualize
       the same way children do.

  II. It has not yet been demonstrated that apes
      can combine signs in grammatical patterns
      to form sentences.

    A. The apes' sequences of signs are often
       confusing and repetitious.

    B. Lana's manipulation of stock sentences
       could be the result of conditioning.

    C. The Gardners' example is inconclusive.

    D. Even Patterson does not claim that her
       apes grasp grammar.

III. Current research at Yerkes Primate Center
      may provide more conclusive answers.

    A. Kanzi combines symbols in what appear
       to be simple grammatical patterns.

    B. The pygmy chimpanzees are beginning to
       understand spoken English.

Shaw 1

Somewhere Between the Word and the Sentence: 3
The Great Apes and the Acquisition of Language   4

Choosing from among the eighty signs in   5
American sign language that she had learned, a
chimpanzee named Lucy selected three and signaled
to her trainer, "Roger tickle Lucy." When Roger
failed to respond to her request and signaled instead, "No, Lucy tickle Roger," the chimpanzee
jumped onto his lap and began to tickle him (Des-   6
mond 43-44). One afternoon, Koko the gorilla,
who was often bored with language lessons, stubbornly and repeatedly signaled "red" when asked
the color of a white towel. She did this even
though she had correctly identified the color
white many times before. At last the gorilla
produced "a minute speck of red lint that had
been clinging to the towel" (Patterson and Linden
80-81). In Atlanta, when a two-and-a-half-year-
old pygmy chimpanzee's mother was taken away for
breeding, the young chimp amazed researchers by
revealing he had been learning "out of the corner
of his eye" symbols that were being taught to his
mother. He hit the symbols for both apple and

3. *Title.* The first part of Shaw's title is an evocative phrase introducing an idea that will be clarified at the end of the paper. The subtitle is an explicit description of her topic.

4. *Paper format.* The title is centered between the left and right margins, about two inches from the top of the page. All pages, including page 1, are numbered with arabic numerals at the upper right-hand corner, about a half-inch from the top, preceded by the writer's last name. The text is double-spaced, with a margin of one inch at the top, bottom, and sides of the paper.

   If your paper does not have a title page, put the following information on four separate lines, double-spaced, in the upper left corner of the first page: your name, your instructor's name, the name and section number of the course, and the date. Then center the title two lines below this information.

5. *Opening paragraph.* Karen Shaw decided to open her paper with three vivid examples that provide an overview of her subject.

6. *Author named in parentheses.* Because the name of the author is not included in a signal phrase, it appears in parentheses along with the page number. (See 54a.)

Shaw 2

ball on a computerized keyboard and pointed to
the objects (Eckholm, "Kanzi" C1).   7

     These and hundreds of similar scenes played   8
out over the past twenty-five years make it clear
that the great apes (chimpanzees, pygmy chimpanzees, gorillas, and orangutans) resemble humans
in language abilities more than had previously
been believed. Just how far that resemblance
extends, however, is a matter of some controversy. Researchers agree that apes have acquired
large vocabularies, but they differ sharply in
interpreting the uses to which these vocabularies
have been put. On balance, the evidence sug-
gests--despite the objections of some skeptics--
that apes have used symbols spontaneously and
creatively and have even learned to conceptualize
with them. It is as yet unknown, however, to
what extent they can combine symbols in grammatical patterns.

     Though apes lack the vocal ability to pro-
duce human sounds, they have acquired fairly
large vocabularies in American sign language
(Ameslan) and in an artificial language on a computerized keyboard. Washoe, an African-born
chimpanzee trained by psychologists Allen and
Beatrice Gardner from 1966 to 1970, learned 160

7. *Author and short title in parentheses.* Because there are two works by Eckholm in the list of works cited, a short form of the title is included in the parentheses. (See 54a.)

8. *Thesis.* Shaw's thesis is carefully articulated in her second paragraph. Ordinarily the thesis would appear in the opening paragraph, but Shaw decided to delay her thesis and begin with a series of vivid examples.

Shaw uses a full paragraph to express her thesis because her conclusions about the ape experiments are complex. Notice that the thesis paragraph surveys the organization of the paper, preparing readers for its main parts and even for some of its subparts. The thesis sentence that appears in Shaw's outline presents the main point more succinctly.

The thesis of the paper is not as dramatic as Shaw thought it would be when she began the paper. Having seen several television shows and having read a few popular articles before fully researching her subject, Shaw was at first convinced that the apes' linguistic abilities were extensive. Later, as she read more widely, she began to doubt her preliminary thesis and even considered reversing it dramatically. On completing her reading, however, Shaw decided that the evidence for the apes' abilities was most convincing, even though their abilities were not as extensive as she had once thought.

signs in Ameslan. Washoe began to learn signs by
spontaneously imitating the Gardners, who used
only sign language in her presence, but she
learned more rapidly when the Gardners took her
hands and molded the signs with them. To determine when Washoe truly knew a sign, the Gardners
applied a rigid criterion: The sign had to be
used "appropriately and spontaneously at least
once a day for fourteen or fifteen consecutive   **9**
days" (Davis 21).

    The largest Ameslan vocabulary claimed for
an ape, 600 signs, is that of Francine Patterson's gorilla Koko, who has lived with Patterson
since 1972. This figure is based on a simple
count, not on the Gardners' strict criterion.
But Patterson has also kept records showing that
Koko has mastered nearly 200 signs as measured by
the Gardners' criterion (Patterson and Linden   **10**
83-84).

    At the Yerkes Primate Center in Atlanta,   **11**
even more rigid criteria have been applied to determine if chimpanzees truly know a symbol. In
studies at Yerkes, researchers judged that the
pygmy chimpanzees Kanzi and Mulika had learned a
symbol only when repeated instances of spontaneous use were consistently followed by behavior

9. *Importance of statistics and other specific evidence.* Shaw uses statistics throughout to support her assertions. Here she provides a concrete explanation of what the Gardners mean by a rigid criterion.

10. *Two authors.* When there are two authors, include both names either in a signal phrase or in the parenthetical reference. Linden did not help Patterson conduct her research, so his name could not be included in the signal phrase. He did, however, coauthor the source in which the statistics appear, so his name is included in the parentheses.

11. *Summarizing without plagiarizing.* When summarizing, Shaw avoids plagiarism by using her own words and sentence structures, not those of the source. Here, for instance, is the passage from Savage-Rumbaugh that Shaw has summarized.

ORIGINAL SOURCE

The criterion used for determining when a word should be listed as a member of Kanzi's and Mulika's vocabulary differs significantly from those used in other studies (Fouts, 1973; Gardner & Gardner, 1971; Terrace, 1979). These criteria required that symbol production appear to be appropriate and that it occur on a specific number of consecutive days without prompting. Because it has been shown that context-appropriate responses can occur without comprehension (Savage-Rumbaugh, 1984b, 1986; Savage-Rumbaugh et al., 1983), a behavioral concordance measure was devised. This measure required that Kanzi and Mulika verify their utterances on 9 of 10 occasions. Only spontaneous utterances were considered to be appropriate candidates for behavioral verification.

For example, if Kanzi requested a trip to the treehouse, he would be told: "Yes, we can go to the treehouse." However, only if he then led the experimenter to this location could a correct behavioral concordance be scored for the word *treehouse*.

verifying that the symbol had been understood.
For example, a spontaneous use of the symbol for
"treehouse" would be counted only if the chimp
also took the researcher to the treehouse
(Savage-Rumbaugh et al. 217).

    In spite of claims made for Washoe, Koko,
and others, however, there is still skepticism
about whether the apes really learn signs or
whether they merely imitate or respond to the
cues of their trainers.[1] Psychologist H. S.
Terrace, the chief trainer of a chimp named Nim,
is one of the most formidable of the skeptics
because he was once a believer. Ultimately Terrace concluded that most of Nim's, Washoe's, and
Koko's signs were responses to deliberate or nondeliberate cues given by trainers immediately before the ape signed (Terrace et al. 899).

    Although Terrace may be correct in asserting
that a high percentage of the apes' signs have
been in response to cues, he and other critics
have not demonstrated that all of them are. The
Gardners and other researchers have performed
elaborate double-blind experiments that prevent
any possibility of cueing, and the apes have performed well in such tests.[2] Sue Savage-Rumbaugh
of the Yerkes Primate Center, who has herself

12. *Use of "et al."* When a source has four or more authors, the last name of the first author followed by "et al." appears either in the signal phrase or in the parentheses. (See 54a.)

13. *Use of information notes.* The number at the end of this sentence refers to an information note at the end of Shaw's paper. Shaw's rough draft contained a long discussion of cueing and the subtle ways it can occur, but the material had to be cut because Shaw was losing her focus on the thesis. She preserved a short passage by putting it in the note. (See pp. 526–527.)

14. *Addressing opposing arguments.* Shaw wisely addresses her opponents' arguments throughout the paper, showing that she knows both sides and that she believes her arguments stand up against the opposition. Here she counters Terrace's conclusion and offers evidence from concrete experiments to support her assertion.

15. *Use of information notes.* The number at the end of this sentence refers to an information note at the end of Shaw's paper. Shaw does not have the space to discuss the double-blind experiments but thinks some readers may want to read about them. The note at the end of the paper provides bibliographic information about a source that discusses these experiments in detail. (See pp. 526–527.)

criticized some of the sign language research,
has taken great care to prevent unconscious
cueing in tests of pygmy chimpanzees' abilities
to master symbols on a computerized keyboard. Because experimenters did not know "the order of
presentations and the location of stimuli," they
could not unintentionally affect the chimp's responses (Savage-Rumbaugh et al. 217).

Perhaps the most convincing evidence that
the apes have not been simply responding to cues
is that they have used signs or symbols spontaneously among themselves, often without a trainer
present. When the Gardners returned Washoe to an
ape colony in Oklahoma, she desperately signaled
to humans from whom she was separated by a moat,
and from the start she signed to the other apes:

> Frustrated by lack of conversational-
> ists, she [Washoe] even tried talking
> to dogs. . . . One particularly memo-
> rable day, a snake spread terror
> through . . . the ape island, and all
> but one fled in panic. This male sat
> absorbed, staring intently at the ser-
> pent. Then Washoe was seen running
> over signing to him, "Come, hurry up."
> (Desmond 42)

16

16. *Indented quotations, ellipsis marks, and brackets.* Quotations longer than four typed lines should be indented ten spaces from the left margin and typed double-spaced. Quotation marks are not used to enclose indented quotations because the format tells readers that the material is a quotation.

It is a sacred rule of research that material should be quoted *exactly* as it appears in a source. Often, however, it is necessary to insert or omit material in a quoted passage. Brackets are used to insert words not in the original source, in this case the name Washoe. Bracketed information often clarifies the quotation or makes it fit grammatically within your text. Ellipsis dots indicate that words have been deleted. The first ellipsis mark in the quotation consists of a period (indicating the end of a sentence) and three dots. The second ellipsis mark appears within a sentence, so it consists simply of three dots. (See 53e.) Notice that the parenthetical reference for an indented quotation, unlike that for an in-text citation, appears after the last sentence period of the quotation and contains no punctuation of its own.

Patterson's gorillas Koko and Michael sign
to one another, with Michael occasionally using
signs that he could have learned only from Koko.
"Even more intriguing," writes Patterson, "is his
variation of the <u>tickle</u> sign depending on whom he
is conversing with" (Patterson and Linden 176).

The most dramatic and moving instances of
chimps signing to one another have involved
Washoe, now under the care of Roger Fouts at Central Washington University. When Washoe had a
baby in 1976, although the baby chimp lived only
a few hours, Washoe signed to it before it died
(Davis 42). Recently another baby chimpanzee
placed in the care of Washoe has mastered more
than fifty signs in American sign language without help from humans. "We only used seven signs
in his presence," says Fouts. "All of his signs
were learned from the other chimps at the laboratory" (qtd. in Toner 24).   17

In addition to showing that apes learn signs   18
and use them spontaneously, the studies suggest a
third important conclusion: Apes can use language, or something like it, creatively. The
precocious pygmy chimpanzee Kanzi, encouraged by   19
his trainers to pick up language the way a child
does rather than through structured sessions with

17. *Indirect source.* When citing the words of a writer or speaker who has been quoted in a source, begin the citation with "qtd. in." (See 54a.)

18. *Use of summary as a transition.* In the first part of this sentence, Shaw summarizes the points she has made so far about the apes' language ability; the summary is an effective transition to the next part of her discussion.

19. *Effective use of evidence.* Shaw draws on many different sources for evocative examples of creative names. Each example or series of examples is followed by a parenthetical reference to its source.

food rewards, has learned to ask for particular films by combining symbols in a creative way. For instance, to request <u>Quest for Fire</u>, a film about early primates discovering fire, Kanzi began to punch symbols for "campfire" and "TV" (Eckholm, "Kanzi" C3). The Gardners' Lucy is **20** reported to have called an onion "cry fruit" and a radish "cry hurt food" (Desmond 40). And Francine Patterson claims that her gorilla Koko has invented many creative names, some of the most clever being "elephant baby" to describe a Pinocchio doll; "finger bracelet" to describe a ring; "white tiger" to describe a toy zebra; "bottle match" to describe a cigarette lighter; and "eye hat" to describe a mask (Patterson and Linden 146).

Apes who invent names are not simply learning by rote. They are adapting language for their own purposes. And those purposes, it turns out, may include lying, joking, and perhaps even swearing. Both Lucy and Koko have been reported to lie (Desmond 201), and Lucy has been clever enough to see through the lies of her trainers (Desmond 102). Ted Crail points out that lies **21** "fall within that part of language which is 'half art.' Lies are different from memorizing or mimicking" (137).

20. *Sample note cards*

> Creative naming   Desmond
>
> p. 40   Lucy: "cry fruit" (onion)
>   "cry hurt food" (radish)
>
> Not all researchers accept these
> and other examples, but Desmond
> says, "Personally, I give the apes
> the benefit of the doubt."   (p. 40)

> Creative naming   Patterson and Linden
>
> p. 146   Koko: "elephant baby" (Pinocchio
>   doll)
>   "finger bracelet" (ring)
>   "white tiger" (toy zebra)
>   "bottle match" (cigarette
>   "eye hat" (mask) lighter)
> Washoe: "smoke string food"
>   (chewing tobacco)
> Lucy: "cry hurt food" (radish)

21. *Author named in signal phrase.* Because the author is named in the signal phrase, only the page number appears in the parentheses. (See 54a.)

Francine Patterson is convinced that Koko   **22**
both appreciates jokes and jokes back in turn
with her trainers. Patterson claims that many of
the apparent "mistakes" made by Koko in her lessons are really attempts to inject variety into
boring classroom drills. For example, when one
trainer asked Koko where she wanted to put some
apple juice, Koko replied first "nose," then
"eye," and then "ear." The trainer retorted,
"Okay, here it goes in your ear." Koko laughed,
signed "drink," and opened her mouth, showing
that she knew very well where the drink belonged
(Patterson and Linden 142-43). Patterson is
aware that many scientists find her anecdotal
evidence of humor unconvincing, but she doubts
whether an experiment that would satisfy them
could be designed for such a subjective activity
as joking (Patterson and Linden 207).

Whether the apes can swear is debatable.
Patterson claims that Koko uses such swear words
as "rotten," "toilet," and "dirty." According to
Patterson, the sign for "dirty," which the trainers used to refer to feces, "became one of Koko's
favorite insults. Under extreme provocation she
will combine dirty with toilet to make her meaning inescapable" (Patterson and Linden 39).

22. *Use of anecdotal evidence.* The narrative example in this paragraph is anecdotal evidence that many researchers would discount. Shaw finds the example intriguing enough to include, but she does make clear at the end of her paragraph that such evidence is not the result of a controlled scientific experiment.

Chimpanzee Nim also began to extend the use of
the sign "dirty," which he was taught to use when
he wanted to go to the toilet, but his trainer
H. S. Terrace refuses to be convinced he was
swearing. He argues that Nim used the sign only
when what he really wanted was to be removed from
an uncomfortable situation (154).

Another important discovery has been that **23**
the apes, just like human children, have learned
to conceptualize with their "words." As Flora
Davis points out, children begin by using the
word "dog" for the family poodle but quickly
learn to extend that name to other dogs, though
perhaps overgeneralizing and using the word also
for cats and other small animals. She points out
that the apes who learned sign language followed
a similar pattern. Washoe first learned the sign
"open" when she wanted to open a door; later,
without prompting, she signed "open" when she
needed help with drawers, jars, and even faucets.
And just like human children, she "tended to
overgeneralize." For instance, she had learned
the word "hurt" for her scratches, bruises, and
scabs, but when she first saw a human navel, she
signed "hurt" (23-24). Sue Savage-Rumbaugh reports that the pygmy chimpanzee Kanzi has also

23. *Importance of topic sentences.* Like this paragraph, almost every one of Shaw's paragraphs opens with a clear topic sentence that focuses the reader's attention on the paragraph's main point. Notice that many of Shaw's topic sentences also clarify the paragraph's connection with ideas that have gone before. In this topic sentence, for example, the phrase "Another important discovery" links the paragraph to earlier paragraphs describing other discoveries.

extended the meanings of the symbols he has
learned:

> He has, for example, used "coke" to re-
> fer to all brands of dark carbonated
> drinks, "rain" to refer to the sprin-
> kling produced from the spray of a
> hose, "tomato" to refer to a variety of
> small, round, red fruits . . . and
> "bread" to refer to all varieties of
> bread, including taco shells. (Savage-
> Rumbaugh et al. 227)

Although the great apes have demonstrated   24
significant language skills, the question remains
whether they can combine signs in grammatical
patterns to form sentences. All human languages
have a grammar, a system through which relations
among words are conveyed. H. S. Terrace's de-   25
scription of grammar echoes that of linguist Noam
Chomsky, after whom Terrace's chimp Nim was named: 26

> Unlike words, most sentences cannot be
> learned individually. Psychologists,
> psycholinguists, and linguists are in
> general agreement that using a human
> language indicates knowledge of a gram-
> mar. How else can one account for a
> child's ultimate ability to create an

24. *Echoing the thesis as a transition.* Shaw shifts smoothly to the second part of her paper by echoing her thesis.
25. *Use of definition.* Shaw introduces this next section of her paper by defining *grammar*. The definition is a good strategy; if grammar is what distinguishes human beings' linguistic capabilities from those of other species, then readers must have a clear understanding of what that distinction is.
26. *Use of long quotations.* Quotations four lines or longer are set off from the text by indenting ten spaces. (See also annotation 16.) Shaw uses only three long quotations in her paper, since too many of them can be disruptive. Notice that Shaw is careful to introduce long quotations with a sentence that makes their significance clear.

Shaw 11

> indeterminate number of meaningful sen-
> tences from a finite number of words?
> (Terrace et al. 891)

It is true that apes have strung together
various signs (for instance, "Roger tickle
Lucy"), but the sequences are often confusing and
repetitious. Nim's series of sixteen signs is a
case in point: "give orange me give eat orange me
eat orange give me eat orange give me you"
(Terrace et al. 895).

Lana, a chimpanzee who learned to communicate in an artificial language on a computerized
keyboard, could tap out about six stock sentences. For example, she might punch "please,"
then a name, then a verb (such as "tickle" or
"groom"), and then "Lana." Such "sentences,"
however, could be conditioned responses involving
little or no understanding of grammar.

The Gardners were impressed by Washoe's
multisign sequences, seeing in them the beginnings **27**
of some grasp of grammar, but these findings have
been disputed. In one frequently cited filmed
sequence, Washoe's teacher placed a baby doll in
a cup. Washoe signed "baby in baby in my drink,"
a series of signs that seemed to make grammatical
sense. Terrace points out, however, that Washoe **28**

27. *A balanced approach.* Although Shaw is critical of some of the claims that have been made about the chimpanzees' and gorillas' grasp of grammar, she presents a balanced view of the evidence. She does not ridicule the researchers' claims or completely discount them; she simply argues, in a rational tone, that the claims have not been adequately proved.

28. *Sample note card*

> Grammar   Terrace et al.
>
> Terrace probably correct in saying
> claims by Gardners and others go
> too far. I would like to believe
> that apes grasp grammar but
> should maybe change my thesis.
> Back off. Read Davis again—this
> time more critically.

had previously been drilled in similar patterns
and that the teacher had pointed to the objects
(Terrace et al. 898).

Of all the apes, it is Patterson's Koko and
Michael for whom the most is claimed, but even
Patterson does not make large claims for her
apes' grasp of grammar. Many of Michael's and
Koko's short sequences make sense, but whether
one can conclude much from the longer sequences
seems doubtful. For instance, when Michael was
asked what "bird" meant, he signed the following:
"Bird good cat chase eat red trouble cat eat
bird." Patterson believes that Michael had seen
a cat catch a bird and was trying to describe the
scene (Patterson and Linden 173). It is certainly possible but, as Patterson herself would
probably admit, hardly proved.

More definite conclusions may come from the   29
Yerkes Primate Center and Language Research Center in Atlanta, where several remarkable pygmy
chimpanzees, most important Kanzi, are being
studied by Duane Rumbaugh and Sue Savage-
Rumbaugh. Pygmy chimpanzees have been little
studied, and few are in captivity, but the Atlanta scientists are convinced that this species
has a more "humanlike intelligence" than the

29. *An open-minded approach.* Although Shaw is not convinced that apes can combine signs in grammatical patterns to form sentences, she acknowledges that current research might prove her wrong.

Shaw 13

other apes. The Rumbaughs are hesitant to say
that Kanzi creates sentences, but they do report
that Kanzi's "two and three word statements are
often made without prompting, systematically add
useful information and represent his own creative
responses to novel situations" (Eckholm, "Pygmy"
B7). Duane Rumbaugh points out that Kanzi prac-   **30**
tices "simple grammatical ordering rules," for
example usually putting actions before objects,
as when he presses symbols for "KEEPAWAY BALLOON"
while playing a game with a balloon (Bower 140).

  One of the most interesting discoveries at
Yerkes is the pygmy chimpanzees' apparent ability
to understand spoken English. For some time
Kanzi's keyboard, carried by attendants wherever
the chimp goes over the fifty-five acres he can
roam, has been equipped with a voice synthesizer
so that a word is spoken each time Kanzi touches
a symbol on the board (Savage-Rumbaugh et al.
230). Kanzi increasingly understands spoken
English and the connection between the spoken
word and the symbol on his keyboard.

  Perhaps the best summation of the current
state of ape language studies comes from biolo-   **31**
gist Robert Seyfarth, who writes that the line
separating humans from other animals "remains

30. *Paraphrasing without plagiarizing.* When paraphrasing, Shaw avoids plagiarism by using her own words and sentence structures, not those of the source, and by putting any borrowed phrases in quotation marks. Here, for instance, is the passage from Bower that Shaw has paraphrased:

ORIGINAL SOURCE

Kanzi's use of symbols on a keyboard to make requests is not as extensive as his language comprehension, Rumbaugh says, but he does practice simple grammatical ordering rules for putting pairs of symbols together in novel ways. For instance, actions usually precede objects in Kanzi's requests; he presses symbols for "KEEPAWAY BALLOON" when he wants to tease a caregiver with a balloon and start a playful fight.

31. *Revision.* The first draft of the paper included a long discussion of Seyfarth's studies of monkeys in the wild. Shaw wisely eliminated this discussion because it introduced a new kind of evidence (all the other examples involve apes learning language from human beings).

Shaw 14

hazily drawn, somewhere between the word and the
sentence" (18). Apes have acquired large vocab-   **32**
ularies and they have used their "words" spontaneously and creatively and seem to be able to
conceptualize with them. But it is still to be
discovered if they can create a complex sentence
with their vocabularies to say, for instance,
"If I refuse to eat this green banana, will I
still be allowed to watch the Bonzo rerun on
television?"

32. *Conclusion.* Shaw's conclusion summarizes her whole argument and satisfies the reader's desire to know where she stands on the issue of the apes' ability to learn language. Here the evocative phrase used for the title is seen in context; this phrase provides a memorable statement of Shaw's final position.

Notes   **33**

[1] The most famous example of cueing involves **34** a horse named Clever Hans whose owner sincerely thought the horse could solve mathematical problems, tapping out the answers with his foot. It was demonstrated that the horse was in fact responding to the involuntary jerks of the owner's head at the point when the correct number of taps had been reached.

[2] For a description of the Gardners' double- **35** blind experiments, see Thomas A. Sebeok and Jean Umiker-Sebeok, "Performing Animals: Secrets of the Trade," Psychology Today Nov. 1979: 78-91.

33. *Format of information notes.* If your paper has information notes, begin them on a separate page. Type the heading "Notes" one inch from the top of the page and centered between the left and right margins. Begin the notes two spaces below the heading. Double-space the notes and indent the first line of each note five spaces from the left margin. The number of the note (corresponding to the number used in the text of the paper) should be raised slightly above the note and separated from it by one space. The number should not be followed by a period or enclosed in parentheses.

34. *Use of information notes.* Information notes are optional; not every research paper has them. Shaw's first note discusses interesting information that did not fit gracefully into the text of her paper. Her second note provides bibliographic information about a source that may be of interest to her readers. This source does not appear in Shaw's list of works cited, so she mentions it here.

35. *Format of the bibliographic reference.* Unlike in the list of works cited, the authors' names are all in normal order in an information note.

Shaw 16

Works Cited   36

Bower, Bruce. "Kanzi Extends His Speech Reach."   37
      Science News 27 Aug. 1988: 140.

Crail, Ted. Apetalk and Whalespeak.   38
      Los Angeles: Tarcher, 1981.

Davis, Flora. Eloquent Animals: A Study in Ani-
      mal Communication. New York: Coward, 1978.

Desmond, Adrian. The Ape's Reflexion. New
      York: Dial, 1979.

Eckholm, Erik. "Kanzi the Chimp: A Life in   39
      Science." New York Times 25 June 1985,
      local ed.: C1+.

---. "Pygmy Chimp Readily Learns Language Skill." 40
      New York Times 24 June 1985, local ed.: A1+.

Patterson, Francine, and Eugene Linden. The   41
      Education of Koko. New York: Holt, 1981.

Savage-Rumbaugh, Sue, et al. "Spontaneous Symbol 42
      Acquisition and Communicative Use by Pygmy
      Chimpanzees (Pan paniscus)." Journal of Ex-
      perimental Psychology 115 (1986): 211-35.

Seyfarth, Robert M. "Talking with Monkeys and   43
      Great Apes." International Wildlife
      Mar.-Apr. 1982: 13-18.

Terrace, H. S. Nim. New York: Knopf, 1979.

36. *Format of the list of works cited.* Begin the list of works cited on a separate page. Type the heading "Works Cited" one inch from the top of the page, centered between the left and right margins and followed by two lines of space. Double-space every entry, with the first line of each entry beginning at the left margin; indent subsequent lines in an entry five spaces from the left margin. Begin each entry with the author's name (or names), giving the first author's name in inverted order and any additional names in normal order. Alphabetize the entire list by the authors' names. Anonymous works should be alphabetized by the title of the work.

    The heading "Works Cited" tells readers that the list includes only the works that have been cited in the paper. If your instructor prefers a list of all the works you consulted, title the list "Works Consulted."

37. *Periodical published weekly.* This bibliographic entry has five parts: the author's name, the title of the article, the name of the periodical, the date of the issue, and the page number or numbers.

38. *Book by a single author.* The bibliographic entry has five parts: the author's name, the title (and subtitle, if any) of the book, the place of publication, the name of the publisher, and the date of publication.

39. *Newspaper article.* This bibliographic entry has six parts: the author's name, the title of the article, the name of the newspaper, the date, the edition, and the page number. (Often there is no edition.)

40. *Two or more works by the same author.* In entries after the first, use three hyphens followed by a period instead of repeating the author's name.

41. *Work by two or three authors.* Invert the name of the first author only and separate it from the next author's name with a comma.

42. *Article in a journal paginated by volume.* This bibliographic entry has six parts: the author's name, the title

Terrace, H. S., et al. "Can an Ape Create a   **44**

Sentence?" <u>Science</u> 206 (1979): 891-902.

Toner, Mike. "Loulis, the Talking Chimp."

<u>National Wildlife</u> Feb.-Mar. 1986: 24.

of the article, the name of the journal, the volume number (the issue number's unnecessary), the year of publication, and the page numbers on which the article appears.

43. *Article in a magazine.* The bibliographic entry has five parts: the author's name, the title of the article, the name of the magazine, the date of the issue, and the page numbers on which the article appears.

44. *Work by four or more authors.* After the name of the senior author (the one listed first), add a comma and *et al.,* Latin for "and others."

55

Alternative systems for documenting sources

To suit their special needs, the various academic disciplines have developed different editorial styles for citing sources in the text of the paper and for including them in a list of works cited. In your papers use the documentation style recommended by your instructor.

Most English classes use the style of in-text citation recommended by the Modern Language Association (MLA) and described in 54. This section surveys two alternative systems of documentation: the author/date style of in-text citation recommended by the American Psychological Association (APA), used in the social sciences; and footnotes or endnotes, an MLA alternative that is sometimes used in history and the humanities. For a list of style manuals in a variety of disciplines, see 55c.

55a APA style (used in the social sciences)

The American Psychological Association (APA) recommends a system of in-text citations that refer to a list of references at the end of the paper.

APA in-text citations

APA in-text citations provide at least the author's last name and the date of publication. For direct quotations, a page number is given as well.

BASIC FORMAT FOR A QUOTATION   Ordinarily, introduce the quotation with a signal phrase that includes the author's last name followed by the date of publication in parentheses. Put the page number (preceded by "p.") in parentheses at the end of the quotation.

As Davis (1978) reports, "If the existence of a

signing ape was unsettling for linguists, it was

also startling news for animal behaviorists"

(p. 26).

When the author's name does not appear in the signal phrase, place the author's name, the date, and the page number in parentheses at the end of the quotation. Use commas between items in the parentheses.

BASIC FORMAT FOR A SUMMARY OR A PARAPHRASE For a summary or a paraphrase, include the author's last name and the date either in a signal phrase or in parentheses at the end. A page number is not required.

According to Davis (1978), when they learned of an

ape's ability to use sign language, both linguists

and animal behaviorists were taken by surprise.

When they learned of an ape's ability to use sign

language, both linguists and animal behaviorists

were taken by surprise (Davis, 1978).

A WORK WITH TWO AUTHORS Name both authors in the signal phrase or parentheses each time you cite the work. In the parentheses, use "&" between the authors' names; in the signal phrase, use "and."

Patterson and Linden (1981) agree that the gorilla

Koko acquired language more slowly than a normal

speaking child.

Directory to the APA system

55a: APA documentation

APA IN-TEXT CITATIONS

APA REFERENCES (BIBLIOGRAPHIC LIST)

PAGES FROM A SAMPLE PAPER: APA STYLE

For pages from a sample paper documented with APA in-text
citations, see pages 593–595.

Directory to footnotes or endnotes

55b: Footnotes or endnotes (an MLA alternative)

NOTE: For a list of style manuals for various disciplines, see pages 599–600.

Koko acquired language more slowly than a normal

speaking child (Patterson & Linden, 1981).

A WORK WITH THREE TO FIVE AUTHORS Identify all authors in the signal phrase or the parentheses the first time you cite the source.

The study noted a fluctuating divorce rate in Mid-

dletown between the 1920s and the 1970s (Caplow,

Bahr, Chadwick, Hill, & Williamson, 1982).

In subsequent citations, use the first author's name followed by "et al." in either the signal phrase or the parentheses.

While the incidence of wife abuse may not be

higher than in the past, the researchers found

that women are more willing to report it (Caplow

et al., 1982).

A WORK WITH SIX OR MORE AUTHORS Use only the first author's name followed by "et al." in all citations.

Communes in the late 1960s functioned like extended

families, with child-rearing responsibilities

shared by all adult members (Berger et al., 1971).

AUTHOR UNKNOWN If the author is not given, either use the complete title in a signal phrase or use the first two or three words of the title in the parenthetical citation.

The UFO reported by the crew of a Japan Air Lines

flight remains a mystery. Radar tapes did not

confirm the presence of another craft ("Strange

Encounter," 1987).

If "Anonymous" is specified as the author, treat it as if it were a real name: (Anonymous, 1987). In the bibliographic references, also use the name Anonymous as author.

CORPORATE AUTHOR If the author is a government agency or other corporate organization with a long and cumbersome name, spell out the name the first time you use it in your paper followed by an abbreviation in brackets. In later citations, simply use the abbreviation.

First citation: (National Institute of Mental Health [NIMH], 1981)

Later citations: (NIMH, 1981)

TWO OR MORE WORKS IN THE SAME PARENTHESES When your parenthetical citation names two or more works, put them in the same order that they appear in the bibliography, separated by semicolons.

AUTHORS WITH THE SAME LAST NAME To avoid confusion, use initials with the last names if your bibliography lists two or more authors with the same last name.

Research by J. A. Smith (1987) revealed that . . .

PERSONAL COMMUNICATION Conversations, memos, letters, and similar unpublished person-to-person communications should be cited by initials, last name, and precise date.

L. Smith (personal communication, October 12,

1987) predicts that government funding of this

type of research will end soon.

Do not include personal communications in the bibliographic references at the end of your paper.

APA references (bibliographic list)

In APA style, the alphabetical list of works cited is entitled "References." The general principles are as follows:

1. Invert *all* authors' names, and use initials instead of first names. With two or more authors, use an ampersand (&) rather than the word "and." Separate the names with commas. Alphabetize the list by authors' names.
2. Use all authors' names; do not use "et al."
3. Place the date of publication in parentheses immediately after the last author's name.
4. Underline titles and subtitles of books; capitalize only the first word of the title and subtitle (as well as all proper nouns).
5. Do not place titles of articles in quotation marks, and capitalize only the first word of the title and subtitle (and all proper nouns). Capitalize names of periodicals as you would capitalize them ordinarily (see 45c). Underline the volume number of periodicals.
6. Use the abbreviation "p." (or "pp." for plural) before page numbers of magazine and newspaper articles and works in anthologies, but do not use them before page numbers of articles appearing in scholarly journals.
7. You may use a short form of the publisher's name as long as it is easily identifiable.

BASIC FORMAT FOR A BOOK

Linden, E. (1986). <u>Silent partners: The legacy of the ape language experiments</u>. New York: Random House.

TWO OR MORE AUTHORS

Patterson, F., & Linden, E. (1981). <u>The education of Koko</u>. New York: Holt, Rinehart and Winston.

Caplow, T., Bahr, H. M., Chadwick, B. A., Hill,
R., & Williamson, M. H. (1982). <u>Middletown fam-
ilies: Fifty years of change and continuity</u>.
Minneapolis: University of Minnesota Press.

AUTHOR UNKNOWN

Contrasting styles of Reagan and Bush on Middle
East. (1990, June). <u>Moment</u>, pp. 18-19.

CORPORATE AUTHOR When the author is an organization, the publisher is often the same organization. In such a
case, give the publisher's name as "Author."

National Institute of Mental Health. (1976). <u>Be-
havior modification: Perspective on a current
issue</u>. Rockville, MD: Author.

EDITORS

Sebeok, T. A., & Umiker-Sebeok, J. (Eds.). (1980).
<u>Speaking of apes</u>. New York: Plenum Press.

TRANSLATION

Miller, A. (1990). <u>The untouched key: Tracing
childhood trauma in creativity and destructive-
ness</u> (H. and H. Hannum, Trans.). New York:
Doubleday.

EDITION OTHER THAN THE FIRST

Lowery, S. A., & De Fleur, M. L. (1988). <u>Mile-
stones in mass communication research: Media
effects</u> (2nd ed.). New York: Longman.

WORK IN AN ANTHOLOGY

Basso, K. H. Silence in western Apache culture.
    (1970). In P. Giglioli (Ed.), Language and
    social context (pp. 67-86). Harmondsworth,
    England: Penguin.

GOVERNMENT DOCUMENT

U.S. Department of State. (1986). Report to Con-
    gress on voting practices in the United
    Nations. Washington, DC: U.S. Government
    Printing Office.

ARTICLE IN A JOURNAL PAGINATED BY VOLUME

Otto, M. L. (1984). Child abuse: Group treatment
    for parents. Personnel and Guidance Journal,
    62, 336-338.

ARTICLE IN A JOURNAL PAGINATED BY ISSUE

Nichols, R. G. (1986). Word processing and basic
    writers. Journal of Basic Writing, 5(2), 81-97.

ARTICLE IN A MAGAZINE

Seyfarth, R. M. (1982, March-April). Talking with
    monkeys and great apes. International Wild-
    life, pp. 13-18.

ARTICLE IN A NEWSPAPER

Cohen, D. L. (1990, June 20). Counselors in ele-
    mentary schools: Children's "prevention spe-
    cialists." Education Week, pp. 1, 14-16.

LETTER TO A PERIODICAL

Hopi, M., & Young, J. (1990). European policies
     serve to prevent homelessness [Letter to the
     editor]. Public Welfare, 48(1), 5-6.

BOOK REVIEW

Crosby, F. (1990). [Review of Equity and gender:
     The comparable worth debate]. Psychology of
     Women Quarterly, 14, 147-148.

COMPUTER PROGRAM

Professional file [Computer program]. (1988).
     Mountain View, CA: Software Publishing Corpora-
     tion.

VIDEOTAPE

Minasian, S. M. (Producer). (1985). World of the
     sea otter [Videotape]. San Francisco, CA:
     Marine Mammal Fund.

TWO OR MORE WORKS BY THE SAME AUTHOR   Use the author's name for first and subsequent entries. Arrange the entries by date, the earliest first.

     Davis, F. (1973). Inside intuition: What we know
          about nonverbal communication. New York:
          McGraw-Hill.

     Davis, F. (1978). Eloquent animals: A study in an-
          imal communication. New York: Coward,
          McCann & Geoghegan.

TWO OR MORE WORKS BY THE SAME AUTHOR IN THE SAME YEAR Cite the works according to the usual style, and arrange them alphabetically by title. Add lowercase letters beginning with "a," "b," and so on, within the parentheses immediately following the year.

> Eckholm, Erik. (1985a, June 25). Kanzi the chimp:
>
> A life in science. The New York Times, pp. C1,
>
> C3.
>
> Eckholm, Erik. (1985b, June 24). Pygmy chimp readily learns language skill. The New York Times,
>
> pp. A1, B7.

PAGES FROM A SAMPLE PAPER: APA STYLE

Following are two pages and a sample list of references taken from a research paper documented with the APA style of in-text citations.

Somewhere Between the Word and the Sentence:
The Great Apes and the Acquisition of Language

Choosing from among the eighty signs in
American sign language that she had learned, a
chimpanzee named Lucy selected three and signaled
to her trainer, "Roger tickle Lucy." When Roger
failed to respond to her request and signaled instead, "No, Lucy tickle Roger," the chimpanzee
jumped onto his lap and began to tickle him (Desmond, 1979, pp. 43-44). One afternoon, Koko the
gorilla, who was often bored with language lessons, stubbornly and repeatedly signaled "red"
when asked the color of a white towel. She did
this even though she had correctly identified the
color white many times before. At last the gorilla produced "a minute speck of red lint that
had been clinging to the towel" (Patterson & Linden, 1981, pp. 80-81). In Atlanta, when a two-
and-a-half-year-old pygmy chimpanzee's mother was
taken away for breeding, the young chimp amazed
researchers by revealing he had been learning
"out of the corner of his eye" symbols that were
being taught to his mother. He hit the symbols

for both apple and ball on a computerized keyboard and pointed to the objects (Eckholm, 1985a,
p. C1).

These and hundreds of similar scenes played
out over the past twenty-five years make it clear
that the great apes (chimpanzees, pygmy chimpanzees, gorillas, and orangutans) resemble humans
in language abilities more than had previously
been believed. Just how far that resemblance
extends, however, is a matter of some controversy. Researchers agree that apes have acquired
large vocabularies, but they differ sharply in
interpreting the uses to which these vocabularies
have been put. On balance, the evidence sug-
gests--despite the objections of some skeptics--
that apes have used symbols spontaneously and
creatively and have even learned to conceptualize
with them. It is as yet unknown, however, to
what extent they can combine symbols in grammatical patterns.

Though apes lack the vocal ability to produce human sounds, they have acquired fairly

The rest of the paper has been omitted.

Somewhere Between

16

References

Bower, B. (1988). Kanzi extends his speech reach. Science News, 134, 140.

Crail, T. (1981). Apetalk and whalespeak. Los Angeles: Tarcher.

Davis, F. (1978). Eloquent animals: A study in animal communication. New York: Coward, McCann & Geoghegan.

Desmond, A. (1979). The ape's reflexion. New York: Dial Press.

Eckholm, E. (1985a, June 25). Kanzi the chimp: A life in science. The New York Times, pp. C1, C3.

Eckholm, E. (1985b, June 24). Pygmy chimp readily learns language skill. The New York Times, pp. A1, B7.

Patterson, F., & Linden, E. (1981). The education of Koko. New York: Holt, Rinehart and Winston.

Savage-Rumbaugh, S., McDonald, K., Sevcik, R. A., Hopkins, W. D., & Rubert, E. (1986). Spontaneous acquisition and communicative use by chimpanzees (Pan paniscus). Journal of Experimental Psychology, 115, 211-213.

55b   Footnotes or endnotes (an MLA alternative)

Although the *MLA Handbook* treats in-text citations as its preferred style (see 54), it also lists traditional notes as an acceptable alternative.

Notes provide complete publishing information, either at the bottom of the page (footnotes) or at the end of the paper (endnotes). A raised arabic numeral in the text indicates that a quotation, paraphrase, or summary has been borrowed from a source; to find the publishing information for that source, readers consult the footnote or endnote with the corresponding number. Notes are numbered consecutively throughout the paper.

TEXT

For instance, Lana once described a cucumber as "banana which-is green."[9]

NOTE

   [9] Flora Davis, <u>Eloquent Animals: A Study in Animal Communication</u> (New York: Coward, 1978) 300.

The first time you cite a source in your paper, give the full publication information for that work as well as the page number of the specific quotation, paraphrase, or summary. The following examples cover the formats that are most frequently encountered.

BASIC FORMAT FOR A BOOK

   [1] Eugene Linden, <u>Silent Partners: The Legacy of the Ape Language Experiments</u> (New York: Random, 1986) 87.

TWO OR MORE AUTHORS

² Roger Fisher and William Ury, <u>Getting to Yes: Negotiating Agreement Without Giving In</u> (Boston: Houghton, 1981) 108.

BOOK WITH EDITOR OR TRANSLATOR

³ Albert Camus, <u>Lyrical and Critical Essays</u>, trans. Ellen Conroy Kennedy, ed. Philip Thody (New York: Knopf, 1968) 8.

UNKNOWN AUTHOR

⁴ <u>The Times Atlas of the World</u>, 5th ed. (New York: New York Times, 1975) 95.

EDITION OTHER THAN THE FIRST

⁵ Brenda Spatt, <u>Writing from Sources</u>, 3rd ed. (New York: St. Martin's, 1991) 78.

MULTIVOLUME WORK

⁶ Robert Graves, <u>The Greek Myths</u>, 2 vols. (New York: Braziller, 1967) 2: 216.

WORK IN AN ANTHOLOGY

⁷ M. H. Abrams, "English Romanticism: The Spirit of the Age," <u>Romanticism Reconsidered</u>, ed. Northrop Frye (New York: Columbia UP, 1963) 64.

ENCYCLOPEDIA OR DICTIONARY

⁸ Mark S. Frankel, "Human Experimentation: Social and Professional Control," <u>Encyclopedia of Bioethics</u>, 1978 ed.

ARTICLE IN A MAGAZINE

9 Matt Clark, "Medicine: A Brave New World," Newsweek 5 Mar. 1984: 65.

ARTICLE IN A JOURNAL PAGINATED BY VOLUME

10 Mary L. Otto, "Child Abuse: Group Treatment for Parents," Personnel and Guidance Journal 62 (1984): 336.

ARTICLE IN A JOURNAL PAGINATED BY ISSUE

11 Randall G. Nichols, "Word Processing and Basic Writers," Journal of Basic Writing 5.2 (1986): 93.

ARTICLE IN A NEWSPAPER

12 Cynthia Gorney, "When the Gorilla Speaks," Washington Post 31 Jan. 1985: B1.

SUBSEQUENT REFERENCES TO THE SAME SOURCE Subsequent references to a work that has already been cited in a note should be given in shortened form. You need to give only enough information so that the reader can identify which work you are referring to — usually the author's last name and a page number. The abbreviations *ibid.* and *op. cit.* are no longer used.

13 Linden 129.

14 Fisher and Ury 16.

15 The Times Atlas 28.

If you are using more than one work by one author or two works by authors with the same last name, cite the author's last name and a shortened title.

[16] Linden, Silent 53.

[17] Linden, Apes 136.

When you use notes as your method of documentation, you may not need a list of works cited, since complete publishing information is given in the notes themselves. Many professors prefer, however, that you include an alphabetized list of the works cited in the paper or a bibliography of the works you consulted, whether or not they were cited. If you do include a list of works cited or a bibliography, use the MLA style described in 54b.

55c A list of style manuals for various disciplines

The *Bedford Handbook for Writers* describes three commonly used systems of documentation: MLA in-text citations, used in English and the humanities (see 54); APA in-text citations, used in psychology and the social sciences (see 55a); and footnotes or endnotes, an MLA alternative (see 55b). Following is a list of style manuals used in a variety of disciplines.

BIOLOGY

Council of Biology Editors. *CBE Style Manual: A Guide for Authors, Editors, and Publishers in the Biological Sciences.* 5th ed. Bethesda, MD: Council of Biology Editors, 1983.

CHEMISTRY

American Chemical Society. *Handbook for Authors of Papers in American Chemical Society Publications.* Washington, D.C.: American Chemical Society, 1978.

ENGLISH AND THE HUMANITIES (SEE 54.)

Gibaldi, Joseph, and Walter S. Achtert. *MLA Handbook for Writers of Research Papers.* 3rd ed. New York: Modern Language Association of America, 1988.

GEOLOGY

Cochran, Wendell, Peter Fenner, and Mary Hills, eds. *Geowriting: A Guide to Writing, Editing, and Printing in Earth Science.* Alexandria, VA: American Geological Institute, 1984.

LAW

Columbia Law Review. *A Uniform System of Citation.* 14th ed. Cambridge, MA: Harvard Law Review, 1986.

LINGUISTICS

Linguistic Society of America. "LSA Style Sheet." Published annually in the December issue of the *LSA Bulletin.*

MATHEMATICS

American Mathematical Society. *A Manual for Authors of Mathematical Papers.* 7th ed. Providence: American Mathematical Society, 1980.

MEDICINE

International Steering Committee of Medical Editors. "Uniform Requirements for Manuscripts Submitted to Biomedical Journals." *Annals of Internal Medicine* 90 (Jan. 1979): 95-99.

PHYSICS

American Institute of Physics. *Style Manual for Guidance in the Preparation of Papers.* 3rd ed. New York: American Institute of Physics, 1978.

PSYCHOLOGY AND THE SOCIAL SCIENCES (SEE 55A.)

American Psychological Association. *Publication Manual of the American Psychological Association.* 3rd ed. Washington, D.C.: American Psychological Association, 1983.

PART XI

Special Types of Writing

56

Writing arguments

In argumentative writing, you take a stand on a debatable issue. The issue being debated might be a matter of public policy: Should religious groups be allowed to meet on school property? What is the least dangerous way to dispose of nuclear waste? Should a state enact laws rationing medical care? On such questions, reasonable persons can disagree.

Reasonable men and women also disagree about many scholarly issues. Psychologists debate the validity of behaviorism; historians interpret the causes of the Civil War quite differently; biologists conduct genetic experiments to challenge the conclusions of other researchers.

Your goal, in argumentative writing, is to change the way your readers think about a subject or to convince them to take an action that they might not otherwise be inclined to take. Do not assume that your audience already agrees with you; instead, envision skeptical readers who will make up their minds after listening to both sides of the debate. To convince such readers, you will need to build arguments strong enough to stand up to the arguments put forward by your opponents (sometimes called *the opposition*).

56a Plan a strategy.

Although thinking critically about your topic is an important first step in all writing, it is especially important in argumentative writing. Planning a strategy for an argumentative essay is much like planning a debate for a speech class. A good way to begin is to list your arguments and the arguments of the opposition and then consider the likely impact of these arguments on your audience. If the arguments of the opposition look very powerful, you may want to rethink your position. By modifying your initial position — perhaps by claiming less or by proposing a less radical solution to a problem — you may have a greater chance of persuading readers to change their views.

Listing your arguments

Let's say that your tentative purpose (which may change as you think about your audience and the opposition) is to argue in favor of lowering the legal drinking age from twenty-one to eighteen. Here is a list of possible arguments in favor of this point of view.

- Society treats eighteen-year-olds as mature for most purposes.
    - They can vote.
    - They can go away to college.
    - At eighteen, men must register with Selective Service and be available for a possible draft.
- Age is not necessarily an indication of maturity.
- The current drinking age is unfair, since many older Americans were allowed to drink at eighteen.
- An unrealistic drinking age is almost impossible to enforce, and it breeds disrespect for the law.
- In European countries that allow eighteen-year-olds to drink, there is less irresponsible teenage drinking than in our country.

Listing the arguments of the opposition

The next step is to list the key arguments of the opposition. Here are some possible arguments *against* lowering the drinking age to eighteen.

- Teenage drinking frequently leads to drunk driving, which in turn leads to many deaths.

— Teenage drinking sometimes leads to date rape and gang violence.

— Alcoholism is a serious problem in our society, and a delayed drinking age can help prevent it.

— If the legal age were eighteen, many fifteen- and sixteen-year-olds would find a way to purchase alcohol illegally.

If possible, you should talk to someone who disagrees with your view or read some articles that are critical of your position. By familiarizing yourself with the views of the opposition, you can be reasonably sure you have not overlooked an important argument that might be used against you.

Considering your audience

Once you have listed the major arguments on both sides, think realistically about the impact they are likely to have on your intended audience. If your audience is the voting age population in the United States, for example, consider how you might assess some of the arguments of each side of the drinking age question.

Looking at your list, you would see that your audience, which includes many older Americans, might not be impressed by the suggestion that age is no sign of maturity or by the argument that because eighteen-year-olds are old enough to attend college they should be allowed to drink. You would decide to emphasize your other arguments instead. Americans who remember a time when young men were drafted, for example, might be persuaded that it is unfair to ask a man to die for his country but not allow him to drink. And anyone who has heard of Prohibition might be moved by the argument that an unrealistic drinking regulation can breed disrespect for the law.

As for the arguments of the opposition, clearly the first one on the list is the most powerful. Statistics show that drunk driving by teenagers causes much carnage on our highways and that teenagers themselves are frequently the victims. To have any hope of convincing your audience, you would need to take this argument very seriously; it would be almost impossible to argue successfully that reducing highway deaths is not important.

Rethinking your position

After exploring both sides of an argument, you may decide to modify your initial position. Maybe your first thoughts about the issue were oversimplified, too extreme, or mistaken in some other respect. Or maybe, after thinking more about your readers, you see little hope of persuading them of the truth or wisdom of your position.

If you were writing about the drinking age, for example, you might decide to modify your position in light of your audience. To have a better chance of convincing the audience, you could argue that eighteen-year-olds *in the military* should be allowed to drink. Or you could argue that eighteen-year-olds should be allowed to drink beer and wine, not hard alcohol. Or you could link your proposal to new tough laws against drunk driving.

56b Frame a thesis and state your major arguments.

A thesis is a sentence that expresses the main point of an essay. (See 2b.) In argumentative writing, your thesis should clearly state your position on the issue you have chosen to write about. Let's say your issue is the high insurance rates that most companies set for young male drivers. After thinking carefully about your own views, the arguments of the opposition, and your audience (the general public), you might state your position like this:

> Although young male drivers have a high accident rate, insurance companies should not be allowed to discriminate against anyone who has driven for the past two years without a traffic violation.

Notice that this is a debatable point, one about which reasonable persons can disagree. It is not merely a fact (for example, that companies do set higher rates for young males). Nor is it a statement of belief (for example, that differing rates are always unfair). Neither facts nor beliefs can be substantiated by reasons, so they cannot serve as a thesis for an argument.

Once you have framed a thesis, try to state your major arguments, preferably in sentence form. Together, your thesis and your arguments will give you a rough outline of your essay. Consider the following rough outline of an essay written by Julian L. Simon, a business professor at the University of Maryland. Simon argues for an easing of restrictions on immigration into the United States. His thesis frames the issue in economic terms, and his major arguments are economic reasons that support his thesis.

> Thesis: Despite claims that increased immigration would hurt the economy, the evidence strongly suggests that new immigrants strengthen the economy in a variety of ways.

— Immigrants do not cause native unemployment, even among low-paid and minority groups.

— Immigrants do not overuse welfare services.

— Immigrants bring high-tech skills that the economy needs badly.

— Immigration is lower than it was in the peak years at the turn of the century.

— Natural resources and the environment are not at risk from immigration.

— Immigration reduces the social costs of the elderly, which can't be cut.

Some of the sentences in your rough outline might become topic sentences of paragraphs in your final essay. (See 5a.)

56c Draft an introduction that states your position without alienating readers.

In argumentative writing, your introduction should state your position on an issue in a clear thesis sentence (see 2b and 56b), and it should do this without needlessly alienating the audience whom you hope to convince. Where possible, try to establish common ground with readers who may not be in initial agreement with your views.

One student, who argued against allowing prayer in public schools, established common ground with readers who disagreed with her by explaining that she once shared their views. Her introduction ends with a clear thesis that states her current position on the issue.

> During most of my school years, the Lord's Prayer was a part of our opening exercises. I never gave it a second thought, and I never heard anyone complain about it. So when prayer in the schools became an issue in the courts, I was surprised to hear that anyone viewed it as a threat to individual rights or as a violation of the division between church and state. But now that I've thought about it, I would not like to see the practice of prayer in the schools reinstituted.

In her first draft, the student began the introduction like this: "I do not think prayer should be allowed in schools." This sentence clearly stated her position, but its blunt tone was likely to alienate readers who favor school prayer. The student wisely decided to establish common ground with her readers before stating her position. Notice that her new thesis statement, at the end of the introduction, is as clear as her original thesis but has a much more reasonable tone.

One way to establish common ground with readers who disagree with your position is to show that you share common values. If your subject is school prayer, for instance, you might show that even though you oppose allowing prayer in schools, you believe in the value of prayer. The writer of the following introduction successfully used this strategy.

> Although the Supreme Court has ruled against prayer in public schools on First Amendment grounds, many people still feel that prayers should be allowed. These people, most of whom hold strong religious beliefs, are well intentioned. What they fail to realize is that the Supreme Court decision, although it was made on legal grounds, makes good sense on religious grounds as well. Prayer is too important to be trusted to our public schools.

Like the writer of the other introduction about school prayer, this writer sounds reasonable. He states his position clearly and firmly in a thesis at the end of the paragraph, but because he takes into consideration the values of those who disagree with him, readers are likely to approach his essay with an open mind.

56d Support each argument with specific evidence.

When presenting the arguments for your position, you will of course need to back them up with evidence: facts, statistics, examples and illustrations, expert opinion, and so on. Depending on the issue you have chosen to write about, you may or may not need to do some reading to gather evidence. Some argumentative topics, such as whether class attendance should be required at your college or university, can be developed through personal experience and maybe questionnaires or interviews. Other debatable topics, such as the extent to which apes can learn language, require library research.

If any of your evidence is based on reading, you will need to document your sources. Documentation gives credit to your sources and shows readers how to track down the source in case they want to assess its credibility or explore the issue further. The style of documentation used in most English classes is described in 54; two other styles are described in 55. Always find out from your instructor which style he or she prefers.

Using facts and statistics

A fact is something that is known with certainty because it has been objectively verified: The capital of Wyoming is Cheyenne. Carbon has an atomic weight of 12. John F. Kennedy was assassinated on November 22, 1963. Statistics are collections of numerical facts: One-half of U.S. households currently own a VCR. North America holds only 4 percent of the world's proven oil reserves; together, Iraq, Kuwait, and Saudi Arabia own 44 percent.

Most arguments are supported at least to some extent by facts and statistics. For example, if you were arguing against mandatory class attendance, you might include facts about the attendance policies of professors in several disciplines; you could also report statistics on the views of students.

Karen Shaw, the student who wrote the research essay on apes and language that is printed in Part X, gathered facts and statistics from printed sources. When she included them in her essay, she documented them, as in the following example.

```
The gorilla Koko has mastered nearly 200 signs

as measured by the Gardners' strict criterion

(Patterson and Linden 83-84).
```

Shaw got this statistic from *The Education of Koko,* a book by Francine Patterson and Eugene Linden. The parenthetical citation at the end of the sentence includes the last names of the authors and the page numbers on which the information appears. (See 54 for more about documentation.)

Using examples and anecdotes

Examples and anecdotes (illustrative stories) alone rarely prove a point, but when used in combination with other forms of evidence, they flesh out an argument and bring it to life. In an essay arguing against mandatory class attendance, you might give examples of class sessions that were obviously a waste of time, maybe because the professor simply read from the textbook or because you were asked to play games that had nothing to do with the subject.

In her research essay, Karen Shaw used many examples from a variety of sources to show that apes are capable of using language creatively (see page 560), and she includes an anecdote to show that the gorilla Koko apparently jokes with her trainers in sign language (see page 562). Shaw is careful not to conclude too much from the anecdote, however. Although she finds it interesting, she does not view it as absolute proof of apes' language ability.

Citing expert opinion

Although they are no substitute for careful reasoning of your own, the views of an expert can contribute to the force of your argument. You might interview an educational psychologist on learning styles, for example, to help support your argument that class attendance is not the only way to learn. Or, if you were arguing in favor of mandatory class attendance, you might interview a dean to learn about academic goals (such as increased tolerance for persons from other cultures) that can be accomplished only through class attendance.

When you rely on expert opinion, you must document your sources. You can summarize or paraphrase the expert's opinion (see 53d) or you can quote the expert's exact words (see 53e). For important advice on appropriate use of written sources, see the charts on pages 512–515.

56e Anticipate objections and refute opposing arguments.

Readers who already agree with you need no convincing, although a well-argued case for their own point of view is always welcome. But indifferent and skeptical readers may resist your arguments because they have minds of their own. To give up a position that seems reasonable, a reader has to see that there is an even more reasonable one. In addition to presenting your own case, therefore, you should review the chief arguments of the opposition and explain what you think is wrong with them.

There is no best place in an essay to deal with the opposition. Often it is useful to summarize the opposing position early in your essay. After stating your thesis but before developing your own arguments, you might have a paragraph beginning "Critics of this view argue that. . . ." But sometimes a better plan is to anticipate objections as you develop your case paragraph by paragraph. Wherever you decide to deal with opposing arguments, do your best to refute them. Show that those who oppose you are not as persuasive as they claim because their arguments are flawed or because your arguments to the contrary have greater weight.

As you refute opposing arguments, try to establish common ground with readers who are not in initial agreement with your views. If you can show that you share your readers' values, they may be able to switch to your position without giving up what they feel is important. For example, to persuade people opposed to shooting deer, a state wildlife commission would have to show that it too cares about preserving deer and does not want them to die needlessly. Having established these values in common, the commission might be able to persuade critics that a carefully controlled hunting season is good for the deer population because it prevents starvation caused by overpopulation. Likewise, if those opposed to hunting want to persuade the commission to ban the hunting season, they would need to show that the commission could achieve its goals by some other feasible means, such as expanding the deer preserve or increasing the food supply to support an increased herd.

People believe that intelligence and decency support their side of an argument. To change sides, they must continue to feel intelligent and decent. Otherwise they will persist in their opposition.

56f Avoid common mistakes in reasoning.

Certain errors in reasoning occur frequently enough to deserve special attention. In both your reading and your writing, you will want to be alert to common mistakes in inductive and deductive reasoning and to certain mistakes known as logical fallacies.

Using inductive reasoning with care

When you reason inductively, you draw a conclusion from an array of facts. For example, you might conclude that a professor is friendly because he or she smiles frequently and talks to students after class or that fifty-five miles per hour is a safer speed limit than sixty-five miles per hour because there are fewer deaths per accident at that speed.

Inductive reasoning deals in probability, not certainty. For a conclusion based on inductive reasoning to be highly probable, the evidence must be sufficient, representative, and relevant. Consider, for example, how you would decide whether to trust the following conclusion, drawn from evidence gathered in a survey:

> **CONCLUSION** The majority of households in our city would subscribe to cable television if it were available.

EVIDENCE In a recent survey, 356 of the 500 households questioned say they would subscribe to cable television.

Is the evidence sufficient? That depends. In a city of 10,000, the 500 households are a 5 percent sample, sufficient for the purposes of marketing research. But in a city of 2 million, the households would amount to one-fortieth of 1 percent of the population, an inadequate sample on which to base an important decision.

Is the evidence representative? Again, that depends. The cable company would trust the survey if it knew that the sample had been carefully constructed to reflect the age, sex, geographic distribution, and income of the city's population as a whole. If, however, the 500 households were concentrated in one wealthy neighborhood, the company would be wise to question the survey's conclusion.

Is the evidence relevant? The answer is a cautious yes. The survey question is directly linked to the conclusion. A question about the number of hours spent watching television, by contrast, would not be relevant, because it would not be about *subscribing* to *cable* television. In addition, a cautious interpreter of the evidence would want to know whether people who *say* they would subscribe tend to subscribe *in fact.* By looking at marketing research done in other cities, the cable television company could determine — through a new round of inductive reasoning — how many of the 356 households who say they would subscribe are likely in fact to subscribe.

Using deductive reasoning with care

When you reason deductively, you draw a conclusion from two or more assertions (called premises).

The police do not give speeding tickets to people driving less than five miles per hour over the limit. Sam is driving fifty-

nine miles per hour in a fifty-five-mile-per-hour zone.
Therefore, the police will not give Sam a speeding ticket.

The conclusion is true only if the premises are true. If the
police sometimes give tickets for less than five-mile-per-hour
violations or if the speedometer is inaccurate, Sam cannot
safely conclude that he will avoid a ticket.

Deductive reasoning can often be structured in a three-
step argument called a *syllogism*. The three steps are the
major premise, the minor premise, and the conclusion:

1. Anything that increases radiation in the environment is
   dangerous to public health. (major premise)
2. Nuclear reactors increase radiation in the environment.
   (minor premise)
3. Therefore, nuclear reactors are dangerous to public health.
   (conclusion)

The major premise is a generalization. The minor premise is
a specific case. The conclusion follows from applying the generalization to the specific case.

Many deductive arguments do not state one of the premises but rather leave the reader to infer it. In the preceding
example, the conclusion would still sound plausible without
the major premise: *Nuclear reactors increase radiation in the
environment; therefore, they are dangerous to public health.*
A careful reader, however, will see the missing premise and
will question the whole argument if the premise is debatable.

Deductive arguments break down if one of the premises
is not true or if the conclusion does not logically follow from
them. For example, consider this argument:

The deer population in our state should be preserved. During
hunting season hundreds of deer are killed. Therefore, the
hunting season should be discontinued.

To challenge this argument, the state's wildlife commission might agree with both the major and minor premises but question whether the conclusion follows logically from them. True, the deer population should be preserved; true, deer are killed during hunting season. However, in an area where deer have no natural enemies, herds become too large for the forest vegetation to support them. The overpopulated herds strip the leaves and bark from the young trees, killing the trees before dying of starvation themselves. The commission might conclude, therefore, that a limited hunting season helps preserve a healthier and more stable population of deer.

Avoiding logical fallacies

Some errors in reasoning are so common that writers and readers call them by name: hasty generalization, non sequitur, false analogy, and so on. Such errors are known as *logical fallacies.*

HASTY GENERALIZATION A hasty generalization is a conclusion based on insufficient or unrepresentative evidence.

> Deaths from drug overdoses in Metropolis have doubled in the past three years. Therefore, more Americans than ever are dying from drug abuse.

Data from one city do not justify a conclusion about the whole United States.

Many hasty generalizations contain words like *all, every, always,* and *never,* when qualifiers such as *most, many, usually,* and *seldom* would be more accurate. Go over your writing carefully for such general statements and make sure that you have enough data to verify your position or that you qualify the statements.

A *stereotype* is a hasty generalization (usually derogatory) about a group. Examples: Women are bad bosses; politicians are corrupt; people without children are self-centered. Stereotyping is common because of our human tendency to perceive selectively. We tend to see what we want to see; that is, we notice evidence confirming our already formed opinions and fail to notice evidence to the contrary. For example, if you have concluded that politicians are corrupt, your stereotype will be confirmed by occasional news reports of legislators being indicted — even though every day the newspapers describe conscientious officials serving the public honestly and well. Generalizations about people must be based on numerous typical cases and not contradicted by many exceptions. And even conclusions that are generally valid — that Americans tend to place a high value on individual rights, for example — will have significant exceptions because what is generally true about groups of people will not be true of all individuals within those groups.

NON SEQUITUR A non sequitur (Latin for "does not follow") is a conclusion that does not follow logically from preceding statements or that is based on irrelevant data.

Mary loves good food; therefore, she will be an excellent chef.

Mary's love of good food does not guarantee that she will be able to cook it well.

FALSE ANALOGY An analogy points out a similarity between two things that are otherwise dissimilar. Analogies can be an effective means of illustrating a point (see 6b), but they are not proof. In a false analogy, a writer falsely assumes that because two things are alike in one respect, they must be alike in others.

If we can put humans on the moon, we should be able to find a cure for the common cold.

Putting humans on the moon and finding a cure for the common cold are both scientific challenges, but the technical problems confronting medical researchers are quite different from those solved by space scientists.

EITHER . . . OR FALLACY The *either . . . or* fallacy is the suggestion that only two alternatives exist when in fact there are more.

> Either learn how to operate a computer or you won't be able to get a decent job after college.

In fact, many occupations do not require knowledge of computers.

FAULTY CAUSE-AND-EFFECT REASONING Careless thinkers often assume that because one event follows another, the first is the cause of the second. This common fallacy is known as *post hoc*, from the Latin *post hoc, ergo propter hoc*, meaning "after this, therefore because of this." Like a non sequitur, it is a leap to an unjustified conclusion.

> Since Governor Smith took office, unemployment of minorities in the state has decreased by 7 percent. Governor Smith should be applauded for reducing unemployment among minorities.

The writer must show that Governor Smith's policies are responsible for the decrease in unemployment; it is not enough to show merely that the decrease followed the governor's taking office.

Demonstrating the connection between causes and effects is rarely a simple matter. For example, to explain why an introductory chemistry course has a very high failure rate, you would begin by listing possible causes: inadequate preparation of students, poor teaching, large class size, unavailability of qualified tutors, and so on. Next you would need to investigate each possible cause by gathering statistical data. For example, to see whether inadequate preparation of students contributes to the high failure rate, you might do a statistical comparison of the math and science backgrounds of successful and failing students. Or to see whether large class size is a contributing cause, you might run a pilot program of small classes and then compare grades in the small classes with those in the larger ones. Only after investigating all of the possible causes would you be able to weigh the relative impact of each cause and then suggest appropriate remedies.

CIRCULAR REASONING AND BEGGING THE QUESTION   Suppose you go to see a doctor about a rash you suddenly developed. "I have a rash," you say to the doctor. "What is your diagnosis?" The doctor answers, "You have allergitis." When you ask, "What's that?" the doctor replies, "It's a rash." This is an example of circular reasoning: No real information has been introduced; by a trick of semantics you have wound up back where you started.

Like circular reasoning, begging the question is a way of ducking the issue. Instead of supporting the conclusion with evidence and logic, the writer simply restates the conclusion in different language.

> Faculty and administrators should not be permitted to come to student council meetings because student council meetings should be for students only.

The writer has given no reason for this position but has merely repeated the point.

APPEALS TO EMOTION   Many of the arguments we see in the media strive to win our sympathy rather than our intelligent agreement. A TV commercial suggesting that you will be thin and sexy if you drink a certain diet beverage is making a pitch to emotions. So is a political speech that recommends electing John D'Eau because he is a devoted husband and father who fought for his country in Vietnam.

The following passage illustrates several types of emotional appeals.

> This progressive proposal to build a large ski resort in the state park has been carefully researched by Fidelity, the largest bank in the state; furthermore, it is favored by a majority of the local merchants. The only opposition comes from narrow-minded, do-gooder environmentalists who care more about trees than they do about people; one of their leaders was actually arrested for disturbing the peace several years ago.

Words with strong positive or negative connotations, such as *progressive* and *do-gooders*, are examples of *biased language*. Attacking the persons who hold a belief (environmentalists) rather than refuting their argument is called *ad hominem*, a Latin term meaning "to the man." Associating a prestigious name (Fidelity) with the writer's side is called *transfer*. Claiming that an idea should be accepted because a large number of people are in favor (the majority of merchants) is called the *bandwagon appeal*. Bringing in irrelevant issues (the arrest) is a *red herring*, named after a trick used in fox hunts to mislead the dogs by dragging a smelly fish across the trail.

In examining your own and other people's writing for errors of logic, you will find that logical fallacies are frequently not so clear-cut that a casual reader can spot them immediately. Often they show up in combination. To recognize such fallacies in your own writing takes discipline, but you can do it if you train yourself to become a skeptical and demanding reader — the kind of person who measures all claims against the evidence.

EXERCISE 56 – 1

Explain what is illogical in the following brief arguments. It may be helpful to identify the logical fallacy or fallacies by name. Answers to lettered sentences appear in the back of the book.

a. All of my blind dates have been embarrassing disasters, so I know this one will be too.

b. If you're old enough to vote, you're old enough to drink. Therefore, the drinking age should be lowered to eighteen.

c. This country has been run too long by old, out-of-date, out-of-touch, entrenched politicians protecting the special interests that got them elected.

d. It was possible to feed a family of four on $70 a week before Governor Leroy took office and drove up food prices.

e. If you're not part of the solution, you're part of the problem.

1. Whenever I wash my car, it rains. I have discovered a way to end all droughts — get all the people to wash their cars.

2. Our current war on drugs has not worked. Either we should legalize drugs or we should turn the drug war over to our armed forces and let them fight it.

3. College professors tend to be sarcastic. Three of my five professors this semester make sarcastic remarks.

4. Although Ms. Bell's book on Joe DiMaggio was well researched, I doubt that an Australian historian can contribute much to our knowledge of an American baseball player.

5. Self-righteous nonsmoking fanatics have eroded our basic individual freedoms by railroading the passage of oppressive antismoking laws that interfere with our natural right to make our own decisions.

6. If professional sports teams didn't pay athletes such high salaries, we wouldn't have so many kids breaking their legs at hockey and basketball camps.

7. Ninety percent of the students oppose a tuition increase; therefore, the board of trustees should not pass the proposed increase.

8. If the president had learned the lesson of Vietnam, he would realize that sending U.S. troops into a foreign country can only end in disaster.

9. A mandatory ten-cent deposit on bottles and cans will eliminate litter because everyone I know will return the containers for the money rather than throw them away.
10. Soliciting money to save whales and baby seals is irresponsible when thousands of human beings can't afford food and shelter.

57

Writing about literature

Most of us know how to read and respond to literature — novels, stories, poems, and plays — in an informal way. "I like it," we say. "What was it about?" we ask. "What made it so powerful?" we might want to know. The purpose of the literary paper is to take our informal judgments about a work and, through reflection and analysis, transform them into reasoned, compelling arguments.

All good writing about literature attempts to answer a question, spoken or unspoken, about the text: "Is Huckleberry Finn a hero?" "Why doesn't Hamlet kill his uncle sooner?" "What makes Emily Dickinson's poems so popular?" The goal of a literary essay should be to answer such questions with a meaningful interpretation, presented forcefully and persuasively.

57a Get involved in the work; be an active reader.

Read the work closely and carefully. Think of the work as speaking to you: What is it telling you? Asking you? Trying to make you feel?

If the work provides an introduction and footnotes, read them attentively. They may be a source of important information. Use the dictionary to look up words unfamiliar to you or words with subtle nuances that may affect the work's meaning.

Rereading is a central part of the process. You should read short works several times, first to get an overall impression and then again to focus on meaningful details. With longer works, such as novels or three-act plays, read the most important chapters or scenes more than once while keeping in mind the work as a whole.

As you read and reread, interact with the work by posing questions and looking for answers. The chart on pages 626–627 suggests some questions about literature that may help you become a more active reader.

Annotating the work and taking notes

Annotating the work is a way to focus your reading. The first time through, you may want to pencil a check mark next to passages you find particularly significant. On a more careful rereading, pay particular attention to these passages and jot down your ideas and reactions in a notebook or (if the book is your own) in the margins of the page.

Here is one student's annotation of a short story by Herman Melville:

No first name? *a person who copies legal documents by hand*

Bartleby the Scrivener: A Story of Wall Street

hesitating

I am a (rather) elderly man. The (nature of my) *verbose*

(avocations) for the last thirty years, has brought *style*

hesitating me into (more than ordinary contact) with (what would)

again (seem) an interesting and somewhat singular set of

men, of whom, as yet, (nothing, that I know of,) has *sure of*

ever been written--I mean, the law-copyists, or *anything?*

scriveners. I have known very many of them, *Even the*

punctuation professionally and privately, and, if I pleased, *makes him*

could relate divers histories, at which good- *seem hesitant.*

more natured gentlemen (might) smile, and sentimental

caution souls (might) weep. But I waive the biographies of

all other scriveners, for a few passages in the *now he*

life of Bartleby, who was a scrivener, the strang- *knows —*

est I ever saw, or heard of. *takes a stand*

Isn't he

Notice how the student has responded to unfamiliar words, raised questions, and noted recurring patterns of language. These annotations may lead the student to an interpretation based on the narrator's habits of speech.

Note taking is also an important part of rereading a work of literature. In your notes you can try out ideas and develop your perspective on the work. Here are some notes one student took on a story by Edgar Allan Poe:

"The Fall of the House of Usher"

House of Usher has two meanings — the building and the family

seeing the building has an emotional impact on the narrator: "with the first glimpse of the building, a sense of insufferable gloom pervaded my spirit"

narrator uses descriptive language that evokes his feelings — "dull," "dark," "soundless," "dreary," "melancholy," "insufferable gloom"

produces feeling of depression in reader too

Who is this narrator? What is his relationship to the Ushers?

Such notes, consisting of observations and questions to yourself, are the raw material out of which you will build an interpretation.

Forming an interpretation

After getting a clearer understanding of the work through rereading and jotting notes, you are ready to start forming an interpretation. Look through your notes and annotations for recurring insights about some aspect of the work, perhaps about its characters, theme, pattern of imagery, or central conflict. Look for insights that reveal meanings in the work that were not obvious to you on a first reading, and make sure you have plenty of details and examples to support your interpretation.

In forming an interpretation, it is important to focus on a central issue. You should avoid trying to do several things at once. You may think, for example, that *Huckleberry Finn* is a great book because it contains brilliant descriptions of scenery, has a lot of humorous moments, but also tells a serious story of one boy's development. This is an interesting, complex response to the work, but your job in writing an essay will be to close in on one issue that you can develop into a sustained, in-depth argument. Your essay's focus might be on how Mark Twain uses humor to make a point or on why Huck's emotional growth is important to the novel's theme or even on how the long passages of scenic description break up the story's action.

57b   Plan your essay.

Think ahead about your essay's purpose, length, and scope. What will you be trying to accomplish? Most short essays necessarily deal with either a broad question about a short work (How does language function in Gwendolyn Brooks's "We Real Cool"? How does James Joyce's "The Dead" confront traditions of love and romance? What might the moth symbolize in Virginia Woolf's "The Death of the Moth"?) or a narrow question about a long work (How does Dickens portray lawyers in *Great Expectations*? How is Hell depicted in *Paradise Lost*? What is the purpose of the comic scenes in *Macbeth*?). Don't take on more than you can handle; you cannot give an exhaustive explanation of the significance of a six-hundred-page novel in a five-page essay.

In addition to thinking about your essay's purpose, length, and scope, spend some time planning its focus and shape. As with any piece of writing, you can best do this by drafting a tentative thesis and sketching an outline. (See also 1c and 1d.)

Questions to ask about literature

GENRE

What kind of work is it? Is it a novel, a short story, a play, a film, a poem? Is it a specialized genre that has conventions of its own, such as a mystery novel, a tragedy, a western, or a sonnet?

PLOT

What happens? Are events revealed in chronological order or are there flashbacks? What patterns do you find in the plot's development? Is there a central conflict? When do events come to a climax? Are there any subplots? Which events are foreshadowed, and which take the reader by surprise? Are any events ironic?

SETTING

When and where do events take place? Does the setting create an atmosphere that reinforces the plot, gives an insight into a character, or hints at the theme of the work?

CHARACTER

Who are the central characters? What seems to motivate them? Which characters change significantly, and what, if anything, have they learned from their experiences? Which characters are well rounded and which are relatively "flat" or stereotypical? How are conflicts between characters resolved?

Questions about literature (continued)

POINT OF VIEW

In a story or novel, who is the narrator and from what point of view does he or she relate the action? In fiction, the most common points of view are *first person* (the narrator is a character in the story who uses the word *I*), *omniscient* (the narrator is the author, who knows things no character possibly could), and *limited omniscient* (the narrator is the author but views most of the action from the perspective of one of the characters). Is the narrator perhaps innocent or naive or self-deceptive?

In a poem, who is the speaker? The speaker may be the poet, but often it is a *persona*, a voice or role that the poet assumes, possibly for dramatic effect. To whom, if anyone, is the voice in the poem speaking?

THEME

What is the overall meaning of the work — the central insight about people or the truth about life that it illustrates?

IMAGERY

What sensory images does the writer evoke most often? How do such images contribute to the work's meaning? Do any recurring images seem symbolic?

NOTE: For more technical matters, such as rhyme and meter in poetry, consult a literature textbook or a reference work on literature.

Drafting a tentative thesis

Your thesis statement should be a strong, assertive summary of your interpretation. Consider, for example, the following successful thesis statements taken from student essays.

> In Stephen Crane's gripping tale "The Open Boat," four men lost at sea discover not only that nature is indifferent to their fate but that their own particular talents make little difference as they struggle for survival.

> Although Medea professes great love for her children, Euripides gives us reason to suspect her sincerity: Medea does not hesitate to use the children as weapons in her bloody battle with Jason, and from the outset she displays little real concern for their fate.

> Obsessed by the desire for revenge, Montresor hopes not only to punish Fortunato but in doing so to avoid capture, demonstrate his cleverness, and degrade his victim.

As in other writing, the thesis of a literary paper cannot be too factual (As a runaway slave, Jim is in danger from the law), too broad (One major theme of American literature is discovery), or too vague (Shakespeare was a brilliant man). (See also 2b.)

In a literary essay, your thesis should usually appear in your introductory paragraph. In the following example, the student writer's thesis is italicized.

> In *Electra*, Euripides depicts two women who have had too little control over their lives. Electra, ignored by her mother, Clytemnestra, has been married off to a farmer and treated more or less like a slave. Clytemnestra has fared even worse. Her husband, Agamemnon, has slashed the throat of their daughter Iphigenia as a sacrifice to the gods. *The experience of powerlessness has taught mother and daughter two very different lessons: Electra has learned the value of*

> traditional, conservative sex roles for women, but
> Clytemnestra has learned just the opposite.

Sketching an outline

Your thesis may strongly suggest a method of organization, in which case you will have little difficulty jotting down your essay's key points. For example, one of the thesis statements given earlier, based on Poe's "The Cask of Amontillado," suggested this informal outline:

> Thesis: Obsessed by the desire for revenge, Montresor hopes not only to punish Fortunato but in doing so to avoid capture, demonstrate his cleverness, and degrade his victim.

> — Montresor's obvious motive — to punish Fortunato for a perceived insult
> — Simple punishment not enough for Montresor, who has other motives as well
>   — to avoid capture
>   — to demonstrate his cleverness
>   — to degrade his victim

After checking through his notes to make sure he had enough material to develop the points listed in his informal outline, the student was ready to begin drafting his essay.

If your thesis does not by itself suggest a method of organization, turn to your notes and begin putting them into categories that relate to the thesis. The student who drafted the tentative thesis based on Euripides' play *Medea* (see page 628) constructed the following formal outline from her notes:

> Thesis: Although Medea professes great love for her children, Euripides gives us reason to suspect her sincerity: Medea does not hesitate to use the children as weapons in her bloody battle with Jason, and from the outset she displays little real concern for their fate.

    I. From the very beginning of the play, Medea is a less than ideal mother.
       A. Her first words about the children are hostile.
       B. Her first actions suggest indifference.

    II. In three scenes Medea appears to be a loving mother, but in each of these scenes we have reason to doubt her sincerity.

    III. Throughout the play, as she plots her revenge, Medea's overriding concern is not her children but her reputation.
       A. Fearing ridicule, she is proud of her reputation as one who can "help her friends and hurt her enemies."
       B. Her obsession with reputation may stem from the Greek view of reputation as a means of immortality.

    IV. After she kills her children, Medea reveals her real concern.
       A. She shows no remorse.
       B. She revels in Jason's agony over their death.

Whether to use a formal or an informal outline is to some extent a matter of personal preference. For most purposes, you will probably find that an informal outline is sufficient, perhaps even preferable. (See 1d.)

57c Support your interpretation with specific evidence from the text.

Although anyone can express an opinion about a literary work, your task in literary analysis is to find examples in the text that confirm the validity of your interpretation and to cite them forcefully enough to convince others of the worth of your interpretation.

    As a rule, each paragraph in the body of your essay should begin with a topic sentence that is clearly interpretive; often it will state one of the points listed in your outline. The rest of the paragraph should consist of details and perhaps quotations in support of your interpretation. Consider, for example, the following student paragraph, which develops one of the points in the preceding outline.

> A woman rejected by the man she loves, Medea is highly sensitive to ridicule. She fears that unless she is hard-boiled, unless she commits the most hideous of crimes in vengeance for Jason's treatment of her, people will laugh at her. Early in the play she says that if she should die in the course of her revenge plot, she would give her enemies "cause for laughter" (line 383). A bit later she tells herself, "Never/Shall you be mocked by Jason's Corinthian wedding,/Whose father was noble, grandfather Helius" (404–6). Her first explanation for her plan to kill the children is "For it is not bearable to be mocked by enemies" (797). When later she is debating whether to kill the children, she asks herself, "Do I want to let go/My enemies unhurt and be laughed at for it?/I must face this thing" (1049–51). Finally, facing Jason after she has killed the children, Medea proclaims, "No, it was not to be that you should scorn my love,/And pleasantly live your life through, laughing at me" (1354–55).

Notice that although the examples in this paragraph are given in chronological order, the student is not simply summarizing the story's plot. Instead, she uses the examples to support an interpretation: that Medea, as portrayed by Euripides, is indeed "highly sensitive to ridicule."

Avoiding simple plot summary

In a literary essay, it is tempting to rely heavily on plot summary and avoid interpretation. You can resist this temptation by paying special attention to your topic sentences. If the opening sentence of a paragraph in the body of your essay states a fact instead of announcing an interpretation, you probably need to rethink your approach. The following rough-draft topic sentence, for instance, led to a plot summary rather than an interpretation.

> As they drift down the river on a raft, Huckleberry and the runaway slave Jim have many philosophical discussions.

The student's revised topic sentence, which announces an interpretation, is much better:

> This theme of dawning moral awareness is reinforced by the many philosophical discussions between Huck and Jim, the runaway slave, as they drift down the river on a raft.

Usually a little effort is all that is needed to make the difference between a plot summary that goes nowhere and a focused, forceful interpretation. As with all forms of writing, revision is key.

57d Observe the conventions of literary papers.

When you are writing a literary paper, it is important to observe certain conventions so that your readers' attention will be focused directly on your argument, not on the details of your presentation.

Referring to authors and titles

The first time you make reference to authors, refer to them by their first and last names: "Virginia Woolf was one of England's most important novelists." In subsequent references, use their last names only: "Woolf's early work was largely overlooked." Do not refer to the author by his or her first name; as a rule, do not use titles such as Mr. or Ms. or Dr.

Titles of short stories, essays, and most poems are put in quotation marks: "The Dead" by James Joyce; "The Death of the Moth" by Virginia Woolf; "High Windows" by Philip Larkin. (See 37d.) Titles of novels, nonfiction books, plays, and epics or other long poems are underlined to indicate italics: *Heart of Darkness* by Joseph Conrad; *I Know Why the Caged Bird Sings* by Maya Angelou; *Macbeth* by William Shakespeare; *Howl* by Allen Ginsberg. (See 42a.)

Referring to characters and events

Refer to each character by the name most often used for him or her in the work. If, for instance, a character's name is Lambert Strether and he is always referred to as "Strether," do not call him "Lambert" or "Mr. Strether." Similarly, write "Lady Macbeth," not "Mrs. Macbeth."

When describing fictional events in a work of literature, use the present tense: "Octavia *demands* blind obedience from James and from all of her children. When James and Ty *catch* two redbirds in their trap, they *want* to play with them; Octavia, however, *has* other plans for the birds." (See also 13b and 28a.)

Referring to parts of works

Be as accurate as possible when referring to subdivisions of a literary work. Avoid using phrases like "the part where." Instead give specific references by using the appropriate descriptive terms: "the final stanza," "the scene in which Hamlet confronts his mother," "the passage that refers to Jane Austen," and so on.

When referring to a specific sentence or paragraph in prose (a novel, story, or nonfiction work), use a page number in a parenthetical notation: "It seemed as if this were the Loom of Time," says Ishmael (185). With poems, refer to specific lines: "Shall I compare thee to a summer's day?" asks Shakespeare (line 1). When discussing a play, give the act number, scene number, and line number, if there is one, separated by periods. Early in *Hamlet*, the stage is set for the appearance of the ghost (1.1.1–12). "Everything that matters in this town has fallen into the hands of a few bureaucrats," says Hovstad in Ibsen's *An Enemy of the People* (1.2). (See 54a.)

Formatting quotations

If a prose quotation takes up fewer than four typed lines, put it in quotation marks and run it into the text of your essay. If it is four lines or longer, set it off from your text by indenting ten spaces from the left margin; when a quotation has been set off from the text, quotation marks are not needed. (See 37b.)

Enclose quotations of three or fewer lines of poetry in quotation marks within your text, and indicate line breaks by a slash. (See 39e.) When you quote more than three lines of poetry, set the quotation off from the text and omit the quotation marks. (See 37b.)

57e If you use secondary sources, document them appropriately and avoid plagiarism.

Many literary essays do not rely on secondary sources—works other than the literary text under discussion. For an example of an essay without secondary sources, see pages 637–641.

Other literary essays use some ideas from sources such as articles or books of literary criticism, biographies of the author, the author's own essays and autobiography, and histories of the era in which the work was written. (For an example of a paper that uses secondary sources, see pages 643–651.) Even if you use secondary sources, your main goal should always be to develop your own understanding and interpretation of the literary work.

Whenever you use secondary sources, you must document them and you must avoid plagiarism. Plagiarism is unacknowledged borrowing — whether intentional or unintentional — of a source's words or ideas. (See 53d.)

Documenting sources

Most literary essays are documented with the system recommended by the Modern Language Association (MLA). This system of documentation is discussed in detail in 54, which is easy to find because its pages have a vertical band in color. For other systems of documentation, see 55.

An MLA in-text citation usually combines a signal phrase with a page number in parentheses:

SAMPLE MLA IN-TEXT CITATION
Arguing that fate has little to do with the tragedy that befalls Oedipus, Bernard Knox writes that "the catastrophe of Oedipus is that he discovers his own identity; and for his discovery he is first and last responsible" (6).

The signal phrase prepares readers for the quotation and names the author; the number in parentheses is the page on which the quotation appears.

The in-text citation is used in combination with a list of works cited at the end of the paper. Anyone interested in knowing the other publishing information about the source can consult the list of works cited. Here, for example, is the works cited entry for the work referred to in the sample in-text citation:

SAMPLE ENTRY IN THE LIST OF WORKS CITED

Knox, Bernard. Oedipus at Thebes: Sophocles'

Tragic Hero and His Time. New York: Norton,

1971.

As you document sources with in-text citations, consult 54a; as you construct your list of works cited, consult 54b.

Avoiding plagiarism

The rules about plagiarism are the same for literary papers as for other research writing. It is wrong to use other writers' ideas or language without giving credit to your source. If an interpretation was suggested to you by another critic's work or if an obscure point was clarified by someone else's research, it is your responsibility to cite the source. If you have borrowed any phrases or sentences from your source, you must put them in quotation marks and credit the author.

For important tips on avoiding plagiarism, see 53d and the charts on pages 512–515.

On the following pages are two sample essays. The first, by Margaret Peel, has no secondary sources. (Langston Hughes's "Ballad of the Landlord," the poem on which the essay is based, appears on page 642.) The second essay, by Jim Dixon, is an example of a paper that has used secondary sources.

reasonable complaint and a gentle reminder that the
complaint is already a week old: "My roof has sprung a
leak. / Don't you 'member I told you about it / Way
last week?" (lines 2-4). In the second stanza, he
appeals diplomatically to the landlord's self-
interest: "These steps is broken down. / When you come
up yourself / It's a wonder you don't fall down"
(6-8). In the third stanza, when the landlord has
responded to his complaints with a demand for rent
money, the tenant becomes more forceful, but his voice
is still reasonable: "Ten Bucks you say is due? /
Well, that's Ten Bucks more'n I'll pay you / Till you
fix this house up new" (10-12).

    The fourth stanza marks a shift in the tone of
the argument. At this point the tenant responds more
emotionally, in reaction to the landlord's threats to
evict him. By the fifth stanza, the tenant has un-
leashed his anger: "Um-huh! You talking high and
mighty" (17). Hughes uses an exclamation point for
the first time; the tenant is raising his voice at
last. As the argument gets more heated, the tenant
finally resorts to the language of violence: "You
ain't gonna be able to say a word / If I land my fist
on you" (19-20).

    These are the last words the tenant speaks in the
poem. Perhaps Hughes wants to show how black people

SAMPLE ESSAY (WITHOUT SECONDARY SOURCES)

Peel 1

Margaret Peel

Professor Welch

English 102

February 2, 1991

Opposing Voices in "Ballad of the Landlord"

Langston Hughes's "Ballad of the Landlord" is
narrated through four voices, each with its own perspective on the poem's action. These opposing
voices--of a tenant, a landlord, the police, and the
press--dramatize a black man's experience in a society
dominated by whites.

The main voice in the poem is that of the tenant,
who, as the last line tells us, is black. The tenant
is characterized by his informal, nonstandard speech.
He uses slang ("Ten Bucks"), contracted words (_'member_,
more'n), and nonstandard grammar ("These steps is
broken down"). This colloquial English suggests the
tenant's separation from the world of convention,
represented by the formal voices of the police and the
press, which appear later in the poem.

Although the tenant uses nonstandard English, his
argument is organized and logical. He begins with a

who threaten violence are silenced. When a new voice
is introduced--the landlord's--the poem shifts to
italics:

> Police! Police!
>
> Come and get this man!
>
> He's trying to ruin the government
>
> And overturn the land! (21-24)

This response is clearly an overreaction to a small
threat. Instead of dealing with the tenant directly,
the landlord shouts for the police. His hysterical
voice--marked by repetitions and punctuated with exclamation points--reveals his disproportionate fear
and outrage. And his conclusions are equally excessive: This black man, he claims, is out to "ruin the
government" and "overturn the land." Although the
landlord's overreaction is humorous, it is sinister as
well, because the landlord knows that, no matter how
excessive his claims are, he has the police and the
law on his side.

In line 25, the regular meter and rhyme of the
poem break down, perhaps showing how an arrest dis-
rupts everyday life. The "voice" in lines 25-29 has
two parts: the clanging sound of the police ("Copper's
whistle! / Patrol bell!") and, in sharp contrast,
the unemotional, factual tone of a police report
("Arrest. / Precinct Station. / Iron cell").

The last voice in the poem is the voice of the
press, represented in newspaper headlines: "MAN
THREATENS LANDLORD / TENANT HELD NO BAIL / JUDGE GIVES
NEGRO 90 DAYS IN COUNTY JAIL (31-33). Meter and
rhyme return here, as if to show that once the tenant
is arrested, life can go on as usual. The language
of the press, like that of the police, is cold and
distant, and it gives the tenant less and less status.
In line 31, he is a "man"; in line 32, he has been
demoted to a "tenant"; and in line 33, he has become a
"negro," or just another statistic.

By using four opposing voices in "Ballad of the
Landlord," Hughes effectively dramatizes different
views of minority assertiveness. To the tenant, assertiveness is informal and natural, as his language
shows; to the landlord, it is a dangerous threat, as
his hysterical response suggests. The police response is, like the language that describes it, short
and sharp. Finally, the press's view of events, represented by the headlines, is distant and unsympa-
thetic.

By the end of the poem, we understand the
predicament of the black man. Exploited by the landlord, politically oppressed by those who think he's
out "to ruin the government," physically restrained by
the police and the judicial system, and denied his

individuality by the press, he is saved only by his
own sense of humor. The very title of the poem suggests his--and Hughes's--sense of humor. The tenant
is singing a <u>ballad</u> to his oppressors, but this ballad
is no love song. It portrays the oppressors, through
their own voices, in an unflattering light: the landlord as cowardly and ridiculous, the police and press
as dull and soulless. The tenant may lack political
power, but he speaks with vitality, and no one can say
he lacks dignity or the spirit to survive.

Langston Hughes
Ballad of the Landlord

Landlord, landlord,
My roof has sprung a leak.
Don't you 'member I told you about it
Way last week?

Landlord, landlord,
These steps is broken down.
When you come up yourself
It's a wonder you don't fall down.

Ten Bucks you say I owe you?
Ten Bucks you say is due?
Well, that's Ten Bucks more'n I'll pay you
Till you fix this house up new.

What? You gonna get eviction orders?
You gonna cut off my heat?
You gonna take my furniture and
Throw it in the street?

Um-huh! You talking high and mighty.
Talk on—till you get through.
You ain't gonna be able to say a word
If I land my fist on you.

Police! Police!
Come and get this man!
He's trying to ruin the government
And overturn the land!

Copper's whistle!
Patrol bell!
Arrest.

Precinct Station.
Iron cell.
Headlines in press:

MAN THREATENS LANDLORD

TENANT HELD NO BAIL

JUDGE GIVES NEGRO 90 DAYS IN COUNTY JAIL

SAMPLE ESSAY (WITH SECONDARY SOURCES)

Jim Dixon

Professor Goldsmith

Literature 110

October 12, 1990

Family as Theater in

Eudora Welty's "Why I Live at the P.O."

The outspoken narrator of Eudora Welty's "Why I Live at the P.O.," known to us only as "Sister," intends to convince us--the world at large--that her family has "turned against" her, led on by her sister, Stella-Rondo. To escape her family, she explains, she has left home and now lives at the P.O., where she is postmistress. As she delivers her monologue, the narrator reveals more about herself than she intends. We see her as a self-centered young woman who enjoys picking fights and provoking melodramatic scenes in which she is the center of attention. Not too far into the story, we realize that others in the family behave as melodramatically as Sister does, and we begin to wonder why. The story's setting may provide the answer: In a small town in Mississippi, sometime after World War II and before television, entertainment is scarce. The members of this family cope with isolation and boredom by casting themselves in a con-

tinuing melodrama, with each person stealing as many
scenes as possible.

   The story's plot, its point of view, and its
characterization all contribute to this theme of the
family as theater. The plot is arranged in scenes,
almost as if it were a theatrical performance, with
Sister playing the starring role. Each scene focuses
on a family member "turning against" her. Scene 1
begins like this: "So the first thing Stella-Rondo did
at the table was turn Papa-Daddy against me" (Welty,
"Why" 47). To announce scene 2, Sister uses similar
phrasing: "Papa-Daddy . . . tried to turn Uncle Rondo
against me" (Welty, "Why" 48). Scene 3 concludes
with another echo: "Stella-Rondo hadn't done a thing
but turn [Mama] against me" (Welty, "Why" 51). And
the final echo, at the end of scene 4, marks the dramatic climax: "There I was with the whole entire house
on Stella-Rondo's side and turned against me" (Welty,
"Why" 52).

   That the story is arranged in dramatic scenes is
no accident. Such stories impressed Eudora Welty as
a child. Describing the stories told by one of her
mother's friends, Welty writes, "What I loved about
her stories was that everything happened in scenes.
I might not catch on to what the root of the trouble
was . . . but my ear told me it was dramatic" (One

14). This same storyteller seems to have inspired Welty to use the first-person point of view in "Why I Live at the P.O." "Years later," writes Welty, "beginning with my story 'Why I Live at the P.O.,' I wrote reasonably often in the form of a monologue that takes possession of the speaker. How much more gets told besides" (<u>One</u> 14)!

The first-person point of view is crucial to the theme of Welty's story. It is both quicker and funnier to <u>show</u> that the narrator is self-centered and melodramatic than it would be to <u>tell</u> it. Sister is definitely the star in the melodrama. She begins her tale with "I," and every event is made to revolve around herself, even her sister's marriage:

> I was getting along fine with Mama, Papa-Daddy and Uncle Rondo until my sister Stella-Rondo just separated from her husband and came back home again. Mr. Whitaker! Of course I went with Mr. Whitaker first, when he first appeared here in China Grove, taking "Pose Yourself" photos, and Stella-Rondo broke us up. (Welty, "Why" 46)

Sister's monologue is, in the words of critic Ann Romines, "a highly elaborated weapon" ("How" 96). Consider, for example, the many catty remarks Sister makes about her enemies: She calls Stella-Rondo's

Mr. Whitaker "this photographer with the popeyes,"
describes Papa-Daddy as someone who "sulks," and says
that Mama "weighs two hundred pounds and has real tiny
feet" (Welty, "Why" 46, 50). As for Stella-Rondo,
the narrator tells us that she uses "cheap Kress
tweezers," her kimono is "some terrible-looking flesh-
colored contraption," and she has brought home "a
peculiar-looking child" (Welty, "Why" 50, 49, 50).

Clearly the narrator's descriptions are exaggerated, and because of this we may be tempted to view
her account of events with skepticism. On the whole,
however, she seems to be right when she tells us that
the entire family has "turned against" her. Much of
the story is presented in dialogue that shows her
family picking on her, and it is unlikely that Welty
would have her completely fabricate the dialogue. In
The Eye of the Story, Welty tells us that a story may
mean what it says or it may mean more than it says,
but "it is not all right, not in good faith, for
things not to mean what they say" (160).

This is not to suggest that the narrator's per-
ceptions of things are always on the mark. She is
probably kidding herself when she announces, at the
beginning of the story, that everything was going
well until Stella-Rondo arrived, because bickering
is clearly a way of life in her family. Her self-

deception is strongest, however, at the end of the
story. "I want the world to know I'm happy," she
proclaims, but we know this is not true. As she herself has just told us, her family makes up nearly the
entire population of China Grove, and China Grove,
whether she likes it or not, is her world. She cannot be happy apart from it. If she wants anyone to
hear her monologue, she will have to return home.
Even her curiosity will tempt her to return home,
though she does not yet see this. "Stella-Rondo may
be telling the most horrible tales in the world about
Mr. Whitaker," she says, "but I haven't heard them"
(Welty, "Why" 56). It is obvious to us that she very
much wants to hear them.

Although the narrator is self-deceptive, she is
not crazy. Welty herself has stated that the narrator is excitable but sane:

> It never occurred to me while I was writing
> this story (and it still doesn't) that I was
> writing about someone in serious mental
> trouble. I was trying to write about the
> way people who live away off from nowhere
> have to amuse themselves by dramatizing
> every situation that comes along by exag-
> gerating it. (Prenshaw 19)

The narrator is not the only one in her family to

exaggerate a situation for dramatic effect. All of
the other key players--Papa-Daddy, Mama, Uncle Rondo,
and Stella-Rondo--do so as well. Papa-Daddy is eager
to steal the first scene. Reacting to Stella-Rondo's
misrepresentation of a remark the narrator has made
about his beard, he plays the role of outraged victim
and even manufactures an insult to keep the attention
on himself. "'Bird's nest'--is that what you call
it?" he says, even though no one has suggested that
his beard resembles a bird's nest (Welty, "Why" 47).
When Stella-Rondo's daughter, two-year-old Shirley T.,
finally grabs center stage, Papa-Daddy retreats to his
hammock in a fit of pique, but only after delivering
this melodramatic exit line: "You can all sit here and
remember my words: I'll never cut off my beard as long
as I live, even one inch, and I don't appreciate it in
you at all" (Welty, "Why" 48).

Mama views the return of her prodigal daughter,
Stella-Rondo, as a moment of high drama. As the narrator puts it, "Mama said she like to made her drop
dead for a second" (Welty, "Why" 46). Although Mama
claims to be "ashamed" of Stella-Rondo for not writing
to the family about Shirley T., she is so effusive in
her praise that we, like the narrator, feel she is
play-acting. And we know she is play-acting when she
claims to believe that Shirley T. is adopted, because

we learn from her later comments that she knows very
well whose child she is. Like the other members of
the family, Mama is quick to pick a fight and provoke
a scene. When the narrator begins digging up her
four-o'clocks to replant at the P.O., Mama's response
is theatrical. Raising the window, she shouts,
"Those happen to be my four-o'clocks. Everything
planted in that star is mine. I've never known you
to make anything grow in your life" (Welty, "Why" 53).

Like everyone else in the family, Uncle Rondo is
not about to be ignored. Making a dramatic entrance
in Stella-Rondo's flesh-colored kimono, he announces,
"I'm poisoned." He has just drunk a bottle of medicine (the main ingredient being alcohol, no doubt),
something he does every Fourth of July. Feeling
dizzy and out of sorts, he plays the role of the in-
valid. Again like the other members of his family,
Uncle Rondo enjoys a fight. When Stella-Rondo tells
him that the narrator has said he looks like a fool in
the flesh-colored negligee (a lie, since Stella-Rondo
herself has said this), he responds with a temper
tantrum. As the narrator describes the scene, he
"tears off the kimono and throws it down on the dirty
floor and puts his foot on it. It had to be sent all
the way to Jackson to the cleaners and re-pleated"
(Welty, "Why" 52). As if he hasn't already caused

enough excitement, the next morning Uncle Rondo throws
a package of firecrackers into the narrator's bedroom,
getting--he thinks--just revenge for the perceived
insult.

Stella-Rondo has gained everyone's attention
simply by returning home, after a two-year absence,
with Shirley T. in tow. This attention, however, is
not enough. Perhaps better than anyone else at picking fights, Stella-Rondo stirs up trouble: fabricating
the story of Shirley T.'s being adopted, misrepresenting the narrator's words about Papa-Daddy's beard,
reacting with an exaggerated sense of injury when she
sees Uncle Rondo in her kimono, and lying to Uncle
Rondo to get her sister into trouble.

As Welty has been careful to show us, the narrator is not the only self-centered, melodramatic member
of this family. Given the family history, we can be
fairly sure that things will soon be back to normal.
The narrator will move back home, and the family,
welcoming the diversion, will no doubt find a way of
turning her homecoming into a new round of excitement.

Dixon 9

Works Cited

Prenshaw, Peggy Whitman, ed. <u>Conversations with
  Eudora Welty</u>. Jackson: UP of Mississippi,
  1984.

Romines, Ann. "How Not to Tell a Story." <u>Eudora
  Welty: Eye of the Storyteller</u>. Ed. Dawn
  Trouard. Kent: Kent State UP, 1989. 94-104.

Welty, Eudora. <u>The Eye of the Story: Selected Essays
  and Reviews</u>. New York: Vintage, 1979.

---. <u>One Writer's Beginnings</u>. New York: Warner,
  1984.

---. "Why I Live at the P.O." <u>The Collected Stories
  of Eudora Welty</u>. New York: Harcourt, 1980.
  46-56.

58

Business letters, résumés, and memos

58a Business letters

In writing a business letter be direct, clear, and courteous, but do not hesitate to be firm if the situation calls for it. State your purpose or request at the beginning of the letter and include only pertinent information in the body. Follow conventions of form and usage, and avoid spelling errors.

Business letters usually follow one of three patterns: full block, block, and semiblock. In full block form, letterhead stationery, giving the return address of the writer (or of the writer's company), is used. Every element of the letter (including date, inside address, salutation, body, close, and signature) is typed flush with the left margin. In block form, the return address of the writer, the close, and the signature are moved to the right. Paragraphs are not indented but begin flush with the left margin. In semiblock form, considered the least formal of the three patterns, the return address, close, and signature are moved to the right, and the beginning of each paragraph is indented five spaces from the left margin.

Type business letters on letterhead stationery or on unlined paper that is at least $5\frac{1}{2}'' \times 8\frac{1}{2}''$. Type on only one side of the paper, single-spacing the body of the letter and double-spacing between paragraphs. The sample letter on the next page, in block form, illustrates the proper placement of each part of a business letter. The return address is followed by the date. (Note that the writer's name is not part of this heading.) The inside address includes the full name, title, and complete address of the person to whom the letter is written. (This information is repeated as the address on the envelope.) The inside address is typed flush left, a few lines below the return address heading. The salutation, or greeting, is typed

BUSINESS LETTER IN BLOCK FORM

Return address ⎯⎯⎯ ⎡ 14 Closter Road
Langdon, ND 58249
⎣ March 12, 1990

Personnel Manager ⎤
Minnesota Public Radio ⎥ Inside
45 East 8th Street ⎥ address
St. Paul, MN 55101 ⎦

Dear Sir or Madam: ⎤⎯⎯ Salutation

I am applying for the summer internship you
listed with the Job Information and Placement
Center at North Dakota State University. I am
currently a sophomore at North Dakota State University, with a major in mass communication and a
minor in English.

As the enclosed résumé shows, I have had a variety of experiences in radio. In addition to
producing the weekly debate show "The Forum" for
the university radio station, KDSU, I have also
taken several upper-level courses in broadcast
journalism and audio production. My job last   Body
summer at KDSU provided an overview of the admin-
istrative aspects of radio, and I believe the internship you offer will give me an opportunity to
acquire specific experience in the production
area of broadcasting.

I would be happy to send you a transcript of "The
Forum." I am available for an interview almost
any time and can be reached at (701) 256-7011.

I look forward to hearing from you.

Close ⎯⎯ ⎡ Sincerely,

Signature ⎯ ⎡ *Barbara C. Hansen*

⎣ Barbara C. Hansen

Enc.

two lines below the inside address. A colon follows the salutation, and the body of the letter begins two lines below the greeting.

In the salutation use *Ms.* if you are writing to a woman whose title or marital status is unknown or if the woman prefers this form of address. If you are not writing to a particular person, you can use the salutation *Dear Sir or Madam* or you can address the company itself — *Dear Solar Technology.*

In block form the close is lined up with the return address and typed two lines below the end of the letter. Common closes are *Yours truly, Very truly yours,* and *Sincerely.* (Note that only the first word of the close is capitalized.) The name of the writer is typed four lines below the close, leaving room for the written signature between the close and the typed name. The name of the writer should not be prefaced by a title or followed by an abbreviation for a title or position. This information can be included in a separate line under the typed name (for example, *Director* or *Sales Manager*).

Other information can be included below the signature and flush with the left margin (for example: *Enc.,* indicating that something is enclosed with the letter; *cc: Mr. Theodore Jones,* indicating that a copy of the letter is being sent to Mr. Jones, a third party; or *JEF:njl,* indicating that JEF [the writer's initials] wrote the letter and njl typed it).

The name and return address of the writer is typed in the upper left-hand corner of the envelope. The addressee's name, title, and complete address are typed just right of the center of the envelope. The letter (which should be about the same width as the envelope) is folded in thirds.

58b Résumés

An effective résumé presents relevant information in a clear and concise form. Every résumé should include name, address, and telephone number; a history of education and employment; a list of special interests or related activities; and

RÉSUMÉ

Barbara C. Hansen
14 Closter Road
Langdon, ND 58249
(701) 256-7011

Position Desired   Internship in News Department

Education
1988 to present   North Dakota State University,
                         Fargo, ND. B.A. in mass communi-
                         cation expected May 1992. Minor
                         in English.

1984-1988   Langdon High School, Langdon, ND.

Experience
Feb. 1989   Producer of "The Forum," a weekly
to present   broadcast on KDSU, the university
                         radio station. Responsibilities
                         include selecting the issues and
                         the participants, moderating the
                         debates.

May—Sept. 1989   Receptionist, KNDK radio station,
                         Langdon, ND. Answered telephones;
                         performed various clerical duties.

Related Interests   Volunteer tutoring in the Moorhead
and Activities   area public schools; basketball;
                         reading.

References   Academic references available from
                         the Job Information and Placement
                         Office at North Dakota State Uni-
                         versity, Fargo, ND 58105.

                         Employment   Ms. Kimberly Quinlan
                         Reference   KNDK Radio Station
                                         Langdon, ND 58249

                         Personal   Mr. Stephen Hurley
                         Reference   45 Main Street
                                         Langdon, ND 58249

information about how to obtain references. You may also include personal information such as date of birth or marital status, but such information is not necessary. Some résumés name the specific position desired. If you are applying for a number of different positions, you may find it more useful to name a broader employment goal.

In the education history, begin with the institution you are currently attending and work backward to your high school, listing degrees and dates of attendance. If you have won special honors, include them. In the employment history, again list your most recent job first and then work backward. Give the dates of employment and the company name and address. You can also list your supervisors. Describe your responsibilities, highlighting those tasks or skills related to the position you are seeking. In listing special interests, concentrate on those related to your employment goal. Instead of listing the names and addresses of references, you can state that references are available on request.

In a résumé, present yourself in the best possible light, but do not distort any of the facts about your experience or qualifications. Select details wisely and your résumé will be a valuable tool.

When you send your résumé, you should include a letter that tells what position you seek and where you learned about it. The letter should also summarize your education and past experience, relating them to the job you are applying for. You may want to highlight a specific qualification and refer the reader to your résumé for more information. End the letter with a suggestion for a meeting, and tell your prospective employer when you will be available.

58c Memos

Business memos (short for *memorandums*) are a form of communication used within a company or organization. Usually brief and to the point, a memo reports information,

BUSINESS MEMO

To: Production and Development personnel

cc: Stephen Dumais

From: Helen Brown

Date: February 26, 1991

Subject: New computers for staff

As you may know, we will be receiving four new personal computers next week to supplement the ones we
already have.   In preparation, I would like you to
take part in an upcoming training program and to
rearrange your work areas to accommodate the new
equipment.

1.   Training program

A computer consultant will teach in-house workshops on
how to use our spreadsheet program.   If you have already tried the program, be prepared to discuss any
problems you have encountered.

Workshops for our two departments will be held in the
training room at the following times:

    Production: March 12, 10:00 a.m. to 2:00 p.m.

    Development: March 15, 10:00 a.m. to 2:00 p.m.

Lunch will be provided in the cafeteria. If you cannot
attend, please let me know by March 1.

2.   Allocation and setup

To give everyone access to a computer, two computers
will be set up in the library for the senior editors,
one in the inner office for the assistant editors, and
one in the front office for the editorial assistants.
At peak times, such as the end of the summer, we may
be able to rent an additional computer.

Editorial assistants in both departments should see me
before the end of this week to discuss preparation of
the work spaces and ordering of supplies.

makes a request, or recommends an action. The format of a memo, which varies from company to company, is designed for easy distribution, quick reading, and efficient filing.

Most memos display the recipient, sender, date, and subject at the top of the page. Many also have a "cc" ("carbon copy") line to indicate additional people to receive a copy. Some companies have preprinted forms (similar to office stationery) for the first page of a memo.

The subject line should describe the subject as clearly and concisely as possible, and the introductory paragraph should get right to the point. The body of the memo should be well organized and easy to scan. To promote scanning, use headings where possible and display any items that deserve special attention by setting them off from the text.

Because readers of memos are busy people, you cannot always assume that they will read a memo word for word. Therefore, you should put important information first or highlight it in some way so that it cannot be missed. If important information (such as a request for a response or action) must come at the end of the memo, put it in a separate paragraph. Readers know from experience that a short paragraph at the end may deserve special attention.

Glossary of Usage

This glossary includes words commonly confused (such as *accept* and *except*), words commonly misused (such as *hopefully*), and words that are nonstandard (such as *hisself*). It also lists colloquialisms and jargon. Colloquialisms are expressions that may be appropriate in informal speech but are inappropriate in formal writing. Jargon is needlessly technical or pretentious language that is inappropriate in most contexts. If an item is not listed here, consult the index. For irregular verbs (such as *sing, sang, sung*), see 27a. For idiomatic use of prepositions, see 18d.

a, an   Use *an* before a vowel sound, *a* before a consonant sound: *an apple, a peach.* Problems sometimes arise with words beginning with *h*. If the *h* is silent, the word begins with a vowel sound, so use *an*: *an hour, an heir, an honest senator, an honorable deed.* If the *h* is pronounced, the word begins with a consonant sound, so use *a*: *a hospital, a hymn, a historian, a hotel.*

accept, except   *Accept* is a verb meaning "to receive." *Except* is usually a preposition meaning "excluding." *I will accept all the packages except that one. Except* is also a verb meaning "to exclude." *Please except that item from the list.*

adapt, adopt   *Adapt* means "to adjust or become accustomed"; it is usually followed by *to*. *Adopt* means "to take as one's own." *Our family adopted a Vietnamese orphan, who quickly adapted to his new surroundings.*

adverse, averse   *Adverse* means "unfavorable." *Averse* means "opposed" or "reluctant"; it is usually followed by *to*. *I am averse to your proposal because it could have an adverse impact on the economy.*

advice, advise   *Advice* is a noun, *advise* a verb: *We advise you to follow John's advice.*

affect, effect   *Affect* is usually a verb meaning "to influence." *Effect* is usually a noun meaning "result." *The drug did not affect the disease, and it had several adverse side effects. Effect* can also be a verb meaning "to bring about." *Only the president can effect such a dramatic change.*

aggravate   *Aggravate* means "to make worse or more troublesome." *Overgrazing aggravated the soil erosion.* In formal writing, avoid the colloquial use of *aggravate* meaning "to annoy or irritate." *Her babbling annoyed* (not *aggravated*) *me.*

agree to, agree with   *Agree to* means "to give consent." *Agree with* means "to be in accord" or "to come to an understanding." *He agrees with me about the need for change, but he won't agree to my plan.*

ain't   *Ain't* is nonstandard. Use *am not, are not* (*aren't*), or *is not* (*isn't*). *I am not* (not *ain't*) *going home for spring break.*

all ready, already   *All ready* means "completely prepared." *Already* means "previously." *Susan was all ready for the concert, but her friends had already left.*

all right   *All right* is always written as two words. *Alright* is nonstandard.

all together, altogether   *All together* means "everyone gathered." *Altogether* means "entirely." *We were not altogether certain that we could bring the family all together for the reunion.*

allude   To *allude* to something is to make an indirect reference to it. Do not use *allude* to mean "to refer directly." *In his lecture the professor referred* (not *alluded*) *to several pre-Socratic philosophers.*

allusion, illusion   An *allusion* is an indirect reference. An *illusion* is a misconception or false impression. *Did you catch my allusion to Shakespeare? Mirrors give the room an illusion of depth.*

a lot   *A lot* is two words. Do not write *alot*. *We have had a lot of rain this spring.* See also *lots, lots of.*

A.M., P.M., a.m., p.m.　Use these abbreviations with numerals: *6:00 P.M., 11:00 a.m.* Do not use them as substitutes for the words *morning* and *evening. I worked until late in the evening* (not *p.m.*) *yesterday.*

among, between　Ordinarily, use *among* with three or more entities, *between* with two. *The prize was divided among several contestants. You have a choice between carrots and beans.*

amoral, immoral　*Amoral* means "neither moral nor immoral"; it also means "not caring about moral judgments." *Immoral* means "morally wrong." *Until recently, most business courses were taught from an amoral perspective. Murder is immoral.*

amount, number　Use *amount* with quantities that cannot be counted; use *number* with those that can. *This recipe calls for a large amount of sugar. We have a large number of toads in our garden.*

an　See *a, an.*

and etc.　*Et cetera* (*etc.*) means "and so forth"; therefore, *and etc.* is redundant. See also *etc.*

and/or　Avoid the awkward construction *and/or* except in technical or legal documents.

angry at, angry with　To write that one is *angry at* another person is nonstandard. Use *angry with* instead.

ante-, anti-　The prefix *ante-* means "earlier" or "in front of"; the prefix *anti-* means "against" or "opposed to." *William Lloyd Garrison was one of the leaders of the antislavery movement during the antebellum period. Anti-* should be used with a hyphen when it is followed by a capital letter or a word beginning with *i.*

anxious　*Anxious* means "worried" or "apprehensive." In formal writing, avoid using *anxious* to mean "eager." *We are eager* (not *anxious*) *to see your new house.*

anybody, anyone　*Anybody* and *anyone* are singular. (See 21d and 22a.)

anymore　Reserve the adverb *anymore* for negative contexts, where it means "any longer." *Moviegoers are rarely shocked anymore by profanity.* Do not use *anymore* in positive contexts. Use *now* or *nowadays* instead. *Interest rates are so high nowadays* (not *anymore*) *that few people can afford to buy homes.*

anyone　See *anybody, anyone.*

anyone, any one　*Anyone,* an indefinite pronoun, means "any person at all." *Any one,* the pronoun *one* preceded by the adjective *any,* refers to a particular person or thing in a group. *Anyone from Chicago may choose any one of the games on display.*

anyplace *Anyplace* is informal for *anywhere.* Avoid *anyplace* in formal writing.

anyways, anywheres *Anyways* and *anywheres* are nonstandard. Use *anyway* and *anywhere.*

as *As* is sometimes used to mean "because." But do not use it if there is any chance of ambiguity: *We canceled the picnic because* (not *as*) *it began raining. As* here could mean "because" or "when."

as, like See *like, as.*

averse See *adverse, averse.*

awful The adjective *awful* means "awe-inspiring." Colloquially it is used to mean "terrible" or "bad." The adverb *awfully* is sometimes used in conversation as an intensifier meaning "very." In formal writing, avoid these colloquial uses. *I was very* (not *awfully*) *upset last night. Susan had a terrible* (not *an awful*) *time calming her nerves.*

awhile, a while *Awhile* is an adverb; it can modify a verb, but it cannot be the object of a preposition such as *for.* The two-word form *a while* is a noun preceded by an article and therefore can be the object of a preposition. *Stay awhile. Stay for a while.*

bad, badly *Bad* is an adjective, *badly* an adverb. (See 26a.) *They felt bad about being early and ruining the surprise. Her arm hurt badly after she slid headfirst into second base.*

being as, being that *Being as* and *being that* are nonstandard expressions. Write *because* or *since* instead. *Because* (not *Being as*) *I slept late, I had to skip breakfast.*

beside, besides *Beside* is a preposition meaning "at the side of" or "next to." *Annie Oakley slept with her gun beside her bed. Besides* is a preposition meaning "except" or "in addition to." *No one besides Terrie can have that ice cream. Besides* is also an adverb meaning "in addition." *I'm not hungry; besides, I don't like ice cream.*

between See *among, between.*

bring, take Use *bring* when an object is being transported toward you, *take* when it is being moved away. *Please bring me a glass of water. Please take these flowers to Mr. Scott.*

burst, bursted; bust, busted *Burst* is an irregular verb meaning "to come open or fly apart suddenly or violently." Its principal parts are *burst, burst, burst.* The past-tense form *bursted* is nonstandard. *Bust* and *busted* are slang for *burst* and, along with *bursted,* should not be used in formal writing.

can, may The distinction between *can* and *may* is fading, but many careful writers still observe it in formal writing. *Can* is traditionally reserved for ability, *may* for permission. *Can you ski down the advanced slope without falling? May I help you?*

capital, capitol *Capital* refers to a city, *capitol* to a building where lawmakers meet. *Capital* also refers to wealth or resources. *The capitol has undergone extensive renovations. The residents of the state capital protested the development plans.*

censor, censure *Censor* means "to remove or suppress material considered objectionable." *Censure* means "to criticize severely." *The library's new policy of censoring controversial books has been censured by the media.*

center around *Center on* and *center in* are considered more logical than *center around. His talk centered on the global buildup of arms in the last five years.*

cite, site *Cite* means "to quote as an authority or example." *Site,* as a verb, means "to situate or locate." *He cited* (not *sited*) *Frank Lloyd Wright to give strength to his argument.*

climactic, climatic *Climactic* is derived from *climax,* the point of greatest intensity in a series or progression of events. *Climatic* is derived from *climate* and refers to meteorological conditions. *The climactic period in the dinosaurs' reign was reached just before severe climatic conditions brought on an ice age.*

compare to, compare with *Compare to* means "to represent as similar." *She compared him to a wild stallion. Compare with* means "to examine the ways in which two things are similar." *The study compared the language ability of apes with that of dolphins.*

complement, compliment *Complement* is a verb meaning "to go with or complete" or a noun meaning "something that completes." *Compliment* as a verb means "to flatter"; as a noun it means "flattering remark." *Her skill at rushing the net complements his skill at volleying. Mother's flower arrangements receive many compliments.*

conscience, conscious *Conscience* is a noun meaning "moral principles." *Conscious* is an adjective meaning "aware or alert." *Let your conscience be your guide. Were you conscious of his love for you?*

contact   Although the use of *contact* to mean "to get in touch with" is common in speech, it is not appropriate in formal writing. If possible, use a precise verb such as *write* or *telephone*. *We will telephone* (not *contact*) *you soon.*

continual, continuous   *Continual* means "repeated regularly and frequently." *She grew weary of the continual telephone calls. Continuous* means "extended or prolonged without interruption." *The broken siren made a continuous wail.*

could care less   *Could care less* is a nonstandard expression. Write *couldn't care less* instead. *He couldn't* (not *could*) *care less about his psychology final.*

could of   *Could of* is nonstandard for *could have. We could have* (not *could of*) *had steak for dinner if we had been hungry.*

criteria   *Criteria* is the plural of *criterion*, which means "a standard or rule or test on which a judgment or decision can be based." *The only criterion for the scholarship is ability.*

data   *Data* is the plural of *datum*, which means "a fact or proposition." Many writers now treat *data* as singular or plural depending on the meaning of the sentence. Some experts insist, however, that *data* can only be plural. *The new data suggest* (not *suggests*) *that our theory is correct.* The singular form *datum* is rarely used.

different from, different than   Ordinarily, write *different from. Your sense of style is different from Jim's.* However, *different than* is acceptable to avoid an awkward construction. *Please let me know if your plans are different than* (to avoid *from what*) *they were six weeks ago.*

differ from, differ with   *Differ from* means "to be unlike"; *differ with* means "to disagree." *She differed with me about the wording of the agreement. My approach to the problem differed from hers.*

disinterested, uninterested   *Disinterested* means "impartial, objective"; *uninterested* means "not interested." *We sought the advice of a disinterested counselor to help us solve our problem. He was uninterested in anyone's opinion but his own.*

don't   *Don't* is the contraction for *do not. I don't want any. Don't* should not be used as the contraction for *does not*, which is *doesn't. He doesn't* (not *don't*) *want any.* (See 27c.)

double negative   Standard English allows two negatives only if a positive meaning is intended. *The runners were not unhappy with* *their performance.* Double negatives used to emphasize negation are nonstandard. *Jack doesn't have to answer to anybody* (not *nobody*).

due to *Due to* is an adjective phrase and should not be used as a preposition meaning "because of." *The trip was canceled because of* (not *due to*) *lack of interest. Due to* is acceptable as a subject complement and usually follows a form of the verb *be. His success was due to hard work.*

each *Each* is singular. (See 21d and 22a.)

effect See *affect, effect.*

e.g. In formal writing, replace the Latin abbreviation *e.g.* with its English equivalent: *for example* or *for instance.*

either *Either* is singular. (See 21d and 22a.) (For *either . . . or* constructions, see 21c and 22d.)

elicit, illicit *Elicit* is a verb meaning "to bring out" or "to evoke." *Illicit* is an adjective meaning "unlawful." *The reporter was unable to elicit any information from the police about illicit drug traffic.*

emigrate from, immigrate to *Emigrate* means "to leave one country or region to settle in another." *In 1900, my grandfather emigrated from Russia to escape the religious pogroms. Immigrate* means "to enter another country and reside there." *Many Mexicans immigrate to the United States to find work.*

eminent, imminent *Eminent* means "outstanding" or "distinguished." *We met an eminent professor of Greek history. Imminent* means "about to happen." *The announcement is imminent.*

enthused Many people object to the use of *enthused* as an adjective. Use *enthusiastic* instead. *The children were enthusiastic* (not *enthused*) *about going to the circus.*

-ess Many people find the *-ess* suffix demeaning. Write *poet,* not *poetess; Jew,* not *Jewess; author,* not *authoress.*

etc. Avoid ending a list with *etc.* It is more emphatic to end with an example, and in most contexts readers will understand that the list is not exhaustive. When you don't wish to end with an example, *and so on* is more graceful than *etc.* See also *and etc.*

eventually, ultimately Often used interchangeably, *eventually* is the better choice to mean "at an unspecified time in the future" and *ultimately* is better to mean "the furthest possible extent or greatest extreme." *He knew that eventually he would complete his degree. The existentialist considered suicide the ultimately rational act.*

everybody, everyone   *Everybody* and *everyone* are singular. (See 21d and 22a.)

everyone, every one   *Everyone* is an indefinite pronoun. *Every one*, the pronoun *one* preceded by the adjective *every*, means "each individual or thing in a particular group." *Every one* is usually followed by *of*. *Everyone wanted to go. Every one of the missing books was found.*

exam   *Exam* is informal. Use *examination* in writing.

except   See *accept, except.*

expect   Avoid the colloquial use of *expect* meaning "to believe, think, or suppose." *I think* (not *expect*) *it will rain tonight.*

explicit, implicit   *Explicit* means "expressed directly" or "clearly defined"; *implicit* means "implied, unstated." *I gave him explicit instructions not to go swimming. My mother's silence indicated her implicit approval.*

farther, further   *Farther* describes distances. *Further* suggests quantity or degree. *Chicago is farther from Miami than I thought. You extended the curfew further than you should have.*

female, male   The terms *female* and *male* are jargon for "woman" and "man." *Two women* (not *females*) *and one man* (not *male*) *applied for the position.*

fewer, less   *Fewer* refers to items that can be counted; *less* refers to general amounts. *Fewer people are living in the city. Please put less sugar in my tea.*

finalize   *Finalize* is jargon meaning "to make final or complete." Use ordinary English instead. *The architect prepared final drawings* (not *finalized the drawings*).

firstly   *Firstly* sounds pretentious, and it leads to the ungainly series *firstly, secondly, thirdly, fourthly,* and so on. Write *first, second, third* instead.

flunk   *Flunk* is colloquial for *fail* and should be avoided in formal writing.

folks   *Folks* is an informal expression for "parents" or "relatives" or "people" in general. Use a more formal expression instead.

further   See *farther, further.*

get   *Get* has many colloquial uses. In writing, avoid using *get* to mean the following: "to evoke an emotional response" (*That music* *always gets to me*); "to annoy" (*After a while his sulking got to me*); "to take revenge on" (*I got back at him by leaving the room*); "to become" (*He got sick*); "to start or begin" (*Let's get going*). Avoid using *have got to* in place of *must*. *I must* (not *have got to*) *finish this paper tonight.*

good, well *Good* is an adjective, *well* an adverb. (See 26.) *He hasn't felt good about his game since he sprained his wrist last season. She performed well on the uneven parallel bars.*

hanged, hung *Hanged* is the past-tense and past-participle form of the verb *hang* meaning "to execute." *The prisoner was hanged at dawn. Hung* is the past-tense and past-participle form of the verb *hang* meaning "to fasten or suspend." *The stockings were hung by the chimney with care.*

hardly Avoid expressions such as *can't hardly* and *not hardly*, which are considered double negatives. *I can* (not *can't*) *hardly describe my elation at getting the job.*

has got, have got *Got* is unnecessary and awkward in such constructions. It should be dropped. *We have* (not *have got*) *three days to prepare for the opening.*

he At one time *he* was commonly used to mean "he or she." Today such usage is inappropriate. (See 17f and 22a for alternative constructions.)

he/she, his/her In formal writing, use *he or she* or *his or her*. For alternatives to these wordy constructions, see 17f and 22a.

hisself *Hisself* is nonstandard. Use *himself*.

hopefully *Hopefully* means "in a hopeful manner." *We looked hopefully to the future.* Do not use *hopefully* in constructions such as the following: *Hopefully, your daughter will recover soon.* Indicate who is doing the hoping: *I hope that your daughter will recover soon.*

hung See *hanged, hung*.

i.e. In formal writing, replace the Latin abbreviation *i.e.* with its English equivalent: *that is*.

if, whether Use *if* in a statement of condition and *whether* to express alternatives. *If you go on a trip, whether it be to Nebraska or New Jersey, remember to bring traveler's checks.*

illusion See *allusion, illusion*.

imminent See *eminent, imminent*.

immoral See *amoral, immoral*.

implement   *Implement* is a pretentious way of saying "do," "carry out," or "accomplish." Use ordinary language instead. *We carried out* (not *implemented*) *the director's orders with some reluctance.*

imply, infer   *Imply* means "to suggest or state indirectly"; *infer* means "to draw a conclusion." *John implied that he knew all about computers, but the interviewer inferred that John was inexperienced.*

individual   *Individual* is a pretentious substitute for *person*. *We invited several persons* (not *individuals*) *from the audience to participate in the experiment.*

ingenious, ingenuous   *Ingenious* means "clever." *Sarah's solution to the problem was ingenious. Ingenuous* means "naive" or "frank." *For a successful manager, Ed is surprisingly ingenuous.*

in regards to   *In regards to* confuses two different phrases: *in regard to* and *as regards*. Use one or the other. *In regard to* (or *As regards*) *the contract, ignore the first clause.*

irregardless   *Irregardless* is nonstandard. Use *regardless.*

is when, is where   These mixed constructions are often incorrectly used in definitions. *A run-off election is a second election held to break a tie* (not *is when a second election breaks a tie*). (See 11c.)

its, it's   *Its* is a possessive pronoun; *it's* is a contraction for *it is.* (See 36c and 36e.) *The dog licked its wound whenever its owner walked into the room. It's a perfect day to walk the twenty-mile trail.*

kind(s)   *Kind* is singular and should be treated as such. Don't write *These kind of chairs are rare.* Write instead *This kind of chair is rare. Kinds* is plural and should be used only when you mean more than one kind. *These kinds of chairs are rare.*

kind of, sort of   Avoid using *kind of* or *sort of* to mean "somewhat." *The movie was kind of boring.* Do not put *a* after either phrase. *That kind of* (not *kind of a*) *salesclerk annoys me.*

learn, teach   *Learn* means "to gain knowledge"; *teach* means "to impart knowledge." *I must teach* (not *learn*) *my sister to read.*

leave, let   *Leave* means "to exit." Avoid using it with the nonstandard meaning "to permit." *Let* (not *leave*) *me help you with the dishes.*

less   See *fewer, less.*

let, leave   See *leave, let.*

liable *Liable* means "obligated" or "responsible." Do not use it to mean "likely." *You're likely* (not *liable*) *to trip if you don't tie your shoelaces.*

lie, lay *Lie* is an intransitive verb meaning "to recline or rest on a surface." Its principal parts are *lie, lay, lain*. *Lay* is a transitive verb meaning "to put or place." Its principal parts are *lay, laid, laid*. (See 27b.)

like, as *Like* is a preposition, not a subordinating conjunction. It can be followed only by a noun or a noun phrase. *As* is a subordinating conjunction that introduces a subordinate clause. In casual speech you may say *She looks like she hasn't slept* or *You don't know her like I do.* But in formal writing, use *as. She looks as if she hasn't slept. You don't know her as I do.* (See prepositions and subordinating conjunctions, 47f and 47g.)

loan Some people object to the use of *loan* as a verb. Use *lend* instead. *Please lend* (not *loan*) *me five dollars.*

loose, lose *Loose* is an adjective meaning "not securely fastened." *Lose* is a verb meaning "to misplace" or "to not win." *Did you lose your only loose pair of work pants?*

lots, lots of *Lots* and *lots of* are colloquial substitutes for *many, much,* or *a lot.* Avoid using them in formal writing.

male, female See *female, male.*

mankind Avoid *mankind* whenever possible. It offends many readers because it excludes women. Use *humanity, humans, the human race,* or *humankind* instead.

may See *can, may.*

maybe, may be *Maybe* is an adverb meaning "possibly." *May be* is a verb phrase. *Maybe the sun will shine tomorrow. Tomorrow may be a brighter day.*

may of, might of *May of* and *might of* are nonstandard for *may have* and *might have. We may have* (not *may of*) *had too many cookies.*

media, medium *Media* is the plural of *medium. Of all the media that cover the Olympics, television is the medium that best captures the spectacle of the events.*

most *Most* is colloquial when used to mean "almost" and should be avoided. *Almost* (not *Most*) *everyone went to the parade.*

must of See *may of*.

myself *Myself* is a reflexive or intensive pronoun. Reflexive: *I cut myself.* Intensive: *I will drive you myself.* Do not use *myself* in place of *I* or *me*. *He gave the flowers to Melinda and me* (not *myself*). (See also 24.)

nauseated, nauseous *Nauseated* means "suffering from nausea." *Nauseous* means "causing nausea." *I feel nauseated* (not *nauseous*).

neither *Neither* is singular. (See 21d and 22a.) For *neither . . . nor* constructions, see 21c and 22d.

none *None* is singular. (See 21d and 22a.)

nowheres *Nowheres* is nonstandard for *nowhere*.

number See *amount, number*.

of Use the verb *have*, not the preposition *of*, after the verbs *could, should, would, may, might*, and *must*. *They must have* (not *of*) *left early.*

off of *Off* is sufficient. Omit *of*. *The ball rolled off* (not *off of*) *the table.*

OK, O.K., okay All three spellings are acceptable, but in formal speech and writing avoid these colloquial expressions for consent or approval.

parameters *Parameter* is a mathematical term that has become jargon for "fixed limit," "boundary," or "guideline." Use ordinary English instead. *The task force was asked to work within certain guidelines* (not *parameters*).

percent, per cent, percentage *Percent* (also spelled *per cent*) is always used with a specific number. *Percentage* is used with a descriptive term such as *large* or *small*, not with a specific number. *The candidate won 80 percent of the primary vote. Only a small percentage of registered voters turned out for the election.*

phenomena *Phenomena* is the plural of *phenomenon*, which means "an observable occurrence or fact." *Strange phenomena occur at all hours of the night in that house, but last night's phenomenon was the strangest of all.*

plus *Plus* should not be used to join independent clauses. *This raincoat is dirty; moreover* (not *plus*), *it has a hole in it.*

precede, proceed *Precede* means "to come before." *Proceed* means "to go forward." *As we proceeded up the mountain, we noticed fresh* *tracks in the mud, evidence that a group of hikers had preceded us.*

principal, principle   *Principal* is a noun meaning "the head of a school or organization" or "a sum of money." It is also an adjective meaning "most important." *Principle* is a noun meaning "a basic truth or law." *The principal expelled her for three principal reasons. We believe in the principle of equal justice for all.*

proceed, precede   See *precede, proceed.*

quote, quotation   *Quote* is a verb; *quotation* is a noun. Avoid using *quote* as a shortened form of *quotation. Her quotations* (not *quotes*) *from Shakespeare intrigued us.*

raise, rise   *Raise* is a transitive verb meaning "to move or cause to move upward." It takes a direct object. *I raised the shades. Rise* is an intransitive verb meaning "to go up." It does not take a direct object. *Heat rises.*

real, really   *Real* is an adjective; *really* is an adverb. *Real* is sometimes used informally as an adverb, but avoid this use in formal writing. *She was really* (not *real*) *angry.* (See 26a.)

reason is because   Use *that* instead of *because. The reason I'm late is that* (not *because*) *my car broke down.* (See 11c.)

reason why   The expression *reason why* is redundant. *The reason* (not *The reason why*) *Jones lost the election is clear.*

relation, relationship   *Relation* describes a connection between things. *Relationship* describes a connection between people. *There is a relation between poverty and infant mortality. Our business relationship has cooled over the years.*

respectfully, respectively   *Respectfully* means "showing or marked by respect." *Respectively* means "each in the order given." *He respectfully submitted his opinion to the judge. John, Tom, and Larry were a butcher, a baker, and a lawyer, respectively.*

sensual, sensuous   *Sensual* means "gratifying the physical senses," especially those associated with sexual pleasure. *Sensuous* means "pleasing to the senses," especially those involved in the experience of art, music, and nature. *The sensuous music and balmy air led the dancers to more sensual movements.*

set, sit   *Set* is a transitive verb meaning "to put" or "to place." Its principal parts are *set, set, set. Sit* is an intransitive verb meaning "to be seated." Its principal parts are *sit, sat, sat. She set the dough* in a warm corner of the kitchen. The cat sat in the warmest part of the room.

shall, will *Shall* was once used as the helping verb with *I* or *we: I shall, we shall, you will, he/she/it will, they will.* Today, however, *will* is generally accepted even when the subject is *I* or *we.* The word *shall* occurs primarily in polite questions (*Shall I find you a pillow?*) and in legalistic sentences suggesting duty or obligation (*The applicant shall file form 1080 by December 31*).

should of *Should of* is nonstandard for *should have.* They *should have* (not *should of*) *been home an hour ago.*

since Do not use *since* to mean *because* if there is any chance of ambiguity. *Since we won the game, we have been celebrating with a pitcher of beer. Since* here could mean "because" or "from the time that."

sit See *set, sit.*

site, cite See *cite, site.*

somebody, someone *Somebody* and *someone* are singular. (See 21d and 22a.)

something *Something* is singular. (See 21d.)

sometime, some time, sometimes *Sometime* is an adverb meaning "at an indefinite or unstated time." *Some time* is the adjective *some* modifying the noun *time* and is spelled as two words to mean "a period of time." *Sometimes* is an adverb meaning "at times, now and then." *I'll see you sometime soon. I haven't lived there for some time. Sometimes I run into him at the library.*

sure and *Sure and* is nonstandard for *sure to. We were all taught to be sure to* (not *and*) *look both ways before crossing a street.*

take See *bring, take.*

than, then *Than* is a conjunction used in comparisons; *then* is an adverb denoting time. *That pizza is more than I can eat. Tom laughed, and then we recognized him.*

that See *who, which, that.*

that, which Many writers reserve *that* for restrictive clauses, *which* for nonrestrictive clauses. (See 32e.)

theirselves *Theirselves* is nonstandard for *themselves. The two people were able to push the Volkswagen out of the way themselves* (not *theirselves*).

there, their, they're *There* is an adverb specifying place; it is also an expletive. Adverb: *Sylvia is lying there unconscious.* Expletive: *There are two plums left. Their* is a possessive pronoun: *Fred and Jane finally washed their car. They're* is a contraction of *they are: They're later than usual today.*

this kind See *kind(s).*

to, too, two *To* is a preposition; *too* is an adverb; *two* is a number. *Too many of your shots slice to the left, but the last two were right on the mark.*

toward, towards *Toward* and *towards* are generally interchangeable, although *toward* is preferred.

try and *Try and* is nonstandard for *try to. The teacher asked us all to try to* (not *and*) *write an original haiku.*

ultimately, eventually See *eventually, ultimately.*

unique Avoid expressions such as *most unique, more straight, less perfect, very round.* Something either is unique or it isn't. It is illogical to suggest degrees of uniqueness. (See 26c.)

usage The noun *usage* should not be substituted for *use* when the meaning intended is "employment of." *The use* (not *usage*) *of computers dramatically increased the company's profits.*

use to, suppose to *Use to* and *suppose to* are nonstandard. Write *used to* and *supposed to* instead.

utilize *Utilize* means "to make use of." It often sounds pretentious; in most cases, *use* is sufficient. *I used* (not *utilized*) *the best workers to get the job done fast.*

wait for, wait on *Wait for* means "to be in readiness for" or "await." *Wait on* means "to serve." *We're only waiting for* (not *waiting on*) *Ruth to take us to the game.*

ways *Ways* is colloquial when used to mean "distance." *The city is a long way* (not *ways*) *from here.*

where Do not use *where* in place of *that. I heard that* (not *where*) *the crime rate is increasing.*

which See *that, which* and *who, which, that.*

while Avoid using *while* to mean "although" or "whereas" if there is any chance of ambiguity. *Although* (not *While*) *Gloria lost money in the slot machine, Tom won it at roulette.* Here *while* could mean either "although" or "at the same time that."

who, which, that Do not use *which* to refer to persons. Use *who* instead. *That*, though generally used to refer to things, may be used to refer to a group or class of people. *Fans wondered how an old man who* (not *that* or *which*) *walked with a limp could play football. The team that scores the most points in this game will win the tournament.*

who, whom *Who* is used for subjects and subject complements; *whom* is used for objects. (See 25.)

who's, whose *Who's* is a contraction of *who is; whose* is a possessive pronoun. *Who's ready for more popcorn? Whose coat is this?* (See 36c and 36e.)

will See *shall, will.*

would of *Would of* is nonstandard for *would have. She would have* (not *would of*) *had a chance to play if she had arrived on time.*

you In formal writing, avoid *you* in an indefinite sense meaning "anyone." (See 23d.) *Any spectator* (not *You*) *could tell by the way John caught the ball that his throw would be too late.*

your, you're *Your* is a possessive pronoun; *you're* is a contraction of *you are. Is that your new motorcycle? You're on the list of finalists.* (See 36e.)

Answers to Lettered Exercises

EXERCISE 8 – 2, page 117

Possible revisions:

a. After a couple of minutes, the teacher walked in smiling.
b. The losing team was made up of superstars who acted as isolated individuals on the court.
c. Because we are concerned about the environment, we keep our use of insecticides, herbicides, and fungicides to a minimum.
d. The aides help the younger children with reading and math, their weakest subjects.
e. My first sky dive, from an altitude of 12,500 feet, was the most frightening experience of my life.

EXERCISE 8 – 3, page 119

Possible revisions:

a. When our team finally acquired an expert backstroker, we won every relay for the rest of the season.
b. The senator's planned trip to Spain and Portugal was canceled because of terrorist activities.
c. When I presented the idea of job sharing to my supervisors, to my surprise they were delighted with the idea.
d. Although outsiders have forced changes on them, native Hawaiians try to preserve their ancestors' sacred customs.
e. Sharon's country kitchen, formerly a lean-to porch, overlooks a field where horses and cattle graze among old tombstones.

EXERCISE 9 – 1, page 125

Possible revisions:

a. The system has capabilities such as communicating with other computers, processing records, and performing mathematical functions.
b. The personnel officer told me that I would answer the phone, welcome visitors, distribute mail, and do some typing.
c. This summer I want a job more than a trip to Disney World.
d. How ideal it seems to raise a family here in Luray instead of in the air-polluted suburbs.
e. Nancy not only called the post office but checked with the neighbors to see if the package had come.

EXERCISE 10 – 1, page 130

Possible revisions:

a. Dip the paintbrush into the paint remover and spread a thick coat on a small section of the door.
b. Some say that Ella Fitzgerald's renditions of Cole Porter's songs are better than any other singer's.
c. SETI (the Search for Extraterrestrial Intelligence) has excited and will continue to excite interest among space buffs.
d. Samantha got along better with the chimpanzees than with Albert. [or . . . than Albert did.]
e. Gunther Gebel-Williams, whom we watched today and who is a star of the Ringling Brothers and Barnum & Bailey Circus, is well known for his training of circus animals.

EXERCISE 11 – 1, page 134

Possible revisions:

a. My instant reaction was anger and disappointment.
b. I brought a problem into the house that my mother wasn't sure how to handle.
c. It is through the misery of others that old Harvey has become rich.
d. A cloverleaf allows traffic on limited-access freeways to change direction.
e. Bowman established the format that future football card companies would emulate for years to come.

EXERCISE 12 – 1, page 139

Possible revisions:

a. He wanted to buy only three roses, not a dozen.
b. Within the next few years, orthodontists will be using as standard practice the technique Kurtz developed.
c. Celia received a flier from a Japanese nun about a workshop on making a kimono.
d. Jurors are encouraged to sift through the evidence carefully and thoroughly.
e. Each state would set into motion a program of recycling all reusable products.

EXERCISE 12 – 2, page 144

Possible revisions:

a. Reaching the heart, the surgeon performed a bypass on the severely blocked arteries.
b. When I was nestled in the cockpit, the pounding of the engine was muffled only slightly by my helmet.
c. Feeling unprepared for the exam, June found the questions as hard as her instructor had suggested they would be.
d. While my sister was still a beginner at tennis, the coaches recruited her to train for the Olympics.
e. To protest the arms buildup, demonstrators set bonfires throughout the park.

EXERCISE 13 – 1, page 150

Possible revisions:

a. We waited in the emergency room for about an hour. Finally, the nurse came in and told us that we were in the wrong place.
b. Newspapers put the lurid details of an armed robbery on page 1 and relegate the warm, human-interest stories to page G-10.
c. Ministers often have a hard time because they have to please so many different people.
d. We drove for eight hours until we reached the South Dakota Badlands. We could hardly believe the eeriness of the landscape at dusk.
e. The question is whether ferrets bred in captivity have the instinct to prey on prairie dogs or whether this is a learned skill.

EXERCISE 14 – 1, page 153

Possible revisions:

a. Disposing of nuclear waste in Antarctica would violate an international treaty.
b. The producer manages the entire operation.
c. Emphatic and active; no change.
d. Escaping into the world of drugs, I rebelled against anything and everything laid down by the establishment.
e. Emphatic and active; no change.

EXERCISE 16 – 1, page 173

Possible revisions:

a. When visitors come, Grandmother just stares at the wall.
b. Dr. Sandford has seen problems like yours many times.
c. Bloom's race for the governorship is futile.
d. New fares must be reported to all of our transportation offices.
e. In Biology 10A a faculty tutor will assign you eight taped modules and clarify any information on the tapes.

EXERCISE 17 – 1, page 178

Possible revisions:

a. It is a widely held myth that middle-aged people can't change.
b. All work-study students must prove that they are enrolled.
c. I crawled on my elbows about ten yards to the trench.
d. When our father was laid off from his high-paying factory job, we learned what it was like to be poor.
e. If you cannot install the computer, you may call the firm's 800 number to get help.

EXERCISE 17 – 3, page 186

Possible revisions:

a. Harriet Glover is the defense attorney appointed by the court. Al Jones has been assigned to work with her on the case.
b. A young graduate who is careful about investments can accumulate a significant sum in a relatively short period.
c. An elementary school teacher should understand the concept of nurturing if he or she intends to be a success.
d. Because Dr. Brown and Dr. Coombs were the senior professors in the department, they served as co-chairpersons of the promotion committee.
e. If we do not stop polluting our environment, we will perish.

EXERCISE 18 – 3, page 191

Possible revisions:

a. Many of us are not persistent enough to make a change for the better.
b. Mrs. Altman's comments were meant to evoke [or provoke] a response from the class.
c. Sam Brown began his career as a lawyer, but now he is a real estate mogul.
d. When Robert Frost died at age eighty-eight, he left a legacy of poems that will make him immortal.
e. This patient is kept in isolation to prevent her from catching our germs.

EXERCISE 18 – 4, page 193

a. I was so angry with the salesperson that I took her bag of samples and emptied it on the floor in front of her.
b. Correct
c. Try to come up with the rough outline, and we will find someone who can fill in the details.
d. "Your prejudice is no different from mine," she shouted.
e. The parade moved off the street and onto the beach.

EXERCISE 18 – 5, page 196

Possible revisions:

a. His fellow club members deliberated very briefly; all agreed that his behavior was unacceptable.

b. The president thought that the scientists were using science as a means of furthering their political goals.
c. Architect I. M. Pei gave our city a new cultural spirit that led to a renaissance.
d. We ironed out the wrinkles in our relationship.
e. Mel told us that he wasn't willing to take the chance.

EXERCISE 19 – 1, page 205

Possible revisions:

a. As I stood in front of the microwave, I recalled my grandmother bending over her old black stove and remembered what she taught me: that any food can have soul if you love the people you are cooking for.
b. It has been said that there are only three indigenous American art forms: jazz, musical comedy, and soap opera.
c. Correct
d. Myra did not tell us about her new job for six weeks, although she saw one or the other of us every day.
e. While on a tour of Italy, Maria and Kathleen sneaked away from their group to spend some quiet minutes with Leonardo da Vinci's *Last Supper*, a stunning fresco painted in the fifteenth century in a Milan monastery.

EXERCISE 20 – 1, page 216

Possible revisions:

a. The city had one public swimming pool that stayed packed with children all summer long.
b. Theo and Fanny had hoped to spend their final days in the old homestead, but they had to change their plans and move together to a retirement home.
c. Why should we pay taxes to support public transportation? We prefer to save energy dollars by carpooling.
d. Suddenly there was a loud silence; the shelling had stopped.
e. As I walked into the living room, a special report flashed onto the TV screen: The space shuttle had exploded.

EXERCISE 20 – 2, page 217

Possible revisions:

a. Because the trail up Mount Finegold was declared impassable, we decided to return to our hotel a day early.
b. Correct
c. The officer must enforce the laws, even when the laws seem unfair.
d. Researchers studying the fertility of Texas land tortoises X-rayed all the female tortoises to see how many eggs they had.
e. The suburbs seemed cold; they lacked the warmth and excitement of our Italian neighborhood.

EXERCISE 21 – 1, page 229

a. Subject: friendship and support; verb: have; b. Subject: rings; verb: are;
c. Subject: Each; verb: has; d. Subject: source; verb: is; e. Subject: windows; verb: were.

EXERCISE 21 – 2, page 232

a. High concentrations of carbon monoxide result in headaches, dizziness, unconsciousness, and even death.
b. Correct.
c. Correct
d. Crystal chandeliers, polished floors, and a new oil painting have transformed Sandra's apartment.
e. Either Alice or Jan usually works the midnight shift.

EXERCISE 22 – 1, page 238

Possible revisions:

a. All students who are taking the school bus to the volleyball game must bring in a permission slip signed by their parents.
b. Correct
c. Late at night, I sometimes saw a priest or a brother entering the side door of the church, his face silhouetted briefly in the moonlight.
d. A climatologist collects weather data from around the world, analyzes the data, and then passes the analyses along to forecasters.
e. If you have any students attending class who are still not on your roster, please send them to the registration office.

EXERCISE 23 – 1, page 247

Possible revisions:

a. The detective photographed the body after removing the blood-stained shawl.
b. In Professor Johnson's class, students are lucky to earn a C.
c. Satanism is a serious problem in our country. Its rites are grotesque perversions of many of Christianity's sacred rituals.
d. The Comanche braves lived violent lives; they gained respect for their skill as warriors.
e. All students can secure parking permits from the campus police office, which is open from 8 A.M. until 8 P.M.

EXERCISE 24 – 1, page 255

a. My Ethiopian neighbor was puzzled by the dedication of us joggers.
b. Correct
c. Sue's husband is ten years older than she.
d. The winners, Julie and he, were unable to attend the awards ceremony.
e. My father always tolerated our whispering after the lights were out.

EXERCISE 25 – 1, page 262

a. In his first production of *Hamlet*, whom did Laurence Olivier replace?
b. Correct
c. Correct
d. Some group leaders cannot handle the pressure; they give whoever makes the most noise most of their attention.
e. One of the women whom Johnson hired became the most successful lawyer in the agency.

EXERCISE 26 – 1, page 270

a. My mechanic showed me exactly where to wrap the wire firmly around the muffler.
b. All of us on the team felt bad about our performance.
c. My mother thinks that Carmen is the more pleasant of the twins.
d. Correct
e. Last Christmas was the most wonderful day of my life.

EXERCISE 27 – 1, page 276

a. Noticing that my roommate was shivering and looking pale, I rang for the nurse.
b. When I get the urge to exercise, I lie down until it passes.
c. Correct
d. The team of engineers watched in horror as the newly built dam burst and flooded the small valley.
e. Correct

EXERCISE 27 – 3, page 284

a. Correct
b. The police are used to helping lost tourists.
c. The whooping crane has been an endangered species since the late 1930s.
d. We often don't know whether he is angry or just joking.
e. Staggered working hours have reduced traffic jams and saved motorists many gallons of gas.

EXERCISE 28 – 1, page 293

a. Correct
b. Watson and Crick discovered the mechanism that controls inheritance in all life: the workings of the DNA molecule.
c. Marion would write more if she weren't distracted by a house full of children.
d. Sharon told me that she had gone to the meeting the day before.
e. Correct

EXERCISE 28 – 2, page 295

Possible revisions:

a. The research assistant reported the results.
b. Parents do not use enough discretion in deciding which television programs their children may watch.
c. As the patient undressed, we saw scars on his back, stomach, and thighs. Child abuse was what we suspected.
d. We noted right away that the taxi driver had been exposed to Americans because he knew all the latest slang.
e. The tailor replaced the buttons, lengthened or shortened the hems, and cleaned and pressed all of the costumes.

EXERCISE 29 – 1, page 305

a. We will make this a better country.

b. There is nothing in the world that TV has not touched on.
c. Did you understand my question?
d. A hard wind was blowing while we were climbing the mountain.
e. The child's innocent world has been taken away from him.

EXERCISE 29 – 2, page 308

Possible sentences:

a. I enjoy riding my motorcycle.
b. Will you help Samantha study for the test?
c. The team hopes to work hard and win the championship.
d. Tom and his brothers miss surfing during the winter.
e. The babysitter let Roger stay up until midnight.

EXERCISE 31 – 1, page 319

a. It is easy to learn how to operate our computers.
b. My grandfather is very old-fashioned.
c. The prime minister is the most popular leader in my country.
d. Pavel hasn't heard from the cousin that he wrote to last month.
e. There are many skyscrapers in New York City.

EXERCISE 31 – 2, page 322

a. an attractive young Vietnamese woman
b. a dedicated Catholic priest
c. her old blue wool sweater
d. Joe's delicious Scandinavian bread
e. many beautiful antique bird cages

EXERCISE 31 – 3, page 324

a. My mother was annoyed at me for coming home late.
b. The noise in the hall was distracting to me.
c. Correct
d. The violence in recent movies is often disgusting.
e. Correct

EXERCISE 32 – 1, page 328

a. Correct
b. The man at the next table complained loudly, and the waiter stomped off in disgust.
c. Instead of eating half a cake or two dozen cookies, I now grab a banana and an orange.
d. Nursing is physically and mentally demanding, yet the pay is low.
e. After I won the hundred-yard dash, I found a bench in the park and collapsed.

EXERCISE 32 – 2, page 331

a. She wore a black silk cape, a rhinestone collar, satin gloves, and high tops.
b. Correct

c. City Café is noted for its spicy vegetarian dishes and its friendly, efficient service.

d. Juan walked through the room with casual, elegant grace.

e. Correct

EXERCISE 32 – 3, page 335

a. We encountered no problems until we reached Cripple Creek, where the trail forked.

b. The Scott Pack, which is a twenty-five-pound steel bottle of air, is designed to be worn on a firefighter's back.

c. Correct

d. Shakespeare's tragedy *King Lear* was given a splendid performance by the actor Laurence Olivier.

e. Correct

EXERCISE 32 – 4, page 341

a. The whiskey stills, which were run mostly by farmers and fishermen, were about twenty miles from the nearest town.

b. At the sound of a starting pistol, the horses surged forward toward the first obstacle, a sharp incline three feet high.

c. Each morning the seventy-year-old woman cleans the barn, shovels manure, and spreads clean hay around the milking stalls.

d. The students of Highpoint are required to wear dull green polyester pleated skirts.

e. You will be unable to answer all the clients' questions or solve all their problems, but you may turn to the directory when difficult issues arise.

EXERCISE 32 – 5, page 343

a. On January 29, 1990, we finally received Ms. Gilroy's reply to our letter of November 16, 1989.

b. The coach having bawled us out thoroughly, we left the locker room with his last, harsh words ringing in our ears.

c. Good technique does not guarantee, however, that the power you develop will be sufficient for Kyok Pa competition.

d. We bought a home in Upper Marlboro, where my husband worked as a mail carrier.

e. Please make the check payable to David Kerr, D.D.S., not David Kerr, M.D.

EXERCISE 33 – 1, page 350

a. We'd rather spend our money on blue-chip stocks than speculate on pork-bellies.

b. Being prepared for the worst is one way to escape disappointment.

c. When he heard the groans, he opened the door and ran out.

d. My father said that he would move to California if I would agree to transfer to UCLA.

e. I quickly accepted the fact that I was literally in third-class quarters.

EXERCISE 34 – 1, page 356

a. If fifty million people say a foolish thing, it is still a foolish thing.

b. No amount of experimentation can ever prove me right; a single experiment can prove me wrong.
c. Don't talk about yourself; it will be done when you leave.
d. The only sensible ends of literature are first, the pleasurable toil of writing; second, the gratification of one's family and friends; and lastly, the solid cash.
e. All animals are equal, but some animals are more equal than others.

EXERCISE 34 – 2, page 357

a. Correct
b. America has been called a country of pragmatists, although the American devotion to ideals is legendary.
c. The first requirement is honesty; everything else follows.
d. I am not fond of opera; I must admit, however, that I was greatly moved by *Les Misérables*.
e. Delegates to the convention came from Basel, Switzerland; Waikiki, Hawaii; Nome, Alaska; and Pretoria, South Africa.

EXERCISE 35 – 1, page 360

a. The second and most memorable week of survival school consisted of five stages: orientation, long treks, POW camp, escape and evasion, and return to civilization.
b. Among the canceled classes were calculus, physics, advanced biology, and English 101.
c. His only desires were for vengeance: vengeance for his father's death, vengeance for his mother's loss of eyesight, vengeance for his own lost youth.
d. For example, when a student in a private school is caught with drugs, he or she is immediately expelled.
e. Correct

EXERCISE 36 – 1, page 364

a. In a democracy anyone's vote counts as much as mine.
b. Correct
c. The puppy's favorite activity was chasing its tail.
d. After we bought J.J. the latest style pants and shirts, he decided that last year's faded, ragged jeans were perfect for all occasions.
e. A crocodile's life span is about thirteen years.

EXERCISE 37 – 1, page 371

a. "Fire and Ice" is one of Robert Frost's most famous poems.
b. As Emerson wrote in 1849, "I hate quotations. Tell me what you know."
c. Joggers have to run up the hills and then back down, but bicyclers, once they reach the top of a hill, get a free ride back down.
d. Correct
e. Historians Segal and Stineback tell us that the English settlers considered these epidemics "the hand of God making room for His followers in the 'New World.' "

EXERCISE 39 – 1, page 381

a. We lived in Davenport, Iowa, during the early years of our marriage.
b. Every night after her jazzercise class, Elizabeth bragged about how invigorated she felt, but she always looked exhausted.
c. Correct
d. Cancer — a disease that strikes without regard to age, race, or religion and causes dread in the most stalwart person — had struck my family. [*or* Cancer, . . . person, . . .]
e. The class stood, faced the flag, placed hands over hearts, and raced through "I pledge allegiance . . . liberty and justice for all" in less than sixty seconds.

EXERCISE 40 – 1, page 387

a. Correct
b. My grandmother told me that of all the subjects she studied, she found economics the most challenging.
c. Correct
d. The first discovery of America was definitely not in A.D. 1492.
e. Turning to page 195, Marion realized that she had finally reached the end of chapter 22.

EXERCISE 41 – 1, page 390

a. We have ordered four azaleas, three rhododendrons, and two mountain laurels for the back area of the garden.
b. Correct
c. Correct
d. We ordered three 4-door sedans for company executives.
e. In 1989, only 102 male high school students in our state planned to make a career of teaching.

EXERCISE 42 – 1, page 393

a. Howard Hughes commissioned the *Spruce Goose*, a beautifully built but thoroughly impractical wooden aircraft.
b. Pulaski was so exhausted he could barely lift his foot the six inches to the elevator floor.
c. Even though it is almost always hot in Mexico in the summer, you can usually find a cool spot on one of the park benches in the town's *zócalo*.
d. Correct
e. One of my favorite novels is George Eliot's *Middlemarch*.

EXERCISE 44 – 1, page 412

a. Correct
b. The quietly purring cat cleaned first one paw and then the other before curling up under the stove.
c. Many states are adopting laws that limit property taxes for homeowners.
d. Your dog is well known in our neighborhood.
e. Correct

EXERCISE 45 – 1, page 417

a. District Attorney Johnson was disgusted when the jurors turned in a verdict of not guilty after only one hour of deliberation.
b. My mother has begun to research the history of her Indian ancestors in North Carolina.
c. Correct
d. Refugees from Central America are finding it more and more difficult to cross the Rio Grande into the United States.
e. I want to take Environmental Biology 103, one other biology course, and one English course.

EXERCISE 47 – 1, page 425

a. idea, words, freedom, movement; b. hands, devil's (noun/adjective), workshop; c. flower, concrete (noun/adjective), cloverleaf; d. censorship, flick, dial; e. Figures, liars

EXERCISE 47 – 2, page 428

a. Every (pronoun/adjective), its (pronoun/adjective), its (pronoun/adjective); b. those, who; c. I, some (pronoun/adjective), that, I, myself; d. who, his (pronoun/adjective); e. No one

EXERCISE 47 – 3, page 431

a. have been; b. can be savored; c. does bring down; d. flock; e. Do scald

EXERCISE 47 – 4, page 433

a. Adjectives: Little, great; b. Adjectives: The (article), American, tolerant; adverb: wonderfully; c. Adjectives: a (article), rotten; adverb: not; d. Adjectives: a (article), thin; adverb: very; e. Adjective: the (article); adverb: faster

EXERCISE 48 – 1, page 442

a. Complete subject: A spoiled child; simple subject: child; b. Complete subject: all facts; simple subject: facts; c. Complete subject: (You); d. Complete subject: nothing except change; simple subject: nothing; e. Complete subject: hope

EXERCISE 48 – 2, page 446

a. Direct object: a hundred fathers; subject complement: an orphan; b. Direct object: the depth of a river; c. Direct objects: your door, your neighbors; object complement: honest; d. Subject complement: a feast of lanterns; e. Indirect object: her father; direct object: forty whacks

EXERCISE 49 – 1, page 452

a. with no side effects (adjective phrase modifying *tranquilizer*); b. on its back (adverbial phrase modifying *carries*); c. of money (adjective phrase modifying *love*), of all evil (adjective phrase modifying *root*); d. in a graveyard (adverbial phrase modifying *begins*), in a river (adverbial phrase modifying *ends*); e. with words (adverbial phrase modifying *can stroke*)

EXERCISE 49 – 2, page 458

a. Though you live near a forest (adverb clause modifying *do waste*); b. who help themselves (adjective clause modifying *those*); c. What is written without effort (noun clause used as subject of the sentence); d. that trots (adjective clause modifying *dog*); e. unless it is practiced on clever persons (adverb clause modifying *is practiced*)

EXERCISE 49 – 3, page 462

a. being sixteen (gerund phrase used as subject complement); b. Concealing a disease (gerund phrase used as subject of the sentence), to cure it (infinitive phrase used as adjective modifying *way*); c. To help a friend (infinitive phrase used as subject of the sentence), to give ourselves pleasure (infinitive phrase used as subject complement); d. bearing gifts (participial phrase modifying *Greeks*); e. being dead (gerund phrase used as object of the preposition *by*)

EXERCISE 50 – 1, page 466

a. complex; who always speaks the truth (adjective clause); b. compound; c. simple; d. complex; If you don't go to other people's funerals (adverb clause); e. complex; who sleep like a baby (adjective clause)

EXERCISE 56 – 1, page 620

a. hasty generalization; b. false analogy; c. emotional appeal; d. faulty cause-and-effect reasoning; e. *either . . . or* fallacy

(Continued from page iv)

Jane Brody, from *Jane Brody's Nutrition Book.* Copyright © 1981 by Jane E. Brody. Reprinted by permission of W. W. Norton & Company, Inc.

Roger Caras, from "What's a Koala?" Copyright 1983 by Roger Caras. First appeared in *Geo* Magazine, May 1983. Reprinted by permission of Roberta Pryor, Inc.

Bruce Catton, from "Grant and Lee: A Study in Contrasts," *The American Story,* Earl Schenck Miers, editor. © 1956 by Broadcast Music, Inc. Reprinted by permission of the U.S. Capitol Historical Society.

Napoleon A. Chagnon, from *Yanomamo: The Fierce People.* Reprinted by permission of Holt, Rinehart and Winston, Publishers.

Barnaby Conrad III, from " 'Train of Kings, the King of Trains' Is Back on Track," *Smithsonian,* December 1983. Reprinted by permission of *Smithsonian.*

Earl Conrad, from *Harriet Tubman.* Reprinted by permission of Paul S. Eriksson, Publisher.

James Underwood Crockett, Oliver E. Allen, and the Editors of Time-Life Books, from *The Time-Life Encyclopedia of Gardening.* © 1977 Time-Life Books Inc. Reprinted by permission of Time-Life Books Inc.

Emily Dickinson, from "The Snake." Reprinted by permission of the publishers and the Trustees of Amherst College from *The Poems of Emily Dickinson,* Thomas H. Johnson, Ed. Cambridge, Mass.: The Belknap Press of Harvard University Press, copyright 1951, © 1955, 1979, 1983 by the President and Fellows of Harvard College. "Opinion is a flitting thing," from *Life and Letters of Emily Dickinson,* edited by Martha D. Bianchi. Copyright 1924 by Martha Dickinson Bianchi. Copyright renewed 1952 by Alfred Leete Hampson. Reprinted by permission of Houghton Mifflin Company.

Annie Dillard, from *Teaching a Stone to Talk.* Copyright © 1982 by Annie Dillard. Reprinted by permission of HarperCollins Publishers.

Erik Eckholm, from "Pygmy Chimp Readily Learns Language Skill," *The New York Times.* Copyright © 1985 by The New York Times Company. Reprinted by permission.

Jane Goodall, from *In the Shadow of Man.* Copyright © 1971 by Hugo and Jane van Lawick-Goodall. Reprinted by permission of Houghton Mifflin Company.

Ellen Goodman, from "Bad Samaritans," *The Washington Post,* March 10, 1984.

Stephen Jay Gould, from "Were Dinosaurs Dumb?" *The Panda's Thumb: More Reflections in Natural History.* Copyright © 1980 by Stephen Jay Gould. Reprinted by permission of W. W. Norton & Company, Inc.

Hillary Hauser, from "Exploring a Sunken Realm in Australia," *National Geographic,* January 1984. Reprinted by permission of the National Geographic Society.

Richard Hofstadter, from *America at 1750: A Social Portrait.* Copyright © 1971 by Beatrice K. Hofstadter, executrix of the estate of Richard Hofstadter. Reprinted by permission of Alfred A. Knopf, Inc.

Langston Hughes, "Ballad of the Landlord." Reprinted by permission of Harold Ober Associates Incorporated. Copyright 1951 by Langston Hughes. Copyright renewed 1979 by George Houston Bass.

Philip Kopper, "How to Open an Oyster." Copyright © 1979 by Philip Kopper. Reprinted by permission of Times Books, a division of Quadrangle/The New York Times Book Co., Inc., from *The Wild Edge: Life and Lore of the Great Atlantic Beachers* by Philip Kopper.

William Least Heat Moon, from *Blue Highways*. Copyright © 1982 by William Least Heat Moon. Reprinted by permission of Little, Brown and Company.

Margaret Mead, from "New Superstitions for Old," *A Way of Seeing*. Reprinted by permission of William Morrow & Company, Inc.

Gloria Naylor, from *Linden Hills*. Copyright © 1985 by Gloria Naylor. Reprinted by permission of Houghton Mifflin Company.

Flannery O'Connor, from "The King of the Birds," *Mystery and Manners*. Copyright © 1969. Reprinted by permission of Farrar, Straus and Giroux, Inc.

Saul K. Padover, from *Jefferson*. Copyright 1942, 1970 by Saul K. Padover. Reprinted by permission of Harcourt Brace Jovanovich, Inc.

Readers' Guide to Periodical Literature, March 1982–February 1983, from entries under "Animal Communications." Copyright © 1982, 1983 by The H. W. Wilson Company. Material reproduced by permission of the publisher.

Paul Reps, from "The Moon Cannot Be Stolen" *Zen Flesh, Zen Bones*. Reprinted by permission of Charles E. Tuttle, Co., Inc., of Tokyo, Japan.

Richard Rodriguez, from "Aria: A Memoir of a Bilingual Childhood." Reprinted by permission of the author. Copyright © 1980 by Richard Rodriguez. First published in *The American Scholar*.

Arthur M. Schlesinger, Jr., from *The Age of Roosevelt: The Crisis of the Old Order*. Copyright © 1957 by Arthur M. Schlesinger, Jr. Reprinted by permission of Houghton Mifflin Company.

Julian Simon, "Immigration for a Stronger America," *The Washington Post*, September 1, 1990.

Lewis Thomas, from "On Societies as Organisms" and "Your Very Good Health," *The Lives of a Cell*. Copyright © 1974 by Lewis Thomas. From "Notes on Punctuation," *The Medusa and the Snail*. Copyright © 1979 by Lewis Thomas. All rights reserved. Reprinted by permission of Viking Penguin, Inc.

James Thurber, from "University Days," *My Life and Hard Times*. Copyright © 1933, 1961 by James Thurber. Published by Harper & Row, Publishers, Inc. Reprinted by permission.

Margaret Visser, from *Much Depends on Dinner* by Margaret Visser. Reprinted by permission of Grove Press and the Canadian publishers, McClelland & Stewart, Toronto.

Olivia Vlahos, from *Human Beginnings*. Published by Viking Penguin Inc. Reprinted by permission of the author.

Alice Walker, from "In Search of Our Mothers' Gardens," *In Search of Our Mothers' Gardens*. Copyright 1967 by Alice Walker. Reprinted by permission of Harcourt Brace Jovanovich, Inc.

E. B. White, from "Here is New York," from *Essays of E. B. White*. Copyright 1949 by E. B. White. Published by Harper & Row, Publishers, Inc. Reprinted by permission of HarperCollins Publishers.

Index

G

H

M

P

R

T